Blogging, Citizenship, and the Future of Media

Blogging, Citizenship, and the Future of Media

edited by
Mark Tremayne

 Routledge
Taylor & Francis Group
New York   London

Routledge is an imprint of the
Taylor & Francis Group, an informa business

Routledge
Taylor & Francis Group
270 Madison Avenue
New York, NY 10016

Routledge
Taylor & Francis Group
2 Park Square
Milton Park, Abingdon
Oxon OX14 4RN

© 2007 by Taylor & Francis Group, LLC
Routledge is an imprint of Taylor & Francis Group, an Informa business

Printed in the United States of America on acid-free paper
10 9 8 7 6 5 4 3 2 1

International Standard Book Number-10: 0-415-97940-4 (Softcover) 0-415-97939-0 (Hardcover)
International Standard Book Number-13: 978-0-415-97940-5 (Softcover) 978-0-415-97939-9 (Hardcover)

No part of this book may be reprinted, reproduced, transmitted, or utilized in any form by any electronic, mechanical, or other means, now known or hereafter invented, including photocopying, microfilming, and recording, or in any information storage or retrieval system, without written permission from the publishers.

Trademark Notice: Product or corporate names may be trademarks or registered trademarks, and are used only for identification and explanation without intent to infringe.

Visit the Taylor & Francis Web site at
http://www.taylorandfrancis.com

and the Routledge Web site at
http://www.routledge-ny.com

Contents

Preface   vii

Introduction: Examining the Blog–Media Relationship   ix

    Mark Tremayne

Part One: Blogging: Research on Blogging Using Content Analysis   **1**

1. Longitudinal Content Analysis of Blogs: 2003–2004   3

    Susan C. Herring, Lois Ann Scheidt, Inna Kouper and Elijah Wright

2. Audiences as Media Producers: Content Analysis of 260 Blogs   21

    Zizi Papacharissi

3. Pundits in Muckrakers' Clothing: Political Blogs and the 2004 U.S. Presidential Election   39

    D. Travers Scott

4. Analyzing Political Conversation on the Howard Dean Candidate Blog   59

    Sharon Meraz

5. Blogging for Better Health: Putting the "Public" Back in Public Health   83

    S. Shyam Sundar, Heidi Hatfield Edwards, Yifeng Hu and Carmen Stavrositu

Part Two: Citizenship: Examining Blog Use, Antecedents and Consequences   **103**

6. Reading Political Blogs During the 2004 Election Campaign: Correlates and Political Consequences   105

    William P. Eveland, Jr. and Ivan Dylko

7. Blog Use Motivations: An Exploratory Study   127

    Barbara K. Kaye

8. Credibility of Political Messages on the Internet: A Comparison of Blog Sources   149

    Lynda Lee Kaid and Monica Postelnicu

9. Blog Readers: Predictors of Reliance on War Blogs   165

   Thomas Johnson and Barbara K. Kaye

Part Three: The Future of Media: Examining the Impact of Blogging on Journalism   185

10. Press Protection in the Blogosphere: Applying a Functional Definition of "Press" to News Web Logs   187

    Laura Hendrickson

11. Blogs Without Borders: International Legal Jurisdiction Issues Facing Bloggers   205

    Brian Carroll and Bob Frank

12. Emergent Communication Networks as Civic Journalism   225

    Lou Rutigliano

13. Citizen Journalism: A Case Study   239

    Clyde Bentley, Brian Hamman, Jeremy Littau, Hans Meyer, Brendan Watson and Beth Welsh

14. Harnessing the Active Audience: Synthesizing Blog Research and Lessons for the Future of Media   261

    Mark Tremayne

Editor   273

Contributors   275

Index   279

Preface: Blog Terminology

The research presented in this book assumes the reader has some familiarity with web culture and blogging. Nevertheless, some terminology is provided here. According to blog veteran and unofficial movement historian Rebecca Blood, the brief etymology of the term "blogs" goes back to the late 1990s and looks something like this: web journal → web log → weblog → wee blogs → blogs. Blogs are distinguished from other websites in their dynamism, reverse chronological presentation and dominant use of the first person. The term "bloggers" refers primarily to those who write them as opposed to those who read them.

Bloggers often provide links to other web content and many have a blog roll: a list of links to favorite blogs as part of site navigation. Bloggers also use links within their posts. Posts are the individual entries a blogger makes, usually time stamped, analogous to stories in a newspaper. Collectively, blogs and the links that connect them are referred to as the blogosphere, a term clearly derivative of the public sphere. Whether the activity that occurs within the blogosphere fits the Habermasian ideal is one topic of this book. "Blog use" is a term most frequently attached to the act of reading blogs; however, as with everything on the web, the old distinctions between sender and receiver are challenged here. On many blogs, readers can (and are encouraged to) leave comments in response to the author's posts. This, too, is rightly considered blog use.

As the book will make clear, it is difficult to generalize about the blogosphere because of its size, diversity of content and variation in format. The blogs at the center of this network have characteristics that those on the periphery often do not share. When one makes a claim about the nature of the blogosphere, it is important to consider which part of it is under consideration. In this book, investigations focus on blogs written in English, primarily those in the United States.

At this early stage of blog development, it is also important to keep in mind when a particular study was conducted. How the blogosphere looked at the turn of the century is not, in many respects, how it looked 5 years later or how it will look 10 years from now. Nevertheless, patterns are beginning to emerge, as the research presented here will demonstrate. Most of the studies presented were conducted within a year of the 2004 U.S. political campaigns, a time when political blogging reached a zenith. Blog rankings in the fall of 2004 were dominated at the top by this category of blog, but a year before and a year later other topics (especially technology) could often be found.

Introduction: Examining the Blog–Media Relationship

MARK TREMAYNE

In the spring of 2005, a 16-year-old boy named Jack[1] from a southern U.S. state decided to tell his parents that he was gay. They did not take it well. Jack's parents decided they had raised him wrong and he was psychologically damaged. They told Jack that he was not on the path God wanted him to be on and that they were sending him to a Christian "straight camp" to get him back on the right track.

Jack responded by doing something other teens have for years: He poured his emotions into a personal journal. However, this journal was a blog on his MySpace.com website that was accessible to his friends and anyone else who might stumble upon it while surfing the web. Jack's personal anguish was evident. (Quotes from his blog will not be used here because a web search would quickly reveal his identity.) He raised the idea of suicide and of harming his parents and was clearly opposed to their plans. In a final posting before leaving for the camp, Jack wrote of his emotional turmoil and included a list of the strict rules he would be living under for the next several weeks.

In a preblog world it is unlikely that Jack's story would have spread much further than his family and circle of friends. However, Jack's blog provided other people a window into his life and a simple means of transmitting what they saw there to others. Within one day of Jack's last precamp post, his story began spreading through the blogosphere, eventually spurring a political demonstration, a state investigation and international news coverage.

First, a fellow MySpace blogger from Jack's home state saw his blog, passed the information along to gay and lesbian activists there and wrote about Jack's situation on his own blog. The activists quickly organized a protest at the camp's headquarters and another blogger, one who also happened to be a news director for a television station in the area, read about the group's plans. The next day, she sent a news crew to cover the protest and the resulting television story got the attention of a columnist at the local newspaper.[2] The columnist's story was followed by national coverage in the gay press and eventually a state investigation of the camp was initiated when someone made a claim of abuse. When the state investigation was terminated due to lack of evidence, the news website for a national television network ran a story about it that included quotes from Jack's blog. A wire service piece sent the story worldwide and it appeared, among other places, on a news website in India.

The impact of all of this on Jack remains unclear. After finishing his stay at the camp, Jack only posted one item regarding his experience, at least in part because of his parents' directives. He is grateful for the support he received but unhappy about being co-opted as a "cause" by activist groups. He was upset about the media coverage but, to some degree, sympathetic. He is angry about the whole experience.

The impact that blogging will have on the future of media is also unclear but the research compiled in this volume provides some answers. It suggests that Jack's case is typical and atypical of the blog–media relationship. Typical is the speed with which the information spread and the events unfolded. Within 2 days dozens of people were picketing the camp's headquarters and within 10 days the story appeared on more than 70 blogs and had found its way into traditional media. However, that the story spread at all is a rarity, so Jack's case is also atypical. It involves what has been called a personal blog or online diary (Herring, Scheidt, Bonus & Wright, 2005; Krishnamurthy, 2002). Although this is the most common type of blog, it usually receives little attention from the mainstream press. Most personal blogs exist in relative isolation, linked to very few other blogs and are therefore mostly unread (Herring et al. 2005).

The examples presented later in this introduction will provide evidence that the greatest impact on mainstream media comes not from personal journals but from political blogs, a subset of what researchers have dubbed filter blogs (Cornfield, Carson, Kalis & Simon, 2005; Halavais, 2002; Herring et al., 2005). The term *filter* is meant to describe the process undertaken by this type of blogger when he or she brings certain items to readers' attention and ignores others. If personal blogs are focused inward, filter blogs are more outwardly focused. Their function is to direct readers to other websites or at least to bring information from those sites to readers' attention. When personal opinion or analysis is offered, it most often addresses a particular topic rather than events in the author's life.

Two of the most common types of filter blogs are those focused on technology and on politics or current events. The latter is of particular interest to researchers in the fields of political science, mass communication and information science. In 2004, political blogs dominated the top of blog rankings such as those published at Technorati.com, Daypop.com and Truthlaidbear.com. These sites rank blogs based on the total number of links they receive from other blogs. A question for researchers has been: Why do a few blogs get all the links while most remain obscure? That question is explored in the next section.

The Blogosphere as a Network

The blogosphere is a classic social network with special qualities that make it ideal for research. First, the communication carried on this network appears primarily in text form and, in most cases, is archived. Contrast this with most social networks in which communication is verbal and unrecorded. In those cases, it can be difficult or impossible to reconstruct the flow of ideas in the network accurately. In the blogosphere, one can trace a piece of information back to the first blogger to mention it. Sites such as Technorati.com allow for blog-specific searches that can quickly isolate a cluster of blogs in which a given topic has been discussed.

Second, the social ties of this network are explicitly designated when a blogger provides a link to another blog. These links come in two forms. There is the blogroll, a list of links provided by a blogger to inform readers of work he or she considers useful or of high quality. This set of links is relatively static and typically appears as part of main-page navigation. A second category of links is more dynamic. Bloggers link to other blogs within their posts, typically to respond to a point another has made or to direct readers to an item the blogger found interesting or useful. Links of both types are directional: I may consider you part of my social network but you may not consider me part of yours. Directionality is important in calculating the centrality of a node in a network. Collectively, these links and the blogs connected by them comprise the blogosphere.

A third special quality of this network is the speed with which it is evolving. All networks evolve, but some change so slowly that questions regarding network dynamics can be difficult to examine. The web, however, has proven to be a useful testing ground for examining questions of network formation (Barabasi, 2002). Researchers took advantage of this quality to isolate two principles of network development: growth and preferential attachment (Barabasi & Albert, 1999). Together, these principles explain how a small number of nodes in a network become heavily linked while most remain isolated. The *growth* of the network favors the original nodes; the old are more likely to have acquired links than the new. New nodes prefer to attach to ones that are already well connected because it is more efficient. In this way, the "rich get richer" and a heavily skewed link distribution results. Figure I.1 illustrates how these principles apply to the blogosphere.

If new blogger X desires a readership, he or she will be most successful if a tie with blogger A or B can be formed (see Figure I.1). These blogs have the greatest number of links, so (a) they likely have the most readers; and (b) search engines will rank them highly because the number of links will generate even more traffic. Blog X linking to blog A or B does not guarantee that those blogs will reciprocate, but it increases the chances of such an occurrence. Search engines allow bloggers to identify who is linking to them quickly and reciprocal linking has developed as a norm in the blogosphere because, to a degree, it is mutually beneficial. The most popular blogs receive so many links, however, that it would be nearly impossible to read and respond to all of them. Other

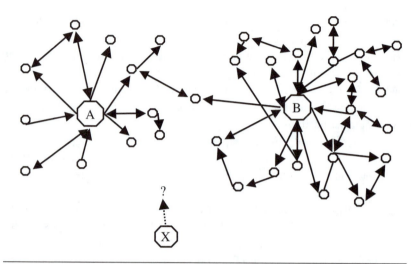

Figure I.1 The blogosphere as a network: hyperlinks determine network centrality.

means of establishing a social tie with these blogs include leaving a comment on the blog or e-mailing the blogger.

However, blogger X may be more interested in personal expression than in generating user traffic. Even if blogger X desires a readership, he or she may spend relatively little time linking to or commenting on others' work. Also, if blogger X desires a readership and invests time in developing social ties, others may not find the content useful or interesting. In all of these cases, the blog will remain in relative isolation with few links coming to it from other blogs. As with most other networks, the vast majority of blogs fall into this category. Most personal blogs, including Jack's blog, are of this type. Nevertheless, as Jack's case proves, even relatively disconnected blogs occasionally have an impact.

The information on a peripheral blog only occasionally reaches a wide audience, but the opposite is true for those at the center of the blogosphere. The hubs of this network are so well connected that anything the authors write will reach a sizable audience (Bar-Ilan, 2005). The audience they have attained affords them importance in the eyes of traditional media; references in the mainstream press expose these blogs to an even wider audience. The following sections expand on the blog–media relationship.

Political Bloggers: How Events and Media Fuel Them

If the Clinton–Lewinsky scandal of the late 1990s is the event that marked the birth of online journalism (Lasica, 2003), the terrorist attacks of September 11, 2001, did the same for blogging. Although blogs began to appear in the late 1990s, it was after 9/11 that the phenomenon spread rapidly. Many of the new blogs focused on the events of that day and President Bush's subsequent war on terrorism. For example, the conservative blog Vodkapundit.com began 4 months after 9/11 with a post titled, "Why Aren't We Bombing Iraq Back to the Stone Age Already?"

On the liberal side, the blog Dailykos.com was started 8 months after 9/11 and included frequent posts regarding the war on terrorism and the buildup to the Iraq invasion. The war proved a boon to bloggers as they provided round-the-clock commentary on its execution. These so-called war blogs typically evolved to include discussion of politics and current events, including, notably, extensive discussion of the 2002 and 2004 U.S. elections.

Other major news events also fueled the current events blogs, including the Asian tsunami of December 2004 and terrorist bombings in London in July 2005. Blogs proved to be an invaluable tool for communication and fund-raising after the tsunami. Sites such as tsunamihelp.blogspot.com were able to mobilize relief efforts and coordinate volunteers. The bombings in London proved to be another big story for bloggers. Using their cell phones, eyewitnesses took pictures of chaos that were posted on blogs within minutes (and on a few forward-thinking news sites such as those run by BBC and MSNBC).

If news events such as these spurred the growth of the blogosphere, the question is, "Why?" Readers could always get the essential information from mainstream news sites, but the blogs provide something different. The best of them offer a service to readers by monitoring the web for the latest unique facets of the stories. Instead of visiting dozens of news sites, a good topical blogger can do that for the reader. Blogs give readers the impression that they are getting unmediated raw information. In the case of eyewitness bloggers, this is almost true. Blogs provide not only the news of the event but also instantaneous written commentary on it. Such speculation is also available on cable television but difficult to access if one is at work. Blogs allow for feedback from readers in the form of comment functions available at many blogs. Even readers who will not leave an opinion (probably the vast majority) get the sense of being part of an event by reading the live discourse of others.

Examples of Blogger Influence: Through the Media

Before any individual blog attained an audience comparable to an established media news site, bloggers could influence events as a collective. A widely cited example of this is the downfall of Senate Majority Leader Trent Lott (Johnson & Kaye, 2004). Bloggers like to take credit for stoking the controversy over Lott's 2002 remarks about Senator Strom Thurmond, which eventually led to Lott relinquishing his leadership position. In truth, Lott's comments were initially reported by "old media"—specifically the *Washington Post*, although the item was not on the front page and was not seized upon by other news outlets. The collective commentary and debate amongst bloggers was enough to keep the story alive and eventually the issue made its way to the cable news talk shows that look to the blogosphere for "the buzz" (Cornfield et al., 2005).

The distance between the blogosphere and the mainstream press appeared even smaller in the fall of 2004 when *60 Minutes* aired the now infamous Dan Rather story regarding President Bush's military record. Within hours of the story's airing, a post appeared on a discussion forum at the conservative website FreeRepublic.com challenging the authenticity of documents in the CBS report. Early the next morning, this post, which pointed out problems with font and spacing in the documents, was noticed by one of the authors of PowerlineBlog.com, an influential blog on the conservative side of the blogosphere, and reprinted there.[3] A reader with experience as a military clerk in the 1970s offered additional evidence of forgery and the story spread rapidly through the blogosphere.

By midmorning, a blogger[4] recreated the documents using Microsoft Word and superimposed the letters posted at CBSNews.com with his: an exact match. By midday, the buzz made it to the authors of AndrewSullivan.com and InstaPundit.com, two blogs consistently at the epicenter of the blogosphere. A few hours later, the story appeared on the DrudgeReport.com and shortly after that the Associated Press ran an item that began, "Questions are being raised about the authenticity of newly unearthed memos." The passive lead allowed omitting the subject: bloggers. Less than 24 hours after the story aired, it had been effectively retracted by news organizations nationwide. It would be weeks, however, before CBS admitted error.

The 2004 elections provided other examples of blog–media relationships. Some bloggers who watched the first presidential debate saw a bulge on President Bush's back and speculated it was a radio receiver. The story eventually found its way to Salon.com and the *New York Times* (Bumiller, 2004). Blogger Sam Wang, a neuroscientist at Princeton, provided regular election polling analysis and was contacted for media interviews, including an appearance on Fox News. Liberal blogger Markos Moulitsas Zúniga, creator of DailyKos.com, attained such a large following that he was routinely cited as an expert by well-respected national publications such as *Newsweek*, despite having no journalistic or political credentials beyond the simple popularity (and power) of his blog (Schrobsdorff, 2005).

It was clear from the DailyKos case that political reporters were paying attention to bloggers—at least bloggers that had sizable audiences. Political scientist and well-known blogger Daniel Drezner and a colleague surveyed 140 journalists to find out which blogs they read. Collectively, they mentioned 125 blogs. Ten blogs accounted for more than half of all mentions. A Nexis search for each of the blogs was compared to the number of mentions each blog received in the survey and a very strong correlation (.84) was found (Drezner & Farrell, 2004). When Drezner and Farrell limited the survey results to national publications, the concentration of blog mentions and the correlation with news coverage was even stronger.

The ability of bloggers to affect news coverage in mainstream media is not limited to political coverage. In July 2005, a pregnant Philadelphia woman, Latoyia Figueroa, disappeared; however, her case did not generate the type of media coverage afforded by the disappearance of Laci Peterson in California. Figueroa was black. Richard Blair, author of the blog Allspinzone.com, decided to help publicize the case and spearheaded an online fund-raising drive for a reward fund. When the reward was announced, mainstream media, including CNN.com, ran the story ("Pregnant Philadelphia mother of one missing," 2005).

Examples of Blogger Influence: Circumventing the Media

The influence of blogs is not limited to their effect on mainstream media. In recent years numerous examples of unmediated blog effects on current events have occurred. The 2004 elections provided several. In August of that year, U.S. Representative Ed Schrock abandoned his reelection bid after a report on Blogactive.com said the Republican from Virginia was gay. A statement on the blog says it is dedicated to outing public officials for what it calls "hypocrisy."

In October 2004, plans by Sinclair Broadcast Group to air an anti-John Kerry documentary on 40 stations were scuttled after a grassroots campaign led by bloggers convinced them it would be bad for business (Gegax, 2004). Liberal bloggers had started a campaign to convince fellow Democrats to sell Sinclair stock and to encourage union and pension funds to sell as well. In 3 days, the stock dropped 15% and groups still holding stock were threatening lawsuits against Sinclair. The company backed down. Later that month the Bush campaign was forced to reedit its final television campaign ad after a report on Dailykos.com pointed out that the original version had been digitally altered (Kurtz, 2004).

In early 2006, George Deutsch, a Bush appointee at NASA, raised the ire of some science bloggers after they discovered his efforts to limit communication from NASA scientist James Hansen regarding the threat of global warming and to change NASA's website so that any mention of "big bang" was also followed by "theory." Blogger Nick Anthis at Scientificactivist.blogspot.com did what could only be described as journalism. He received a tip from an old colleague of Deutsch's that his resume was inaccurate: He had no college degree from Texas A&M. Anthis checked with records at the university and confirmed the tip. His post generated a flurry of discussion within the blogosphere and Deutsch was eventually fired (Revkin, 2006).

The impact of web information on real world events is not limited to the political arena. One example from outside the beltway occurred in October 2005. Although not labeled as a blog, the website Hoopshype.com shares some blog characteristics, posting items from local newspapers and other websites about the NBA under the heading "Rumors." One item concerned the potential availability of Hornet's center Jamaal Magloire and was read by Milwaukee

Buck's General Manager Larry Harris. Harris followed up on the rumor with a phone call and within 48 hours a trade was agreed upon (Ballard, 2005).

Mainstream Media: Coping With Bloggers

The examples outlined here provide some evidence of the growing influence of amateur news and information providers. Their influence stems from several factors. First, they have outsider status. Like television news in the 1950s, they are seen by users as conduits to raw information, somehow less corrupted by power than their predecessors. Second, some have attained a large audience. Regardless of whether they "should" have an audience, they do, and with it comes power. Third, they have the "power of the collective" (Halavais, 2002). Even if many individual blogs have just a few hundred regular readers, collectively the blogosphere can generate a louder "buzz" (Cornfield et al., 2005). Through individual link choices, this collective bestows upon a select few the "power of authority."

Blogs represent a threat to mainstream media in a number of ways. As the rapid expansion of the cable universe inevitably led to a slow decline of audience share for the old broadcast networks, so too can we expect a decline in use of preweb media. Unlike cable television, for which content production is expensive and channels number in the hundreds, blog content is cheap to produce, is free to the consumer and numbers its channels in the millions.

How do legacy media handle the challenge? Some media companies are responding by shedding old assets, as the recent sale of Knight Ridder demonstrates. For the companies that "stick it out," three stages to dealing with the increasingly active audience are apparent.

First, mainstream media attacked the blogs. They were insignificant, filled with errors and lacking in credibility. Some of this continues but this stage is mostly finished. Second, mainstream media embraced the blogs—an "if you can't beat 'em, join 'em" approach evidenced by nearly universal adoption and incorporation of the word "blog" on major newspaper and broadcast news websites. Often, what were once called columns are now called blogs. Also, some of the most popular writers in the real blogosphere have been hired by mainstream outlets, providing further evidence of the movement's success (and a possible sign of its impending failure). Finally (this stage is just beginning), mainstream news organizations will learn from bloggers how to take advantage of active citizen–readers to generate better product and lower costs. In the final chapter of this book, I will return to this theme and, after a review of research on the blog phenomenon, suggest some ways in which we can expect media to adapt in this changing environment.

Organization of This Book

In addition to this introduction, the book consists of three parts, each corresponding to part of the title, *Blogging, Citizenship and the Future of Media*.

The first part is dedicated to setting the stage. What generalizations can we make about the nature of blogging? Is the blogosphere an interactive forum where lively discussion of important issues takes place? Can we see journalism being exercised in this arena? Content analyses from leading blog researchers are presented to answer these questions.

Chapter 1 and chapter 2 examine independent random samples of blogs. Herring and colleagues sampled over time to identify trends in the structure, content, and authorship of blogs. Papacharissi found blogs that were largely self-referential and lacking in original journalistic content.

Chapter 3 and chapter 4 concern the world of political blogging. In an examination of two top conservative blogs and two top liberal blogs, Scott finds evidence that *some* of the traditional functions of news are apparent but rarely is there firsthand reporting. Instead, bloggers continue a trend toward punditry in the media. Meraz examined thousands of posts on the Howard Dean for president blog and examines the discourse for evidence of deliberation and meaningful issue discussion.

Finally, Sundar and colleagues (chapter 5) closely examine one corner of the blogosphere: 47 blogs about mental health. Rather than an abundance of medical expertise, they found these blogs to be primarily personal in nature.

Readers of blogs are the focus of the second section of the book. How are blog readers different from the rest of the population and what are the consequences of their use? Chapter 6 examines two samples of blog readers to explore these questions. Eveland and Dylko find that online news use, participation in discussion forums and listening to talk radio predict blog use. They also find a relationship between blog reading and political participation.

Chapter 7 explores the motivations of blog use. Kaye found 10 motivation categories including blog characteristics that appealed to users and the ability of blogs to facilitate personal fulfillment.

Chapter 8 is an experiment in blog credibility. Kaid and Postelnicu found that study participants rated blog content credible at equivalent rates, regardless of the authorship of the blog (content was controlled).

Chapter 9 examines the users of war blogs. Johnson and Kaye found these bloggers to be disproportionately male, conservative and trusting in government. Although they represent only a fraction of online news consumers, they depend on blogs particularly for information about the war in Iraq.

The final section consists of studies concerned with the ramifications of the blog phenomenon for traditional media. Chapter 10 and chapter 11 focus on changes in the law that may result from bloggers' entrance into the arena of mass communication. Hendrickson suggests expanding the functional definition of the press to accommodate the activities of some bloggers; Carroll and Frank discuss the chilling effect bloggers face from international legal challenges to their right to publish.

Chapter 12 and chapter 13 present cases studies in citizen-based journalism. Rutigliano identifies three types of journalistic blogs and suggests that their structures affect the kind of work produced on them. Bentley and colleagues describe their experiences with MyMissourian.com, a natural experiment in blending professional journalistic norms with amateur reporting.

Finally, in chapter 14, I look to the growing body of blog research and suggest themes that have implications for the future of journalism.

References

Ballard, C. (2005, October 28). Believe the hype. CNN.com. Available from http://sportsillustrated.cnn.com/2005/writers/chris_ballard/2010/2027/magloire.trade/index.html.

Barabasi, A. -L. (2002). *Linked: The new science of networks*. Cambridge, MA: Perseus Publishing.

Barabasi, A. -L., & Albert, R. (1999). Emergence of scaling in random networks. *Science, 286*, 509–512.

Bar-Ilan, J. (2005). Information hub blogs. *Journal of Information Science, 31*(4), 297–307.

Bumiller, E. (2004, October 9). The mystery of the bulge in the jacket. *The New York Times*, p. 15.

Cornfield, M., Carson, J., Kalis, A. & Simon, E. (2005). Buzz, blogs, and beyond. From http://pew.org.

Drezner, D., & Farrell, H. (2004). *The power and politics of blogs*. Paper presented at the American Political Science Association, Chicago.

Gegax, T. T. (2004, October 20). Stolen honor. *Newsweek*. Available from http://www.msnbc.msn.com/id/6293163/site/newsweek/.

Halavais, A. (2002, October). *Blogs and the social weather*. Paper presented at the Internet Research 3.0 meeting, Maastricht, The Netherlands.

Herring, S., Scheidt, L. A., Bonus, S. & Wright, E. (2005). Weblogs as a bridging genre. *Information, Technology and People, 18*(2), 142–171.

Johnson, T., & Kaye, B. (2004). Wag the blog: How reliance on traditional media and the Internet influence credibility perceptions of Weblogs among blog users. *Journalism & Mass Communication Quarterly, 81*(3), 622–642.

Krishnamurthy, S. (2002, October). *The multidimensionality of blog conversations: The virtual enactment of September 11*. Paper presented at the Internet Research 3.0 meeting, Maastricht, The Netherlands.

Kurtz, H. (2004, October 29). A final volley of commercials. *Washington Post*. Available from http://www.washingtonpost.com/wp-dyn/articles/A7424-2004Oct7428.html.

Lasica, J. D. (2003). Internet journalism and the Starr investigation. In T. Rosenstiel & A. S. Mitchell (Eds.), *Thinking clearly*. New York: Columbia University Press.

Pregnant Philadelphia mother of one missing. (2005, July 27). CNN.com. Available from http://www.cnn.com/2005/US/2007/2027/Philadelphia.missing/index.html.

Revkin, A. (2006, February 8). A young Bush appointee resigns his post at NASA. *The New York Times*, p. 13.

Schrobsdorff, S. (2005, December 29). Kos-eye view. *Newsweek*. Accessed April 2006 from http://www.msnbc.msn.com/id/10629288/site/newsweek/.

Notes

1. Because of his age and his critical, or at least conflicted, feelings regarding media coverage of his blog I have chosen to protect his identity. Jack is not his real name.
2. This reconstruction of the sequence of events is based, in part, on personal correspondence among the newspaper columnist, the assignment editor at the local television station and me on June 14, 15 and 17, 2005.
3. See PowerlineBlog.com, September 9, 2004, 7:51 a.m.
4. Littlegreenfootballs.com.

Part One

Blogging: Research on Blogging
Using Content Analysis

1
Longitudinal Content Analysis of Blogs: 2003–2004

SUSAN C. HERRING, LOIS ANN SCHEIDT,
INNA KOUPER AND ELIJAH WRIGHT

Introduction

In the past several years, blogs—frequently modified webpages containing dated entries listed in reverse chronological sequence—have gone from relative obscurity to immense popularity. Blogs are popular in part because they enable easy, inexpensive self-publication of content for a potentially vast audience on the world wide web, and because they are more flexible and interactive than previous publication formats, print or digital (Herring, Scheidt, Bonus & Wright, 2005). The rapid efflorescence of the blogosphere—the universe of available blogs—has also been fertilized by a series of external events over the past few years that have inspired blogging activity: terrorist acts, war, political campaigns and natural disasters. Blogging about these events has attracted the attention of the mainstream news media, further contributing to the popularization and adoption of this new mode of computer-mediated communication.

Scholarly research about blogging has also blossomed in recent years. Much of it has focused on blogs concerned with external events (known as "filters" because they "filter" information from other sources on the web; Blood, 2002) and the impact of bloggers as "citizen journalists" (Gillmor, 2003; Lasica, 2002, 2003), "public intellectuals" (Park, 2003) and "opinion leaders" (Delwiche, 2004). The most linked-to, hence presumed most influential, bloggers are known as the "A" list (Trammell & Keshelashvili, 2005). Other research has examined blogs as a new communication genre, using content analysis (Herring, Scheidt et al., 2004, 2005; Papacharissi, 2004), rhetorical analysis (Miller & Shepherd, 2004) and ethnographic interviews (Nardi, Schiano & Gumbrecht, 2004) to characterize the forms, functions and audiences of blogs, as well as people's motivations for blogging.

In all of this research, the blogging phenomenon is represented as dynamic and evolving. As yet, however, no research to our knowledge has empirically investigated how blogs or blogging practices change over time, or how external events shape blogging practice.

This chapter begins to address this lack by presenting the results of a longitudinal content analysis of blogs randomly sampled between March 2003 and April 2004. This was a troubled year in world politics: The United States began pre-emptive bombing of Iraq amid global protests on March 19, 2003, closely followed by the "shock and awe" blitz on Baghdad by the United States and the United Kingdom. One year later, terrorist bombings in Madrid led another ally, Spain, to withdraw its troops from Iraq around the time of the first outbreak of civil war in Najaf. At the same time, closely watched by the rest of the world, the 2004 U.S. presidential race was heating up after Howard Dean, the leading challenger of George W. Bush's presidency and the first candidate to make effective use of blogging (Kerbel & Bloom, 2005), ruined his chances for election by screaming at a campaign rally on January 29, 2004, and John Kerry cinched the Democratic party nomination on March 2, 2004.

During this event-filled year, the number of active blogs more than quadrupled. Mass media coverage of blogs also increased dramatically, bringing blogs into the mainstream consciousness (Drezner & Farrell, 2004). Against this backdrop, we collected and analyzed three random samples, totaling 457 blogs, at 6-month intervals. Our primary goal was to assess the extent to which the characteristics of blogs, as described in previous research, remained stable or changed during this active period. Our findings reveal longitudinal trends that support earlier characterizations, as well as variation that suggests responsiveness to external events.

The remainder of this chapter is organized as follows. As background for the presentation of our research question and methodology, the next section reviews literature on growth of the blogosphere, blogging in response to external events and structural and functional characteristics of blogs. Three categories of results of our longitudinal analysis are then presented and discussed: change over time, stability over time and variability. In concluding, we identify challenges associated with longitudinal blog analysis and suggest directions for future research.

Background

Growth of the Blogosphere

Blogs have come a long way since Turnbull (1999) first introduced them to *The Scotsman*'s readership as "the latest Internet craze." Earlier that year two software products that automated blog creation, Blogger and Pitas, were released to the public (Blood, 2002). In the first few months after Blogger's release, the site gained 10 to 20 new users per day, ending the year with 2,300 registered users. By the end of January 2001, Blogger had registered 117,970 users, a 5,029% increase in 13 months (Turnbull, 2001).

The number of blogs continued to grow at an exponential rate, although estimates vary depending on the methods used to count blogs (see Herring et al., 2005). At the beginning of our data collection period in March 2003, the blog-tracking site blo.gs reported 350,000 active blogs (Herring, Scheidt et al., 2004); by late September 2003, that number had doubled (Herring, Kouper, Scheidt & Wright, 2004). In early 2004, surveys found that between 2 and 7% of American adult Internet users (between 1.06 and 3.71 million people) had created blogs (Lenhart, Horrigan & Fallows, 2004). According to blo.gs and Technorati (another blog-tracking service), the number of active blogs around the end of our data collection period in April 2004 was between 1.5 and 2 million.

Estimates including blog-hosting services such as LiveJournal, DiaryLand and Xanga were much higher during the same period. In October 2003, the Perseus Corporation estimated that 4.12 million blogs had been created (Henning, 2003), although many of them were inactive. By the end of the first quarter of 2004, this estimate had risen to 31.6 million blogs, most of which were personal journals (Henning, 2005).[1]

Response to External Events

As the number of active blogs has grown, so too has their ability to respond to the world around them. After the events of 9/11, traditional media outlets could not keep up with the original reporting and man-on-the-street commentary found in blogs (Stone, 2004). On September 11, 2001, veteran blogger Dave Winer reported that "[m]ost of the major news sites are inaccessible, but news and pictures are reaching us through e-mail, Webcams and the blog community" (Winer, 2001). Blog posting increased in amount and frequency in the week after 9/11, as did the number of comments per post and the number of posts per individual blogger (Krishnamurthy, 2002).

Bloggers have also shown that they can ignite the traditional media's interest in a topic. For example, in 2002 when traditional media did not respond with significant outcry over U.S. Senator Trent Lott's racist remarks at Strom Thurmond's 100th birthday party, bloggers took over the story with such vigor that traditional media outlets were forced to renew their coverage (Shachtman, 2002). Lott's eventual resignation has been attributed to the influence exerted by bloggers. Similarly, blogs have shone a light onto stories missed by the traditional media, thereby acting as agenda setters for the mass media (Bloom, 2003; Delwiche, 2004).

Bloggers as Journalists

Media attention to blogs has grown in proportion to the increase in the number of blogs published. In their study of blog influence, Drezner and Farrell (2004) found that only 11 news articles published between 1995 and 1999 used the term "blog"; by 2003 that number had grown to 647. Part of the interest of the mainstream media stems from the perception of blogging as an alternative form of journalism (Blood, 2003; Bloom, 2003; Gillmor, 2003; Lasica, 2002, 2003; Welch, 2003).

However, although some of the most read A-list bloggers are professional journalists (Park, 2003), most bloggers would not call themselves journalists (Lasica, 2002) and do not even dream of becoming journalists (Cook, 2005). Their writing would not qualify as journalism because most blogs "focus on narrow subject matter of interest to a select but circumscribed niche. And the blogs that do contain bona fide news are largely derivative, posting links to other blogs and, in many cases, print journalism" (Andrews, 2003).

Warbloggers

Among the blogs that have attracted the most media attention are the so-called warblogs. Warbloggers are filter bloggers who express their views on current political events. In recent years, they have addressed post-9/11 issues, in particular the wars in Afghanistan and Iraq. Early warbloggers were labeled "a hawkish bunch" (Cavanaugh, 2002), but more recent accounts have credited warbloggers with the rise of antiwar sentiments (Chesher, 2005).

Warblogging differs from journalistic blogging in that most warbloggers write their commentary at a safe distance from the action on which they comment (Cavanaugh, 2002). To publish their commentaries, they depend on the mainstream media for the details that populate their writings. Other warblogs are written by those in the field—in particular by members of the armed forces, embedded reporters, Iraqis, or others who write about their firsthand experiences (Thompson, 2003). Whether issuing firsthand accounts or commentary on published news, warbloggers differ from mainstream news media in their open inclusion of personal outlook in their writing (Wall, 2004).

The period of our data collection and analysis coincides with the onset of U.S. hostilities and the official declaration of war against Iraq—a highly controversial topic in the blogosphere. The Iraq war was also made a central issue by bloggers in the 2004 U.S. presidential election campaign. (For the role played by blogging in the campaign, see, for example, Bloom, 2003, and Kerbel & Bloom, 2005.)

Content Analysis of Blogs

Content analysis has been used to analyze the structure, purpose and themes found in high-profile blogs. Lawson–Borders and Kirk (2005) analyzed campaign blogs of political candidates during the 2004 U.S. presidential election. They found that the blogs were primarily social diaries and organizing tools for the candidates. Trammell and Keshelashvili (2005) conducted a content analysis of 209 single-authored A-list blogs drawn from Popdex. The list included blogs written by men and women; the men produced primarily filter blogs and the women wrote more blogs in the styles of diaries. Trammell and Keshelashvili (2005) found that all of the A-list blogs included elements of self-revelation and that metadiscourse about blogging was a common theme.

Content analysis methods have also been used to analyze ordinary blogs. Herring, Scheidt et al. (2004, 2005) employed content analysis as a means to characterize blogs as a genre. In a random sample of 203 blogs selected from the blog-tracking site blo.gs in spring 2003, the authors found that the average English-language blog had a single author, focused on personal events in the blogger's life, contained relatively few links and received few comments. Papacharissi (2004) conducted a quantitative content analysis of a random sample of 260 blogs hosted by Blogger.com and found similar results. Papacharissi characterizes blogs as having more in common with diaries than with independent journalism.

In a follow-on study that added 154 blogs to their original sample, Herring, Kouper et al. (2004) found that ordinary bloggers were female nearly as often as male and young (teens or young adults) as often as adult. However, gender and age of bloggers varied according to blog type: Adult males wrote almost all of the filter blogs and young females wrote the largest proportion of personal journal (diary) blogs.

Recent research suggests that there may also be cultural differences in blogging practices. In their content analysis of 358 random Polish-language blogs drawn from the blog-hosting service blog.pl, Trammell, Tarkowski, Hofmokl and Sapp (2006) found that Polish bloggers are more often female (nearly 75%) and younger than English-language bloggers; they are often elementary and middle-school ages. Similarly to Scheidt (2006), however, Trammell and her colleagues found that the themes of young Polish female bloggers' posts tend to focus on the emotional impact of the life events that they are relaying.

The present study goes beyond previous research by incorporating a longitudinal perspective. Our primary research question concerns the extent to which the characteristics of random English-language blogs and blog authors (e.g., as identified by Herring, Scheidt et al., 2004, 2005; Herring, Kouper et al., 2004; Papacharissi, 2004) remained stable or changed between 2003 and 2004. The answer to this question has implications for understanding the nature of emergence and change in new media, and for predicting future trends in blogging practice.

Methodology

Data

The data for this study are three samples of blogs collected randomly at roughly 6-month intervals. During March and April 2003, 203 blogs were collected; 154 blogs were collected on September 29 and September 30, 2003, and 100 blogs were collected on April 12 and April 13, 2004, for a total of 457 blogs. All three samples were obtained by using the random blog selection feature of the blog-tracking website blo.gs. At the time, the blo.gs site tracked the largest number of blogs from the most diverse sources. (The site has since been bought by Yahoo! and the random selection feature disabled.) Individuals could contact blo.gs to have their blogs tracked, and lists of updated blogs were imported by blo.gs every hour from antville.org, blogger.com, pitas.com and weblogs.com. Later in the study period, blo.gs also began tracking some blogs from LiveJournal and other blog-hosting sites.

To create coherent corpora that would lead to optimally interpretable results, for the purpose of this study we excluded non-English-language blogs, photo and audio blogs and instances of blog software used for nonblog purposes (e.g., news aggregators, community center events calendars, retail/advertising). We also excluded blogs containing fewer than two entries, to ensure that the blogs were not one-time experiments. Thus, generalizations from this study apply only to active, English-language, text-based blogs. These constituted the majority of blogs available during the period under investigation.[2]

Analytical Methods

Content analysis (Bauer, 2000; see Bates & Lu, 1997; Ha & James, 1998; McMillan, 2000, for applications of content analysis methodology to websites) was conducted to identify and quantify structural and functional properties of the blogs in the three corpora. We coded for 22 categories, including blogger characteristics, blog type, blog software used and textual and interactive features of the first (most recent) entry. These codes are a reduced set of those developed and described in greater detail in Herring, Scheidt et al. (2004, 2005).

Blogger characteristics include gender, age, occupation (if indicated) and identity indicators (e.g., choice of name, inclusion of photo). We searched for this information throughout the entire blog. *Blog type* codes include filter, personal journal and k(nowledge)-log. A blog was coded as one of the first three types if a clear majority of its entries exhibited the labeled content; blogs with a roughly balanced mix of content were coded as "mixed" and blogs whose content indicated a purpose other than those described here were coded as "other." Blog type was usually identifiable from the title, blog description (if any) and entries on the blog's home page. Finally, the *first blog entry* was coded for number and nature of links (e.g., to other blogs or news sources), number of comments received and presence of images. We also measured text length by counting the number of words and sentences in the first entry of each blog.

The spring and fall 2003 samples were coded by three out of the four authors, who achieved better than 80% agreement on code assignment, and the spring 2004 sample was coded by the third author. Coding for all three samples was checked for consistency by the first author. The findings are reported in this chapter using descriptive statistics with a focus on comparison across the three samples. Because multiauthored blogs are infrequent in the samples (see Table 1.4) and raise separate issues about blog authorship, most of the findings are reported for single-authored blogs only.

Results

The results of the longitudinal content analysis can be grouped into three categories: change, stability and variability. Change indicates that certain characteristics of blogs show a clear pattern of increasing or decreasing over time. Stability refers to characteristics that do not change appreciably over time. Variability indicates results that do not show a clear directional pattern, but rather fluctuate from sample to sample.

Change Over Time   An examination of the structural characteristics of entries in single-authored blogs reveals that despite the general expectation that the web will generate more and more multimedia content (Herring, 2004), the blogs in our corpus became increasingly text-based. Over time, bloggers tended to post longer entries with more words and more sentences that included fewer images. Blogs also became less connected to each other (see Table 1.1) and to the rest of the web as the average number of links per entry decreased. The results for these structural characteristics are summarized in Table 1.1. Change over time in the average number of words per entry is also represented graphically in Figure 1.1. As Table 1.1. shows, even in the first sample, the frequency of images per entry is very low (0.11). The average number of links per entry also started out low (0.65), considering popular claims about the overall connectivity of the blogosphere (e.g., Blood, 2002). In light of

Table 1.1 Structural Characteristics of Blog Entries

	Number of words	Number of sentences	Number of images	Number of links	Number of comments
Spring 2003	202.95	15.17	0.11	0.65	0.40
Fall 2003	224.51	17.87	0.04	0.43	0.64
Spring 2004	299.62	22.05	0.04	0.47	0.39

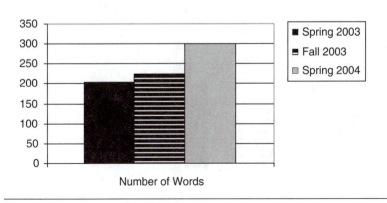

Figure 1.1 Average number of words in blog entries.

this, although the amount of measurable change is slight, the fact that images and links decreased rather than held constant or increased is noteworthy. The number of comments per entry fluctuated, but also remained low overall (0.4, 0.6, 0.4).[3]

It is often claimed that computer-mediated communication encourages anonymity. The data from the three samples do not support this claim; rather, most of the blog authors provided some identifiable personal information. This tendency increased over time: 65.9, 77.3 and 78.6% of authors in the three samples, respectively, used their first name or their full name. In particular, the use of first names increased over time; in contrast, pseudonyms and blogs in which no name was given decreased steadily. These results are summarized in Table 1.2 and represented graphically in Figure 1.2. The tendency for first names to increase at the expense of all other name types suggests that first names were emerging as the conventional means of blogger self-reference during this period.

Table 1.2 Blogger Name Types

	Spring 2003	Fall 2003	Spring 2004
No name	14 (8%)	8 (5.7%)	4 (4.5%)
Pseudonym	43 (24.4%)	23 (16.3%)	13 (14.6%)
First name (or transparently derived nickname)	57 (32.4%)	74 (52.5%)	44 (49.4%)
Full name	59 (33.5%)	35 (24.8%)	26 (29.2%)
Other	1 (0.6%)	—	1 (1.1%)
First name and initial	2 (1.1%)	1 (0.7%)	—
Initial and last name	—	—	1 (1.1%)
Total	176 (100%)	141 (100%)	89 (100%)

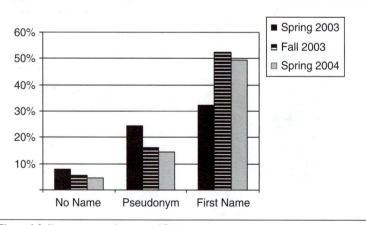

Figure 1.2 No names, pseudonyms and first names.

A majority of bloggers also explicitly or implicitly gave some indication of their occupation. More than half of the bloggers were students in all three samples (see Table 1.3), although the frequency fluctuated somewhat over time. The second most frequent occupation was information technology work (programmers, webmasters, system administrators, etc.); its frequency increased from 15.4% in spring 2003 to 16.2% in fall 2003 to 20.4% in spring 2004. Although the numbers involved are small, we include this finding because it is contrary to what we expected based on the popular view that blogging is increasingly being adopted by "ordinary," less technically sophisticated users.

Stability Over Time Two main characteristics of the blogs in our corpus remained stable over time: the number of blog authors and the presence of an image (typically a photograph) of the author on the home page of the blog. An overwhelming majority of blogs were created and maintained by one author (Table 1.4). In an almost equal number of cases, the blogs lacked an image of the blog author (Table 1.5). This last practice contrasts with the practice in personal home pages (Bates & Lu, 1997) and contributes to the impression that these blogs are primarily textual documents. In addition, the blogging software used to host and publish blogs remained stable overall, despite some fluctuations. Blogger was the preferred publishing software in all three samples (67.9, 77.5 and 67.4%, respectively), while various other blog software types gained or lost users over time. Over the 13-month period, Movable Type and Pitas lost ground, and LiveJournal and Blogdrive gained in popularity.

Table 1.3 Occupation of Blog Authors for Whom Occupation Could Be Determined

	Spring 2003	Fall 2003	Spring 2004
Student	53 (50.9%)	62 (59.0%)	30 (55.6%)
Teacher/faculty	11 (10.6%)	2 (1.9%)	3 (5.6%)
IT worker	16 (15.4%)	17 (16.2%)	11 (20.4%)
Other[a]	24 (23.1%)	24 (22.9%)	10 (18.5%)
Total	104 (100%)	105 (100%)	54 (100%)

[a] Occupations in this category were encountered fewer than 10 times in all three samples.

Table 1.4 Number of Blog Authors

	Spring 2003	Fall 2003	Spring 2004
One author	176 (91.2%)	141 (92.8%)	89 (89.0%)
Multiple authors	17 (8.8%)	11 (7.2%)	11 (11.0%)
Total	193 (100%)	152 (100%)	100 (100%)

Table 1.5 Presence of Author Image on Blog Home Page

	Spring 2003	Fall 2003	Spring 2004
No image	128 (81%)	104 (80%)	60 (80%)
Image	30 (19%)	26 (20%)	15 (20%)
Total	158 (100%)	130 (100%)	75 (100%)

Table 1.6 Blogging Software Used

	Spring 2003	Fall 2003	Spring 2004
Blogger	106 (67.9%)	107 (77.5%)	58 (67.4%)
Movable Type	19 (12.2%)	14 (10.1%)	5 (5.8%)
Pitas	12 (7.7%)	—	3 (3.5%)
Radio	6 (3.8%)	—	—
Blogdrive	—	6 (4.3%)	8 (9.3%)
LiveJournal	—	5 (3.6%)	3 (3.5%)
TypePad	—	3 (2.2%)	3 (3.5%)
Other	13 (8.4%)	3 (2.1%)	6 (7%)
Total	156 (100%)	138 (100%)	86 (100%)

However, none of these fluctuations affected the overall dominance of Blogger. The frequencies for the most common types of blogging software used in the samples are shown in Table 1.6.

Variability Over Time The largest number of features displays a pattern of variability, according to which the first and third samples pattern together in contrast with the second sample. This variable pattern is evident for blogger gender, blogger age, blog type and link type. It is also evident to some extent for number of comments, student bloggers and use of Blogger software. Gender of blog authors is shown in Table 1.7 and represented graphically in Figure 1.3. A majority of bloggers are male in Sample 1 and Sample 3, whereas in Sample 2 males and females are represented nearly equally (with a slight female majority).

Table 1.7 Gender of Blog Authors

	Spring 2003	Fall 2003	Spring 2004
Male	95 (54%)	68 (48.2%)	51 (57.3%)
Female	74 (42%)	70 (49.6%)	36 (40.4%)
Unknown	7 (4%)	3 (2.1%)	2 (2.2%)
Total	176 (100%)	141 (100%)	89 (100%)

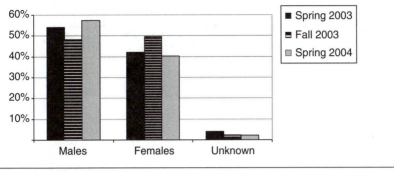

Figure 1.3 Gender of blog authors.

Table 1.8 Age of Blog Authors

	Spring 2003	Fall 2003	Spring 2004
Adult	105 (64.8%)	50 (38.2%)	42 (47.2%)
Teenager	44 (27.2%)	50 (38.2%)	23 (25.8%)
Young adult	13 (8%)	31 (23.7%)	24 (27%)
Total	162 (100%)	131 (100%)	89 (100%)

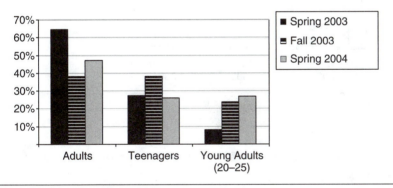

Figure 1.4 Age of blog authors.

Regarding age, adult bloggers predominate in Sample 1 and Sample 3, whereas Sample 2 has equal numbers of adults and teenagers. The percentage of young adults (aged 20 to 25) increases across the three samples. These patterns are shown in Table 1.8 and Figure 1.4.

Blog type exhibits similar variation. Although not as common as personal journals overall, filter blogs are more frequent in Sample 1 and Sample 3 than in Sample 2; personal journals show the inverse pattern. Mixed blogs pattern with personal journals; k-logs and blogs classified as "other" were infrequent in all three samples. The frequencies of all blog types are shown in Table 1.9.

Table 1.9 Blog Type

	Spring 2003	Fall 2003	Spring 2004
Personal journal	115 (65.3%)	105 (74.5%)	60 (67.4%)
Filter	25 (14.2%)	9 (6.4%)	14 (15.7%)
K-log	7 (4%)	3 (2.1%)	2 (2.2%)
Mixed	22 (12.5%)	21 (14.9%)	10 (11.2%)
Other	6 (3.4%)	3 (2.1%)	1 (1.3%)
Unknown	1 (0.6%)	—	2 (2.2%)
Total	176 (100%)	141 (100%)	89 (100%)

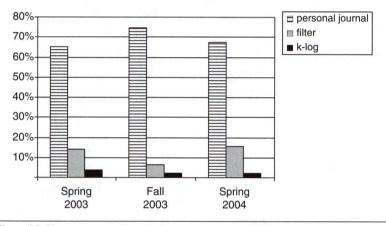

Figure 1.5 Blog type: personal journal, filter and k-log.

Figure 1.5 graphically represents the distribution of personal journals, filters and k-logs.

Even the links in the first entries show this pattern of variation for some link types. Links to news sources and other websites are more frequent in Sample 1 and Sample 3 than in Sample 2, whereas entries with no links are most frequent in Sample 2. Links to other blogs (considered by Blood, 2002, to be an essential characteristic of the blog genre), in contrast, were surprisingly infrequent and tend to decrease over time. These findings are summarized in Table 1.10.

Finally, the first and third samples also differ from the second in terms of number of comments received on entries (Table 1.1), number of student

Table 1.10 Link Types

	Spring 2003	Fall 2003	Spring 2004
No links	120 (61.2%)	112 (76.7%)	65 (70.7%)
Links to other blogs	11 (5.6%)	8 (5.5%)	2 (2.2%)
Links to news sources	13 (6.6%)	6 (4.1%)	8 (8.7%)
Links to other websites created by blogger	4 (2%)	2 (1.4%)	—
Links to websites created by others	47 (24%)	16 (11%)	17 (18.5%)
Internal blog links	1 (0.5%)	2 (1.4%)	—
Total	196 (100%)	146 (100%)	92 (100%)

bloggers (Table 1.5) and use of Blogger software (Table 1.6). All of these are highest in Sample 2.

Discussion

Despite the relatively brief time span covered in this study (13 months), some changes were evident in the characteristics of the blogs sampled. During the study period, blog entries became more textual, supporting the trend identified in Herring (2004) towards renewed popularity of textual forms of CMC. Blog authors increasingly presented themselves by their first name and decreasingly by other means, suggesting convergence towards a convention of friendly, informal self-identification. These changes may reflect the fact that blogs were still relatively young and emergent as a mode of computer-mediated communication in 2003 and 2004.

At the same time, many characteristics of the blog genre remained fairly stable during this period. Consistent with earlier findings, the frequency of links and comments in blog entries remained low. This finding is contrary to the popular characterization of the blogosphere as interconnected and conversational (see also Herring, Kouper et al., 2005). The longitudinal evidence also supports the earlier characterization of most blogs as single-authored, personal diaries (Herring, Scheidt et al. 2004, 2005; Papacharissi, 2004). The overall predominance of personal over news content, together with the low incidence of links to news sources, argues against any simple equation of blogging with "citizen journalism" (Gillmor, 2003). Moreover, the stability of these findings suggests that the blog genre had already taken on these characteristics by spring 2003.

It remains to explain the pattern of variability according to which many characteristics of blog content and blog authors differed between samples 1 and 3 and sample 2. We suggest that these characteristics are interrelated and that the variation reflects variation in external events—specifically, in the concentration and nature of the newsworthy events taking place at the time during which the three samples were collected.

Although the entire 13-month period was active in terms of news about the Iraq war, more important events—especially those relating to Iraq—took place just before the spring 2003 and spring 2004 samples than before the fall 2003 sample. September was a relatively quiet news month, with the exception of the stabbing of the Swedish foreign minister in a department store on September 10 and Estonia's announcement that it would join the European Union on September 14. These events did not attract much attention in the blogosphere.

In contrast, spring 2003 saw the outbreak of the Iraq war and the "shock and awe" bombing of Baghdad. Spring 2004 saw the Madrid bombings, the start of civil war in Iraq and John Kerry's unseating of Howard Dean in the U.S. Democratic presidential primaries. Both periods were followed by a dramatic rise in new blog creation compared to the number of new blogs created after September 2003 (Sifry, 2004), as shown in Figure 1.6.

We suggest that the events around the time of Sample 1 and Sample 3 triggered more blogging about those events, in addition to inspiring more people to start blogging. Although we did not code for the subject matter of blogs in this study, indirect evidence from the characteristics that we analyzed supports this view. The number of filter blogs was highest in the first and third samples, as were the numbers of male bloggers and adult bloggers. By definition, filter blogs comment on external events and thus are more likely to link

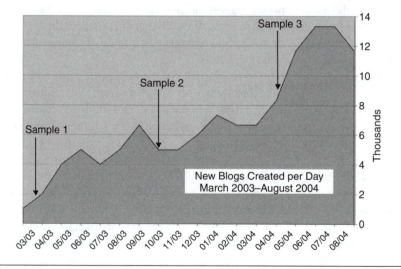

Figure 1.6 New blogs created after each sampling point. (Modified from Sifry, D., 2004, *Sifry's Alerts*. Retrieved February 16, 2006, from http://www.sifry.com/alerts/archives/000419.html.)

to news sources and other websites. Filter blogs are also written most often by adult males (Herring, Kouper et al., 2004; Trammell & Keshelashvili, 2005).

Conversely, the second sample included the highest proportion of personal journal blogs, fewer links, more students and more equal numbers of women and young people, more of whom used easily accessed Blogger software. This pattern suggests what blogs might look like in calmer times. As such it has implications for the future of blogging, since, in a larger historical perspective, times of peace are more common than times of war.

Conclusion

This study presented what we believe is the first longitudinal content analysis of blogs. More longitudinal analysis is needed as the blog genre continues to evolve and expand its range of uses. In particular, research is needed on multimedia modes of blogging such as photoblogs and audio and video blogging, which increased in popularity after our data collection period, as well as on the recent phenomenon of podcasting. It may be that the increase in textuality we observed from 2003 to 2004 was accompanied by an increasing specialization in multimedia elsewhere in the repertoire of blog types. Understanding the forces operating in this process of differentiation could have broader implications for the study of the evolution of new media formats.

This research was carried out at a historically significant moment: during the first year of the controversial U.S.-led war against Iraq. However, it did not analyze blog content specifically about the war or other news events. We do not know, for example, to what extent the filter bloggers in our samples were "warbloggers." Future longitudinal research should focus on the themes that are blogged about to probe in greater depth the relationship between blogging and the external world. The present study suggests that this relationship has a gender dimension, in line with the public man / private woman dichotomy identified in previous research (Elshtain, 1993): external bloggers are more often male than female. This dynamic also calls for further exploration.

Perhaps the greatest challenge in analyzing blogs longitudinally lies in identifying comparable samples at different points in time. In this study, we used blogs randomly selected by the blog-tracking site blo.gs, which more or less ensured that we were drawing from the same sources, even though blo.gs expanded its coverage somewhat during the period of our data collection. The random selection service has since been discontinued, however, constraining our ability to extend the methodology of this study to later samples. Stable tools for identifying, tracking and searching blogs are essential to facilitate longitudinal analysis of the blogosphere, as well as to enhance the functionality of blogs.

References

Andrews, P. (2003). Is blogging journalism? *Nieman Reports, 57*(3), 63–64. Retrieved April 24, 2006, from http://www.nieman.harvard.edu/reports/03-3NRfall/V57N3.pdf.

Bates, M. J., & Lu, S. (1997). An exploratory profile of personal home pages: Content, design, metaphors. *Online and CD Review, 21*, 331–340.

Bauer, M. W. (2000). Classical content analysis: A review. In M. W. Bauer & G. Gaskell (Eds.), *Qualitative researching with text, image, and sound: A practical handbook* (pp. 131–151). London: Sage Publications.

Blood, R. (2002). Introduction. In J. Rodzvilla (Ed.), *We've got blog: How weblogs are changing our culture* (pp. ix–xiii). Cambridge MA: Perseus Publishing.

Blood, R. (2003). Weblogs and journalism: Do they connect? *Nieman Reports, 57*(3), 61–62. Retrieved April 24, 2006, from http://www.nieman.harvard.edu/reports/03-3NRfall/V57N3.pdf.

Bloom, J. (2003, August). The blogosphere: How a once-humble medium came to drive elite media discourse and influence public policy and elections. *Proceedings of the annual meeting of the American Political Science Association.* Philadelphia: American Political Science Association. Retrieved April 24, 2006, from http://www.uoregon.edu/~jbloom/APSA03.pdf.

Cavanaugh, T. (2002). Let slip the blogs of war. In J. Rodzvilla (Ed.), *We've got blog: How weblogs are changing our culture* (pp. 188–197). Cambridge, MA: Perseus Publishing. Retrieved March 24, 2006, from http://www.ojr.org/ojr/workplace/1017770789.php.

Chesher, C. (2005, May). *Blogs and the crisis of authorship.* Presented at the meeting of the Blogtalk Downunder, Sydney. Retrieved May 24, 2005, from http://incsub.org/blogtalk/?page_id=40.

Cook, T. (2005, May). *Up against reality: Blogging and the cost of content.* Presented at the meeting of the Blogtalk Downunder, Sydney. Retrieved May 24, 2005, from http://incsub.org/blogtalk/?page_id=42.

Delwiche, A. (2004, May). *Agenda-setting, opinion leadership, and the world of Web logs.* Paper presented at the Annual Conference of the International Communication Association, New Orleans, LA.

Drezner, D., & Farrell, H. (2004, September). The power and politics of blogs. *Proceedings of the annual meeting of the American Political Science Association.* Chicago, IL: American Political Science Association. Retrieved November 30, 2004, from http://archive.allacademic.com/publication/getfile.php?file=docs/apsa_proceeding/2004-08-18/30340/apsa_proceeding_30340.PDF&PHPSESSID=d99a266b9d5b3aa8aad8c907a2cdbf1e.

Elshtain, J. B. (1993). *Public man, private woman: Women in social and political thought,* 2nd ed. Princeton, NJ: Princeton University Press.

Gillmor, D. (2003). Moving toward participatory journalism. *Nieman Reports, 57*(3), 79–80. Retrieved April 24, 2006, from http://www.nieman.harvard.edu/reports/03-3NRfall/V57N3.pdf.

Ha, L., & James, E. L. (1998). Interactivity reexamined: A baseline analysis of early business Web sites. *Journal of Broadcasting and Electronic Media, 42*, 457–474.

Henning, J. (2003). The blogging iceberg—Of 4.12 million hosted weblogs, most little seen, quickly abandoned. Perseus Development Corporation White Papers. Retrieved July 6, 2006, from http://www.perseus.com/blogsurvey/.

Henning, J. (2005, April 12). The blogging geyser. Perseus Development Corporation White Papers. Retrieved July 6, 2006, from http://www.perseus.com/blogsurvey/geyser.html.

Herring, S. C. (2004). Slouching toward the ordinary: Current trends in computer-mediated communication. *New Media & Society, 6*(1), 26–36.

Herring, S. C., Kouper, I., Scheidt, L. A. & Wright, E. (2004). Women and children last: The discursive construction of weblogs. In L. Gurak, S. Antonijevic, L. Johnson, C. Ratliff & J. Reyman (Eds.), *Into the blogosphere: Rhetoric, community, and culture of weblogs.* Minneapolis: University of Minnesota Press. Retrieved March 24, 2006, from http://blog.lib.umn.edu/blogosphere/women_and_children html.

Herring, S. C., Kouper, I., Paolillo, J. C., Scheidt, L. A., Tyworth, M., Welsch, P., Wright, E. & Yu, N. (2005). Conversations in the blogosphere: An analysis "from the bottom up." *Proceedings of the Thirty-Eighth Hawaii International Conference on System Sciences (HICSS-38)*. Los Alamitos: IEEE Computer Society Press. Retrieved April 24, 2006, from http://ella.slis.indiana.edu/~herring/blogconv.pdf.

Herring, S. C., Scheidt, L. A., Bonus, S. & Wright, E. (2004). Bridging the gap: A genre analysis of weblogs. *Proceedings of the 37th Hawaii International Conference on System Sciences (HICSS-37)*. Los Alamitos: IEEE Computer Society Press. Retrieved April 24, 2006, from http://www.blogninja.com/DDGDD04.doc.

Herring, S. C., Scheidt, L. A., Bonus, S. & Wright, E. (2005). Weblogs as a bridging genre. *Information, Technology & People, 18*(2), 142–171.

Kerbel, M. R., & Bloom, J. D. (2005). Blog for America and civic involvement. *The Harvard International Journal of Press/Politics, 10*(4), 3–27. Retrieved March 24, 2006, from http://www.uoregon.edu/~jbloom/BlogforAmerica.pdf.

Krishnamurthy, S. (2002, October). *The multidimensionality of blog conversations: The Virtual Enactment of September 11*. Presented at the meeting of the Internet Research 3.0: NET / WORK / THEORY, Association of Internet Researchers (AoIR), Maastricht, The Netherlands.

Lasica, J. D. (2002, April 18). Blogging as a form of journalism. *USC Annenberg Online Journalism Review*. Retrieved March 24, 2006, from http://www.ojr.org/ojr/lasica/1019166956.php.

Lasica, J. D. (2003). Blogs and journalism need each other. *Nieman Reports, 57*(3), 70–73. Retrieved April 24, 2006, from http://www.nieman.harvard.edu/reports/03-3NRfall/V57N3.pdf.

Lawson–Borders, G., & Kirk, R. (2005). Blogs in campaign communication. *American Behavioral Scientist, 49*(4), 548–559.

Lenhart, A., Horrigan, J. B. & Fallows, D. (2004, June). Content creation online. Pew Internet and American Life Project. Retrieved April 24, 2006, from http://www.pewinternet.org/pdfs/PIP_Content_Creation_Report.pdf.

McMillan, S. J. (2000). The microscope and the moving target: The challenge of applying content analysis to the World Wide Web. *Journalism and Mass Communication Quarterly, 77*(1), 80–98.

Miller, C. R., & Shepherd, D. (2004). Blogging as social action: A genre analysis of the weblog. In L. Gurak, S. Antonijevic, L. Johnson, C. Ratliff & J. Reyman (Eds.), *Into the blogosphere: Rhetoric, community, and culture of blogs*. University of Minnesota Press. Retrieved March 24, 2006, from http://blog.lib.umn.edu/blogosphere/blogging_as_social_action_a_genre_analysis_of_the_blog.html.

Nardi, B., Schiano, D. & Gumbrecht, M. (2004). Blogging as social activity, or, would you let 900 million people read your diary? *Proceedings of computer-supported cooperative work 2004*. Retrieved March 24, 2006, from http://home.comcast.net/%7Ediane.schiano/CSCW04.Blog.pdf.

Papacharissi, Z. (2004, May). *The blogger revolution? Audiences as media producers*. Paper presented at the Annual Conference of the International Communication Association, New Orleans, LA.

Park, D. (2003, October). *Bloggers and warbloggers as public intellectuals: Charging the authoritative space of the weblog*. Paper presented at Internet Research 4.0, Toronto, Canada.

Scheidt, L. A. (2006). Adolescent diary weblogs and the unseen audience. In D. Buckingham & R. Willett (Eds.), *Digital generations: Children, young people and new media*. London: Lawrence Erlbaum Associates. Retrieved March 28, 2006, from http://loisscheidt.com/linked/2006/Adolescent_Diary_Blogs_and_the_Unseen_Audience.pdf. 193–210.

Shachtman, N. (2002, December 23). Blogs make the headlines. *Wired News*. Retrieved March 24, 2006, from http://www.wired.com/news/culture/0,1284,56978,00.html.

Sifry, D. (2004, October 10). State of the blogosphere, October 2004 (Part 1). *Sifry's Alerts*. Retrieved March 25, 2006, from http://www.sifry.com/alerts/archives/000387.html.

Sifry, D. (2006, February 6). State of the blogosphere, February 2006. Part 1: On blogosphere growth. *Sifry's Alerts*. Retrieved February 16, 2006, from http://www.sifry.com/alerts/archives/000419.html.

Stone, B. (2004). *Who let the blogs out? A hyperconnected peek at the world of weblogs*. New York: St. Martin's Press.

Thompson, G. (2003). Blogs, warblogs, the public sphere, and bubbles. Retrieved March 24, 2006, from http://www.svsu.edu/~glt/Transformations_piecerev.pdf.

Trammell, K. D., & Keshelashvili, A. (2005). Examining the new influencers: A self-presentation study of A-List blogs. *Journalism & Mass Communication Quarterly, 82*(4), 968–982.

Trammell, K. D., Tarkowski, A., Hofmokl, J. & Sapp, A. (2006). Rzeczpospolita blogów [Republic of blog]: Examining the motivations of Polish bloggers through content analysis. *Journal of Computer-Mediated Communication, 11*(3). Retrieved July 3, 2006, from http://jcmc.indiana.edu/vol11/issue3/trammell.html.

Turnbull, G. (1999, August 30). Log on for the latest Internet craze. *The Scotsman.* Retrieved through EBSCO.

Turnbull, G. (2001, February 26). The state of the blog: Part 1: Blogger past. *WriteTheWeb.* Retrieved November 28, 2004, from http://writetheweb.com/Members/gilest/old/106/.

Wall, M. A. (2004, May). *Blogs of war: The changing nature of news in the 21st century.* Presented at the Annual Conference of the International Communication Association, New Orleans, LA.

Welch, M. (2003). Blogworld and its gravity. *Columbia Journalism Review, 42*(3), 21–27.

Winer, D. (2001, September 11). Bulletin: Terrorist attack in NY. *DaveNet.* Retrieved March 25, 2006, from http://davenet.scripting.com/2001/09/11/bulletinTerroristAttackInNy.

Notes

1. Since the time of the data collection for this study, the blogosphere continues to grow. By February 2006, Technorati was estimating that the blogosphere was over 60 times the size it was in 2003 (Sifry, 2006).

2. We did not draw random blogs from blog-hosting services such as LiveJournal and Xanga (other than those tracked through blo.gs) because the infrastructure and the blogging practices of those services, especially in 2003, seemed sufficiently different to warrant separate treatment. The patterns identified in the present analysis may not apply to blogs hosted on those services.

3. About half of the blogs in all three samples did not allow comments on entries because that was the default setting of the blog software used or because the author had deactivated the comment option. The average numbers of comments received for blogs that allowed comments are still low and show a similar pattern of fluctuation across the three samples (0.9, 1.3, 0.7).

2

Audiences as Media Producers: Content Analysis of 260 Blogs

ZIZI PAPACHARISSI

Advertised by Blogger.com as "push-button publishing for the people," blogs provide the opportunity for amateur journalism and personalized publishing. Some of the most frequently cited blogs are hosted by journalists, like Andrew Sullivan (andrewsullivan.com) and Mickey Kaus (kausfiles.com). A weblog or blog is a webpage that consists of regular or daily posts, arranged in reverse chronological order and archived (e.g., Herring, Kouper, Scheidt & Wright, 2004). Blogs present a significant topic of study because they provide the opportunity to study media audiences as content producers instead of content consumers (Dominick, 1999; Papacharissi, 2002a, 2002b).

Blogs provide media consumers with an audience and a relatively audible voice; they also offer a virtual space where information ignored by mainstream media can be published. As Andrew Sullivan (2002) argues, blogging is "arguably the most significant media revolution since the arrival of television," providing the ability to "make arguments, fact-check them and rebut them in a seamless and endless conversation" (A4). In addition, this study adds to the body of literature examining the role of the Internet as a revitalizer of social relations, together with growing research on the social potential of the Internet revealing beneficial and harmful behavioral consequences of Internet use (Katz & Aspden, 1997; Kraut et al., 1998, 2002; Nie & Erbring, 2000). Extensive studies of blogs have demonstrated their ability to create online networks social contact (e.g., Herring, Scheidt et al. 2004; Herring, Kouper et al., 2004).

Communication researchers have studied personal home pages in the past (Dominick, 1999; Papacharissi, 2002a, 2002b; Walker, 2000), but they have not focused on blogging, which is different because it: (a) utilizes more user-friendly software; (b) sometimes presupposes a journalistic approach; and (c) dictates a diary-like format and orientation. This study analyzes a random sample of all such blogs to determine content characteristics and speculate on gratifications obtained from sustaining them. This approach should help us consider audiences as producers of media content, determine whether this technology extends the traditional boundaries of journalism and address the personal and social gratifications of blogging.

Blogging as Self-Expression and Social Connectivity

The advent of new media technologies—specifically, personalized publishing—has provided communication researchers with the opportunity to examine media audiences not just as consumers, but also as producers of mass media. Numerous aspects of creative online activity have thus been unveiled, focusing on self-expression, use of rhetorical strategies, socialization and display of alternative content. In an analysis of the rhetorical construction of self in personal websites, Smith (1998) studied strategies webpage hosts use to present the self and invite communication, revealed through a case study of a personal website focusing on fuller figured people. Smith explained how online tools allowed individuals to project their identity and establish connections with online audiences. Specifically, he constructed a taxonomy of web-based invitational strategies, identifying the following:

feedback mechanisms (e-mail, guestbook and others)
vertical hierarchies (the position of items on the page, from top to bottom)
personal expertise
external validation (awards bestowed upon the site)
direct address
personality

In the same vein, Dominick (1999) conducted a content analysis of personal home pages and found that the typical page had a brief biography, a counter or guest book and links to other pages. For Dominick, the manner in which individuals used links on their personal home pages as a means of social association was of special interest because people indirectly defined themselves and their social status by listing their interests and linking to other sites. Webpage hosts also sought positive reinforcement and social contact by inviting visitors to e-mail them or sign and view their "guestbooks" (collections of visitor signatures and comments). Even though most webpages did not contain much personal information, the strategies used for self-representation online were very similar to those used in face-to-face settings.

Walker examined several personal home pages qualitatively to study self-presentation online and found that several authors used personal home pages as a back-up for online interaction or to create and support a specific identity. The Internet facilitated expressions of connectedness through the use of hyperlinks and, at the same time, constrained personal expression through templates that enforced a certain type of structure and content (Walker, 2000).

This focus on self-presentation was further investigated by Papacharissi (2002a), who combined survey and content analysis to understand the utility of personal home pages for their creators. Even though most web authors created a page for information- and entertainment-related purposes, several sustained one for self-expression purposes and to communicate with friends and family. Fewer used them for professional advancement or to pass time. The research also revealed that those less socially active and less satisfied with their lives tended to see the webpage as a way of passing the time and spent more time editing their pages and using the Internet. Overall, the results indicated that this medium further pronounced existent personality predispositions, allowing those who were social to become even more so, while those socially removed became more engrossed in solitary Internet-related activities.

A more extensive follow-up content analysis by Papacharissi (2002b) revealed that the creative potential of personal home pages was somewhat limited by personal home page providers, who inadvertently influenced page design for the less experienced users by providing specific design tools and templates. Therefore, AOL and MSN users were directed to less inventive and more limiting formats, and Geocities users were guided to create more original pages by tools that allowed greater innovation. These findings can be applied to blogs to understand variations in content, expressive strategies and the utility of blogs for individual users. Moreover, a study of content and design templates offered by blog providers can help determine how individual creativity is enhanced or compromised by the extent of publishing services offered.

Recent studies focusing on blogs have demonstrated bloggers' tendency to follow the templates provided by blogging venues faithfully. For instance, in a content analysis of a random sample of blogs, Scheidt and Wright (2004) found that bloggers did not deviate from the standard layout of the blog host and mostly used slightly altered templates provided by the blog venue. Most individual customization was located within a sidebar area, standard with most templates. The lack of visual customization points to the influence exerted by the design and tools offered by the blogspace provider and the primary function of blogs as tools of personal expression and connectivity, rather than artistic creativity.

The focus of this study, then, is to examine descriptive elements of blogs and possible gratification obtained from authoring them, while at the same time investigating the journalistic potential of this medium. Several studies suggest that the journalistic potential of blogs is frequently exaggerated in popular folklore, at the expense of more meaningful social objectives sustained by blogs (i.e., Herring et al., 2005; Herring, Kouper et al., 2004; Herring, Scheidt et al., 2004). Research on personal home pages, a precursor of blogs, also supports the social utility of the medium.

Several blogs feature information on national, local and personal news. Although blogs do not necessarily feature the extensive news content of online news sites, they do allow for personalization of news items and interactive communication with other bloggers and potential audience members; this could be conceived as an alternate form of online journalism. Therefore, this study also includes the informational utility of blogs and assesses the quality of news items present on blogs.

To examine blogs as a new communication genre, the study focuses on general descriptive elements of blogs and centers on elements of content, structure and design. An examination of content should expand our understanding of the overall utility of the blog. Structure and design attest to the type of communication blogs support and encourage. Therefore, this study is guided by two research questions:

RQ1: What are descriptive elements of blogs?

RQ2: How are the content, structure and design of blogs interrelated?

Method

Sample and Procedures

The initial phase of this research focused on extensive perusal of blogs by collecting information on their characteristics, sketching out a codebook and code sheet for the content analysis, taking notes and conducting informal interviews with a handful of bloggers. Blog providers offer web-based tools that allow bloggers to edit and update information online and instantaneously. This service is offered in exchange for some personal information; advanced services and support are usually offered at a monthly fee. Many blogs feature personal musings, while others focus on family communication, displaying news items, listing author interests and links or all of these combined.

The information collected during the initial phase of research informed the design of the codebook and code sheet, which were pilot tested on a small sample of blogs by two coders who had been properly trained to check for accuracy and intercoder reliability of the coding instrument. The research questions were investigated by employing a content analysis of a random sample of 260 blogs. If the web address led to a site that no longer existed, had switched focus or had mistakenly been identified as a portal by the search engine, that listing was skipped and the next one sampled, based on the sampling interval.

Because Blogger.com was the primary host of blogs at the time the study was conducted and because it was a pioneer in providing blogging space and the services that facilitate the practice, the complete sample for the study was randomly drawn from the user directories of Blogger.com, employing a random sampling interval with a random starting point. Random sampling intervals and the starting point were calculated so as to ensure representative and comprehensive sampling from this blogging service. Blogger provides the software and hardware that render blogging convenient and accessible to large audiences. It also enjoys wide appeal and had a reputation for drawing a variety of bloggers at the time at which the study was conducted.

Given the lack of previous research on blogs, the focus of the study was descriptive and explanatory. Therefore, the content analysis focused on descriptive characteristics, structural features, content, design and estimated uses and gratifications of blogs. An attempt was made to record information regarding the gender and occupation of bloggers in instances when they were clearly stated on the webpage.

The coders began by recording the URL and page title of the blog and also recording the age of the blog and the latest date on which the content had been updated. The age of the blog was calculated by visiting its archives and counting the months for which it was active, with the average blog age at 11.10 months (SD = 12.51), and blog age ranging from less than a month to a total of 56 months (mode = 5 months). The date on which the blog was last updated provided some indication on the currency of the information presented and the interest of the author in maintaining the blog. Based on information provided on the blog, the two coders were able to determine the gender of 181 bloggers (male = 52.5; female = 47.5). This gender distribution is closely aligned with the gender distribution reported in studies of other blog domains (e.g., Herring, Kouper et al., 2004), thus partially supporting the representativeness of the sample.

Bloggers tended to be students (21.6%) or appeared to be employed as computer consultants or programmers (12.5%), although it is important to keep in mind that we were only able to obtain this information for half (50.4%) of our sample through the blog site. Because the items involved information clearly present on the site, the two coders reached complete intercoder agreement. Reliability for all content analysis variables was calculated using the Perreault and Leigh (1989) reliability index:

$$I_r = \{[(F_o/N) - (1/k)][k/(k-1)]\}^{0.5}, \text{ for } F_o/n > 1/k$$

where F_o is the observed frequency of agreement between coders, N is the total number of judgments and k is the number of categories.

This index accounts for coder chance agreement and the number of categories used and is sensitive to coding weaknesses. Reliability scores can range from 0 to 1, with higher scores indicating greater intercoder agreement.

Structure

The coders recorded structural elements reflective of the organization of the blog, focusing on textual extensiveness and the use and manipulation of templates. Extensiveness was captured by counting the number of words featured on the blog index page. We focused on the index page as exemplary and typical of the content of the blog. Because blogs are structured like diaries, with a central index page typically featuring the most or the last few recent entries, the index page served as an adequate reflection of blog textual extensiveness. The decision to select a blogger template and the tendency to deviate from it were also recorded, the latter by employing a 5-point Likert scale, ranging from 1 (no template manipulation) to 5 (a lot of template manipulation). The two coders reached complete agreement on extensiveness and template use and .92 intercoder reliability on template manipulation.

Design

Coded design features included innovation, vividness, interactivity and sophistication. These measures were adapted from previous research involving personal home pages and online journalism (Papacharissi, 2002a, 2002b; Walker, 2000). Interactivity was measured on a semantic differential scale, employing a few items so as to investigate how bloggers present material online. Interactivity is a central and fragmented concept typically employed to gauge the overall responsiveness of new media. Definitions of operationalizations of interactivity vary, depending on the context and medium.

Rogers (1995) defined interactivity as "the degree to which participants in a communication process can exchange roles and have control over their mutual discourse." Rafaeli (1988) emphasized variable degrees of medium responsiveness, distinguishing among two-way (noninteractive) communication, reactive communication and fully interactive communication. Applied to the context of online publishing, Ha and James (1998) conceptualized interactivity on commercial sites on the basis of five dimensions: playfulness; (availability of) choice; connectedness to the audience; ability for information collection; and reciprocity. Steuer's (1992) explication of interactivity and vividness as key components of online environments was also consulted because it focuses on these two dimensions to describe virtual environments like the Star Trek Holodeck or the imaginative environments created through books, which have more in common with the virtual environment that bloggers create and present to a potential audience. Papacharissi (2002b) used a similar definition to measure the interactivity of personal home pages. Therefore, Steuer's and Ha and James' work influenced the manner in which design features of blogs were measured in this study.

Consequently, vividness was operationalized as the degree to which the home page presented a sensorially rich environment. The vividness items were phrased in a 5-point semantic differential form and asked the coders to record:

amount of text—ranging from 1 ("little text") to 5 ("just text"); .89 intercoder reliability

degree to which the page attempted to create a graphical user interface (GUI) between host and user—ranging from 1 ("not GUI oriented") to 5 ("very GUI oriented"); .94 intercoder reliability

presence of graphics—ranging from 1 ("no graphics") to 5 ("many or a wide variety of graphics"); .96 intercoder reliability

A highly vivid blog included several graphics, animation and several audiovisual elements, whereas a blog low in vividness was mostly textual.

Interactivity in this study was operationalized as the degree to which the page could be manipulated as well as the degree to which the blogger invited interaction with visitors, to allow for connectedness and reciprocity in communication. Four items were employed to measure interactivity, using a 5-point semantic differential scale. The coders recorded:

> degree to which the blogger directly addressed potential readers—ranging from 1 ("no address") to 5 ("direct address"); .91 reliability
>
> degree to which the blogger invited feedback—ranging from 1 ("no feedback") to 5 ("various different forms of feedback"); .95 reliability
>
> whether the blogger just listed interests or used a more narrative structure to present interests (it was assumed that the narrative structure would engage the user more than a dry list of links)—ranging from 1 ("list") to 5 ("narrative"); reliability at .94
>
> whether the content of the blog could be manipulated, allowing the user to select among the different offerings of the site or even interact with it and its host—ranging from 1 ("content not manipulated at all") to 5 ("content easily manipulated"); .92 reliability

Adapting from Papacharissi (2002a and 2002b), a highly interactive blog provided e-mail and ICQ author information and employed a narrative style through which the author directly addressed the audience and delved into personal thoughts and sharing interests. A blog low in interactivity was usually less inviting, contained fewer feedback mechanisms, and consisted of a simple list of interests or links.

Innovation and sophistication were also measured by single items on a 5-point scale. Adapted from previous research, innovation was operationalized as the degree to which a person presented a page that deviated from the standard templates and tools provided by the webpage service (Papacharissi, 2002a and 2002b). This was not inclusive of the sophistication of blog code because a page can be amateurish and still reflect an effort to move away from templates. Sophistication was measured by recording how advanced or complex the code of the blog was. To determine this, coders looked through templates provided by bloggers and the HTML source code so as to make valid and reliable assessments. Intercoder reliability for innovation and sophistication reached .92 and .89, respectively.

Content

Several aspects of blog content were recorded for this study. Coders were asked to describe, in their own words, the content of each blog. To supplement the open-ended coding of blog content orientation, a coding category titled "focus of diary" asked the coders to browse through the entire blog and then select from specific categories that accurately described the focus of the blog, such as:

personal (strictly a diary format)
interests (collection of links and information, including news)
family (facilitates family communication)
combination (covers two or more categories)
personal views (not a diary, but focused on expression of personal opinion)
creative expression (artistic endeavors)
support (health and other support offered)
fan page (exclusive coverage of fan interests)
other

In selecting a category, coders were asked to consider what the blog was predominantly about. Coders also recorded the presence and focus of links featured on the blog; these are typically gathered on the index page because the rest of the blog site is usually reserved for the display of archives. The presence of feedback mechanisms was also noted, including e-mail, listservs, guestbooks, counters, contact forms, webrings or other communities, ICQ or other forms of feedback. In the intercoder reliability testing of these variables, the two coders reached complete agreement.

An attempt to describe the language featured on the website using a quantitative instrument was made by recording the formality of the language employed and the use of humor. Future studies can focus on a smaller sample and gather more qualitative and detailed information on language used. The purpose of this study was to work with a large sample and gather general information on the tone employed by bloggers. Using a semantic differential scale ranging from 1 (formal) to 5 (informal), coders read through the blogging entries featured on the website and assigned blogs respective ratings.

If a blogger wrote in incomplete sentences, not paying much attention to grammar, syntax, spelling or etiquette, then that qualified the tone as informal. Informal pages were more impromptu, fragmented, light and direct, usually tackling less conventional topics or discussing topics in a less conventional manner. Formal blogs, on the other hand, were written carefully with strict observation of grammatical conventions and general decorum. They appeared to be more planned, serious and organized. Blogs that combined a less planned or conventional approach, but were written carefully and in an organized manner, were defined as moderately (3) formal or informal. Slight deviations from extreme formality or informality were assigned ratings of 2 and 4, respectively. This operationalization of formality was conveyed to coders through training and produced an intercoder reliability rating of .90.

The content analysis also attempted to record the use of humor in blogs because humor is frequently employed together with an informal tone. The coders simply recorded the presence or absence of humor and the presence or absence of humorous devices (sarcasm, irony, self-deprecation, joking, offensive language, other), refraining from operationalizing humor on a continuum and resorting to more subjective judgments. Even though it is possible to identify the presence of humor, determining how funny or unfunny something is on a semantic differential continuum is a matter of personal taste.

The two coders reached complete agreement on the presence/absence of humor and the categories of offensive language, other and regular joking. Sarcasm was operationalized as the use of caustic language and coded with intercoder reliability at .89. Irony was operationalized as a humorous focus on the contrast between how things appear as opposed to how they really are and coded with intercoder reliability at .91. Self-deprecation was defined as a humorous attempt effected by making fun of oneself and coded with .95 intercoder reliability.

The coders also noted the amount of personal information provided by the host on a 5-point scale ranging from 1 ("none") to 5 ("a lot"), with intercoder agreement at .95. A second item targeted the same concept and asked the coders to record how well they thought they knew the person after having read the page. The range was from 1 ("hardly know this person at all") to 5 ("know this person well"); reliability was .93.

Finally, having read the blog, coders were asked to take notes, record observations and speculate on possible motivations and gratifications obtained from sustaining a blog. The basis for these observations was founded on a uses and gratifications (U&G) framework, assuming that individuals pursue media-related behaviors based on specific predispositions or motives and social–psychological characteristics. U&G has been recommended for the study of new media technologies (Newhagen & Rafaeli, 1996; Rubin & Bantz, 1987) and has been used to examine different types of Internet use (Kuehn, 1994; Papacharissi, 2002a, 2002b; Papacharissi & Rubin, 2000).

According to this perspective, relatively active audiences select particular media to satisfy felt needs, which are influenced by a number of social and psychological factors that affect media selection and use (Rubin, 1994). Even though U&G typically employs self-report measures to gauge individual motives and gratifications obtained, this content analysis asked coders to speculate on the possible motivations and gratifications of bloggers as a precursor to possible surveys of bloggers that might follow in future research.

Blogs actually present voluntarily offered self-reported accounts of individual thoughts and opinions. Coders were shown motives and gratifications employed in previous media and new media research as examples of categories they might encounter. They were also advised to steer away from these conventional categories, if necessary, so as to include new motives that might be specific to the use of blogging. Open-ended observations were recorded and recoded into specific categories based on the frequency with which certain categories occurred. These findings are reported in the following section, in response to RQ1.

Results

RQ1: Descriptive Elements of Blogs

The first research question focused on obtaining a systematic description of the essential elements of blogs by focusing on blog structure, design and content. Average word count for blogs was 2,327 words (SD = 12,021), with a maximum value of 188,857 and minimum value of 4 words. Almost all blogs employed some type of template provided by Blogger (99.2%), indicating that was the most convenient way for most authors to post material. Bloggers chose to manipulate this template significantly (6.4%), somewhat (23%), a little (24.2%) or not at all (46.4%). This implied that most blogs featured an index page that adopted a diary-like look, with links to blogger interests, other blogs and archives of previous postings. Therefore, in most cases, the blog resembled an electronic version of a diary. Unlike conventional diaries, however, which are frequently held private and may even feature a lock to guard the privacy of contents, these electronic diaries are open and available to mass potential audiences.

Relating to design features, blogs tended to be rather textual (M = 3.83; SD = 1.12), with little or no presence of a graphical user interface (M = 1.80; SD = 0.93) or graphics (M = 1.52; SD = 0.78). Unlike personal home pages, blogs featured a more diary-like format, which accounted for the lack of a vivid interface or use of multimedia decor. Bloggers, in their majority, viewed these Internet-related tools as the means to publish their personal musings and did not seem interested in employing interactive tools to project a multisensorial sense of self online. Tellingly, the vividness composite scale constructed by averaging these three items produced a mean score of 1.82 (SD = 0.78; alpha = 0.74), indicating blogs that were moderate to low in vividness.

In this sample, bloggers tended to address their potential audiences somewhat (M = 2.94; SD = 1.03); solicited a moderate amount of feedback (M = 2.16; SD = 1.06); tended to present their thoughts primarily in a narrative, diary-like or stream-of-consciousness format (M = 3.41; SD = 0.974); and invited content manipulation (M = 3.57; SD = 1.37) in the sense that they combined text with a list of links to blog archives, friends' blogs and other interest links, thus inviting the reader to select instead of passively read specified content. Blogs tended to be slightly more interactive than vivid, but still only interactive at a moderate level (M = 2.80; SD = 0.52; alpha = 0.53). In terms of blog innovation, blogs did not deviate from the template norm (M = 1.97; SD = 1.02) and revealed a moderately sophisticated crop of online publishers (M = 2.01; SD = 0.98).

The closed-ended categorization of blogs revealed a similar focus, with the majority of blogs possessing a personal orientation (strictly a diary format, 76.3%) and others falling under the following categories:

family (facilitates family communication, 0.8%)
combination (covers two or more categories, 0.8%)
personal views (not diary, but focused on expression of personal opinion, 1.2%)
creative expression (artistic endeavors, 2.4%)
support (health and other support offered, 0.4%)
fan page (exclusive coverage of fan interests, 0.8%)
other (0.4%)

The open-ended coding of content confirmed these categories and distribution. News links were present on several pages with a different focus (15.5%). The news content typically included links to alternative and mainstream news stories that related to popular culture interests of bloggers. Presence of links to current events or stories pertaining to the political sphere was very limited. For these sites, the presence of mainstream (1) to alternative (5) links and news stories was recorded on a semantic differential scale and indicated that most news links or stories on blogs came from a fairly even combination of alternative and mainstream news sources (M = 2.64; SD = 1.25).

Most blogs adopted a diary, self-reflective format; therefore, the modal value for total number of links present was 0. Links, however, were present on several blogs at a varying degree (M = 19; SD = 25) and covered a wide range of topics including, but not limited to, computer news, alternative news, fan information, links to other bloggers and family, and political, religious, music and art interests. Feedback mechanisms were present on 54% of all blogs; bloggers chose or combined e-mail (48.8%), listservs (3.5%), guestbooks (4.3%), counters (3.6%), contact forms (8.7%), webrings or other communities (2.8%), ICQ (3.6%) or other forms of feedback (10.8%).

Blogs were overwhelmingly informal (M = 3.69; SD = 0.83), tackling unconventional and intimate topics with a whimsical, direct and deeply personal tone. Most bloggers did employ humor in general (54.7%) and humorous blogs relied on sarcasm (42.7%), irony (32.5%), self-deprecation (39.2%), jokes (29.2%), offensive language (13.9%) or any other type of humor (0.8%). Very few pages featured offensive visual or verbal material, humorous or not (4.3%). Most blogs featured a moderate amount of personal information (M = 2.22; SD = 0.98). While the purpose of blogs is to supply information, frequently the display of information is selective and so referential that readers do not feel they know the bloggers intimately (M = 2.18; SD = 0.99)—an understandable fact, given the complexity of individual personalities.

Coders observed significant overlap in the speculated uses and gratifications obtained from authoring a blog. Several bloggers took advantage of the diary-like format of the blog to explain their motivation and expectations from authoring the blog, so this information was easy to obtain. Most bloggers specified their primary motivation for authoring the blog:

personal expression (60.4%)
personal expression and the ability to show off a creative side or artistic work (10.6%)
personal expression and the provision of information (14.6%)
personal expression and social communication with friends (8.6%)
passing the time (2.7%)
completing coursework (0.4%)
entertainment (0.8%)
family communication (0.8%)
relating to profit (0.4%)
professional advancement (0.8%)
support for a cause (0.4%)

Bloggers sustained these websites with the expected gratification of primarily self-fulfillment obtained from the ability to express themselves freely online (83%). Coders were able to estimate this based on the writings of the bloggers, who frequently elaborated on their appreciation of the expressive opportunities blogging provides. Several bloggers valued their websites as opportunities for professional advancement and used them to feature their professional skills (3.2%). Others were appreciative of the opportunity to share information with others online (5.5%) or to sustain social communication with their circle of family and friends (5.9%), or of the entertainment (1.2%) or pass time (1.2%) functions of blogging.

RQ2: Relationships Between Descriptive Elements of Blogs

In coding for the descriptive elements of blogs, this study examined the content, structure and design of blogs. These evaluative items had not been used in previous research, yet they captured the appeal of blogs for blog producers and audiences on a continuum. Therefore, they were grouped and factor analyzed to determine whether they represented dimensions of an evaluative scale employed when assessing the general appeal or utility of blogs. This also provided a meaningful manner through which to organize descriptive elements of blogs along different dimensions.

The first factor was a combination of innovation, sophistication, use of graphics, presence of a graphical interface and level of feedback, which was termed Creativity. Even though this factor included feedback, interactivity and vividness items, it seemed that the combination of items reflected blogs with elaborate construction, thus marking design-related creativity. The mean score for the five-item creativity factor was 1.89 (SD = 0.80) and the coefficient alpha for this creativity scale was 0.89. The second factor combined level of formality, amount of text, presence of direct audience address and ability to manipulate content. These four items reflected a tendency to use the page as a forum to write and express one's beliefs, ideas and emotions; therefore, this factor was labeled Expressiveness (M = 3.51; SD = 0.82; alpha = 0.74).

Finally, the third factor included the presence of personal information, the sense that readers felt they knew the blogger well and the presence of a narrative structure. This three-item factor was labeled Intimacy because it represented the tendency to share private information of an intimate nature online (M = 2.60; SD = 0.82; alpha = 0.79). Different from expressiveness, intimacy reflected not simply the tendency to share information, but to disclose information of a personal nature. Table 2.1 presents the results of the factor analysis in more detail.

Relationships between elements of blogs were further explored by examining correlations or ANOVA plots, depending on the nature of the data. Creativity was negatively related to expressiveness ($r = -.34$; $p < .001$) and posi-

Table 2.1 Factor Analysis of Blog Elements

	Component		
	1	2	3
Creativity			
Innovation		−.16	.25
Presence of GUI interface	87	−.18	.01
Use of graphics/multimedia	73	−.20	−.10
Feedback level	.67	.05	.40
Sophistication	.89	−.12	.21
Expressiveness			
Presence/dominance of text	−.29	.73	.03
Direct address of audience	.10	.79	.01
Formal	−.14	.60	.04
Content manipulated	−.22	.74	.09
Intimacy			
List/narrative	−.01	.19	.62
Inclusion of personal information on page	.15	.04	.93
How well do you think you know this person?	.26	.03	.88

Note: A principal components analysis, with a varimax rotation, an eigenvalue of 1 or greater and a 60/40 criterion yielded these factors. After the varimax rotation, the three factors explained 68.12% of the retained variance. Factor 1, Innovation, explained 35.21% with an eigenvalue of 4.23; Factor 2, Personal Information, 23.21% with an eigenvalue of 2.79; and Factor 3, Expressiveness, 9.70% of the retained variance with an eigenvalue of 1.17.

tively related to the level of intimacy (r = .31; p < .001), indicating that creative blogs were no less likely to share personal information; they simply did so in a less textual and expressive manner. Similarly, creativity was positively related to the presence of links (r = .52; p < .001), reluctance to use a template (F (1, 244) = 9.23; p < .01) and greater manipulation of a blog template (r = .69; p < .001). Creatively inclined bloggers were likely to feature more links on their pages and modify the standard blog template substantially.

Creative blogs were also less likely to employ humor in general (F (1, 249) = 8.55; p < .01), especially irony (F (1, 236) = 7.92; p < .01) or self-deprecation (F (1, 241) = 24.27; p < .001), thus confirming the findings of the factor analysis. Humor implies a degree of informality, an element included under the expressiveness dimension of blogs, which, in this study, was negatively related to creativity. Feedback was an element of the creativity dimension of blogs, so, understandably, creative blogs were likely to include feedback mechanisms, including e-mail (F (1, 250) = 140.04; p < .001), listservs (F (1, 250) = 5.43; p < .05), guestbooks (F (1, 250) = 7.69; p < .01), contact forms (F (1, 250) = 7.94; p < .01) and ICQ information (F (1, 249) = 15.00; p < .001).

Expressiveness was negatively related to creativity and positively associated with blog intimacy level (r = .24; p < .001). Expressiveness was also negatively associated with the presence of links (r = −.16; p = .01), indicating that blogs adopting a dominantly textual and informal tone were less likely to display numerous links. Interestingly, highly expressive blogs that featured news items were more likely to include alternative over mainstream news-related information (r = −.51; p = .001).

In this sample, female bloggers were slightly more likely to be expressive than male bloggers, although it is important to keep in mind that these data were not available for all bloggers in the sample (F (2, 248) = 22.6; p < .001). Expressive bloggers were more likely to employ humor in general (F (1, 248) = 18.14; p < .001)—especially sarcasm (F (1, 247) = 27.4; p < .001), irony (F (1, 234) = 6.11; p = .01) and self-deprecation (F (1, 239) = 83.71; p < .001)—and to employ offensive language in a humorous context (F (1, 245) = 5.18; p < .05). Tellingly, expressiveness is not inclusive of feedback and therefore did not relate to any feedback mechanisms in a statistically significant manner.

Positively associated with expressiveness and creativity, intimacy was also related to the tendency not to use a template (F (1, 244) = 9.23; p < .01) or to manipulate one significantly (r = .30; p < .001) and to present blogs extensive in word use (r = .19; p < .01). This indicated the need to go beyond the norm when presenting personal information textually and visually. Intimacy was also the only dimension to be associated with the focus of the blog, revealing that blogs containing information of a more intimate nature were more likely blogs combining the diary focus with other interests, blogs dedicated to family communication and blogs employed for the expression of personal views (F (1, 244) = 9.23; p < .01). Female bloggers were slightly more likely than male bloggers to share information of an intimate personal nature, although these findings are compromised by the lack of such data for the entire sample (F (8, 244) = 4.30; $p < .001$).

Blogs containing information of a more intimate nature were likely to feature use of sarcasm (F (1, 243) = 6.62; $p = .01$), irony (F (1, 229) = 15.61; $p < .001$), self-deprecation (F (1, 235) = 22.82, $p < .001$) and offensive language in a humorous context (F (1, 241) = 4.57; $p < .05$). These blogs also employed feedback mechanisms selectively in support of the positive correlation between intimacy and creativity, featuring presence of an e-mail address (F (1, 244) = 8.29; $p < .01$), use of a listserv (F (1, 244) = 6.72; $p < .01$), presence of a guestbook (F (1, 244) = 4.16; $p < .05$), reference to webrings or other online communities (F (1, 244) = 4.23; $p < .05$) and the provision of ICQ information (F (1, 243) = 6.09; $p < .01$).

Discussion

This content analysis revealed that blogs, on average, feature personalized accounts of information that resemble the diary format more than the independent journalism ideal. This is consistent with previous findings reported by Herring, Scheidt et al. (2004), who concluded that popular accounts frequently overstate "the extent to which blogs are interlinked, interactive, and oriented towards external events, and underestimate the importance of blogs as individualistic, intimate forms of self-expression."

The present study found that these template-influenced online diaries were frequently extensive and verbose, offered moderate interactivity and made little use of a graphical user interface or multimedia tools. The online diary metaphor serves the blogging context well because these online daily musings are disorganized, frequently fragmented, and largely self-referential. The format of blogs is aligned with author uses and gratifications because these self-reflective accounts seem primarily to serve the purpose of personal expression and provide the perceived gratification of self-fulfillment; thus, they comply with the organization, format and utility that serve the individual user best.

Still, blogs present an interesting diversion from the traditional diary format in that, unlike written diaries, the privacy of which is cautiously guarded by their authors, blogs are open for all to browse. In fact, several blogs are authored for the explicit purpose of perusal by friends, family members and the occasional accidental browser. Therefore, they present an interesting paradoxical combination of private and public information that challenges our conventional understanding of the private and public sphere and follows in the tradition of new media technologies that empower the individual to project personal experiences, usually considered private, to a mass audience. Blogs allow the private domain to become public and privatize a portion of the public sphere. Unlike diaries, which are frequently written to express secrets or private thoughts of the individual for the individual, blogs are written to be read.

While most blogs adopt the diary format, not all information featured on blogs is of a private nature. Indeed, even though personal expression presented the primary focus, use and gratification in this sample, the display of interests and sharing of information presented the second most important function, focus and gratification obtained from blogs. Blogs frequently combined the display of personal and social or news-related information, thus challenging and personalizing the conventional news format. Personalization in online journalism implies that the user is allowed to customize his or her news page; however, in blogging, personalization refers to a true melange of private and public information, the social utility of which is ambiguous, but determined solely by the blogger.

Nonetheless, imposing journalistic aspirations upon all blogs may be limiting; blogs are oriented toward providing individuals with a public forum that can be used to provide news of a personal or a general nature. While traditional journalism provides individuals with pictures of a world they cannot experience firsthand, to paraphrase Walter Lippman, blogs operate in the opposite direction, broadcasting the pictures in our heads back to a worldwide audience.

The statistical analyses that identified three primary descriptive dimensions of blogs and investigated the relationships among blogs' descriptive elements indicated that most blogs were not creative, in the sense that they did not rely on a graphical user interface, did not make extensive use of multimedia elements, did not employ innovative or sophisticated design and did not invite feedback on blog content. Thus, these blogs were primarily low-tech affairs of a self-referential nature.

The findings on expressiveness, which was negatively associated with creativity, indicated that whatever blogs lacked in creativity, they made up in expressiveness. Most blogs were moderately to very expressive, implying that the presence of text dominated the entire page, the tone was primarily informal and that bloggers addressed their potential audiences in a very direct manner and created a blog structure that allowed visitors to browse through the entire contents of the blog. Thus, bloggers acknowledged potential audiences and invited them to all aspects of these online diaries, even though, ultimately, bloggers were not focused on feedback and therefore not too concerned with what their potential audiences had to say about their blogs.

Finally, intimacy (or the presence and divulgence of personal information through use of a narrative structure) was present in creative and expressive pages, indicating that, no matter what the author's approach to storytelling was, blogging endeavors were about the display of intimate thoughts, information and insight. Bloggers tended to share intimate information by employing humorous contexts.

To summarize, blogs in this sample presented low-tech, self-referential, verbose attempts to display personal thoughts and information, with little interest for how these thoughts would be received by an audience. The tendency for blogs to support more personally oriented communication has also been identified by recent research, which separated A-list blogs (popular publicized blogs), blogs that are somewhat interconnected and the majority of sparsely socially connected and less conversational blogs (Herring et al., 2005).

Psychology, literature and popular culture have frequently toyed with the idea that individuals keep diaries of personal experiences with the subliminal hope that eventually these diaries will be read by a third person. Blogs allow individuals to play with this desire to have personal memoirs published, awarding their authors with personal gratification, publicity and perhaps a sense of assurance that these private thoughts matter. In a culture saturated with private information on celebrities and public figures, blogs allow their authors to become public and gain a compromised expression of notoriety. Future studies could explore how blogs further blur the distinction between private and public information online, thus redefining how private and public space is perceived. Additional studies of larger samples and surveys of bloggers could lead to information that illuminates the utility of blogs for the individual and society.

Viewed as the latest trend in online use and publishing, blogs present a personalized, self-referential and self-serving use of the Internet, a medium first introduced as informational that then established a following based on the social communication avenues it provided. Blogs present a turn to self-involved uses of the Internet, which are becoming more prevalent. They also create an interesting contrast between earlier uses of the Internet, studied by communication scholars as more socially focused and oriented. Future studies should examine uses of the Internet and blogging to determine whether in fact they have become more self-serving and to clarify the impact this turn could have on the social capital generated by new media.

References

Blogger.com. (2004). Retrieved January 2004 from www.blogger.com.

Dominick, J. (1999). Who do you think you are? Personal home pages and self-presentation on the World Wide Web. *Journalism and Mass Communication Quarterly, 76*(4), 646–658.

Ha, L., & James, E. L. (1998). Interactivity reexamined: A baseline analysis of early business Web sites. *Journal of Broadcasting and Electronic Media, 42*(4), 457–474.

Herring, S. C., Kouper, I., Paolillo, J. C., Scheidt, L. A., Tyworth, M., Welsch, P., Wright, E. & Yu, N. (2005). Conversations in the blogosphere: An analysis "from the bottom up." From BROG: The (We)Blog Research on Genre Project, at http://www.blogninja.com/, accessed June 2005.

Herring, S. C., Kouper, I., Scheidt, L. A. & Wright, E. (2004). Women and children last: The discursive construction of Weblogs. In L. Gurak, S. Anotnijevic, L. Johnson, C. Ratliff & J. Reyman (Eds.), *Into the blogosphere: Rhetoric, community and culture of Weblogs.* http://blog.lib.umn.edu/blogosphere/women_and_children.html.

Herring, S. C., Scheidt, L. A., Bonuns, S. & Wright, E. (2004). Bridging the gap: A genre analysis of Weblogs. *Proceedings of the 37th Hawaii Interaction Conference on System Sciences* (HICSS-37). Los Alamitos: IEEE Press.

Katz, J. E., & Aspden, P. (1997). A nation of strangers? *Communications of the ACM, 40*(12), 81–86.

Kraut, R., Kiesler, S., Boneva, K., Cummings, J., Helgeson, J. & Crawford, A. (2002). Internet paradox revisited. *Journal of Social Issues, 58*(1), 49–74.

Kraut, R., Patterson, M., Lundmark, V., Kiesler, S., Mukophadhyay, T. & Scherlis, W. (1998). Internet paradox: A social technology that reduces social involvement and psychological well-being? *American Psychologist, 53*, 1017–1031.

Kuehn, S. A. (1994). Computer-mediated communication in instructional settings: A research agenda. *Communication Education, 43*, 171–183.

Newhagen, J. E., & Rafaeli, S. (1996). Why communication researchers should study the Internet: A dialogue. *Journal of Communication, 46*(1), 4–13.

Nie, N., & Erbring, L. (2000). Internet and society: A preliminary report. IT & Society 1 (1), 275–283. From http://www.stanford.edu/group/sigss/itandsociety/v01i01/v01i01a18.pdf.

Papacharissi, Z. (2002a). The self online: The utility of personal home pages. *Journal of Broadcasting & Electronic Media, 46*(3), 346–368.

Papacharissi, Z. (2002b). The presentation of self in virtual life: Characteristics of personal home pages. *Journalism and Mass Communication Quarterly, 79*(3), 643–660.

Papacharissi, Z., & Rubin, A. M. (2000). Predictors of Internet use. *Journal of Broadcasting & Electronic Media, 44*, 175–196.

Perreault, W., & Leigh, L. (1989). Reliability of nominal data based on qualitative judgments. *Journal of Marketing Research, 26*(2), 135–148.

Rafaeli, S. (1988). Interactivity: From new media to communication. In R. P. Hawkins, J. M. Wiemann & S. Pingree (Eds.), *Advancing communication science: Merging mass and interpersonal process* (pp. 100–134). Newbury Park, CA: Sage.

Rogers, E. M. (1995). *Diffusion of innovations.* New York: Free Press.

Rubin, A. M. (1994). Media uses and effects: A uses-and-gratifications perspective. In J. Bryant & D. Zillmann (Eds.), *Media effects: Advances in theory and research* (pp. 417–436). Hillsdale, NJ: Lawrence Erlbaum.

Rubin, A. M., & Bantz, C. R. (1987). Utility of videocassette recorders. In J. G. Salvaggio & J. Bryant (Eds.), *Media use in the information age: Emerging patterns of adoption and consumer use* (pp. 181–195). Hillsdale, NJ: Lawrence Erlbaum.

Scheidt, L., & Wright, E. (2004). Common visual design elements of Weblogs. From BROG: The (We)Blog Research on Genre Project, at http://www.blogninja.com/, accessed June 2005.

Smith, M. J. (1998). E-merging strategies of identity: The rhetorical construction of self in personal Web sites (doctoral dissertation, Ohio University, 1998). *Dissertation Abstracts International, 59*, 4315.

Steuer, J. (1992). Defining virtual reality: Dimensions determining telepresence. *Journal of Communication, 42*(4), 73–93.

Sullivan, A. (2002, October 13). An honest blogger will never make a quick buck. *Sunday Times*, A4.

Walker, K. (2000). "It's difficult to hide it": The presentation of self on Internet home pages. *Qualitative Sociology, 23*(1), 99–120.

3

Pundits in Muckrakers' Clothing: Political Blogs and the 2004 U.S. Presidential Election

D. TRAVERS SCOTT

During the 2004 U.S. presidential campaign, blogs arrived as a political communications medium. Tales of intrepid citizen journalists scooping and fact-checking the corrupt mainstream media (MSM) became conventional wisdom through a series of events, culminating in the Memogate controversy. A content analysis of four leading political blogs during the final 14 weeks of the campaign, however, challenges this narrative as more exception than common practice. While the blogs studied were found to perform traditional news functions, key aspects of blogging mythology and rhetoric, such as original reporting, circumvention of mainstream media, alternative sources and—perhaps most significant in terms of political communications and democracy, suggesting action in response to news and information—were surprisingly rare. Rather than vigilante muckrakers, bloggers were activist media pundits, raising questions about their true role in political communication.

Backstory: Blogging and Memogate

For several years, blog authors and their fans championed accounts of indefatigable bloggers sniffing out under-the-radar stories and challenging mainstream media. They compiled a litany of moments in which blogs influenced, supplanted, surpassed or scooped MSM, such as the Trent Lott/Strom Thurmond scandal (Gill, 2004; Kennedy School of Government Case Program, 2004) and *New York Times* Editor Howell Raines' resignation (Regan, 2003). Celebrities emerged, such as Baghdad blogger Salam Pax, whose postings Grove Press published as a book (Pax, 2003) and Glenn Reynolds, whose *Instapundit* was drawing an estimated 50,000 unique visitors each weekday before the election season began in earnest (Kennedy School of Government Case Program, 2004).

The medium evolved, incorporating photography, video, audio, satellite positioning and mobile technologies (Glaser, 2004c; Lasica, 2003). Conferences, university courses, and books addressed blogs, as did early adopters in fields as diverse as library science (Thomsen, 2002), education (Embrey, 2002), demographics (Whelan, 2003) and medicine (Brown, 2003). Journalists were particularly interested and struggled to articulate a place within U.S. media for bloggers, variously described as citizen journalists (Andrews, 2003; Outing, 2003; Williams, 2003), "adopt-a-journalist" critical observers (Glaser, 2004a), MSM fact-checkers and ideological watchdogs (Glaser, 2004b) and mainstream journalists operating in more immediate, speculative or opinionated modes (Weintraub, 2004). News bloggers, with their frequent disregard for traditional journalistic objectivity, were lauded for introducing voice and personality (Grossman, 2004) to "a media world that's otherwise leached of opinions and life" (Jarvis, quoted in Welch, Jensen & Reeves, 2003).

As 2004 unfolded, blogs moved beyond the technorati. Studies showed relatively few active bloggers and readers, but a dizzying rate of increase from previous years (Perseus Development Corporation, 2003; Pew Internet and American Life Project, 2005). Researchers, politicians and media critics noted blogs' influence among niche audiences, particularly in media and politics (Drezner & Farrell, 2004; Glaser, 2003; Richards, 2004). Some news bloggers surpassed readerships of traditional print outlets such as *The Chicago Tribune* or *The Dallas Morning News* (Lasica, 2004); many received press credentials to the 2004 Democratic (Weiss, 2004) and Republican (Grossman, 2004) National Conventions.

A few crossed over to MSM, as when *Washington Monthly* acquired Kevin Drum's political news blog, *Calpundit.com*, and rechristened it *Political Animal* (Grossman, 2004). *Time* magazine declared many blogs had "lost their amateur status forever" during what may be "a golden age of blogging" (Grossman, 2004). In early 2004, blog researcher Alex Halavais had suggested that news blogging had not "even come close to a tipping point yet" (Glaser, 2004c). By summer's wane, the point would be reached.

On September 8, 2004, CBS News' *60 Minutes II* addressed questions regarding President Bush's fulfillment of service obligations in the Texas Air National Guard. They exhibited damaging memos purportedly written by Lt. Col. Jerry B. Killian, Bush's Guard supervisor, of which they had also delivered copies to the White House that morning. Nineteen minutes into the broadcast, the authenticity of the memos was challenged on conservative message board FreeRepublic.com. Four hours later, a post by "Buckhead" argued that the typography of the memos was inconsistent with period typewriters (Wallsten, 2004a, 2004b; Wasserstein, 2004).

Buzz spread through blogs and discussion forums, sparking a flurry of research and, among liberal blogs, counterresearch. The story escalated to gossip site *The Drudge Report*, followed by talk radio, cable news, and mainstream broadcast and print (Wallsten, 2004a; Wasserstein, 2004). Buckhead was identified as Harry W. MacDougland, an Atlanta lawyer with no typography expertise but strong conservative Republican ties. Questions over whether he worked independently or had been fed information did not prevent CBS anchor Dan Rather from ultimately apologizing and, separately, announcing his retirement. After an internal investigation, CBS dismissed four top journalists from their news division (Steinberg & Carter, 2005).

The bloggers had arrived. Postelection, a *Wall Street Journal* editorial compared Memogate to Henry V of England's 1415 defeat of the larger French army at Agincourt, proclaiming it "a great historical development in the history of politics in America" (Noonan, 2004). By year's end, Merriam–Webster announced that "blog" had been the most requested definition from its online dictionaries in 2004 (*Boston Herald*, 2004), and ABC News named bloggers their People of the Year (ABC News, 2004). The mythic narrative was writ large: Savvy citizen muckrakers of the blogosphere had brought the despotic media/political establishment to its knees, heralding a new era of insurgent democracy and fulfilling the Internet's early egalitarian promise. Analysis of the actual practices of four leading political blogs, however, would suggest that candidates were not the only sources of election-season hyperbole.

A Study of Political Blogs

Conceptual Framework

This project aimed to examine the contribution of blogs to the U.S. political communications system. It drew upon theories of sociological news functions, a conceptual framework with a rich history in communications research. Fundamental theories were employed in an effort to address fundamental questions: Are bloggers journalists? What were their sources of information? Were they providing new interpretations or responses to events? Was repurposed news merely recycled or reshaped somehow?

News functions—the purposes that news fulfills in a society—originated in Lasswell's canonical essay, "The Structure and Function of Communication in Society" (1948). Lasswell posited that communication in society performed three functions: *surveillance* of the environment, *correlation* of the components of society in making a response to the environment, and *transmission* of the social inheritance (p. 51). Although numerous theorists have expanded this list, this study focused on surveillance and correlation because many additional functions theorized by scholars such as Lazarsfeld and Merton (1949), Wright (1959) and Gans (2003) can be seen as variants or subcategories of surveillance and correlation.

However, Wright's definitions of these functions were used because they were particularly cogent in relation to journalism. Wright defined *surveillance* as essentially newsmaking: "the collection and distribution of information concerning events in the environment, both outside and within any particular society" (1959, p. 16). *Correlation* he defined as the editorial or propaganda side of communications, the "interpretation of information about the environment and prescription for conduct in reaction to these events" (p. 16).

By analyzing the content of news blogs and their posts, this study expected to find blogs performing news functions of surveillance and correlation. From anecdotal evidence and blogosphere rhetoric, it was expected that their sources would include a diverse array of original reporting, alternative news and mainstream media and provide information, analysis and insights unavailable in the staid halls of MSM. They would provide multiple perspectives, suggest responsive actions and challenge their sources through insightful edits, interpretations and juxtapositions.

Methodology

Over the final 14 weeks of the 2004 U.S. presidential campaign, the content of four blogs was analyzed. These English-language U.S. blogs each had regular and substantial political content, and each appeared often in the Top 20[1] rankings of popularity or influence created by 13 measurement tools[2] and 10 peer/media opinion lists.[3] The blogs observed were:

> *InstaPundit* (instapundit.com), Glenn Reynolds and guests' libertarian–conservative take on politics and current events.
>
> *Talking Points Memo* (talkingpointsmemo.com), Joshua Micah Marshall's liberal writing on politics.
>
> *Daily Dish* (andrewsullivan.com), Andrew Sullivan's conservative writing on politics, gay issues and current events.
>
> *Daily Kos* (dailykos.com), Markos Moulitsas Zúniga and collective members' liberal take on news and politics.

From July 20 to November 5, 2004, these blogs were checked daily and all posts and updates from the previous day's 24-hour period were examined. Posts were coded into one of three categories: (a) *Electoral* posts contained any reference to participants or organizations involved in the 2004 election campaign; (b) *Personal* posts did not contain electoral content but explicitly mentioned the blogger's personal life, activities, feelings or experiences; and (c) *Other* posts included all remaining blog posts.

Electoral posts were examined for indicators of surveillance and correlation, as well as for the sources of their information. *Surveillance* was indicated by original newsgathering content, non-web content (gathering and bringing information into the online news realm) and watchdog fact-checking of other media. *Correlation* was indicated by calls to action aiming to mobilize readers, interpretive manipulations of source materials and use of adjunct bloggers to add multiple perspectives to stories. The *sources* for material related in posts were broken into two primary categories: direct experience and media. Media sources were divided into news and non-news sources, and news sources were categorized as mainstream or alternative across a variety of media (e.g., print, broadcast, web). Non-news sources were likewise categorized (e.g., other blogs, businesses, humor sites). Finally, classification was made of sourcing elements (e.g., text, graphics, photo, audio and/or video) and methods (e.g., citation, quotation, hypertext link or combination).

To assess validity of measurement, coding reliability tested between two coders on 300 posts chosen through systematic random subsampling. Each post was coded for 39 variables: 39 variables × 300 posts = 11,700 total. Overall agreement among coders was found in 11,289/11,700 variables or 0.96 crude agreement. Note that the tracking of several variables that were rarely present created high degrees of agreement among coders. Individual variables' crude agreement ranged from 0.85 to 1.0. To take into account chance agreement, kappa (κ) coefficients were calculated for these variables and are indicated as appropriate.

Findings

During this study, the four blogs published a cumulative total of 5,730 posts. Electoral posts discussed a range of matters, such as campaign strategy, analysis of media coverage, and regional polls. Personal posts tended to be "behind-the-scenes" glimpses of running the blog or diary-esque vignettes of the blogger's life, such as Andrew Sullivan (2004b) describing a bout with a bronchial infection. Other posts ranged from the regular announcement of open discussion forums at *Daily Kos* to addresses of politics or current events that affected politics, but did not directly reference an election. Although *Daily Kos* and *InstaPundit* were roughly twice as prolific as *Daily Dish* and *Talking Points Memo*, across all four blogs, electoral posts were predominant, comprising 64.9% of the total. Other posts made up roughly a third; only 6.9% were personal posts. Calculation of a kappa coefficient for post categorization yielded κ = .78, high agreement beyond chance.

The proportion of post types was similar for three of the four blogs: *Daily Dish*, *Daily Kos* and *Talking Points Memo* each contained roughly 70% or more electoral posts, 15% other posts, and a small percentage of personal posts. With *InstaPundit*, however, electoral and other posts were almost equal at approximately 45%, due to main blogger Glenn Reynolds' frequent postings on science, cooking, and other topics. Overall, although expectations were met in that electoral posts were the majority category for each blog, the preponderance of other posts over personal posts was unexpected, given the highly touted subjective and individualistic nature of the medium.

Surveillance[4]   These blogs were expected often to perform the news function of surveillance—that is, newsgathering. Surveillance was indicated by reporting on any event observed in physical or media worlds. This included applying original research to fact-check media reports. Among all four blogs, surveillance occurred even more frequently than anticipated, in 93.5% (κ = .86) of electoral posts, showing that these blogs placed a premium on this function.

A typical act of surveillance was to alert readers to an article of interest, as when *Daily Dish* pointed out a rare instance of President Bush acknowledging gay and lesbian issues: "He said it! *The Washington Blade* has found a reference by the president to the word 'gay'" (Sullivan, 2004c). Similarly, *Daily Kos* surveyed a broadcast news outlet as well as a polling organization in this post on the Alaskan Senate race: "Tony Knowles is still maintaining his narrow lead in the polls. A DSCC poll show [*sic*] a 48–44 lead among 'definite' voters, 47–43 among 'likely' voters. The latest KTUU poll shows a much narrower race" (Moulitsas, 2004d).

Correlation   The second focus of analysis was on the news function of correlation—editorializing, or connecting, interpreting and suggesting action in response to events. This was expected to occur to a degree at least commensurate with that of surveillance, due to blogging's reputation for vociferous, polyvocal opinions. In addition, correlation was expected to be fairly consistent across blogs. The three indicators of correlation were calls to action (e.g., links to a petition), manipulation of source material to emphasize something originally unapparent (e.g., pulling out a significant quote buried deep in an article) or connecting multiple perspectives on events by using adjunct bloggers (e.g., guests or members of the blogging collective). Correlation appeared far less often than surveillance, in only 27.7% (κ = .89) of posts. This was consistent across the four blogs. Most predominant was the use of adjunct bloggers, which occurred in 15.8% (κ = .98) of posts. For example, in this excerpt from *Daily Kos*, a collective member begins point-by-point refutation of early Memogate blogging:

> As everyone on the planet no doubt knows by now, the hard-right of the freeper[5] contingent—specifically, *LittleGreenFootballs*, a site which frequently is cited for eliminationist rhetoric and veiled racism, and *Power Line,* a site linked to with admiration by such luminaries as Michelle Malkin and Hugh Hewitt—discovered that if you used the same typeface, you could make documents that looked almost—but not exactly—like the TANG[6] documents discovered by CBS News.... I do not believe there is any truly "new" information here, but I hope to condense it in one easy-to-digest reference. So here are some point-by-point findings re: the "forgeries."
>
> First Claim (LittleGreenFootballs): "The documents can be recreated in Microsoft Word."
>
> What the LGFer did to "prove" this was to type a Microsoft Word document in Times New Roman font, and overlay it with the original document.... First, of course, in order to do this, he first had to reduce the document so that the margins *were* the same, since the original PDF

distributed by CBS is quite a bit larger. Then he superimposed the two documents, such that the margins on all sides lined up (Hunter, 2004, paragraphs 1–8, emphasis original).

Across all blogs, interpretive manipulations of source material occurred in 8.9% (κ = .84) of posts. This generally took the form of emphasizing passages not prioritized in the original. In this *Daily Dish* post, the quote Sullivan selected had been buried in the last third of a *Washington Post* transcript of John Edwards' 3500+ word speech to the Democratic National Convention:

> Edwards was also smart to bring together two important themes of this convention: unity and war. Here's the critical passage:

> The truth is, the truth is that what John and I want, what all of us want [is] for our children and our grandchildren to be the first generations that [grow] up in an America that's no longer divided by race. We must build one America. We must be one America, strong and united for another very important reason: because we are at war (Sullivan, 2004f, paragraphs 1 and 2).

Calls to action appeared in only 6.8% (κ = .57) of posts, but this was not equally distributed among blogs. At 11.5%, *Daily Kos* had 2 to 3 times more calls to action than the other three blogs. A frequent call was candidate fund-raising for the "dKos Dozen," as in this example during the Republican National Convention:

> Okay. Here it goes.

> As you listen to McCain tonight, give.

> As you listen to Giuliani, give.

> Every time you hear a media pundit say something blatantly wrong, or biased, or asinine, give.

> Every time you think that the Republicans may, just may pull this thing off, give.... This is crunch time now (Moulitsas, 2004c, paragraphs 1–9).

Moulitsas linked to the websites of eight candidates he had endorsed, as well as to a page on his site that provided information and fund-raising totals. Surprisingly rare for an election season was exhortation or instruction for voting.

Sources   The sources for posts were categorized as in the *media* environment or in the actual, physical environment—that is, *direct experience*. Surprisingly, media sources were by far more common, appearing in 91.8% (κ = .88) of posts. News media sources, such as the *New York Times*, appeared in 60% (κ = .93) of posts, and non-news media, such as the blog *Power Line*, appeared in 64% (κ = .85) of posts. *Talking Points Memo* particularly utilized news media sources, which appeared in 70.9% of its posts. *InstaPundit* relied more on non-news media sources, which appeared in 76.6% of its posts. Far less frequent overall was original reporting of direct experience (including fact-checking the media), which appeared in only 12.1% (κ = .76) of posts. Furthermore, less consistency was found in direct experience sourcing. *Daily Dish* and *InstaPundit* sourced direct experience in only 6.5 and 7.3% of posts, respectively, compared to *Daily Kos* and *Talking Points Memo* with 14.2 and 24.9%, respectively.

Media and direct experience sourcing appeared in this *Daily Kos* post on Kerry's speech at the Democratic National Convention: "'Help is on the way'...hurry the hell up! (Reuters pic.)...'I want an America that relies on its own ingenuity and innovation—not the Saudi royal family.' Be still be [*sic*] beating heart!...*He hit it out. Way out*" (Moulitsas, 2004a, paragraphs 1–7, emphasis original). Direct experience also took the form of rumor and buzz, as when *Daily Dish* contrasted a tied Gallup poll with insider information: "I hear all sorts of different things—how the Bush internals are looking good, how the Dem GOTV operation is on fire, etc. etc. But I doubt anyone really knows how this will turn out" (Sullivan, 2004e, paragraph 3). This *Talking Points Memo* post described Marshall's mix of sources:

> I do a fair amount of original reporting for this site. But most of what I do is, inevitably, a matter of mining other news sources for bits and pieces of information and piecing them together with other pieces of information, showing too-little-noticed connections or explaining or trying to interpret their meaning (Marshall, 2004a, paragraph 6).

However, as previously noted, whether juxtaposed or standing alone, direct experience appeared far less often than media sources.

Media sources were examined in further depth, beginning with news media. These were expected to include a vibrant mix of mainstream and alternative outlets from a variety of channels and often juxtaposed. It was expected that alternative media sources would rival if not surpass MSM. However, mainstream news sources appeared in 49.5% (κ = .90) of posts, whereas alternative news outlets appeared in only 19% (κ = .91). Mainstream news sources were dominated by print outlets, such as the *Washington Post*, appearing in 33.0% (κ = .81) of posts. Here, for example, *Talking Points Memo* blogger Joshua Micah Marshall described his intent in blogging a *New York Times* article:

> I just read this article in the *Times*, billed as Cheney's counterattack against the Democratic ticket, figuring it would be filled with various distortions and untruths I could pick apart.

Really, though, there's not much there to pick apart, because there's simply not much there. Some boiler plate [*sic*] about raising taxes, the troop funding vote run-around and some stuff about John Edwards hair— that's about it.

If the *Times* author is reasonably conveying Cheney's message, it's awfully weak stuff (Marshall, 2004b, paragraphs 1–3).

Mainstream broadcast news outlets such as CBS News followed, appearing in 16.6% (κ = .81) of posts. Wire services (e.g., Reuters), web-only sources (e.g., Google News) and unlinkable mainstream news sources (e.g., books or the subscription-only online *Wall Street Journal*) were all in the single digits (κ = .67, .58 and 1.0, respectively). Among alternative news outlets, print again dominated, with 9.6% (κ = .58) of posts sourcing publications such as *The Weekly Standard* or *Village Voice.*

Web-only alternative news sources ran a close second, appearing in 8.2% (κ = .70) of posts, as when *Daily Kos* quoted a *Salon.com* article about the suspicious bulge in President Bush's jacket during the debates (Blades, 2004). Alternative unlinkable news sources, such as subscription newsletter *The Hotline*, appeared in 1.9% (κ = .67) of posts. Alternative broadcast news sources, including the much lauded *The Daily Show with Jon Stewart*, appeared only in 0.8% (κ = 1.0) of posts.

Juxtaposing alternative and mainstream sources within a post appeared in only 8.5% (κ = .83) of posts, as when *InstaPundit* drew upon the *National Review* and CNN (among others) in dissecting the claims of Kerry and John O'Neill having been in Cambodia:

> Cambodia update: John Cole notes that John O'Neill says he was in Cambodia on a Swift Boat. He says this hurts O'Neill's credibility. ... But it's worth noting that O'Neill was in Vietnam longer than Kerry.

> Update: Okay, O'Neill has responded. ... Here's the key bit from CNN suggesting an inconsistency on O'Neill's part:

> O'Neill said no one could cross the border by river and he claimed in an audio tape that his publicist played to CNN that he, himself, had never been to Cambodia either. But in 1971, O'Neill said precisely the opposite to then President Richard Nixon.

> O'NEILL: I was in Cambodia, sir. I worked along the border on the water.

> NIXON: In a swift boat?

> O'NEILL: Yes, sir (Reynolds, 2004b, paragraphs 1–9).

Non-news media sources, expected to appear frequently, were sorted into five categories: organizations or businesses (e.g., Amazon.com, The Heritage

Foundation, the White House), other blogs, the blogger's blog or website, an individual (e.g., speaking directly with a person, reader e-mail, blog comments or a personal website, including any site whose domain name or title was an individual's name) and other miscellaneous sources (e.g., humor sites, historical archives). The blogs sourced non-news media in 64.0% ($\kappa = .85$) of posts. Other blogs were the most common type, appearing in 32.1% ($\kappa = .82$) of posts. Organizations or businesses, the blogger's blog or site and individual sources each appeared about half as often ($\kappa = .68, .83, .88$, respectively). Other miscellaneous sources appeared in only 5.1% ($\kappa = .53$) of posts.

Unlike the fairly consistent pattern of findings thus far, in non-news sources there was greater variance by blog. *InstaPundit* relied most on other blogs, as in the post, "The biggest ad buy of the campaign: (via *PoliPundit*.) You can see the ad online here, if you're interested" (Reynolds, 2004a, paragraph 1). Reynolds first linked to the mainstream web news source Yahoo! News, then the blog *PoliPundit*, followed by another miscellaneous source, the political ad website *Ashley's Story*.

In contrast, *Daily Kos* relied most on organizations or businesses. Here, for example, Moulitsas linked first to a previous post in his blog and then to a business, Amazon.com: "Before I wrote my review of Lakoff's new book, *Don't Think of an Elephant*, it stood at 325 on Amazon's rankings. Right now it's sitting at #12, and reached as high as #8 for a bit" (Moulitsas, 2004b, paragraphs 1–3). Finally, *Daily Dish* relied most heavily upon individuals, and *Talking Points Memo* most often used itself as a non-news media source.

The manner of citing news and non-news media sources was also examined. It was expected that the blogs would use primarily text-based citations, links and quotations, but that, capitalizing on the multimedia capabilities of the web, graphics, photographs, audio and video would also often appear. However, each of the blogs was consistently a text-based enterprise. Multimedia elements appeared at most in about 2.0% ($\kappa = .84$) of posts. In contrast, 61.6% ($\kappa = .86$) of posts cited, quoted and linked to a source, as does this *Daily Dish* post with *Salon.com*:

> Reaganites versus Bush: Doug Bandow joins the growing throng of principled conservatives unwilling to give Bush a second term. Money quote:

> Quite simply, the president, despite his well-choreographed posturing, does not represent traditional conservatism—a commitment to individual liberty, limited government, constitutional restraint and fiscal responsibility. Rather, Bush routinely puts power before principle.

> One wonders why this kind of piece isn't published by the *Weekly Standard* or *National Review* (Sullivan, 2004d, paragraphs 1–3).

Consistency

The overall consistency of findings across these leading political blogs in their news functions and sources suggests that, despite ideological differences, they served similar communicative functions in similar manners. Such consistency was further supported by longitudinal analysis of data, which showed high synchronicity of activity among the four blogs. As expected, a modest but real upward trend in surveillance and correlation was observed as the election approached.

Also as expected, blogging spiked around the Democratic (July 26 to July 29) and Republican (August 30 to September 2) national conventions and on Election Day (November 2). Unique spikes of surveillance or correlation had been expected at times; however, in general, the two were remarkably uniform in their rises and falls and in their proportions, with surveillance consistently appearing in roughly 20 more posts than correlation. Only on election day did this vary, when surveillance spiked dramatically, appearing in almost eight times more posts than correlation.

Memogate: Contrasting Examples

Controversy surrounding CBS News' use of likely forged documents in reporting on President Bush's Texas Air National Guard service was a moment of substantial and unprecedented media exposure for blogs. Bloggers played a central role in questioning the authenticity of the documents, and this episode has become part of the mythic media narrative concerning the growing importance of bloggers. However, much discussion of the event by MSM and bloggers verged on synecdoche, suggesting that the original reporting and investigation of Memogate bloggers was typical blogging activity.

Close examination of data from the blogs studied in this project during the first 2 weeks[7] of Memogate does not reveal activity as significant as Memogate hype would lead one to expect. The modest increases (with one exception) and several decreases in activity among these four blogs seem not quite on par with Henry V's defeat of the superior French army at Agincourt. Admittedly, they are a small sample, yet they represent, if not central blogs in Memogate, nevertheless four of the most widely read and influential political blogs. My point is not to generalize to all political blogging from these four, but to offer them as a counterpoint to the blogging generalizations made in regard to Memogate.

Although Memogate was clearly one of the more significant campaign events, during its first two weeks (most of its period of salience), among the blogs studied in this project, surveillance overall only increased by 4.6%. Their number of electoral posts actually decreased by 7.4%. Original reporting of direct experience—the much-trumpeted "citizen journalism"—decreased by 4.8%. Correlation overall decreased by approximately the same amount, as did the multiple perspectives and networked know-how of adjunct bloggers—their efficient distributed labor force noted frequently in Memogate stories. The investigative activities of manipulating source material to reveal hidden points of importance also decreased by a small amount. One correlation indicator did increase dramatically by 50.0%: calls to action. This was driven primarily by a fund-raising drive for candidates at *Daily Kos* and instructions from *InstaPundit* to read certain blogs or articles on a variety of topics (not predominantly Memogate).

In terms of sources, news media increased by 10%, and this was equal among mainstream and alternative outlets. Juxtapositions of mainstream and alternative news sources also increased by 5.3%. Yet, despite other blogs being drivers of the Memogate story, their sourcing increased by only half as much as that and, as for circumventing the dreaded MSM, sourcing non-news outlets increased by even less. These data are not offered to discredit the work of Memogate bloggers, but rather as evidence to suggest that their achievements may be atypical.

Blogging Myths and Realities

While these data show, as expected, that the blogs studied performed traditional news functions, what was unexpected was how rarely these were performed traditionally: via firsthand reporting of events directly experienced in the physical world. Instead, the focus was mediated reporting. They performed surveillance and correlation primarily upon stories and information published by various news outlets, blogs, businesses and other sources. This seemed, if not directly to contradict, at least to question the generalizability of the conventional narrative of bloggers functioning as intrepid amateur reporters, carrying out original newsgathering and unrestrained by journalistic conventions.

If the political blogs in this project performed surveillance more on media sources than direct experience, and even more so during a major blogging event such as Memogate, it suggests a journalistic shift. Bloggers—or at least these four bloggers, although there is no particular reason to think of them as distinct from other popular political blogs—have taken the tools of the Fourth Estate and used them *on* the Fourth Estate, applying the news functions to the news "functioners." Akin to a citizen auditing the IRS or a theater critic leaping on stage, bloggers blur the line between producer/consumer and reality/mediation—a typical new-media perspective (Bolter & Grusin, 1999; Manovich, 2001). It is not merely that they have tools to create news, but that they see a fundamental lack of separation between newsmakers and news consumers.

Furthermore, bloggers' surveillance of news media suggests punditry more than journalism, specifically media punditry. Eleanor Clift, David Broder, William Safire and Clarence Page are contemporaries in a long tradition of political punditry, and Roger Ebert or Michiko Kakutani in a tradition of cultural criticism; however, comparatively much less common are pundits of media and news, such as Howard Kurtz or the short-lived *Brill's Content* magazine. Although the 24-hour news cycle and proliferation of outlets may have spurred media reflexivity (Gans, 2003), that is not the same as outsider analysis. The act of media punditry may be coming into its own via bloggers who, for the most part—and this is a fuzzy, degenerating division—operate outside or in opposition to MSM.

However, bloggers not only define and amplify the emerging role of the media pundit, but also alter the notion of punditry by occasionally performing traditional journalistic reporting, again blurring the line between producer and audience. Combined with their blatant ideological stances, this suggests a new conceptualization that might be more accurately referred to not as insta-pundits but rather as *activist pundits*. These bloggers collapse some distinction between political and media punditry because they do not strictly separate those realms. Many consider journalists wholly integrated actors in the political system, rather than members of the Fourth Estate. Therefore, bloggers' media punditry *is* political punditry.

Given that punditry has been shown to be a factor in affecting public perception of news media (Domke, Watts, Shah & Fan, 1999; Watts, Domke, Shah & Fan, 1999), this reconceptualization from journalist to pundit does not lessen bloggers' potential importance. If anything, it shows political blogging in general and Memogate in particular as a continuation of the strategic use of media punditry, which Domke et al. suggest "should be conceptualized as a product of the complex interactions of candidates and their handlers with journalists during the course of a presidential campaign" (p. 54).

The worrisome implication for viewing bloggers as pundits is their potential role as components in the process described by Bennett (1990, 2003) and Bennett and Manheim (2001) in which journalists take cues from elite political actors to define subjects of public discourse—a reversal of traditional democratic ideals. Similarly, McChesney sees punditry's ascent, as in the case of Fox News Channel's profitable substitution of punditry for conventional journalism, as part of a larger trend of declining investigative journalism and overreliance on public relations that "plays directly into the hands of powerful commercial interests" (2004, p. 81). If, as this project argues, bloggers represent an expansion of punditry more than a resurgence of muckraking, then this may be a trend neither revolutionary nor welcome.

While these findings suggest that political blogs are not as revolutionary as the discourse around events such as Memogate suggests, bloggers do represent a new media force. However, the dissonance between mythic blogging narratives and actual activities suggests a hybrid of some concern: activist pundits operating under the rhetoric of watchdog journalism. During this election cycle, *The Daily Show* host, Jon Stewart, famously attacked the hosts of CNN's *Crossfire* for being "partisan hacks" carrying out a sham of political commentary and debate. Stewart was not alone in suggesting that partisan hackery, with its resultant demoralization of the electorate and negative impact on democracy, represents the current state of punditry.

Ironically, while cheering on Stewart, many bloggers may have been practicing or on the verge of practicing partisan hackery. One can easily see potential slippage of bloggers from scrappy, upstart challengers to apparatchik pawns of sophisticated strategic communication campaigns. In the case of Memogate, the quick response and Republican connections of the first questioners fueled conspiracy theories of White House involvement. Although individual cases of blog manipulation are debatable, in the wake of scandals such as Trent Lott, Memogate, and the false identity of White House press corps member Jeff Gannon/James Guckertt, any political communications specialist who does *not* include bloggers in his or her strategic plans is unwise. While the current watchdog rhetoric of the blogging media narrative may provide an aura of integrity for now, cracks soon began to show among veteran bloggers and readers. As one reader of *Daily Dish* complained during the height of Memogate:

> I got a good laugh from your post on the "factual superiority of the blogosphere" because I did learn a lot of facts from blogs about the "CBS memos."

> From the right-wing blogs, I learned that the memo font matches MS Times-Roman, and nothing else. From the left-wings blogs, I learned that the memo font matches IBM Press-Roman, and nothing else.

> From the right-wing blogs, I learned that small horizontal variation in spacing is proof of "kerning" and therefore computer generation. From the left-wing blogs, I learned that small vertical variation in alignment is proof of mechanical action and therefore typewriter creation.

> I learned that the right-wing facts are certainly true, as noted by *Washington Post* experts, and the left-wing facts are certainly true, as established by the *Boston Globe.*

> From the right-wing blogs, I learned that a trusted expert is one who writes to Glenn Reynolds, offering to withhold any opinion on any topic if only the good [p]rofessor will end the stream of right-wing e-mail abuse. This guy's pleading uncertainty proves to Mickey Kaus and a waiting world that the *Globe* is full of crap.

> From the left-wing blogs, I learned that a trusted expert is a long-time Kevin Drum poster who suddenly reveals (without evidence) that he was an IBM typewriter salesman and therefore has knowledge that apparently belongs to no other living human. This guy's self-proclaimed

certainty proves to *Dailykos* [*sic*] and a waiting world that the *Washington Post* is full of crap.

From all blogs, I learned that the low resolution of the documents nullifies all supposed "facts" that contradict any locally favored *facts*.

From all my reading, I learned the comforting fact that we can all choose our facts as we please and yet still go to bed at night sure that all of *our* facts have survived the rigorous scrutiny that only the blogosphere can provide (Sullivan, 2004a).

Such sarcasm smacks of disillusionment with partisan hackery in the guise of watchdog journalism. Indeed, Sullivan's announcement of a blogging hiatus in February 2005 alluded to limitations of the medium antithetical to thorough investigation and deliberation:

The ability to keep on top of almost everything on a daily and hourly basis just isn't compatible with the time and space to mull over some difficult issues in a leisurely and deliberate manner. Others might be able to do it. But I've tried and failed.... I hope that after, say, nine months, I'll return to blogging full-steam with perhaps a new direction or approach to refresh the material. A little distance from the blogosphere might be helpful in that as well (Sullivan, 2005).

The ultimate potential for blogging, I suggest, lies in a question that has yet to be answered: Can the distributed labor of networked bloggers and blog readers effectively substitute for—or at least significantly complement—standardized, professionally trained, paid staffs of journalists, editors, fact-checkers, watchdogs, ombudsmen, activists and pundits? Once the inevitable first blog hoaxes or inaccuracies are widely reported—shades of Wikipedia—how will blogs regain credibility? (One is reminded of the mid-1990s' claim, "But I saw it on the Internet!" mutating from an assertion of credibility to an ironic comment on the unreliability of the medium.)

Furthermore, will some bloggers, seeking greater financial rewards, attempt to grow beyond their ideological niches and follow the path of mass media in homogenizing their fare, in effect destroying the very things that make them unique? Do, as Sullivan suggests, the real-time expectations of blog readers push the 24-hour news cycle even further? On one hand, journalists in theory are more careful, now that they have bloggers looking over their shoulders. On the other hand, might bloggers' competition and further acceleration of the news cycle lead to more inaccuracies exactly of the sort upon which bloggers feed?

Indeed, the first great online news triumph—Matt Drudge's breaking of the Clinton–Lewinsky scandal—turned out to be less of a scoop than a shortcut through journalism standards: The mainstream news organizations working on the story had not finished fact-checking it before Drudge went public. While he is still an active player, Drudge has not exactly become a respected mainstream journalist, but is more often regarded as a pawn by which strategic communications teams get their messages noticed by the legitimate news. Do blogs await his fate? A worst-case scenario for blogs might be that they do not become a new and significant check-and-balance in news and civic debate, but rather a new and significant force in tabloidism.

During the course of this study, blogs came into their own as political communications forces that I argue are best understood as activist media punditry. Since Memogate, blogs have fueled controversies such as the Gannon/Guckertt identity and political exploitation of the Schiavo right-to-die case. This project, although admittedly limited to a small sample during a specific and unique observational period, has strived to provide quantitative measures of blog activities. It is hoped such information will help separate blog realities from rhetoric.

Whether blogs will maintain credibility among their readers, evolve into online tabloids or assimilate into the existing political communications machine remains to be seen. However, future communications media will certainly come into adoption with spectacular hype and applications, as did telephony, telegraphy, motion pictures, radio, television, VCRs and each iteration of the Internet. Understanding their true functions and applications will require understanding the spectacular technologies and technology spectacles that preceded them.

References

ABC News. (December 30, 2004). People of the year: Bloggers. Retrieved February 12, 2005, from http://abcnews.go.com/WNT/PersonOfWeek/story?id=372266andpage=1.

Adar, E., Adamic, L.A., Zhang, L., and Lukose, R.M. (2004). Implicit structure and the dynamics of blogspace. Presentation to the Thirteenth International World Wide Web Conference, Workshop on the Weblogging Ecosystem: Aggregation, Analysis and Dynamics. New York, May 18, 2004. Retrieved May 25, 2004, from http://www.blogpulse.com/papers/www2004adar.pdf.

Andrews, P. (2003). Is blogging journalism? [Electronic version]. *Nieman Reports, 57*(3), 63–64. Retrieved May 23, 2004, from http://www.nieman.harvard.edu/reports/03-3NRfall/V57N3.pdf.

Bausch, P., Haughey, M. & Hourihan, M. (2002). *We blog: Publishing online with Weblogs.* Indianapolis, IN: Wiley Publishing Inc.

Bennett, W. L. (1990). Toward a theory of press–state relations in the United States. *Journal of Communication, 40*(2), 103–125.

Bennett, W. L. (2003). *News: The politics of illusion,* 5th ed. San Francisco: Longman.

Bennett, W. L., & Manheim, J. B. (2001). The big spin: Strategic communication and the transformation of pluralist democracy. In Bennett, W. L. & Entman, R. M. (Eds.), *Mediated politics: Communication in the future of democracy* (pp. 279–298). New York: Cambridge University Press.

Blades, M. (2004). Science Friday: Save this man's job—Vote Kerry. *Daily Kos.* Retrieved October 29, 2004, from http://www.dailykos.com/story/2004/10/29/4517/5631.

Blood, R. (2002). The Weblog handbook: Practical advice on creating and maintaining your blog. Cambridge, MA: Perseus Publishing.

Bolter, J. D., & Grusin, R. (1999). *Remediation: Understanding new media.* Cambridge, MA: The MIT Press.

Boston Herald. (December 1, 2004). From blogs to cicadas: 2004's most looked-up words. [Electronic version]. Retrieved December 14 from LexisNexis database.

Brown, H. (2003, April 26). Netlines. *British Medical Journal, 326*(7395), 938. Retrieved February 23, 2004, from Proquest database.

Domke, D., Watts, M. D., Shah, D. V. & Fan, D. P. (1999). The politics of conservative elites and the liberal media argument. *Journal of Communication, 49*(4), 35–58.

Drezner, D., & Farrell, H. (2004, July). *The power and politics of blogs.* Presentation to the 2004 American Political Science Association. Retrieved August 15, 2004, from http://www.utsc.utoronto.ca/~farrell/blogpaperfinal.pdf.

Embrey, T. R. (2002, December). You blog, we blog. *Teacher Librarian, 30*(2), 7. Retrieved February 23, 2004, from Proquest.

Gans, H. (2003). *Democracy and the news.* New York: Oxford University Press.

Gill, K. E. (2004). *How can we measure the influence of the blogosphere?* Presentation to the Thirteenth International World Wide Web Conference, Workshop on the Weblogging Ecosystem: Aggregation, Analysis and Dynamics. New York, May 18, 2004. Retrieved May 25, 2004, from http://faculty.washington.edu/kegill/pub/www2004_blogosphere_gill.pdf.

Glaser, M. (2003, November 18). Media critics rave (and kvetch) about the Internet's impact. *Online Journalism Review.* Retrieved November 23, 2003, from http://www.ojr.org/ojr/glaser/1069197815.php.

Glaser, M. (2004a, February 11). "Watchblogs" put the political press under the microscope. *Online Journalism Review.* Retrieved February 16, 2004, from http://ojr.org/ojr/glaser/1076465317.php.

Glaser, M. (2004b, May 5). To their surprise, bloggers are force for change in big media. *Online Journalism Review.* Retrieved May 28, 2004, from ojr.org/ojr/ethics/1085527295.php.

Glaser, M. (2004c, May 11). Scholars discover Weblogs pass test as mode of communication. *Online Journalism Review.* Retrieved May 25, 2004, from http://www.ojr.org/ojr/glaser/1084325287.php.

Grossman, L. (2004, June 21). Meet Joe Blog. Time, 163, 25, p. 65-70.

Hunter. (2004). TANG typewriter follies; Wingnuts wrong. *Daily Kos.* Retrieved April 22, 2005, from http://www.dailykos.com/story/2004/9/10/34914/1603.

Kennedy School of Government Case Program. (2004). "Big media" meets the "bloggers": Coverage of Trent Lott's remarks at Strom Thurmond's birthday party. Cambridge: Harvard College.

Lasica, J. D. (2003). Blogs and journalism need each other. [Electronic version]. *Nieman Reports, 57*(3), 70–74. Retrieved May 23, 2004, from http://www.nieman.harvard.edu/reports/03-3NRfall/V57N3.pdf.

Lasica, J. D. (2004, May 5). Surf's down as more netizens turn to RSS for browsing. *Online Journalism Review.* Retrieved May 11, 2004, from http://ojr.org/ojr/workplace/1083806402.php.

Lasswell, H. D. (1948). The structure and function of communication in society. In Schramm, W. (Ed.), *Mass communications* (pp. 102–115). Urbana: University of Illinois Press.

Lazarsfeld, P. F., & Merton, R. K. (1949). Mass communication, popular taste and organized social action. In Schramm, W. (Ed.), *Mass communications* (pp. 459–480). Urbana: University of Illinois Press.

Manovich, L. (2001). *The language of new media.* Cambridge, MA: The MIT Press.

Marshall, J. M. (2004a). I do a fair amount…. *Talking Points Memo.* Retrieved April 22, 2005, from http://www.talkingpointsmemo.com/archives/week_2004_07_18.php.

Marshall, J. M. (2004b). I just read…. *Talking Points Memo.* Retrieved April 22, 2005, from http://www.talkingpointsmemo.com/archives/week_2004_07_25.php.

McChesney, R. W. (2004). *The problem of the media.* New York: Monthly Review Press.

Moulitsas, M. (2004a). Kerry theme: "Help is on the way." *Daily Kos.* Retrieved April 22, 2005, from http://www.dailykos.com/story/2004/7/29/224223/466.

Moulitsas, M. (2004b). Lakoff book surges. *Daily Kos.* Retrieved April 22, 2005, from http://www.dailykos.com/story/2004/9/21/124721/483.

Moulitsas, M. (2004c). Nag time. *Daily Kos.* Retrieved April 22, 2005, from http://mrdc.dailykos.com/story/2004/9/29/153149/390.

Moulitsas, M. (2004d). OK-Sen; AK-Sen: Updates. *Daily Kos.* Retrieved April 22, 2005, from http://www.dailykos.com/story/2004/10/21/13622/278.

Nardi, B. (2004, June 11). Blogging for the rest of us. Presentation to Digital Media Working Group at University of Washington, Seattle. From author's notes.

Noonan, P. (November 4, 2004). So much to savor. [Electronic version]. *Wall Street Journal.* Retrieved November 10, 2004, from LexisNexis database.

Outing, S. (2003, October 15). Advancing citizen blogs on news sites. *Editor and Publisher.com.* Retrieved May 23, 2004, from http://www.editorandpublisher.com/eandp/columns/stop-thepresses_display.jsp?vnu_content_id=2002027.

Pax, S. (2003). *Salam Pax: The clandestine diary of an ordinary Iraqi.* New York: Grove Press.

Perseus Development Corporation. (2003, November 26). The blogging iceberg: Of 4.12 million hosted Weblogs, most little seen, quickly abandoned. Retrieved June 17, 2004, from http://www.perseus.com/blogsurvey/thebloggingiceberg.html.

Pew Internet and American Life Project. (2005, January 25). A decade of adoption: How the Internet has woven itself into American life. Retrieved January 29, 2005, from http://www.pewinternet.org/PPF/r/148/report_display.asp.

Regan, T. (2003). Weblogs threaten and inform traditional journalism. [Electronic version]. *Nieman Reports, 57*(3), 68–70. Retrieved May 23, 2004, from http://www.nieman.harvard.edu/reports/03-3NRfall/V57N3.pdf.

Reynolds, G. (2004a). The biggest ad buy of the campaign. *InstaPundit.* Retrieved April 22, from http://instapundit.com/archives/018520.php.

Reynolds, G. (2004b). Some election (and post-election) thoughts. *InstaPundit.* Retrieved April 22, from http://instapundit.com/archives/week_2004_10_31.php.

Richards, A. (2004, May 20). Interview. *The Larry King Show.* Transcript retrieved May 25, 2004, from http://www.cnn.com/TRANSCRIPTS/0405/20/lkl.00.html.

Stauffer, T. (2002). Blog on: The essential guide to building dynamic weblogs. New York: McGraw-Hill/Osbourne.

Steinberg, J., & Carter, B. (2005, January 11). CBS dismisses 4 over broadcast on Bush service. [Electronic version]. *The New York Times,* section A, p. 1. Retrieved February 10, 2005, from LexisNexis database.

Sullivan, A. (2004a). Email of the day. *Daily Dish.* Retrieved April 22, 2005, from http://www.andrewsullivan.com/index.php?dish_inc=archives/2004_09_12_dish_archive.html#109513548417617171.

Sullivan, A. (2004b). Coming up for air: *Daily Dish.* Retrieved April 22, 2005, from http://andrewsullivan.com/index.php?dish_inc=archives/2004_07_18_dish_archive.html.

Sullivan, A. (2004c). He said it! *Daily Dish.* Retrieved April 22, 2005, from http://www.andrewsullivan.com/index.php?dish_inc=archives/2004_10_31_dish_archive.html.

Sullivan, A. (2004d). Reaganites versus Bush: *Daily Dish.* Retrieved April 22, 2005, from http://www.andrewsullivan.com/index.php?dish_inc=archives/2004_09_05_dish_archive.html.

Sullivan, A. (2004e). Could it be any closer? *Daily Dish.* Retrieved April 22, 2005, from http://www.andrewsullivan.com/index.php?dish_inc=archives/2004_10_31_dish_archive.html#109928665104987021.

Sullivan, A. (2004f). Bush versus unity: *Daily Dish.* Retrieved April 22, 2005, from http://www.andrewsullivan.com/index.php?dish_inc=archives/2004_07_25_dish_archive.html#109107438046531465.

Sullivan, A. (2005). The *Dish* as you've known it. *Daily Dish.* Retrieved April 22, 2005, from http://www.andrewsullivan.com/index.php?dish_inc=archives/2005_01_30_dish_archive.html#110723289508671920.

Thomsen, E. B. (2002). Internet column: Blogging, anyone? *Collection Building, 21*(2), 76. Retrieved February 24, 2004, from Proquest database.

Wallsten, P. (2004a, September 12). The race to the White House; no disputing it: Blogs are major players. [Electronic version]. *Los Angeles Times,* section A, p. 22. Retrieved February 10, 2005, from LexisNexis database.

Wallsten, P. (2004b, September 18). The race to the White House; GOP activist made allegations on CBS memos. [Electronic version]. *Los Angeles Times,* section A, p. 18. Retrieved February 10, 2005, from LexisNexis database.

Wasserstein, B. (2004, September 19). Bloggers' "moment" doesn't make for a revolution. [Electronic version]. *Los Angeles Times,* section M, p. 1. Retrieved February 10, 2005, from LexisNexis database.

Watts, M. D., Domke, D., Shah, D. V. & Fan, D. P. (1999). Elite cues and media bias: Explaining public perceptions of a liberal press. *Communication Research, 26,* 144–175.

Weintraub, D. (2004, January 14). Politics and beyond: An inside look at *The California Insider*. *Online Journalism Review*. Retrieved June 12, 2004, from http://ojr.org/ojr/workplace/1074119409.php.

Weiss, J. (2004, May 10). Blogs colliding with traditional media: Convention credentials expected for Web logs. [Electronic version]. *The Boston Globe*.

Welch, M., Jensen, M. & Reeves, J. (2003). Blogworld and its gravity. [Electronic version]. *Columbia Journalism Review, 42*(3), 20–26. Retrieved May 23, 2004, from Proquest database.

Whelan, D. (2003). In a fog about blogs. [Electronic version]. *American Demographics, 25*(6), 22. Retrieved May 23, 2004, from Proquest database.

Williams, L. (2003, October 10). The blogger as citizen journalist. *Cadence90*. Retrieved November 24, 2003, from http://www.cadence90.com/blogs/2003_10_01_Nixon_archives.html#106580374740640747.

Wright, C. R. (1959). *Mass communications: A sociological perspective*. New York: Random House.

Notes

1. Or higher if Top 20 was not available.
2. Emerging blog tools attempt to determine the influence of individual blogs through predominantly mathematic methods that are inherently problematic (Adar et al., 2004; Gill, 2004) but represent the best tools available.
3. Peer and media opinions are included due to the social nature of blogging, as Nardi (2004) and others (Bausch, Haughey & Hourihan, 2002; Blood, 2002; Stauffer, 2002) have extensively described.
4. The remainder of this analysis focuses solely on electoral posts unless otherwise indicated.
5. Term for far-right online activists, derived from the *FreeRepublic.com* discussion boards.
6. Texas Air National Guard.
7. The CBS News piece aired September 8, 2004, with nearly immediate blogging response and next-day coverage from mainstream media. This section examines the period of September 8–22, 2004.

4
Analyzing Political Conversation on the Howard Dean Candidate Blog

SHARON MERAZ

Introduction

A recent Pew Internet Report (2004) dispelled the fear that the Internet is being used like an echo chamber to support only like-minded viewpoints. In criticizing the theory of selective exposure, the report concluded that the Internet actively contributes to democratic discourse by exposing Internet news users to more arguments than traditional media does. Though the report included alternative news sites and candidate websites, it did not do any specific analysis of 2004 presidential candidate blogs.

Before the 2004 presidential election, there was little serious attempt by candidates to engage citizens in conversations online on the candidate website. In the 1996 Republican convention, Klinenberg and Perrin (2000) found that of five candidates, Pat Buchanan made the only attempt; however, he simulated the scenario of citizen conversation online by manually posting excerpts of user messages. U.S. Senatorial and gubernatorial candidates quickly adopted the candidate website through the 1996 to 1998 period (D'Alessio, 2000), but as Galley–Stromer (2000) pointed out, interactivity was superficial. A similar lack of interactivity on candidate websites in the 2000 U.S. presidential election led Browning (2002) to conclude that "not since the advent of the World Wide Web a decade ago have technology issues meant [s]o little in the presidential campaign—or have efforts to draw voters to commercial political Web sites met with so little success" (p. 149).

Though approximately 88% of U.S. senatorial candidates had candidate websites in 2000, interactivity was confined to such campaigning/mobilizing features such as downloading candidate posters, buying candidate products, volunteering and fund-raising. In a review of website home pages for U.S. house representatives during the 1996 to 2001 period, Jarvis and Wilkerson (2005) found an avoidance of audience engagement, suggesting an early hesitation on the part of government officials to embrace the Internet for two-way communication with citizens. The lack of usage of the candidate website for direct citizen engagement was also mirrored in other European countries (Norris, 2003) and in the United Kingdom (Ward & Gibson, 2003).

On March 15, 2003, U.S. presidential contender Howard Dean became the first candidate to openly encourage citizen political conversations on his campaign website through the use of a candidate blog. As opposed to using the blog primarily as a one-way personalized communicative device (a common characteristic of most blogs), the Dean campaign used its blog as a discussion forum, amassing thousands of user comments until his withdrawal from the race in February 2004.

The blog as candidate forum for citizen discussion was later implemented on the candidate websites of 2004 Democratic presidential hopefuls John Edwards and Wesley Clark, the eventual Democratic nominee John Kerry and Republican incumbent president George W. Bush. Dean's continued legacy as the blogging politician is evident in the current political blogging surge by U.S. politicians such as Illinois Senator Barak Obama, House Speaker Dennis Hastert, Congressman John Conyers and 2008 Democratic presidential hopeful John Edwards.

This chapter focuses attention on the first influential candidate blog—the Howard Dean 2004 presidential campaign blog—specifically examining the nature and quality of citizen political conversation. In acknowledging Dean's public enthusiasm for encouraging political conversation on the candidate website, this chapter examines to what extent Dean's candidate blog achieved citizen empowerment and open, active deliberation. This chapter also contributes initial quantitative research toward an understanding of the candidate blog's place within the 2004 presidential election, political communication research, online campaigning and democratic dialogue and discourse.

Literature Review

Theoretical Review

This study pulls from theories on deliberation, conversational analysis and community formation to examine the role, function and diversity of political conversation on the Dean candidate blog. Deliberation theory is a vital theory in the study of political conversation. As Burkhalter, Gastil and Kelshaw (2002) have pointed out, deliberation theory is mired in definitional ambiguity; however, several foundational theorists have agreed upon prevailing characteristics of deliberative discourse.

Deliberation is essentially defined as reasoned public political discourse, dialogue or conversation that is egalitarian, rational–critical and inclusive as opposed to private intrapersonal deliberation (Barber, 1984; I. Cohen, 1989; Habermas, 1989; Dryzek, 1990; Fishkin, 1991; Benhabib, 1992; Bohman, 1996; Gutmann & Thompson, 1996; J. Cohen, 1997; Goodin, 2000; Baoill, 2004). Ryfe (2002) noted that good deliberation involves an "advancement of claims, presentation of evidence and consideration of counterfactual data" (p.359). Deliberative conversation must entail reason-giving or argumentation based on factual information as opposed to emotive appeals (Benhabib; Matthews, 1994), although scholars dispute the role that emotion plays in the sexism of argumentation (Benhabib & Cornell, 1987; Young, 1990).

Participants are encouraged to speak intelligently, be civil and polite (Papacharissi, 2004), actively process arguments and allow mutual respect, considerateness and empathy to guide argumentation and decision making (Fishkin, 1991, 1995; Benhabib, 1996; Gutmann & Thompson, 1996) so that the entire spectrum of viewpoints is taken into account without privileging any particular perspective (Mill, 1972; Fishkin, 1991, 1995; Matthews, 1994). Scholars stress the benefits of deliberation, which include an increased tolerance or understanding of others' viewpoints (Gutmann & Thompson; Warren, 1996a, 1996b), a more selfless, public-minded and self-reflective form of democratic citizenship (Dewey, 1954), increased communicative abilities (Gastil, 1993; Bohman, 1996; Gutmann & Thompson; J. Cohen, 1997; Sanders, 1997) and increased political knowledge. As a result of deliberation, citizens should increase political participation, autonomy and individual self-efficacy (Warren 1996b; Fishkin & Luskin, 1999).

In explaining how individuals deal with dissonant information, a pertinent communication theory is Petty and Cacioppo's (1986) elaboration likelihood model (ELM). In ELM theory, influence can occur only after exposure and attention to the message, and elaboration occurs when people think about the issue-relevant information. Individuals exposed to a message might scrutinize the information presented, and this high-effort cognitive activity is considered the central or the high route to persuasion. Individuals take the peripheral route when they depend on such shortcuts to information processing as the source's perceived credibility and the source's trustworthiness. Factors such as the strength of the argument, the receiver's initial position compared to the argument advanced, the receiver's motivation to engage in elaboration and receiver's ability to engage in elaboration affect determine whether the central or the peripheral route is taken to elaboration.

The discussant's self-efficacy can help explain route-processing choice in partisan political conversational networks. Noelle–Neumann's spiral of silence theory (1973, 1980) is meant to explain the powerful effects of mass media. In controversial issue conversations, people determine whether their opinion is part of the majority or the minority. If an individual's opinion is unsupported or against majority opinion, he or she tends to be silenced. The spiral of silence suggests a spiral effect—the more people are silent, the more they become silenced as minority opinions are less represented among opinions. The theory states that individuals can determine whether their opinions fall within the majority or the minority, and this status determination exerts an impact on their decision to speak or be silent.

In examining how political discussant community forms on the Internet, it is vital to pull from theories that explain how individuals self-select into desired communities. Homophily theory suggests that people are attracted to similarity instead of difference, which has important ramifications within conversational networks (McPherson, Smith–Lovin & Cook, 2001). The first homophily study in sociological literature was traced to Lazarsfeld and Merton's (1954) study on friendship processes in Hilltown and Craftown, where they identified two types of homophily: status homophily (demographic factors) and value homophily (shared beliefs and values). In this "birds of a feather flock together" principle, geographical, organizational and role foci are powerful structural forces that induce homophily. With new technologies, shared interests may be the main organizational principle that brings like-minded people together.

Homophily theory underlies Sunstein's (2000, 2002) work on hate group polarization and cybercascades theories within the Internet online community. Sunstein (2001) sees the Internet's effect as deleterious to democracy because it enhances fragmentation, insulation and enclave deliberation. According to Sunstein (2002), this fragmentation can lead to more extreme positions, limited argument pools and informational cybercascades due to the tilt of homogeneous influence. Though Sunstein (2000) realized the significance of insularity to forming movements, developing activism, creating new ideas and securing minority involvement in early online communities, he connected negative long-term effects of homogeneous community discussion to a fragmentation of the public sphere into a realm of counterpublics.

Online Conversation and Deliberation Theory

In terms of online discussion spaces, some authors have intentionally and unintentionally examined aspects of deliberation theory. Papacharissi (2004) examined 287 discussion threads in political Usenet newsgroups for civility. The author made a distinction between civility and politeness and found that fewer than 30% of total messages were uncivil, impolite or both. Hill and Hughes (1998) examined AOL chats and discovered that postings were battling ideas from different viewpoints. Rafaeli and Sudweeks (1997) examined 44 randomly sampled bulletin boards and found that more than 60% of the messages were direct responses to previous messages.

Capella, Price and Nir (2002) tested argument repertoire or the number of relevant reasons stated in support of and against the discussant's opinion in a real-time, multiwave, multigroup-moderated space with 60 groups of citizens. The authors found that participants in online group discussions had higher argument repertoires and greater substantive issue exchanges within group discussions.

To date, few scholars have devoted academic attention to assessing blogs as forums for deliberative interpersonal discussion. In her qualitative assessment of blogs as debate forums for the invasion of Iraq, Roberts–Miller (2004) found they were lacking in true argumentation and reason-giving. Baoill (2004) critiqued the blog format for its heavy time commitment, emphasis on early mover status and lack of supportive infrastructure for rational–critical debate.

Political Conversation and Composition of Political Discussant Networks

Some scholars see democratic benefit in all political conversation (Kim, Wyatt & Katz, 1999; Wyatt, Katz & Kim, 2000). Separating personal conversation from political conversation, Wyatt et al. examined informal conversation among like-minded individuals in a population of 1,029 adults. The authors found that all political conversation, regardless of whether it was conducted at home, at work or in organizations, resulted in greater opinionation and political participation. Using the same data set, Kim et al. found that issue-specific conversation was a determinant of willingness to argue. Issue-specific and general political conversations were determinants of argument quality, while general political conversation was related to campaigning.

The composition of a network—that is, whether it is homogeneous or heterogeneous—can have effects on the ability of political conversation to drive real-world participation, an essential aspect of political campaigns (Mutz, 2002a; Ulbig & Funk, 1999; McLeod et al., 1999b). Mutz found that political disagreement or cross-cutting conversations created intrapersonal ambivalence and interpersonal social accountability, making it less likely for a person to vote and to participate in partisan campaigning. Ulbig and Funk showed that conflict-avoidant people resist participation in such political activities as political protest, campaign support activities or interpersonal discussion of politics. Yet, many scholars agree that heterogeneous networks increase a participant's diversity of opinion and knowledge (McLeod et al., 1999b; Price, Capella & Nir, 2002; Mutz, 2002a).

Environmental factors and the participant's majority or minority status can affect political discussion in conversational networks (Scheufele, Nisbet, Brossard & Nisbet, 2004; Huckfeldt, 2001; Huckfeldt, Beck, Dalton, Levine & Morgan, 1998; Kenny, 1994; Huckfeldt & Sprague, 1987, 1988, 1991). In a series of studies on face-to-face, dyadic political discussant networks, Huckfeldt and Sprague (1987, 1988, 1991, 1998) found that political minorities' opinions were consistently misinterpreted and undercut by majority participants and that disagreement was less well tolerated between majority and minority dyads when compared with majority and majority dyads. Mardsen (1987) found evidence to support the persistent disadvantaged position of minority participants in majority spaces.

Scholars do not agree on the impact of online discussion on the diversity of discussion. Stromer–Galley (2003) interviewed 69 people from Usenet and Yahoo! chat spaces and found that most respondents confronted heterogeneous and diverse opinions. Chaffee et al. (2001) debunked the principle of selective exposure as strongly connected to partisan press and theories of propaganda in relation to traditional media; however, their findings supported a tendency to gravitate to attitude-consistent versus counterattitudinal messages on the candidate's campaign website.

Though very little work has been done on analyzing political conversation on political blogs, link analysis studies suggest deep partisan segmentation in the blogosphere. Welsch (2005) found that right-leaning political blogger Glenn Reynolds (Instapundit) cited more URLs, with no overlap to left-leaning political blogger Duncan Black's (Atrios) link citations. Adamic and Glance (2005) examined the relationship between the 2004 presidential election and the political blogosphere through taking a single day's snapshot of over 1,000 blogs and charting 40 influential blogs for 2 months preceding the November 2004 presidential election. In assessing blogroll links and page citation links, the authors found that 91% of the links remained within partisan communities.

Role of Traditional Media in Political Conversation

Several studies also examine the relationship between interpersonal conversation and the traditional media, revealing the former's dependence on the latter for discussion material (Simon & Xenos, 2000; Scheufele & Nisbet, 2002; Scheufele, 2002; McLeod et al., 1999a, 1999b; Kim et al., 1999). The majority of studies on the relationship between media and interpersonal discussion have examined the relative importance of different mass media. Capella et al. (2002) found no connection between online conversations and exposure to traditional media. McLeod et al. (1999a) also found no direct connection between media use and discussion forum participation. Scheufele (2002) found that newspapers were the most influential medium in issue-based political discussion. In a later study, Scheufele et al. (2004) found that face-to-face networks with greater heterogeneity were more likely to use hard news content in newspapers. Mutz and Martin (2001) found that mainstream news media, particularly newspaper and television, exposed individuals to more dissimilar views than interpersonal conversation did.

Studies are already emerging on the relationship between the blogosphere and mainstream media. Drezner and Farrell (2004) conducted an online survey on blog readership among 140 editors, reporters, columnists and publishers. The authors found that though 125 blogs were cited, the top 10 blogs accounted for 54% of all the mass media blog citations. Marlow (2004), creator of Blogdex, examined referential information for a 3-year period through analysis of hyperlinks. In examining 310 known URLs from 4,728 articles derived through querying the LexisNexis database, Marlow found that journalists were prone to read weblogs popular or prominent in the blog search engine's listing of top blogs.

Hypotheses and Research Questions

This study sought to present some initial quantitative assessments of the nature, quality and diversity of citizen political conversation on the Dean candidate blog. Dean's candidate blog lacked heavy moderation, rule-governed conduct and time allotment for discussion. The blog discussion space did have some specific rules: It was moderated to some extent, members had an honor code of conduct, pseudoidentity was enforced by e-mail recognition and conversation was guided on topic by specific open threads. But, unlike real-world deliberative forums, there were no set limits on the size of blog community membership, no geographical strictures on membership and no set time frames for conversation; individual identity could be fluid if blog participants elected to adopt multiple pseudonyms. In relationship to the degree of familiarity among blog participants, the candidate blog could also be considered a network of weak ties so that most members were primarily virtual acquaintances.

Many prior studies have found a battling of differing viewpoints on online discussion forums (Hill & Hughes, 1998; Stromer–Galley, 2003), and some studies have found that partisan blogs link to blogs of shared political viewpoints (Welsch, 2005; Adamic & Glance, 2005). As a candidate partisan space, this study hypothesized that more supportive than dissenting opinions would be expressed about the candidate—namely, from supporters:

> Hypothesis 1: More supportive than dissenting statements will be made about the Dean candidate from Dean supporters.

In keeping with the findings of the lack of communicative power of minorities in majority, face-to-face, political discussant networks (Huckfeldt & Sprague, 1987, 1988, 1991, 1998), this study hypothesized that nonsupporter minorities who post dissenting opinions would be prone to post fewer issue-based, reason-based dissenting opinions than supporters who post dissenting opinions. Minority dissenting opinion would also be taken less seriously than majority dissenting opinion so that there should be greater dismissing and less willingness to engage minority dissenting opinion from nonsupporters than majority dissenting opinion from supporters. The following hypotheses were advanced:

> Hypothesis 2: Nonsupporter dissenting opinions will be less reason-based and issue-based than supporter dissenting opinions.
> Hypothesis 3: Supporters will be more likely to dismiss and less likely to engage dissenting nonsupporter opinion than dissenting supporter opinion.

As a blog partisan space, it is understood that there will be pressures to conform and push the blog towards homogeneity of opinion; however, it will be difficult to dismiss all dissenting opinion. Mutz and Martin (2001) found that media provided more dissenting, crosscutting viewpoints than interpersonal discussion. This study hypothesized that there would be survival of disagreement through referencing dissenting opinion from the media when references were made to media in blog postings.

> Hypothesis 4: Media opinion will provide a significant source of supportive and dissenting opinion when cited in interpersonal communication on the candidate blog because media content is more diverse in opinion and more prone to report negatively instead of positively on candidate issues.

Past studies have shown a relationship between media use and interpersonal conversation (Scheufele, 2002; Scheufele & Nisbet, 2002; Simon & Xenos, 2000; McLeod et al., 1999a, 1999b; Kim et al., 1999). Former blog studies have also found a strong relationship between blog content and media content (Drezner & Farrell, 2004; Marlow, 2004). As a campaign blog, this study questioned the role and relationship of media–citizen conversations.

> Research Question (RQ) 1: For posts that explicitly mentioned media, which media were cited? Were traditional media sources more popular than nontraditional media sources?

As defined in the prior outline of deliberation theory, one of the goals of interpersonal discussion and deliberation is to elucidate and clarify issues. During election time, the media are often discredited with too great a focus on candidate image, "horse-race" coverage and negative news (Jamieson & Campbell, 1992; Patterson, 1993, 2000; Kendall, 2000). As an open forum, this study asked to what extent the blog format filled a void through focusing on issue discussion as opposed to candidate image discussion.

> RQ 2: To what extent did blog participants engage in discussion of issues on the Dean candidate blog as compared with nonissue discussion?

This study also sought to examine to what extent political conversation on the candidate blog approached some of the classic deliberative ideals. McLeod et al. (1999b) identified network size as related to network heterogeneity, stating that political conversation networks tend towards greater diversity and heterogeneity in opinions and network composition. Diversity of opinion can be measured in the balance of supportive to dissenting opinion permitted on the candidate blog.

> RQ 3: To what extent were blog participants posting positive postings as opposed to negative postings about other candidates on the Dean candidate blog?

As deliberation theory highlights (Barber, 1984; I. Cohen, 1989; Habermas, 1989; Dryzek, 1990; Fishkin, 1991; Benhabib, 1992; Bohman, 1996; Gutmann & Thompson, 1996; J. Cohen, 1997; Goodin, 2000; Baoill, 2004), for a proper rational conversation to occur, there must be a logical relationship between former and subsequent opinions as well as a presentation of evidence. This study posed the following additional research questions:

RQ 4: To what extent were postings supported by an appeal to reason-giving?

RQ 5: To what extent were postings related to previous postings or the current thread?

Methodology

The Dean blog grew to sustain thousands of user posts on a daily basis. On each day, the campaign bloggers posted a series of threaded posts open for blog participant discussion. Because of the sheer volume of postings and to test the advanced hypotheses and research questions most effectively, this study elected to examine discussion threads on days that had the highest probability for issue discussion, deliberation and media engagement. The Dean blog maintained archives of all blog discussions from the day of the blog creation—March 15, 2003—to current. In an effort to narrow the time period, within the month of January 2004, debate days, caucus day for Iowa and primary day for New Hampshire were selected for discussion examination. This yielded a data set of 6 nonsuccessive days in 2004: January 4 (television debate), January 6 (radio debate), January 11 (television debate), January 19 (Iowa caucus), January 22 (television debate) and January 27 (New Hampshire primary).

This narrowing of the data set still yielded a message stream of over 30,000 posts. In an attempt to make analysis of the postings more manageable, a systematic random sampling of every 10th posting was chosen for analysis from each threaded discussion posting per day. From approximately 129 new threads across the 6-day period, this systematic random sampling yielded a data set of 3,066 messages for content analysis. The decision was also made to do manual coding with the codebook versus computer-assisted coding with Diction and VBPro. The unit of analysis was the assertion within blog posts and each post was coded through all of the questions for presence or absence of related criteria as they pertained to the hypotheses and research questions. In coding each post in relation to the codebook, an absence of characteristics were denoted by "0" or left blank.

Each blog post was coded for whether it mentioned issues or nonissues. Nonissue discussion was categorized according to whether it was an assertion about candidate qualifications and character (image characteristics), campaigning (writing letters, getting out the vote, grassroots efforts, "real-world" meetings such as meetups) or support/endorsement (polls, open declarations of support, public and private endorsements). Because coding was handled at the level of the assertion within the blog post, each post could be coded through multiple categories for the presence/absence of issues/nonissues.

To capture dissent, each blog post was also coded for whether it was an overt dissenting post from a supporter or a nonsupporter. Nonsupporters would usually identify themselves as nonsupporters through negative e-mail addresses or openly through declaring support for another candidate. If the post was instead a response from a supporter to a nonsupporter's or supporter's dissenting opinion, the response was coded for how it responded to the dissenting opinion. Categories were collapsed into two simple macrocategories: engagement/deliberation with the blog posting and nonengagement/dismissing of blog posting.

The nonengagement/dismissing of the blog posting captured all responses that did not engage the dissenter with reasoned opinion, but opted instead for name-calling, ordering the poster to leave or dismissing the poster as not worthy of attention. Postings were also coded for whether they mentioned other Democratic candidates or the Republican candidate, and for the affective tone of the posting—that is, whether the tone was positive or negative. To keep the coding scheme at a higher level analysis, distinctions were not made for different candidates, and the post was coded based on the mention of the first Democratic candidate. As an initial exploratory study, the main idea in this coding analysis was to examine whether diverse viewpoints were encouraged.

A post was related to the thread if it kept on subject or if it was related to earlier posts within the same thread. A post was coded as a reason-giving post if it cited substantive reasons for its opinion as opposed to nonfact-based, purely emotional reasoning. Reasons based on personal, selfish reasons or simple affective statements (e.g., "I like the candidate because he looks presidential") were not coded as reason-giving posts. If the post mentioned at minimum one substantive reason, it was coded as a reason-giving post. No attempt was made to establish the veracity of reasons; the point of this code was to establish whether posters reached out to evidence and made rational–critical attempts to back their opinions.

To capture media coverage, each post was coded for whether it made explicit reference to media. Included in these media categories were television/television websites, newspaper/newspaper websites, radio/radio websites, newsmagazines/newsmagazine websites, noncandidate blogs, candidate blogs, Internet-only news sites (e.g., Salon) and other news sources (Gallup, Zogby). A later category was added, the blog participants' websites or blogs, after initial intercoder reliability revealed this source to be a significant media reference for many posters. The post was also coded for whether it presented supportive or dissenting media content towards Dean, as well as whether it delivered an active critique of the media or media figures associated with the quoted media source.

To assess intercoder reliability, 10% of posts for each day of the 6-day period were randomly chosen and coded using the devised codebook. Using Holsti's coefficient of reliability formula, coefficients ranged between 85 and 92% for the different variables. One coder content analyzed the remaining 2,759 of the 3,066 posts. To facilitate quantitative analysis, codes were initially entered into a spreadsheet application and eventually pulled into a statistical package to aid further statistical analysis.

Results

Diversity of Discussion and Dissent

Hypothesis 1 and several of the research questions centered on the nature of discussion and dissent on the candidate blog in terms of deliberative ideals and democratic discourse tenants. Hypothesis 1 predicted that Dean supporters would post more supportive than dissenting statements about the candidate. Examining the full data set of posts over the 6-day period for dissenting assertions from supporters and nonsupporters revealed that the blog was primarily used as a supportive mechanism.

Table 4.1 provides a breakdown of the dissenting posts from supporters and nonsupporters for the period under analysis. Surprisingly, nonsupporter dissent was almost nonexistent; only 131 of 3,066, or approximately 4%, of all blog posts could be clearly identified as presenting dissenting opinion from nonsupporters. Dissenting opinion from supporters more than doubled that from nonsupporters: 285 of the 3,066 posts, or slightly over 9%, represented dissenting opinion from supporters.

As Hypothesis 1 posited, supporters were more likely to post supportive postings (M = 461.83; SD = 117.70) about the candidate than nonsupportive postings (M = 47.5; SD = 31.36), and this difference was significant [$t(5.06)$ =

Table 4.1 Number of Dissenting Blog Posts From Nonsupporters and Supporters by Day

Date	Nonsupporters	Supporters
Jan. 4[a]	30 (8%)	19 (5%)
Jan. 6	21 (6%)	12 (3%)
Jan. 11	6 (2%)	29 (7%)
Jan. 19	60 (9%)	87 (13%)
Jan. 22	10 (2%)	72 (12%)
Jan. 27	4 (1%)	66 (10%)

[a] Numbers reflect the total post number per day, and the percentages reflect the percentage of total dissenting blog posts for that specific day for nonsupporters and supporters.

8.332; $p < .05$], with equal variances not assumed. A surprising finding was that nonsupporters were also more likely to post supportive postings (M = 489; SD = 142.92) about the candidate than nonsupportive postings (M = 21.83; SD = 21.13), and this difference was also significant [$t(5.219) = 7.921$; $p < .05$, with equal variances not assumed]. As these two findings suggest, there were no significant differences in a comparison of supportive postings [$t(10) = 0.359$; $p > .05$] or nonsupportive postings [$t(10) = -1.667$; $p > .05$] between supporters and nonsupporters. Though Hypothesis 1 was proved, it must be noted that supporters and nonsupporters tended to post more supportive than dissenting content concerning the candidate.

Table 4.1 provides further quantitative explanations of the significant results. In reference to nonsupporters, the total number of dissenting posts dropped from 9% of posts on January 19 to 2% on January 22 and 1% on January 27. On the supporter end of dissenting posts, dissent maintained upward movement until January 19, then began slightly dipping past January 22. The reason for these declines in dissenting posts for both groups past January 22 was due to a change in the design of the blog system to include comment registration. Before January 22, citizens could have added posts without authenticating with username and password. The addition of a required registration for adding comments on January 22 enabled dissenters to be tagged by e-mail, thus allowing the Dean headquarters to moderate the blog through blocking specific e-mail addresses from being able to post or removing posts from dissenters or "trolls."

The result of this change in the design of the network was to quash dissent from nonsupporters and, to a lesser extent, supporters. It became increasingly more difficult to voice dissent past January 22, particularly for nonsupporters. On the last day of the 6-day examination, 10 times more posts voiced dissent from supporters than from nonsupporters. The design of the blog facilitated identification and curtailing of any dissent presented from nonsupporters.

Hypothesis 2 predicted that nonsupporter dissenting opinion would be less reason based and issue based than supporter dissenting opinion would be. Table 4.2 provides a summary of the nature of dissenting opinion for supporters and nonsupporters. To test Hypothesis 2, independent sample t-tests were run: one for the relationship between dissenting opinion and issue content for the two groups of blog participants and another for dissenting opinion and reason-based content for the two groups of blog participants. Though there was a surface difference between dissenting opinion based on reason-giving for supporters (M = 13.16; SD = 12.77) and nonsupporters (M = 3.33; SD = 2.07), this difference failed to reach significance [$t(6) = 1.863$; $p > .05$].

Similarly, though there was a difference between dissenting opinion based on issues for supporters (M = 14.5; SD = 12.52) and nonsupporters (M = 3.67; SD = 1.56), this difference also failed to reach significance [$t(6) = 2.027$; $p > .05$]. In other words, the dissenting posts from supporters and nonsupporters

Table 4.2 Dissenting Blog Post Content by Supporter/Nonsupporter Throughout 6-Day Period

Topic	Supporter (%)	Nonsupporter (%)
Issues	13	5
Personal qualifications	6	3
Support	9	3
Campaigning	16	3
Advice-giving	33	1
Reason-giving	18	3

Table 4.3 Supporter Blog Post Reaction Numbers to Supporter/Nonsupporter Dissent

	Supporter		Nonsupporter	
Date	Engage	Dismiss	Engage	Dismiss
Jan 6	9	2	2	22
Jan 11	2	1	5	19
Jan 19	10	4	13	26
Jan 22	26	4	3	33
Jan 29	63	4	7	12

were equally likely to contain similar percentages of issue- and reason-based content. For the data set under investigation, there was no support for non-supporters suffering from an increased lack of self-efficacy when compared to supporters.

Hypothesis 3 predicted that majority supporters would be more likely to dismiss and less likely to engage dissenting nonsupporter opinion than dissenting supporter opinion. Table 4.3 provides descriptive statistics in support of Hypothesis 3 regarding supporter dismissal of dissenting opinion from nonsupporters. Only the latter five data points were used in the analysis because of no data for the first data point on January 4. As the results highlighted, supporters were more likely to dismiss or less likely to engage in constructive discussion with dissenting opinion from nonsupporters ($M = 20.6$; $SD = 11.15$) when compared with supporters ($M = 3$; $SD = 1.41$). This result was significant [$t(8) = 3.502$; $p < .05$].

From these results, it is apparent that when supporters engage in constructive dialogue with dissenting opinion, they seem more willing and motivated to do so if the source is someone who is a supporter or someone who already agrees with their viewpoint and shares their support of the candidate. If dissent appears to be from a nonsupporter, supporters are more likely to use dismissive coping techniques such as flaming and name-calling, as opposed to constructive dialogic and deliberative techniques of engagement.

RQ 3 questioned the extent to which the blog allowed diverse opinion based on positive support for other candidates in addition to Dean. As expected, of the 25% of posts that mention other Democratic candidates, approximately 75% have a negative tone towards the Democratic candidate. As Table 4.4 shows, there was a greater tendency to make negative statements about other Democratic candidates (M = 79.67; SD = 31.15) than positive statements (M = 27.5; SD = 5.01), revealing significant differences between the groups [$t(5.259)$ = 4.050; $p < .05$] when equal variances are not assumed for the groups. This finding is more pronounced when blog participants' positive and negative statements about the Republican incumbent president are examined. There is less positive support for George W. Bush than for any of the competing Democratic candidates: Slightly over 10% of posts mention Bush; over 90% have a negative tone towards him.

Overall, the majority of posts are negative towards other candidates. At a higher level of analysis, these findings support previous blog studies that show a split in the blogopshere along partisan lines: In this study, the majority of positive posts about other candidates were for democratic candidates as opposed to the Republican candidate. However, this study illuminates another finding: There are also splits within shared partisan camps. As this study's results highlight, there was a greater tendency to post negative statements about other Democratic candidates.

RQ 4 questioned to what extent posts were backed by reason-giving. Postings without reason-giving were more likely to dominate the discussion stream (M = 413; SD = 127.7) when compared to postings that included opinions (M = 97.83; SD = 27.32), revealing significant differences between the two categories of postings [$t(5.46)$ = 5.911; $p < .05$], with equal variances not assumed. Throughout the 6-day period, only 20% of blog posts mentioned reasons for opinions in their posts; the majority of comments lacked supportive argumentation or evidenced opinion.

However, though posts lacked reason-giving, over 80% of posts throughout the 6-day period were related to the thread or to earlier posts in the thread. Examination of the blog postings throughout this period highlighted that the majority of posts were related to prior (M = 410; SD = 160.03) as opposed to unrelated (M = 100; SD = 45.19) postings; this difference was significant

Table 4.4 Descriptive Statistics on Negative/Positive Opinions From Supporters/Nonsupporters of Other Democratic Candidates

	N	Mean	SD	Std. error from mean
Negative	6	79.67[a]	31.15	2.05
Positive	6	27.5	5.01	12.72

[a] Independent t-test reveals means to be significantly different with equal variances not assumed: $t(5.259) = 4.050$; $p < .05$.

([$t(6)$ = 4.554; p < .05]). In answer to RQ 5, it was apparent that blog conversation leaned towards relatedness on specific threads, suggesting that the Dean online community remained fairly unified in discussion when guided by the Dean campaign bloggers' open threads.

Traditional Media and Diversity of Interpersonal Discussion

In keeping with prior studies that found media content to be a significant source of diversity in conversation Hypothesis 4 correctly predicted that media content would be equally as likely to be a significant source of dissenting opinion as supportive opinion when cited in interpersonal communication on the candidate blog.

Table 4.5 provides the descriptive statistics of supporting to dissenting media content mentions through the day-to-day period under investigation. Comparison of dissenting opinion from media (M = 40; SD = 6.39) with supportive opinion from media (M = 32.5; SD = 11.95) through the 6-day period revealed no significant differences when equal variance was a tenable assumption [$t(10)$ = 1.36; p > .05]. The lack of a significant difference between supportive and dissenting media content highlighted the ability of media to sustain dissent within the candidate blog. The inherent diversity of media content enabled it to sustain diverse discussion and to balance interpersonal communication on the candidate blog with negative and positive opinions.

RQ 1 questioned which media source was most cited during the time period under investigation. The results in Table 4.6 show that over 25% of blog postings explicitly mention a media source. According to Table 4.6, over 50% of media mentions cite television news and/or a television website. Newspapers and/or newspaper websites are rarely mentioned; approximately 10% of posts mention media. One of the most interesting aspects of the media breakdown is the phenomenon of bloggers pointing to their own website: 8% direct attention to their website.

This finding is interesting because it shows that, within the candidate blog environment, there was an increased role for supporter activism and par-

Table 4.5 Blog Posts Citing Supportive or Dissenting Media Content Throughout 6-Day Period

Date	Supportive (%)	Dissenting (%)
Jan. 4[a]	42	48
Jan. 6	67	33
Jan. 11	59	41
Jan. 19	44	56
Jan. 22	64	36
Jan. 27	55	45

[a]Each day totals 100%.

Table 4.6 Blog Posts Media Mentions Throughout 6-Day Period

Type of media	Source cited (%)
Television	52
Other places	14
Newspapers	12
Own site	8
Other blogs/noncandidate	5
Newsmagazines	4
Radio	3
Internet news	2
Candidate blog	0
Total	100
(Valid cases)	(784)

ticipation. Supporters were encouraged to gain self-efficacy and a sense of empowerment so that they referenced themselves and pointed to their individual websites within their blog postings. It is apparent that blog participants were involved not only in discussion but also in active content creation in support of their candidate.

The results in Table 4.7 break down the media mentions by day and provide greater quantitative detail about the blog–media relationship. On January 4, Howard Fineman wrote a highly critical front-page article about Dean in *Newsweek*; the result was that on January 4, 16% of media mentions were newsmagazines, the second highest media cited after television. On January 27, Dean gave a speech to his supporters in Iowa over national TV. Television dubbed his cheerful scream at the end of his speech the "Iowa scream." Television's persistence in replaying the speech in Iowa was highlighted in the blog's discussion of this coverage on January 19: Over 70% of media mentions were related to television, significantly more than any other day for television citations.

Similarly, as supporters tracked poll numbers on January 28 for the New Hampshire primary, the spike of 24% for other media mentions relates to the citing of poll figures from Zogby and Gallup, nontraditional news organizations. These findings support that blog conversations closely followed the media coverage so that there was evidence of spikes in blog conversation around key media events. This critical finding provides strong evidence of the relationship between the candidate blog and media coverage. Spikes or "burstiness" in these blog conversational streams can be directly related to events and media coverage of those events.

Table 4.7 Blog Posts Mentioning Media Type by Day (percentages)

	Jan. 4	Jan. 6	Jan. 11	Jan. 19	Jan. 22	Jan. 27
Television	35	28	56	71	65	53
Newspapers	11	19	22	3	10	6
Noncandidate blogs	3	2	6	3	4	10
Radio	7	7	1	3	3	2
Candidate blogs	1	2	—	—	—	—
Newsmagazines	16	8	1	—	1	2
Other	12	17	4	12	12	24
Own blog	15	17	10	8	5	3
Total	100%	100%	100%	100%	100%	100%
(Valid cases)	(373)	(361)	(409)	(679)	(587)	(656)

Many of these discussions about media involved an active critique of media coverage. Of the total amount of postings that mentioned media, almost 10% of blog postings were openly critical of media coverage. This finding brings to light the complex relationship between the candidate blog and the media: One in every ten postings had negative sentiments about the nature of media coverage. The candidate blog provided a forum for participants to discuss and comment critically on the nature and quality of media coverage.

Nature of Discussion

The first research question involved a comparison of issue to nonissue discussion on the candidate blog. An examination of the content of blog postings for the 6-day period revealed that discussing issues was not a popular activity on the blog. The results presented in Table 4.8 show that discussants on the candidate blog were more likely to discuss nonissue aspects of the campaign (M = 496.33; SD = 253.06) than issues (M = 80.33; SD = 11.48). With equal variances not a tenable assumption, this difference was significant [$t(5.02)$ = 4.023; $p < .05$].

Further assessment of this research question through descriptive statistics reveals interesting qualitative findings as to the nature of issue discussion.

Table 4.8 Descriptive Statistics of Issue to Nonissue Blog Post Content

	N	Mean	SD	Std. error from mean
Nonissue	6	496.33[a]	253.06	103.31
Issue	6	80.33	11.48	4.69

[a] Independent *t*-test reveals means to be significantly different with equal variances not assumed: $t(5.02)$ = 4.023; $p < .05$.

Table 4.9 Blog Post Content by Day

Date	Issues (%)	Personal (%)	Campaigning (%)	Support/endorsement (%)
Jan. 4a	24	29	13	25
Jan. 6	22	31	18	26
Jan. 11	24	42	21	19
Jan. 19	11	32	41	56
Jan. 22	11	33	30	35
Jan. 27	12	28	27	50
(Valid cases)	(482)	(984)	(824)	(1,171)

[a] Percentages across the days are not meant to total to 100% because posts were coded across multiple categories.

Table 4.9 provides a breakdown of the 6-day aggregates into single-day periods for the issue and nonissue discussion categories. The later one moves in the campaign, as presented by later dates within the time period under study, the more nonissue discussion tends to dominate posting content.

In Table 4.9, we can see that postings mentioning candidate support and endorsements as well as campaigning doubled from January 4, the first day of the 6 day period, to January 27, the last day of examination. In sharp contrast, issue discussion was at a high on the first day of observation at 24% but fell by 50% on the last day of examination. Image discussion remained fairly high over the time period at approximately 30% on January 4 and January 27, rising to over 40% on January 11. Overall, three of the four categories experienced the same relative level or an increase when compared to issue discussion. Issue discussion was the only category that visibly fell throughout the 6-day period under observation.

Discussion

Could website communities and forums be a new breeding ground for attitude-consistent messaging as Chaffee et al. (2001) noted? Theorists such as Cass Sunstein (2001, 2003) have also cautioned that the Internet could encourage more partisan dialogue than democratic dialogue. With the continuous growth in web-based social software tools such as blogging software, wikis, My Space, Friendster and FaceBook, the significance of interpersonal communication to the political communication process promises to increase in the near future, potentially among the younger generation.

Howard Dean's creative push of social network technologies in the 2004 presidential election has also emphasized the potential significance of these participatory technologies to future online political campaigning and citizen engagement. With blogging currently on the rise among U.S. politicians such as Barak Obama, Denis Hastert and John Edwards, the embrace of social networking tools and blogging technologies such as podcasting and video blogging is almost guaranteed in the 2006 and 2008 U.S. election cycles. This increased usage of web-based tools and social software by political candidates in current political campaigns makes it essential that political communication scholars begin to assess the relationship between usage of these technologies and democratic citizenship.

Results from this preliminary study of Dean's campaign blog revealed that it was more of a place for supporters to self-organize, endorse the candidate, campaign and discuss candidate image as opposed to a place designed for diverse interpersonal opinion sharing and deliberative democratic discourse. This finding can give credence to Mutz's (2001) earlier finding that cross-cutting conversations often increase intrapersonal ambivalence and reduce early campaign participation and engagement in political activities among those in support of a candidate.

In this respect, this study's findings provide strong evidence that the candidate blog was primarily used as a place for supporter grassroots organizing. This alignment of the candidate blog with supporters was further emphasized when the campaign implemented a comment registration system empowering the blog administrators to moderate blog postings via the participant's IP and e-mail addresses. The result of this blog registration feature was to limit non-supporter disagreement on the candidate blog by setting up virtual boundaries and signposts on the nature, quality and tone of dissenting comments.

The decision to limit the analysis of the blog's political conversation to debate days and primary days was done in an attempt to capture the maximum possible issue discussion. On debate days, the candidate blog was often turned into a forum for reiterating the strengths of the candidate through live blogging of the televised debates in rolling minute-by-minute commentary. The primary elections' days often involved a discussion of ground-level activities used to convince voters to support the Dean candidate on the candidate blog. However, this study's findings on the lack of blogger issue discussion supports past studies, which have found that voters prefer image discussion to issue discussion (Weaver et al., 1981).

Overall, the Dean blog conversations emphasized support and endorsement, campaigning and image attribute discussion as opposed to engaging, diverse issue discussion. This finding emphasizes the role that the candidate blog played in mobilizing grassroots supporters across geographical space. Supporters often pointed to their own content on personal blogs, personal websites, and databases. Participants felt encouraged not only to share their opinions but also to engage in the act of web content creation. This more active and participatory role for supporters promises to have a huge impact in future election campaigns as participatory technologies continue to make web content creation much easier.

This study provided several noteworthy findings on nonsupporters' participation on the candidate blog. Findings provide some support for the disadvantaged position of the minority nonsupporter in terms of communicative inabilities and majority perception. Much of the past work on face-to-face communication by Huckfeldt and Sprague (1987, 1988, 1991, 1998) was tied to geography and face-to-face conversation dyads. Though the online environment can support more open, weaker heterogeneous ties (Granovetter, 1973, 1983), the campaign blog seemingly provided a partisan cue or online signal of the blog's main perspective.

Though the study's findings found no difference between nonsupporters and supporters in terms of issue-based and reason-based dissent, majority supporters were more prone to dismiss nonsupporter dissenting comments with low-cognitive, peripheral route processing. This lack of engagement with nonsuppoters' dissenting posting was evident through the dismissing techniques used by supporters in reacting to nonsupporters' dissenting posts. As Sunstein (2001, 2003) warned, there is a tendency for online discussion to emphasize polarization and groupthink philosophies resulting in an echo chamber effect: the accentuation of the dominant philosophy by the majority opinion to the exclusion or disengagement of alternative, dissenting opinion. At the same time, though, this cocooning of public opinion in support of a candidate on the said candidate's blog can be seen as germane and essential to creating a safe, nurturing environment for supporters to campaign for their candidate.

Interpreting this study's findings leads to the cautionary conclusion that the campaign blog does support dissent; however, it is primarily the dissent from those already of like minds. These findings provide some evidence of the survival of selective exposure and attention on the candidate blog in terms of interpersonal discussion. A highly significant finding was the role that the media played in permitting disagreement to survive due to their diverse content offerings. Though attempts were made to silence dissenting nonsupporter interpersonal discussion through comment registration, the mass media's role as provider of raw material for discussion played a vital role in providing balanced, diverse and alternative perspectives on the candidate blog.

This study had some limitations. Due to the small record set, researchers are cautioned to sample greater data points in the future to arrive at more conclusive findings. It was also hampered by the selection of disconnected data points and sampling of messages. Additionally, the selection of primary days and debate days could have functioned to skew or distort the findings. Future studies could designate a set block of time and examine the universe of messages for that full time period.

However, as a high-level macroanalysis of the blog's discussion environment, this study provides early findings on the role of the candidate blog in encouraging interpersonal political communication in the 2004 presidential election. With the growth of blogging guaranteed in future online political campaigns, it provides a vital preliminary analysis of the relationship between candidate blogging technologies and citizen political discussion.

References

Adamic, L. A., & Glance, N. (2005). The political blogosphere and the 2004 U.S. election: Divided they blog. H. P. Labs. Available online at http://www.hpl.hp.com/research /idl/papers/politicalblogs/.

Baoill, A. (2004). Weblogs and the public sphere. *Into the Blogsophere.* Available online at http:// blog.lib.umn.edu/blogosphere/weblogs_and_the_public_sphere.html.

Barber, B. (1984). *Strong democracy: Participatory politics for a new age.* Berkley: University of California Press.

Benhabib, S. (1996). Democracy and difference: contesting the boundaries of the political. Princeton, N.J.: Princeton University Press

Benhabib, S. (1992). *Situating the self: Gender, community, and postmodernism in contemporary ethics.* New York: Routledge.

Benhabib, S., & Cornell, D. (1987). *Feminism as critique: On the politics of gender.* Minneapolis: University of Minnesota Press.

Bohman, J. F. (1996). *Public deliberation: Pluralism, complexity, and democracy.* Cambridge, MA: MIT Press.

Browning, G. (2002). *Electronic democracy: Using the Internet to transform American politics.* New Jersey: Cyberage Books.

Burkhalter, S., Gastil, J. & Kelshaw, T. (2002). A conceptual definition and theoretical model of public deliberation in small face-to-face groups. *Communication Theory, 12*(4), 398–422.

Capella, J. H., Price, V. & Nir, L. (2002). Argument repertoire as a reliable and valid measure of opinion quality: Electronic dialogue during the Campaign 2000. *Political Communication, 19,* 73–93.

Chaffee, S. H., Saphir, M. N., Graf, J., Sandvig, C. & Sup Hahn, K. (2001). Attention to counterattitudinal messages in a state election campaign. *Political Communication, 18,* 247–272.

Cohen, I. (1989). Structuration theory: Anthony Giddens and the constitution of social life. New York: St. Martin's Press.

Cohen, J. (1997). Deliberation and democratic legitimacy. In J. Bohman & W. Rehg (Eds.), *Deliberative democracy: Essays on reason and politics* (pp. 67–91). Cambridge, MA: MIT Press.

D'Alessio, D. (2000). Adoption of the World Wide Web by American political candidates, 1996–1998. *Journal of Broadcasting & Electronic Media, 44*(4), 556–568.

Dewey, J. (1954). *The public and its problems.* Athens, OH: Swallow.

Drezner, D. W., & Farrell, H. (2004*). The power and politics of blogs.* Presented at the American Political Science Association, Chicago, IL.

Dryzek, J. (1990). *Discursive democracy: Politics, policy, and political science.* New York: Cambridge University Press.

Fishkin, J. S. (1991). *Democracy and deliberation: New directions for democratic reform.* New Haven, CT: Yale University Press.

Fishkin, J. S. (1995). *The voice of the people: Public opinion and democracy.* New Haven, CT: Yale University Press.

Fishkin, J. S., & Luskin, R. C. (1999). Bringing deliberation to the democratic dialogue. In M. McCombs & A. Reynolds (Eds.), *The poll with a human face: The national issues convention experiment in political communication* (pp. 3–38). Mahwah, NJ: Lawrence Erlbaum.

Galley–Stromer, J. (2000). On-line interaction and why candidates avoid it. *Journal of Communication,* vol. 50, no. 4, 111–132.

Gastil, J. (1993). *Democracy in small groups: Participation, decision making, and communication.* Philadelphia: New Society.

Granovetter, M. (1983). The strength of weak ties: a network theory revisited. *Sociological Theory,* vol. 1, 201–233

Granovetter, M. (1973). The strength of weak ties. *The American Journal of Sociology,* vol. 78, no. 6, 1360–1380.

Gutmann, A., & Thompson, D. (1996). *Democracy and disagreement.* Cambridge, MA: Harvard University Press.

Habermas, J. (1989). *The structural transformation of the public sphere: An inquiry into a category of bourgeois society.* Cambridge, MA: MIT Press.

Hill, K. A., & Hughes, J. E. (1998). *Cyberpolitics: Citizen activism in the age of the Internet.* Lanham, MD: Rowman & Littlefield Publishers Inc.

Huckfeldt, R. (2001). The social communication of political expertise. *American Journal of Political Science, 45*(2), 425–438.

Huckfeldt, R., Beck, P. A., Dalton, R. J., Levine, J. & Morgan, W. (1998). Ambiguity, distorted messages, and nested environmental effects on political communication. *The Journal of Politics, 60*(4), 996–1030.

Huckfeldt, R., & Sprague, J. (1987). Networks in context: The social flow of political information. *The American Political Science Review, 81*(4), 1197–1216.

Huckfeldt, R., & Sprague, J. (1988). Choice, social structure, and political information: The information coercion of minorities. *American Journal of Political Science, 32*(2), 467–482.

Huckfeldt, R., & Sprague, J. (1991). Discussant effects on vote choice: Intimacy, structure, and interdependence. *The Journal of Politics, 53*(1), 122–158.

Jamieson, K.H., & Campbell, Karlyn. (1992). *The interplay of influence: news, advertising, politics, and the mass media.* Belmont, California: Wadsworth

Jarvis, S. & Wilkerson, K. (2005). Congress on the Internet: messages on the home pages of U.S. house of representatives, 1996 to 2001. *Journal of Computer-Mediated Communication, 10*(2). Available online at http://jcmc.indiana.edu/vol10/issue2/jarvis.html

Johnson, S. (2001). *Emergence: The connected lives of ants, brains, cities and software.* Scribner: New York.

Kendall, K. (2000). *Communication in the presidential primaries: candidates and the media, 1912-2000.* Westport, Connecticut: Praegar.

Kenny, C. (1994). The microenvironment of attitude change. *The Journal of Politics, 56*(3), 715–728.

Kim, J., Wyatt, R. O. & Katz, E. (1999). News, talk, opinion, participation: The part played by conversation in deliberative democracy. *Political Communication, 16*, 361–385.

Klinenberg, E., & Perrin, A. (2000). Symbolic politics in the information age: The 1996 Republican presidential campaigns in cyberspace. *Information, Communication and Society, 3*(1), 17–38.

Lazarsfeld, P. F., & Merton, R. K. (1954). Friendship as a social process: A substantive and methodological analysis. In M. Berger (Ed.), *Freedom and control in modern society* (pp. 18–66). New York: Van Nostrand.

Mardsen, P. V. (1987). Core conversation networks of Americans. *American Sociological Review, 52*(1), 122–131.

Marlow, C. (2004). *Audience structure in the Weblog community.* Presented at the Association for Education in Journalism and Mass Communication, New Orleans.

Matthews, D. (1994). *Politics for the people: Finding a responsible public voice.* Chicago: University of Illinois Press.

McLeod, J. M., Scheufele, D. A. & Moy, P. (1999a). Community, communication, and participation: the role of the mass media and interpersonal conversation in local political participation. *Political Communication, 16*, 315–336.

McLeod, J. M, Scheufele, D. A., Moy, P., Horowitz, E. M., Holbert, R. L., Zhang, W., Zubric, S. & Zubric, J. (1999b). Understanding deliberation: The effects of conversation networks on participation in a public forum. *Communication Research, 26*(6), 743–774.

McPherson, M., Smith–Lovin, L. & Cook, J. M. (2001). Birds of a feather: Homophily in social networks. *Annual Review of Sociology, 27*, 415–44.

Mill, J. S. (1972). *Utilitarianism, on liberty, and considerations of representative government.* London: Everyman.

Mutz, D. (2002a). The consequences of cross-cutting networks for political participation. *American Journal of Political Science, 46*(4), 838–855.

Mutz, D. (2002b). Cross-cutting social networks: Testing democratic theory in practice. *American Political Science Review, 96*(1), 111–126.

Mutz, D., & Martin, P. S. (2001). Facilitating communication across lines of political difference: The role of the mass media. *American Political Science Review, 95*(1), 97–113.

Noelle–Neumann, E. (1973). Return to the concept of powerful mass media. In H. Eguchi & K. Sata (Eds.), *Studies in broadcasting: An international annual of broadcasting science* (pp. 67–117). Tokyo: Nippo Hoso Kyokai.

Noelle–Neumann, E. (1980). Mass media and social change in developed societies. In G. C. Wilhoit & H. de Bock (Eds.), *Mass communication review yearbook* (pp. 657–678). Beverly Hills, CA: Sage.

Norris, P. (2003). Preaching to the converted? Pluralism, participation and party Websites. *Party Politics*, 9(1), 21–45.

Papacharissi, Z. (2004). Democracy online: Civility, politeness, and the democratic potential of online political conversation groups. *New Media and Society*, 6(2), 259–283.

Patterson, T. (2000). *Doing well, doing good: How soft news and critical journalism are shrinking the news audience and weakening democracy and what news outlets can do about it.* Massachusetts: Harvard University.

Patterson, T. (1993). *Out of order.* New York: Alfred A. Knopf.

Petty, R. E., & Cacioppo, J. T. (1986). *Communication and persuasion: Central and peripheral routes to attitude change.* New York: Springer–Verlag.

Pew Internet & American Life Project. (2004). *The Internet and democratic debate.* Available online at http://www.pewinternet.org/.

Price, V., Capella, J. N. & Nir, L. (2002). Does disagreement contribute to more deliberative opinion? *Political Communication*, 19, 95–112.

Rafaeli, S., & Sudweeks, F. (1997). Networked interactivity. *Journal of Computer-Mediated Communication*, 2(4). Available online at http://jcmc.indiana.edu/vol2/issue4/rafaeli.sudweeks.html

Roberts–Miller, T. (2004). Parody blogging and the call of the real. *Into the Blogosphere.* Available online at http://blog.lib.umn.edu/blogosphere/parody_blogging.html.

Ryfe, D. M. (2002). The practice of deliberative democracy: A study of 16 deliberative organizations. *Political Communication*, 19, 359–377.

Sanders, L. M. (1997). Against deliberation. *Political Theory*, 25, 347–376.

Scheufele, D. A. (2002). Examining differential gains from mass media and their implications for participatory behavior. *Communication Research*, 29(1), 46–65.

Scheufele D. A., & Nisbet, M. C. (2002). Being a citizen online: New opportunities and dead ends. *Press/Politics*, 7(3), 55–75.

Scheufele D. A., Nisbet, M. C., Brossard, D. & Nisbet, E. (2004). Social structure and citizenship: Examining the impacts of social setting, network heterogeneity, and informational variables on political participation. *Political Communication*, 21, 315–338.

Simon, A. & Xenos, M. (2000). Media framing and effective public deliberation. *Political Communication*, vol. 17, no. 4.

Stromer-Galley, J. (2003). Diversity of political conversation on the Internet: Users' perspectives. *Journal of Computer-Mediated Communication*, 8(3). Available online at http://jcmc.indiana.edu/vol8/issue3/stromergalley.html

Sunstein, C. (2000). Deliberative trouble? Why groups go to extremes. *Yale Law Journal*, 110(1), 71–119.

Sunstein, C. (2001). *Republic.com.* Princeton, NJ: Princeton University Press.

Sunstein, C. (2002). The law of group polarization. *The Journal of Political Philosophy*, 10(2), 175–195.

Ulbig, S. G., & Funk, C. L. (1999). Conflict avoidance and political participation. *Political Behavior*, 21(3), 265–282.

Ward, S., & Gibson, R. (2003). On-line and on message? Candidate Websites in the 2001 general election. *British Journal of Politics and International Relations*, 5(2), 188–205.

Warren, M. E. (1996a). Deliberative democracy and authority. *American Political Science Review*, 86, 8–23.

Warren, M. E. (1996b). What we should expect from more democracy. Radical democratic responses to politics. *Political Theory*, 24, 241–270.

Weaver, D. Graber, D., McCombs, M., & Eyal, C. (1981). *Media agenda setting in a presidential election: issues, images, and interest.* New York: Praegar.

Welsch, P. (2005). Revolutionary vanguard or echo chamber? Political blogs and the mainstream media. Available online at http://www.blogninja.com/index.php.

Wyatt, R. O., Katz, E. & Kim, J. (2000). Bridging the spheres: Political and personal conversation in public and private spaces. *Journal of Communication*, vol. 50, no. 1, 71–92

Young, I. (1990). *Justice and the politics of difference.* Princeton, NJ: Princeton University Press.

5

Blogging for Better Health: Putting the "Public" Back in Public Health

S. SHYAM SUNDAR, HEIDI HATFIELD EDWARDS,
YIFENG HU AND CARMEN STAVROSITU

Blogs have received a lot of press lately because many members of the press have started blogging. Given the widespread diffusion of the underlying RSS (really simple syndication) technology, blogs have become commonplace in the online media landscape. Most high-profile bloggers are political journalists and most of the scholarly attention thus far has focused on the impact of this new venue on civic participation and the future of democracy. Relatively little media and scholarly attention has been paid to personal blogs that discuss topics other than politics. For example, the burgeoning number of health blogs has gone virtually unnoticed in mainstream media and the academic discourse about blogs.

Our investigation is an effort to remedy this shortcoming by focusing on health blogs and stimulate a research agenda in this direction. We begin by considering technological factors characterizing the blog as a tool of mass communication and discuss the ensuing psychological considerations. Using this framework, we examine a sample of mental-health blogs in an effort to understand their nature and characteristics with a view to enhancing our theoretical understanding of this new medium of communication and articulating its role in the future of health communication.

Blog Technology and Mass Communication

As a highly personalized medium through which one can reach a mass audience (Trammel & Kiousis, 2005), blogs offer a number of advantages over traditional mass communication. A primary distinguishing feature is their ability to involve the reading public in an integral way. Blogs are not professionally gatekept in the same manner as traditional media. Instead, they rely on individual users to generate and verify content on a continual basis. Bloggers and blog readers, therefore, are creators as well as consumers of information on the Internet, embodying the ideal of "receiver as source" (Sundar & Nass, 2001).

In their typology of online sources, Sundar and Nass (2001) argue that, in addition to the traditional sender of communication ("visible sources"), the medium ("technological source") and the recipients ("receiver sources") can also be construed as sources in the online realm. The latter category is classified further based on the level of analysis as "audience as source" and "self as source," referring respectively to receivers as a collective and as individual users. Blogs operationalize both these types of receiver sources in that they simultaneously serve as a venue for contribution of content by the reader (be it the blogger or someone offering comment on an existing blog entry) and dissemination of information compiled by a multitude of fellow readers.

Audience as Source

To the extent the blog is seen as a repository of information, musings and experiences compiled by archiving blogger activities, as well as commenter contributions, it is a collective effort that operationalizes the "audience as source" conceptualization. This is akin to wikipedia, where users collectively construct the content. Such a collaborative approach to construction of communication messages is inherently appealing as evidenced by the proliferation of products and features in new media that thrive on audience input. E-commerce giant amazon.com is well known for its use of collaborative filtering in being able to indicate what other users who browsed the product that a prospective buyer is considering have purchased on the site. NewYorkTimes.com routinely publishes the most e-mailed stories of the day; investment sites announce the most popular stocks and Apple's iTunes site indicates the most downloaded songs, to mention just a few examples.

Empirical evidence shows the popularity of such collaborative venues on the web. When news stories are ostensibly selected by other users of an online service, they are rated as significantly higher in liking and quality than when the same stories are attributed to news editors (Sundar & Nass, 2001). What this means is that gatekeeping by collective others triggers a heuristic relating to the bandwagon effect ("if others think this is good information, then I must, too"). This is quite likely the case with all collaborative systems that afford input from other sources.

The bandwagon effect has received support in news aggregator sites such as Google News wherein the collective voice has been shown to influence news selection (Knobloch–Westerwick, Sharma, Hansen & Alter, 2005) as well as perceptions of underlying news stories (Sundar, Knobloch–Westerwick & Hastall, in press). Therefore, indicators of external input, especially in collectivity, can profoundly influence our consideration and perception of information.

Blogs represent an even stronger sense of collective voice by allowing the users to not simply select but actually contribute content and sometimes even edit and shape the nature of content. As Scott (2004a, 2004b) points out, blogs feature a strong sense of community, characterized by peer review (Johnson

& Kaye, 2004) and cross-referencing of each others' blogs and other sources of online information. Therefore, the bandwagon heuristic cued by blogs is likely to have a significant impact on our perceptions of content. How we view particular health issues, including symptoms we feel and beliefs we hold about treatment options, may be largely dictated by the collective negotiation of information and opinions in the blogosphere.

Self as Source

For the blogger, the technology allows for an operationalization of "self as source." As Sundar (2006) points out, there is something very seductive about serving as a source, be it as a gatekeeper or as an information provider. He argues that the "me-ness" fostered by interactive features that allow users to be sources is the reason behind the popularity of customization practices in recent years.

Blogs have the potential to cue a strong sense of me-ness, given the deeply personal nature of the online diary-keeping or journal-writing function afforded by them. Yet, this information is public in that it is disseminated to a vast audience of lurkers and commenters, making it mass communication. As Nardi, Schiano, Gumbrecht and Swartz (2004) point out, blogs have relative advantages over other forms of mass communication via the web. They allow for a great deal of flexibility in integrating other communication tools such as e-mail, online social networks and bulletin boards without being as intrusive as e-mail. They feature a medium-level of interactivity in that they fall between listservs that signify a high level and websites, which tend to be static. Blogs have a culture of frequent updating, with latest posts appearing at the top, and offer tremendous archiving and linking functions. They allow long narratives and are generally considered a forum for personal commentary. In more ways than one, blogs place central emphasis on the self (i.e., the blogger).

Given this, blogs may be viewed with the lens of the agency model of customization, which proposes that the self as source is the key mediator (see Figure 5.1) between technological affordances and psychological outcomes (Sundar, 2006). It argues that "technological variables embedded in media systems affect the nature and psychology of our interactions with content as well as other humans by essentially highlighting the importance of our own selves."

Fundamentally, the model would posit that the agency felt by bloggers is likely to have significant psychological consequences by way of involvement, identity and control. The constant activity engendered by blogging is likely to put the blogger in a position of self-importance as content creator; more important, it results in cognitive engagement with the blog. Blogs also offer a glorious vehicle for expressing one's identity. Bargh, McKenna and Fitzsimons (2002) found experimental evidence suggesting that we are likely to express our true selves in Internet interactions and actual selves in face-to-face settings, with the former constituting a more accurate representation of one's identity.

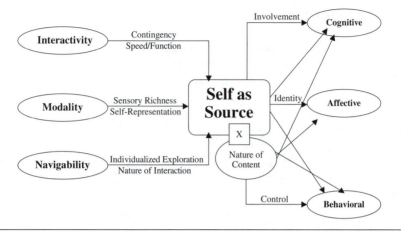

Figure 5.1 Agency Model of Customization

To be able to express this freely on an ongoing basis can be liberating as well as positively reinforcing, leading to positive attitudes toward the activity and blogosphere in general. The authorship and ownership felt by bloggers can give them a sense of agency and autonomy that, according to self-determination theory (Ryan & Deci, 2000), is intrinsically motivating. The enhanced sense of personal control afforded by blogging can therefore be a powerful predictor of action by way of more blogging and making full use of this technology.

In sum, the agency vested by blog technology on the blogger is cognitively involving, affectively ego gratifying and behaviorally empowering in a manner that allows users with health problems to tackle their illnesses and pursue creative outcomes proactively. As a vehicle of mass communication, blogs offer lurkers a strong bandwagon heuristic with which to evaluate the flood of health-related information available on the web. Blogs epitomize the "publicness" in public health. Given these functions, it is imperative for us to gain an academic understanding of the blogosphere, especially pertaining to particular health topics—most notably those that are stigmatized in the offline world. Given its rapid diffusion and enormous implications for public health, literature has to be built around the identity of bloggers (who they are), their motivations for blogging (why they blog) and the nature of blogs (what they say).

Blogs and Health Communication

A report of the Pew Internet and American Life Project (2005) showed that eight out of ten Internet users have looked for health information online. As one of the most recent and popular online applications, blogs have developed into an important form of health information dissemination. Despite the fact that the Internet has become a common tool for health information seeking and that most blog directories include health blogs, we were unable to find a single article on health blogs. Much communication scholarship focuses on political blogs or news blogs (e.g., Johnson & Kaye, 2004; Reese, Rutigliano, Hyun & Jeong, 2005). However, according to a recent survey, blogs are more likely to deal with personal issues than politics or current events. The AOL survey found that, by July 2005, nearly 50% of bloggers in the United States kept a blog because it served as a form of therapy. Only 16.2% were interested in journalism and 7.5% in political information.

Who Blogs?

Research is in its nascent stages in terms of the characteristics and composition of bloggers. However, some patterns have already emerged in describing the overall blogger population.

A few sparse studies have revealed, for instance, that in terms of authorship there are gender differences, although the direction is not always clear. While some scholars have found that the blogosphere is slightly dominated by female authors (e.g., Perseus, 2003), others have found the contrary (e.g., Viégas, 2005). This inconclusiveness is most likely due to different blog genres that the researchers examined. One other study also indicated cross-cultural differences in terms of bloggers (Su, Wang, Mark, Aiyelokun & Nakano, 2005). While the male–female balance is weighted only slightly more in favor of men in the West, this imbalance is considerably more pronounced in favor of men in Eastern cultures. Examining personal/hobby versus political blogs, Su, Wang and Mark (2005) also found that political blogs, compared to personal blogs, are dominated by older bloggers. Furthermore, the same study showed that political bloggers reveal more about their identity than do personal bloggers.

While far from comprehensive, this range of findings indicates some incipient trends characterizing bloggers at large. However, asking "Who blogs?" for mental health bloggers in particular might reveal profound implications for the unique roles that blogs might play in the lives of so many mentally afflicted individuals, diagnosed or not. It might reveal who these voices are, as well as the motivations behind them.

Thus, our first research question *RQ1* asked: Who are mental health bloggers?

Starting from the already initiated trends mentioned earlier, in an attempt to illustrate mental health blogger characteristics, gender differences would first need to be addressed. This is of utmost importance, considering that women continue to report considerably higher rates of psychological distress than men and they maintain more emotionally intimate relationships, including participation in social networks (see Kawachi & Berkman, 2001). It becomes reasonable to expect that, first, there will be more women mental health bloggers than male bloggers and, second, that female bloggers will disclose more information about themselves than will males.

Furthermore, considering the finding by Su, Wang & Mark (2005) that political bloggers tend to be older than personal bloggers, we could expect that personal mental health blogs are more likely to be authored by younger bloggers, compared to professional mental health blogs. The expertise necessary for in-depth knowledge on any highly specialized topic, such as politics, or implied in the notion of "profession," also implicitly assumes a close connection to age, in that expertise is typically acquired over time, as one grows older.

Finally, past research also indicates that political bloggers reveal more about their identity than do personal bloggers (Su, Wang & Mark, 2005). This is typically assessed via the online profile containing personal identifiers that authors choose to reveal or not. We might infer, therefore, that self-disclosure via online profiles fades in importance for personal bloggers, whose main motivation for blogging is the very act of self-disclosure and self-presentation, whereas political bloggers' main goal is to provide social commentary. Thus, in the first case, the whole blog is about self-disclosure, so personal identifiers stated in a profile are not so crucial, as opposed to political bloggers, for whom the online profile is about the only space that can accommodate any personal information. Considering that mental health patients typically have to contend with a high degree of social stigma, it would be safe to expect generally low levels of personal identifiers.

Why Blog?

Literature is emerging about general motivations for blogging. Previous research shows five general motivations: autobiographical narratives, commentary, catharsis, muse and community forum (Nardi et al., 2004). However, for health blogs, especially mental health blogs, other motivations may exist. Literature on why people use the Internet helped us identify three particularly relevant motives for mental health bloggers: social connectedness, coping and identity formation.

Blogging to Connect   Although blogs tend to have a dominant contributor rather than multiple users contributing to an online discussion, Blanchard (2004) argues that blogs have the capacity to be virtual communities. For example, bloggers may link to others' sites and interact with readers through comments sections. Su et al. (2005) also suggest that blogrolls, trackback links and comments reveal a blogger's social connections. (A *blogroll* is a side-list of links to other blogs that the blogger recommends on his or her front page.) This connectedness to others leads to social support. Social support has "important causal effects on health, exposure to stress and the relationship between stress and health" (House, 1987, p. 136). In terms of types of online social support, most frequently exchanged online support messages offer informational support and emotional support (Braithwaite, Waldron & Finn, 1999). Information is critical to health-related decisions (Owen, Fotheringham & Marcus, 2002). One of the leading sources of online health information is support groups that bring together patients with similar ailments (Lasker, Sogolow & Sharim, 2005). In fact, online discussion groups are ranked as being more informative than visits to doctors' offices (Boberg et al., 2003) and rated as "the best source of technical medical knowledge" because they provide "medical referrals, practical coping tips, in-depth information" (Ferguson, 1999).

Online health information seeking not only empowers users to make health decisions, but also brings emotional comfort, which might be associated with strong treatment effects. Traditional online discussion groups, such as bulletin boards, offer much needed emotional support. According to Bass et al. (2006), newly diagnosed cancer patients who go online to seek information about their disease have a more positive attitude and are more active in participating in their treatment. Also, the convenience and privacy of access, anonymity and lack of judgment offer stigma-free consultations and support networks without the need to establish extensive personal relationships steeped in obligations related to dependency and reciprocity (Walther & Boyd, 2002).

While connection to a larger community of people with similar interests may be an important motivation for bloggers, coping with personal issues is also a potentially powerful motivator.

Blogging to Cope   As Nardi et al. (2004) found, many bloggers use the medium to tell the story of their lives and for catharsis. This may be particularly important for people dealing with mental health issues because research shows that "[q]uestioning and reformulating one's life story can renew a sense of meaning and possibility" (Ridgway, 2001). The journaling function of blogs permits the kind of narrative expression conducive to sharing detailed personal histories. This may also be important to the health community because, as Ridgway notes, "Narratives help practitioners understand and respect diversity within the value base, culture, lived experience and life context of people served" (p. 336). Turkle (1999) notes that two psychological effects of cyberspace include *acting out*, in which individuals deal with unresolved conflicts on the cyber stage, and *working through* "significant personal issues" using "cybersociality to reach for new resolutions" to problems. Research indicates that these effects can have an impact on individuals' lives. For example, Bargh and McKenna (2004) found that membership in online forums for two stigmatized groups (homosexuals and fringe political groups) led to participants revealing the stigmatized aspect of themselves to family and friends. Furthermore, others with similar health problems may also benefit from reading narrative-style health blogs.

Some researchers also theorize that individuals use the Internet to affirm their sense of personal identity (Turkle, 1999). When they put forth an idea on the web and receive positive feedback, they have a sense of reification (Bargh

& McKenna, 2004). Responses that affirm individual components of self serve to help users construct their identities.

Blogging to Construct Identity   As noted previously, blogs serve to facilitate identity construction through self-reflection and social interaction (Bortree, 2005). Research shows that the Internet offers multiple ways for users to explore their identities—for example, by experimenting with personae through interactive communities (Turkle, 1999), presenting themselves on personal webpages (Papacharissi, 2002), interacting with special interest groups through online bulletin boards (Scodari & Felder, 2000) and blogging (Bargh & McKenna, 2004; Bortree; Huffaker & Calvert, 2005; Trammel & Keshelashvili, 2005). According to theorists, the Internet allows exploration of one's "self" that may not be comfortably explored in normal social interaction in everyday dealings with others (see Turkle, 1999). The Internet has been lauded as a forum in which stigmatized groups (such as homosexuals) may safely explore their identities. Early online identity formation research has focused on group forums (see, e.g., Bargh & McKenna, 2004; Turkle); however, newer research is exploring the impact of blogs on identity construction (Bortree, 2005; Huffaker & Calvert, 2005; Trammel & Keshelashvili, 2005).

Turkle (1999) equates experimenting with online personae with a stage in adolescent development in which young people engage in relatively consequence-free experimentation that helps shape their "core self" or social identity. Each element of identity is tested and matures through this testing. Turkle argues that often an individual's different identities do not fully develop or mature and that cyberspace allows people to explore unresolved stages of identity development.

The social stigma of mental illness may lead people to stifle that part of their identities in normal social situations, but the illness may be a large part of their subjective sense of self. Thus, there is a disconnect between the "felt" self and the social identity (Turkle, 1999). Blogs provide an outlet—a place to express individual identity while also seeking a social identity with others through shared experiences and meaning.

Based on the literature, we proposed research question *RQ2*: Why do people blog about mental health issues?

Nature of Mental Health Blogs

The dearth of scholarly investigations of blogs in general has already been mentioned. Descriptions of the overall nature of blogs along content- and format-related dimensions are just as scarce.

Blogs have been recently characterized as a medium for "self-disclosure" (Trammel & Keshelashvili, 2005). While home pages may present personal information as well, they tend to be self-focused and "transmission" oriented (Carey, 1975). Blogs, on the other hand, blend the individual forum of the personal web home pages with the more interactive format elements specific to blogs, such as feedback incorporation (in the form of comments) and the inclusion of other communication tools.

Some studies have also identified three blog formats: diary/journals, filters and notebooks (Trammell & Keshelashvili, 2005). Diaries and journals tend to focus on thoughts and feelings of the bloggers. Filter blogs post materials from other sources and contain little original material. Notebooks are distinguished by lengthy essays that may contain internal or external sources. A fourth category is a mix of these three types.

Based on these initial general findings, research question *RQ3* asks specifically: What is the nature of mental health blogs?

Considering the previously mentioned blog typology, when turning the question of format and content to the particulars of mental health blogs, we could assume that personal mental health blogs will tend to follow the diary or journal format (what we labeled "narrative") more, while professional ones will take the form of filter or notebook blogs (combined in our "link/digest" label).

In terms of content, building on previous research on health-related online support groups, gender differences could be expected again. Burleson (2002) found that in online support groups, females tend to exchange mainly verbal and nonverbal messages of emotional support, whereas males tend to give support by way of doing instrumental activities to assist others. These results are consistent with those from offline social support research (Burleson; Freimuth, Stein & Kean, 1989; Rakowski et al., 1990) and lead us to expect that females will tend to adopt a more emotional tone in writing and males might lean towards a more informational one.

Given the exploratory nature of our project, relationships between these two main content and format variables and others included in our codebook will also be examined for potentially revealing and insightful findings.

Methods

An exploratory content analysis was conducted to examine and describe the landscape of mental health blogs. McMillan (2000) suggested that the fast-paced web and the rapidly changing online content pose specific challenges to the process of coding and data collection. However, given their open content archives, blogs should not be prone to these threats and are indeed comparable to traditional media for purposes of content analysis.

Sample

To be able to conduct an efficient random sampling of mental health blogs specifically, we first performed an online search for mental health directories. Upon quick scrutiny, only two of the ones we found seemed to contain a sufficient number of mental health blogs. One consistent problem that arose in the other directories was that most blogs listed did not actually deal directly with any particular mental health disease. From these two directories, 47 mental health blogs, dealing with a wide range of diseases (e.g., depression, bipolar disorder, borderline personality disorder, etc.) were analyzed. Any blog that did not seem to address a mental health disorder directly was discarded.

Units of Analysis

Three units of analysis were considered in this content analysis: blogs, posts and comments. A post was defined as any entry authored and posted by the blog owner on any given day. A comment was defined as any entry authored and posted by a reader in reply to any of the blog owner's posts.

Procedures

All 47 mental health blogs included in the sample were coded for blog-, post- and comment-related variables, based on our three units of analysis.

Blog Variables The blog-level variables were

> author profile (information about the author)
> author gender (male, female, cannot tell)
> author age (20 or younger, 20–30, 30–40, 40–50, 50 or older, cannot tell)
> author expertise (coded as personal [patients] or professional [medical personnel])
> blog's mission statement (used as a proxy for blogger's motivation, operationalized as yes or no, and qualitatively coded when mission statement was included)
> blog's topic (yes or no)
> blog's style (narrative or link compilation/digest)
> reader access (read + comment or read only)
> blog's format (text only, text + static pictures, text + animated pictures, text + pictures + audio/video clips)
> size of blogroll (number of other blogs listed and linked to by the author)
> number of external links (present on the main blog website)
> number of recommendations (any products, such as books, music or medication, listed by the author on the main blog website as recommendations for blog readers)
> number of categories (categories that the author constructed to organize blog entries by topics)
> frequency of blog updating (assessed by randomly selecting a month from the life span of the blog and counting the days in which the author had posted any number of posts)

Post Variables From the randomly selected month meant to serve as an assessment of the blog's frequency of updating, we examined the posts issued from the first and last days of the month. Our first post-related variable was post amount, assessed by counting the number of posts on the first and last days of the month. For the rest of the variables in this category, we only looked at the first post issued on each of these two days: post size (the number of words of the post), post nature (causes, symptoms, diagnosis, treatment and coping, recovery, prevention and other) and post content (emotional, informational, mix and other). A post was considered emotional when authors speaking about the diseases with which they were afflicted maintained a focus on emotional aspects throughout the post. For example, one post reported the author's emotional reaction to the disease and its treatment by explicitly disclosing feelings of hope or hopelessness, frustration or satisfaction. Informational posts, on the other hand, were those that provided specific facts about the workings of—and advice regarding—a certain disease (related to treatment and coping, causes and symptoms, medication, etc.). A mix consists basically of relatively equal occurrences of each so that a dominant tone could not be established. The other category included any post that was not substantial in its emotional or informational weight, as well as posts clearly unrelated to the author's mental health disorder.

Comment Variables   From each of the two posts selected, we first determined the number of comments by counting those posted in reply to both of the selected posts. Subsequently, we decided to examine only the first comment for each of the two posts and coded for the following variables: comment size (number of words in the comment) and comment content (emotional, informational, mix, other). The same considerations apply in the definition of comment content as in post content. In sum, for each blog, we examined two posts per month and one comment per post in terms of their size and content.

Coding Reliability   All coding was conducted by two coders trained in coding procedures and familiar with the code book. To examine reliability, a subset of 10 out of the 47 blogs was independently coded by both coders so that intercoder reliability could be computed. The reliability index was calculated by computing the percent agreement for the variables examined in this study; overall, this agreement amounted to 90%.

Results

Who Blogs?

Authors of mental health blogs range from mental health care professionals and advocates to caregivers to patients. Examples of professionals identified in the blogs include psychiatrists, psychologists, nurses and at least one attorney who advocates for mental health care issues in his region. Caregivers tend to be family members: husbands, wives, partners and parents of people who have a mental health illness. Patients are those bloggers who disclose conditions diagnosed by health care professionals or in some cases seem to self-diagnose where it is not clear whether they have a specific condition or have been treated for one. Some are recovering, while others write about the daily struggle with their diseases. These categories of bloggers are not necessarily discrete. Caregivers may also be dealing with mental health issues of their own, as may health care professionals. For example, one psychologist revealed in her blog that she sees a therapist and takes an antidepressant to combat depression.

Content analysis findings indicate that most mental health blogs are overwhelmingly personal and therefore are authored by patients (85.1%). The rest are professional, authored by any of the professional categories mentioned previously (8.5%).

With respect to disclosure, only 72.3% of bloggers put up an online profile and even less (40.4%) include a mission statement. 78.7% have a clear topic identified. As for the authors, 48.9% are females and 23.4% are males (as gender was read off from authors' profiles directly, 27.7% could not be identified). As expected, the most represented age group is the 20- to 30-year-old group (14.8%), followed by those 30 to 40 years old (10%) and the 40- to 50-year-old group (4.3%) and those 50 years old or older (4.3%).

Gender differences for degree of personal identifiers were also noticed, in that more females (91.3%) put up a profile than males (72.7%), χ^2 (2) = 11.63; p < .01. Personal (80%) rather than professional (50%) blogs had a higher rate of profile disclosure, χ^2 (2) = 9.86; p < .01.

Why Blog?

Blogging to Connect   Quantitative and qualitative analyses indicate that social connectedness is a significant motivation for blogging. Of those who had apparent missions, a majority said they were writing for themselves, although many also stated that their purpose for the blog included helping others. One blogger's mission indicates this dual purpose:

> Much of what I will write about will be for my sake, but if other sufferers of social anxiety read this and can gain some sort of comfort from the fact that they are not alone, then that's great also.

Several stated more altruistic reasons for their blogs in terms of connecting with a larger community, including advocating for better mental health care in their real communities and educating others about alternative therapies:

> I'm creating this blog to help people recover from depression using alternative, nonmedical (drug-free) approaches... I want to share what I've learned about healing from depression, and I want everyone to know that there are ways to get better—without horrible side effects and even if you can't tolerate medication.

The bloggers in this study write with a sense of engagement. Even the narrative type of stream-of-consciousness blogs appear to be written with others in mind—sometimes other bloggers or the web public, sometimes people who have affected them positively or negatively (and who may or may not read the blog) and sometimes people who they know will not respond. For example, one young woman's entries are often written to a deceased male friend. While the dialogue is controlled by the blog author, giving him or her the "last word" on a given topic or issue, we often see the process by which the writer develops ideas, incorporating new information, ideas and attitudes he or she gets from sources seen and unseen by the reader. On average, there are 1.87 comments per post. The size of comments centers around 38.48 words and a majority (85%) of comments give emotional support to the bloggers; only 2.1% are informational (4.3% are uncategorizable).

Bloggers respond to comments readily available to readers, conversations they have had in their real life, things they have read, etc. as they discuss their thoughts, feelings and beliefs in their blogs. As one blogger noted in a post, "i started this thing in May of last year, and at first i didnt think anybody would care to read it, but i see i was wrong. i have met some pretty wonderful people thru this blog." This blogger read and responded to comments on her site and clearly had established friendships with her readers. Furthermore, as is consistent with other types of blogs, some of the mental health blogs in this study have links to blogs that the bloggers read. More than one blog in the sample analyzed commented on another blogger's posts, which was evident by the screen names they used.

Social connectedness may also be a function of online activity. For example, our data show a highly significant correlation between number of posts and blogroll size. The more one posts, the larger the size of his/her blogroll; Pearson's $r = .30$; $p < .05$. Another highly significant correlation is between blogroll size and number of comments: The bigger the size of the blogroll, the higher the number of comments, Pearson's $r = .46$; $p < .001$. This is perhaps due to the interaction among bloggers.

Blogging to Cope and Construct Identity

I want to learn about what is happening to me. I want to be knowledgeable enough to be able to know when it's going to happen or what might trigger it. I want to be knowledgeable enough that when someone learns about it and looks at me like I'm crazy, I can explain that I'm not crazy... just a little broken. I want to meet other people like me and I want to learn from them. And, once I'm in a position to do so, I want to be able to help others to cope with their disease. I know this won't kill me, but I have a feeling that it's not one of those things that won't make me stronger. So...we'll see how it goes.

Almost half (48.5%) of the posts dealt with treatment and coping, 11.8% focused on symptoms and 1.2% referred to causes; 38.8% dealt with other, unrelated, issues. Clearly, coping with the disease is a significant motivation for blogging. For example, bloggers write about how symptoms affect their everyday lives: "i've had real trouble fighting whatever mood state keeps me from getting in the shower every day [sic]." They also write about coping with treatment options, as indicated in this post by a caregiver: "Despite a small hiccup a week before Xmas things have been running smoothly. The halperidol depo is doing it's [sic] job perfectly and we've had several weeks of normality."

We found that blogging about mental health provides writers with a forum to explore the stigmatized parts of themselves. As one blogger wrote:

> I've never felt able to be completely frank about my mental health. This is partly because I have a job and don't want everyone to know everything. And it's partly because I still have "issues" around shame and stigma. I know intellectually that there is nothing to feel shame/stigma about…But wherever those feelings come from they're strong. (And actually some of those feelings are pretty understandable when you read some of the shit written about mental illness by people who should know better.)

The blogger's last statement illustrates another reason people choose to blog: to be a counterargument to messages they believe do not accurately portray their disease, dilemma or issues important to them. For example, one woman expresses frustration that doctors or other experts are "judging" people in her situation, and her blog offers a different perspective. She states that her blog is for people like her and for the medical community. She writes:

> If you are a doctor, *please* take the time to read through my entries…I think this is a far better place to start (*the horse's mouth, so to speak…*) than an article written by someone possibly judging and not really understanding (emphasis in original).

Turkle talks about creating online identities that may or may not mirror real life. People can create "site-specific online personae" (1999, p. 644). Although Turkle was describing individuals' interactions within Internet groups, an analysis of the mental health blogs indicates the authors may have more than one blogger identity. When analyzing one of the blogrolls, we found that several people in our sample had another blog that focused on a subject other than mental illness. A man who feels stigmatized by his disease wrote that he blogs in other arenas, but chose to begin the mental health blog because it gave him a safe place "to be completely frank" about his mental health.

Nature of Mental Health Blogs

In terms of format-related characteristics, most blogs have a narrative style (87.2%), are text only (68.1%), personal in nature (85.1%) and allow readers to read and comment (91.5%). Of bloggers, 85.1% do not organize their posts by creating categories, and 74.5% do not include other communication tools on their blog site. Of the 25.5% who do, the most common communication tools take the form of links to other online networking services such as MySpace, Flickr or Friendster.

In terms of content, 55.3% of posts are emotional, compared to 18.8% that are informational, 14.1% a mix, and 11.8% uncategorizable/other.

Relationship tests between content and format and other variables revealed some expected, but also a few unexpected, findings. As expected, most personal blogs have a narrative style (90%), as opposed to 50% of the professional blogs, $\chi^2 (2) = 10.65$; $p < .01$. Furthermore, personal blogs get updated more frequently (M = 7.85; SD = 1.15) than professional blogs (M = 7.00; SD = 3.62), F(2, 44) = 2.82; $p < .10$.

Interestingly, however, professional blogs receive significantly more comments (M = 6.25; SD = 1.68) than personal ones (M = 1.05; SD = 0.53), F(2, 44) = 4.42, $p < .05$. Also surprisingly, text-only blogs elicit the least number of comments (M = 0.63; SD = 0.61), compared to text + picture (M = 3.5, SD = 0.92) and text + audio + video (M = 4.44; SD = 3.42), F(2, 44) = 3.52, $p < .05$.

Surprisingly, no significant gender differences were found in terms of post content. Males and females did not differ in the emotional versus informational tone adopted in writing.

In sum, qualitative and quantitative analyses revealed specific mental health blog trends for each of the three dimensions we investigated. With respect to bloggers' characteristics, it was revealed that most bloggers are young (20 to 30 years old) women patients (i.e., diagnosed with a mental disorder by a mental health professional).

Furthermore, most bloggers reveal personal identifiers; women do so more than men, and patients do so more than professionals. In terms of motivations, most bloggers appear to write mainly for themselves, but with an awareness of their audience, from whom they welcome feedback. For example, most authors allow readers not only to read, but also to comment. Social connectedness is revealed by the positive relationships between blogroll size and number of comments, as well as between blogroll size and number of posts. Bloggers use posts to cope with a disease significantly more than to talk about causes, symptoms or diagnosis. As for identity construction, our analysis indicates the authors may have more than one blogger identity and use blogging as a tool to explore multiple facets of their identities.

Finally, with regard to the nature of mental health blogs, most content revolves around the issues of treatment and coping, and is mostly emotional in nature, whether it is in the form of bloggers' posts or readers' comments. Surprisingly, these content-specific patterns do not appear to vary as a function of bloggers' gender.

Discussion

This study represents a modest first attempt at collecting baseline data about the nature of health blogs and bloggers. We hope that it sets the stage for a broader program of research that rigorously analyzes the content of health blogs and catalogs their role in health communication on the Internet.

The fact that most of the mental-health blogs we read were text only, personal in nature and followed a narrative style suggests that this technology is not used for its fancy features but because it fills a particular need. Blogs clearly offer a particular forum for expression distinct from other venues of health communication. To begin with, they seem to encourage expression of emotion, which bodes well for this venue acting as an effective vehicle for realizing therapeutic psychological benefits for patients and caregivers with pressing health issues. Research on online social support has upheld the relative superiority of emotional over informational support in coping effectiveness (Hersh, 2005).

One surprising finding in our study pertains to the lack of gender differences with respect to the nature of blog content—that is, emotional versus informational. This finding implies that mental health blogs provide a unique space enabling men, just as women, to reveal emotional issues and troubles related to mental health problems. It seems blogs allow users to transcend traditional gender roles, resulting in a more open, liberated and perhaps truer expression of one's attitudes, beliefs and feelings. The relatively greater proportion of emotional content suggests a self-avowedly cathartic role assigned to this technology by its users.

The idea of self-expression for its own sake is akin to diary-keeping, and psychology research has long demonstrated the use of journaling for coping via catharsis. Alternatively, expression with the intent of sharing one's emotions with others through the site is an effort to catalog one's experience publicly and may indicate a need for social support. Future research should attempt a rigorous examination of the nature of the writing to infer conscious and subconscious intentions behind blogging.

Our data suggest that mental-health bloggers are generally oblivious to the volume of commenting activity on their sites, given the absence of a significant correlation between number of posts and number of comments. This suggests the primacy of the journaling need over that of seeking social support. It also implies that health blogs do not exist for ego gratification, quite unlike political blogs that serve as soapboxes for pundits wanting to hold forth on pet topics. Future research will stand to benefit by examining specific ways in which health blogs differ from other types of blogs so that we can better understand the unique role of this technology for this particular content domain.

For instance, the identity-enhancing function of blogs is particularly relevant for the mentally ill. Because mental health is often stigmatized in the public dialogue, mental health bloggers find unique freedom in this online forum to explore aspects of their identities that are often hidden in everyday interactions. They seek to understand how the disease makes them who they are. As one woman wrote in her blog, "But where do I fit in? I want to fit in somewhere. I want help from someone who'll completely understand and really cares for my well-being. I want to be someone. My own someone." In addition to exploring their own identities, mental-health bloggers are able to experiment with multiple identities with possibly beneficial therapeutic outcomes.

Even as blog authors control the content of their blogs, they write with a sense of engagement to an unseen audience and seem to encourage feedback from readers. A large majority allows readers to comment on posts. Nevertheless, the unique characteristic of blogs as an online self-publishing forum is important to the authors, several of whom expressed the idea that their blogs are the voice they perceive as absent in the public dialogue about their disease. To that extent, blogs serve as an alternative to mainstream media messages about mental health, including those found on health websites, and serve to provide an important inside perspective from the real experts—the mentally ill themselves. They also allow for detailed experiential exposition of their condition without the lens and intrusion of a doctor-patient, counselor-patient, or group therapy setting, thus helping them reveal and cogitate over every minor detail pertaining to their experience of the illness.

Our methodology of inferring motives and psychological benefits by analyzing content patterns and use of formal features of blog technology is indeed a unique way to approach an academic understanding of this new medium of expression, but it is not without its methodological pitfalls.

One of the methodological challenges faced by our study was the random sampling technique. Initially, we conducted an online search for mental health directories that would allow us to randomly select a number of blogs. After a few trials, it became evident that most of the blogs listed in those particular directories did not deal specifically with mental health. Therefore, the dearth of rigorously constructed directories indicates that snowball sampling might prove more useful and appropriate, by selecting mental health blogs listed on a given blog's blogroll.

One other challenge is the difficulty in describing the blogger population, for two reasons. First, in this description, researchers are forced to rely on the information disclosed by the bloggers; second, the accuracy of this information cannot be verified. Furthermore, the nature of blogs makes it even harder, if not impossible, to describe blog audiences, whether they comment or lurk.

Overall, however, this study clearly highlights the importance of self in blogging, thus lending support to the agency model. There is plenty of evidence to suggest a high level of involvement with one's illness through the blog and also a major preoccupation with negotiating one's identity. This is manifested even behaviorally—for instance, an interesting finding revealed that personal mental-health blogs get updated more frequently than professional ones. This pattern is indicative of an enhanced sense of agency amongst patients, when it comes to taking control over their health. Patients now have a space where they can deal with their suffering by taking an active approach and by mapping their trajectory for recovery. In this respect, mental health blogs have the real potential to put the public back into public health.

References

AOL (2005, September 16). AOL survey says: People blog as therapy. Politics, news, gossip are not top motivators for bloggers. Retrieved March 31, 2006, from http://media.timewarner.com/media/newmedia/cb_press_view.cfm?release_num=55254441.

Bargh, J. A., & McKenna, K. Y. A. (2004). The Internet and social life. *Annual Review of Pyschology, 55*, 573–590.

Bargh, J. A., McKenna, K. Y. A. & Fitzsimons, G. M. (2002). Can you see the real me? Activation and expression of the "true self" on the Internet. *Journal of Social Issues, 58*(1), 33–48.

Bass, S. B., Ruzek, S. B., Gordon T. F., Fleisher, L., McKeown–Conn, N. & Moore, D. (2006). Relationship of Internet health information use with patient behavior and self-efficacy: Experiences of newly diagnosed cancer patients who contact the National Cancer Institute's Cancer Information Service. *Journal of Health Communication, 11*(2)

Blanchard, A. (2004). Blogs as virtual communities: Identifying a sense of community in the Julie/Julia Project. Retrieved March 15, 2006, from http://blog.lib.umn.edu/blogosphere/blogs_as_virtual.html.

Boberg, E. W., Gustafson, D. H., Hawkins, R. P., Offord, K. P., Koch, C., Wen, K-Y. et al. (2003). Assessing the unmet information, support and care delivery needs of men with prostate cancer. *Patient Education and Counseling, 49*, 233–242.

Bortree, D. S. (2005). Presentation of self on the Web: An ethnographic study of teenage girls' Weblogs. *Education, Communication & Information, 5*(1), 25–39.

Burleson, B. R. (2002). Introduction to the special issue: Psychological mediators of sex difference in emotional support. *Communication Reports, 15*, 1–4.

Carey, J. W. (1975). A cultural approach to communication. *Communication, 2*, 1–22.

Ferguson, T. (1999, March). E-patients prefer e-groups to doctors for 10 of 12 aspects of healthcare. *The Ferguson Report, 1*. Retrieved June 21, 2005, from http://www.fergusonreport.com/articles/fr039905.htm.

Freimuth, V. S., Stein, J. A. & Kean, T. J. (1989). *Searching for health information: The cancer information service model*. Philadelphia: University of Pennsylvania.

Hersh, A. (2005, May). *I know how you feel: A person-centered approach to supportive messages in online breast cancer groups*. Paper presented at the Annual Convention of the International Communication Association, New York.

House, J. S. (1987). Social support and social structure. *Sociological Forum, 2*, 135-146.

Huffaker, D. A., & Calvert, S. L. (2005). Gender, identity, and language use in teenage blogs. *Journal of Computer-Mediated Communication, 10*(2), article 1. Retrieved March 28, 2006, from: http://jcmc.indiana.edu/vol10/issue2/huffaker.html.

Johnson, T. J., & Kaye, B. K. (2004). Wag the blog: How reliance on traditional media and the Internet influence credibility perceptions of Weblogs among blog users. *Journalism & Mass Communication Quarterly, 81*(3), 622–642.

Kawachi, I., & Berkman, L. F. (2001). Social ties of mental health. *Journal of Urban Health: Bulletin of the New York Academy of Medicine, 78*(3), 458–467.

Knobloch–Westerwick, S., Sharma, N., Hansen, D. L. & Alter, S. (2005). Impact of popularity indications on readers' selective exposure to online news. *Journal of Broadcasting and Electronic Media, 49*(3), 296–313.

Lasker, J. N., Sogolow, E. D. & Sharim, R. R. (2005). The role of an online community for people with a rare disease: Content analysis of messages posted on a primary biliary cirrhosis mailing list. *Journal of Medical Internet Research, 7*(1), e10. Retrieved June 21, 2005, from http://www.jmir.org/2005/1/e10/.

McMillan, S. J. (2000). The microscope and the moving target: The challenge of applying content analysis to the World Wide Web. *Journalism and Mass Communication Quarterly, 77*(1), 80–98.

Nardi, B. A., Schiano, D. J., Gumbrecht, M. & Swartz, L. (December 2004). Why we blog. *Communications of the ACM, 47*(12).

Owen, N., Fotheringham, M. J. & Marcus, B. H. (2002). Communication technology and health behavior change. In K. Glanz, B. K. Rimer & F. M. Lewis (Eds.), *Health behavior and health education*, 3rd ed. (pp. 510–529). San Francisco: Jossey–Bass.

Papacharissi, Z. (2002). The presentation of self in virtual life: Characteristics of personal home pages. *Journalism & Mass Communication Quarterly, 79*(3), 643–660.

Perseus. (2003, October 4). The blogging iceberg: Of 4.12 million Weblogs, most little seen and quickly abandoned. Retrieved March 31, 2006, from http://www.perseusdevelopment. com/survey/news/releases/release_blogs.html.

Pew Internet and American Project. (2005, May). Health information online. Retrieved June 5, 2005, from http://www.pewinternet.org/PPF/r/156/report_display.asp.

Rakowski, W., Assaf, A. R., Lefebvre, R. C., Lasater, T. M., Niknian, M. & Carleton, R. A. (1990). Information-seeking about health in a community sample of adults: Correlates and associations with other health-related practices. *Health Education Quarterly, 17*, 379–393.

Reese, S. D., Rutigliano, L., Hyun, K. & Jeong, J. (2005, August). *Mapping the blogsphere: Citizen-based media in the global news arena.* Paper presented at the Annual Convention of the Association for Education in Journalism and Mass Communication, San Antonio, TX.

Ridgway, P. (2001). Restorying psychiatric disability: Learning from first person recovery narratives. *Psychiatric Rehabilitation Journal, 24*(4), 335–344.

Ryan, R. M., & Deci, E. L. (2000). Self-determination theory and the facilitation of intrinsic motivation, social development, and well-being. *American Psychologist, 55*(1), 68–78.

Scodari, C., & Felder, J. L. (2000). Creating a pocket universe: "Shippers," fan fiction, and *The X-Files* online. *Communication Studies, 51*(3), 238–257.

Scott, L. C. (2004a, August). *Late modern life and the rise of the "blogosphere": Can new media meet life's new challenges?* Paper presented at the Annual Convention of the Association for Education in Journalism and Mass Communication, Toronto, Canada.

Scott, L. C. (2004b, August). *Deliberative communities online: Towards a model of civic journalism based on the blog.* Paper presented at the Annual Convention of the Association for Education in Journalism and Mass Communication, Toronto, Canada.

Su, N. M., Wang, Y. & Mark, G. (2005). Politics as usual in the blogsphere. *Proceedings of the 4th International Workshop on Social Intelligence Design* (SID 2005).

Su, N. M., Wang, Y. & Mark, G., Aiyelokun, T., & Nakano, T. (2005). Bosom buddy afar brings a distant land near: Are bloggers a global community? Proceedings of the 2nd International Conference on Communities and Technologies.

Sundar, S. S. (2006, June). *Self as source: Agency and customization in interactive media.* Paper presented at the 56th Annual Conference of the International Communication Association, Dresden, Germany.

Sundar, S. S., Knobloch–Westerwick, S. & Hastall, M. R. (in press). News cues: Information scent and cognitive heuristics. *Journal of the American Society for Information Science and Technology.*

Sundar, S. S., & Nass, C. (2001). Conceptualizing sources in online news. *Journal of Communication, 51*(1), 52–72.

Trammel, K. D., & Keshelashvili, A. (2005). Examining the new influencers: A self-presentation study of A-list blogs. *Journalism & Mass Communication Quarterly, 82*(4), 968–982.

Trammel, K. D., & Kiousis, S. K. (2005, August). *Agenda-setting and blogs: Issue and attribute salience influence on celebrity Web sites.* Paper presented at the Annual Convention of the Association for Education in Journalism and Mass Communication, San Antonio, TX.

Turkle, S. (1999). Looking toward cyberspace: Beyond grounded sociology. *Contemporary Sociology, 28*(6), 643–648.

Viégas, F. B. (2005). Bloggers' expectations of privacy and accountability: An initial survey. *Journal of Computer-Mediated Communication, 10*(3), article 12. http://jcmc.indiana.edu/vol10/issue3/viegas.html.

Walther, J. B., & Boyd, S. (2002). Attraction to computer-mediated social support. In C. A. Lin & D. J. Atkin (Eds.), *Communication technology and society: Audience adoption and uses* (pp. 153–188). Cresskill, NJ: Hampton Press.

Part Two
Citizenship: Examining Blog Use,
Antecedents and Consequences

6

Reading Political Blogs During the 2004 Election Campaign: Correlates and Political Consequences

WILLIAM P. EVELAND, JR. AND IVAN DYLKO

With the introduction of each new medium during the past century, a pattern of research begins; it typically starts with a description of the content and users and then moves toward understanding the effects of the medium (e.g., see Cantril & Allport, 1935, in the case of radio and Charters, 1933, in the case of movies). The same process occurs when new forms within a given medium are introduced or become popular. About a decade or so ago, for instance, considerable research attention was paid to understanding the content and effects of, and listeners to, political talk radio (e.g., Davis, 1997; Hofstetter, Donovan, Klauber, Cole, Huie & Yuasa, 1994). Later, the focus of attention shifted to the next new medium: the Internet and world wide web (e.g., D'Alessio, 1997).

Most recently, blogs have garnered the attention of journalists and the public after the September 11, 2001, terrorist attacks and the American invasion of Iraq in 2003 (e.g., Johnson & Kaye, 2004). Most important, perhaps, political blogs became a prominent topic in the public discourse of the 2004 presidential election campaign. For instance, we conducted an informal content analysis of major newspapers using LexisNexis and found 175 articles containing the terms "blog" or "weblog" in their headlines or lead paragraphs during the 2004 general election campaign.

Who are the people who read political blogs? Does political blog reading have important implications for democratic participation? Following the tradition of research on each new medium as it begins to diffuse, the purpose of this chapter is to contribute to our understanding of the users of political blogs, how the use of political blogs relates to the use of other forms of news media, perceptions of media bias and, finally, how the use of political blogs relates to political interest, knowledge and participation. Based on two separate studies conducted in the fall of 2004, our findings in many ways confirm prior research on blogs and other "new" technologies. But, they also offer some additional insights into and even some contradictions of what the existing research on political blogs has revealed.

Defining Blogs

When the first blogs emerged in the late 1990s (e.g., Jensen, 2003), they were primarily webpages that contained many links, offered mostly "personal information" (Dearstyne, 2005, p. 39) and were easy to update (Gruhl, Guha, Liben–Nowell & Tomkins, 2004). The blogosphere (the universe of blogs on the web) has been expanding at a fast pace for several years (Bar–Ilan, 2005). According to the search engine Technorati (2006), there were more than 32.4 million blogs available on the Internet as of the end of March 2006.

Today's blogs can generally be characterized as easily created, frequently updated websites that offer the newest information on the top of the page. They contain numerous hyperlinks that are often accompanied by commentary regarding the destination of the link (Wall, 2005). Levels of technological sophistication and resulting capabilities in any given blog may vary, but several intrinsic characteristics apply across much of the blogosphere, including the tendency to link from the blog to related content and the ability of readers to comment on blog postings. The recent rhetoric in popular and semischolarly sources suggests that, as with most new technologies, there are utopian and dystopian perspectives on the new Internet-based forms of mass media (e.g., Dearstyne, 2005; Reese, Rutigliano, Hyun & Jeong, 2005; Stoll, 1996; Sunstein, 2001).

Users and Uses of Blogs

The growing popularity of blogs among Internet users has been widely acknowledged (Bar–Ilan, 2005; Pew Internet and American Life Project, 2005b). Among all Internet users, one quarter used alternative sources, such as blogs, to get campaign news in 2004 (Pew Internet and American Life Project, 2005a). In its most recent study, Pew (2005b) reported that 27% of American Internet users read blogs—a percentage that translates into 32 million Americans having read blogs by the end of 2004. Nine percent of Internet users claim to have read *political* blogs "frequently" or "sometimes" (Pew, 2005b). Besides simply reading a blog, 12% of online Americans participated by posting on the blogs and 7% created a blog (Pew, 2005b). Despite these figures, the majority of Internet users (62%) still did not have a clear understanding of the meaning of the word "blog" (Pew, 2005b).

Research by the Pew Internet and American Life Project (2005b) also indicates that blog readers today are much like the early adopters of the Internet (see Eveland & Dunwoody, 1998) and other new communication technologies (see Rogers, 1986): younger, better educated, more affluent and more likely to be male than their nonreading counterparts. If the popularity of blogs continues to grow at the rate of the past few years, the characteristics of blog readers are likely to follow the traditional diffusion path of successful new communication technologies and slowly shift to mirror typical Internet users and then typical members of the broader public (Pew, 2005a).

Beyond this description of the typical new communication technology adopter, to date there is limited evidence on the characteristics of blog readers. Aside from the nationally representative Pew surveys, most studies rely on self-selected convenience samples of blog readers responding to surveys from links posted on blogs (e.g., Johnson & Kaye, 2004; Kaye, 2005). Such data are common at the beginning of a research program on a new technology, at least in part because probability samples of the wider population will not capture a sufficient number of respondents who are using the new medium.

However, there are also significant problems with making firm inferences from these data (see Bimber, 1999), which the authors acknowledge (e.g., Johnson & Kaye, 2004, p. 627). In particular, it is difficult to draw conclusions about the characteristics of blog users compared to nonusers when data are gathered *only* from blog readers and when the sample of blog readers is a convenience sample drawn from a small, nonprobability sample of blogs out of the universe of tens of millions of blogs. Thus, most of what we know about the users of blogs should be considered very tentative—more "hypotheses to be further tested" than "firm conclusions."

Moreover, as more individuals begin to use blogs, the descriptive characteristics of users are likely to change toward greater typicality of the population, just as they did with the Internet as a whole (U.S. Department of Commerce, 2002). Thus, we will consider the findings of most of the past research on political blogs, in conjunction with what we know about users and effects of other recently diffused technologies, as hypotheses to be tested for confirmation.

Political Blog Reading and Other Forms of Communication

There is an interesting symbiosis between news media use—online and potentially even in traditional print and television sources—and political blogs. First, in the political realm, much of the grist for the blog mill *is* mainstream media reports. That is, many political blog postings include links to and commentary on reports from the mainstream press. Thus, blogs seem to encourage readers to expose themselves to at least some mainstream media, even if they imply some flaws in this content. Moreover, mainstream media have begun to report on blogs and refer to information posted in blogs (Euro RSCG Magnet, 2005); thus, mainstream media may be stimulating blog readership as well. Also, many mainstream journalists are co-opting the blog format formally (through their media organization) or informally (on their own) by maintaining political blogs (MSNBC, 2005; *The Washington Post*, 2005; *Cyberjournalist*, 2005).

Thus, we should expect that readership of political blogs and mainstream media is likely to be positively correlated, or at least not negatively correlated. As with computer and Internet use generally (e.g., Cai, 2005; Robinson, Kestnbaum,

Neustadtl & Alvarez, 2000), it is unlikely that use of blogs will lead to a time displacement of news media. In fact, the evidence suggests that political blog readers appear to be more likely to obtain news than nonusers (Pew, 2005b).

Johnson and Kaye (2004) argued that blog readers are individuals who became disenchanted with traditional media (which they distrust) and as a result turned to blogs for political information. In their study, blog readers considered mainstream media to be "only 'somewhat' credible" (p. 630). It is not clear, however, whether this is any different from those who do not read blogs because the credibility of mainstream media has been declining for years, beginning long before the rise of blogs (Jones, 2004). Of course, the causality question of whether those who distrust traditional media are drawn to blogs or whether reading blogs leads individuals to question the credibility of mainstream media is not a question that they, or we, could appropriately answer. But, it does suggest that perceptions of media bias or credibility may be associated with reading blogs.

Johnson and Kaye (2004) argued that blogs are analogous to political talk radio in form and in content. In terms of content, talk radio and political blogs include clearly opinionated content and a theme of critiquing mainstream media reports for inaccuracy, incompleteness and outright bias. Thus, it makes sense to expect that those who read political blogs are also likely to listen to political talk radio. In terms of form, Johnson and Kaye correctly note that both formats allow limited "audience" response—through phone calls on talk radio and through comments sections on blogs.

The interactive format of most blogs begs another question: What is the relationship between reading blogs and discussing politics in other online and face-to-face contexts? Some work suggests that individuals would be more likely to participate in political discussions online because of anonymity and/ or the ease of self-selecting into groups of similar others no matter what the rarity of one's views might be (e.g., Norris, 2002; Stromer–Galley, 2002). On the other hand, it is likely that those who have an interest in learning others' opinions and expressing their own opinions would be likely to do so not just within the blog format, but also via e-mail, discussion groups and in face-to-face interaction.

Political Correlates of Blog Reading

Even more so than for a description of blog users, the empirical literature tells us very little about the political correlates—whether cause or effect—of reading political blogs. But, there is some conjecture and even some limited evidence that blog readers tend to be politically conservative (Johnson & Kaye, 2004). Thus, we should expect to find a relationship between reading blogs and political ideology and presidential candidate choice in the 2004 campaign.

Johnson and Kaye (2004) also reported that more than half of their respondents believed that using blogs made them more politically involved and almost 90% believed that their knowledge about politics and general news had increased since they had started reading blogs. Although self-reports of media effects are problematic from a validity standpoint,[1] from this preliminary evidence we can hypothesize that reading blogs may be correlated with political participation as well as political knowledge when directly measured instead of asked as self-reports.

Study 1 Method

Sample

To examine the correlates and consequences of blog reading, a two-wave panel survey of web users was conducted. The survey solicited participants from a commercial online panel constructed by the company EasyMail Interactive, which e-mailed participants the survey participation request; interested panel members were directed to a web-based survey. Data for the pre-election survey (Wave I) were gathered between October 20 and 25, 2004. Postelection data (Wave II) were gathered between November 3 (the day after the election) and November 10. The sample size at Wave I was 430, and 298 of the Wave I respondents completed the Wave II questionnaire. Because all analyses include the blog reading variable and this variable was measured only in the second wave of the questionnaire, analyses are based on only those respondents who completed both waves of the questionnaire.

Measures

The central variable in this study was political blog reading. In the questionnaire, blog reading was measured in Wave II by asking respondents, "How many days last week did you get news from a political blog (weblog)?" with response options of 0 through 7 days. The mean of this variable was 0.51 (SD = 1.50) with a mode and median of 0. Given the skew of this variable, it was converted to a dichotomy representing those who did (coded 1) and those who did not (coded 0) read a political blog in the prior week (M = 0.15; SD = 0.35). Indicating that approximately 15% of our respondents had read political blogs, this mean is reasonably close to the estimate of 9% of Internet users reading political blogs by the Pew study reported later as Study 2 (see also Pew Internet and American Life Project, 2005b). That study employed a probability sample, increasing our confidence in the representativeness of at least this aspect of our findings.

Three key potential demographic correlates of blog reading were measured. Education was measured as an ordinal variable with six response options ranging from having a high school diploma or less (coded 1) through holding some form of graduate degree (coded 6). The modal respondent (2) had attended some college but did not graduate; the mean was slightly higher (M = 2.93; SD = 1.52). The average respondent was approximately 51 years old (SD

= 14.92), which is likely a reflection of the nature of recruitment for this type of study. Gender was a dichotomy, with females coded as 2 and males coded as 1; the sample was 58% male.

In addition to demographics, potential communication and political correlates of blog reading were assessed. Political interest was measured in Wave I as the average of two questions on a 10-point scale from "not at all interested" to "very interested." One question asked about interest in national politics and the other asked about interest in the 2004 presidential campaign in particular (M = 7.76; SD = 2.31; r = .76). General political knowledge was measured during Wave I using the standard Delli Carpini and Keeter (1993) five-item index. Five items were scored as 0 if incorrect or missing and 1 if correct. They were then averaged and multiplied by 100 to generate a "percentage correct" score (M = 79.11; SD = 22.60; α = 0.46).

Political ideology was measured as the average of two Wave I items—one for economic ideology and one for social ideology—on a 7-point scale from "very liberal" (1) to "very conservative" (7) (M = 4.32; SD = 1.50; r = .74). Political participation was measured in Wave II using items typical of recent political communication research (e.g., Scheufele, M. Nisbet, Brossard & E. Nisbet, 2004). Five separate questions asked respondents to report whether or not they had engaged in four behaviors over the course of the prior year (donating money, attending a rally, writing a letter to an elected official and displaying a political button, sticker or sign) plus whether or not they had voted in the 2004 election (M = 0.36; SD = 0.24; α = 0.56).

Finally, 2004 vote choice was measured in Wave II among those who reported voting for president, with choices of Bush, Kerry, Nader and other. Because only 3% of all respondents reported voting for someone other than one of the two major party candidates, this variable was recoded as a dichotomy to reflect voting for Kerry or Bush, with Kerry as the high value. Using this measure, Kerry received the votes of 39% of respondents.

In addition to demographic and political variables, numerous forms of communication were measured in Wave II. Traditional news use was an average of two items measuring days per week (0 through 7) during the last week watching national television news and reading a newspaper (M = 4.17; SD = 2.27; r = .31). Political discussion was a single-item measure of days per week during the last week discussing politics (M = 4.50; SD = 2.27). Talk radio listening was also a single-item measure of days per week during the last week listening to talk radio (M = 1.47; SD = 2.31). Late-night comedy viewing was a single-item measure of days per week during the last week watching late-night comedy programs (M = 1.15; SD = 1.90). Cable news exposure was measured as days during the last week that the respondent reported watching cable news for at least 15 minutes (M = 3.27; SD = 2.90).

Online news use was the average of two items tapping days per week reading news on the websites of (a) network or cable news organizations; and (b) print newspaper organizations (M = 1.81; SD = 2.13; r = .44). Online political discussion was measured using three items for which respondents reported the number of days during the last week that they (a) discussed politics over e-mail; (b) read an Internet discussion of politics; and (c) posted to an Internet discussion about politics (M = 1.19; SD = 1.54; α = 0.67). Finally, perceptions of media bias were measured in Wave I as the mean of three items for which respondents assessed the bias in (a) local television news; (b) national television network news; and (c) local daily newspapers as biased in favor of their views, generally unbiased or biased against their views on a scale from 1 to 3, with "bias against" coded as the highest value (M = 2.22; SD = 0.46; α = 0.74).

Study 2 Method

Sample

To provide an internal replication of our original data gathering, especially given the nonprobability nature of that sample, we also conducted a secondary analysis of data gathered by the Pew Internet and American Life Project.[2] These data employed a nationally representative telephone survey of 2,200 respondents shortly after the 2004 presidential election. The study employed a split-ballot technique, so some questions were only employed on form A and others only on form B. This presented some problems for us in making a full replication of the findings of Study 1, as we will discuss later. To make our findings comparable to Study 1, we excluded all respondents to the Pew study who reported that they never went online to use e-mail or the world wide web (approximately 40% of the sample).[3]

Measures

Blog reading was measured by asking respondents, "How often do you get news from online columns or blogs such as Talking Points Memo, the Daily Kos, or Instapundit?" Response options were "regularly" (coded 2), "sometimes" (coded 1) or "hardly ever or never" (coded 0). The mean of this variable was 0.13 (SD = 0.43) with a mode and median of 0. As for Study 1, given the skew of this variable, it was converted to a dichotomy representing those who do (coded 1) and those who hardly ever or never (coded 0) get news from political blogs (M = 0.09; SD = 0.29).

Four relevant demographic variables were also available. Education was measured as an ordinal variable with four response options ranging from less than a high school diploma (coded 1) through college degree or more (coded 4). The modal respondent (2) had attended some college but did not graduate; the mean was slightly higher (M = 3.11; SD = 0.91). The average respondent was approximately 44 years old (SD = 15.33). Gender was coded as a dichotomy with females coded as 2 and males coded as 1; the sample was 51% female.

In addition to demographics, potential communication and political correlates of blog reading were also available. Political ideology was measured by the question, "In general, would you describe your political views as..." with options of "very conservative" (coded 1), "conservative" (coded 2), "moderate" (coded 3), "liberal" (coded 4) and "very liberal" (coded 5) (M = 2.79; SD = 0.93). Political participation was measured by asking respondents to report whether or not they had engaged in four behaviors over the course of the prior year (donating money, attending a rally, calling people on the phone to encourage them to vote and going to people's homes to encourage them to vote for a particular candidate) plus whether or not they had voted in the 2004 election (M = 0.24; SD = 0.17; α = 0.46).

Finally, 2004 vote choice was measured with choices of Bush, Kerry or other. Because only 1% of all respondents reported voting for someone other than one of the two major party candidates, this variable was recoded as a dichotomy to reflect voting for Kerry or Bush, with Kerry as the high value (and "others" set to missing). Using this measure, Kerry received the votes of 43% of respondents.

Numerous forms of communication were also measured. Unfortunately, the nature of the split ballot design of the study meant that all questions about politically oriented television and radio programs were on the alternate form of the survey from the (crucially important for our purposes) Internet measures described later. The exception was newspaper use, which was measured as an average of two items tapping reading of local newspapers and national newspapers with response options of "regularly" (coded 2), "sometimes" (coded 1) or "hardly ever or never" (coded 0) (M = 0.82; SD = 0.60; r = .19).

Online news use was the average of three items tapping reading of news from online television news sites, online newspaper sites and "online newsmagazine and opinion sites such as Slate.com or National Review" using a 3-point scale (0 to 2) from "hardly ever or never" through "regularly" (M = 0.45; SD = 0.47; α = 0.53). Online political discussion was measured as the average of three items tapping whether respondents had (coded 1) or had not (coded 0) sent or received political e-mails, tried to persuade others to vote for a particular candidate via e-mail and engaged in online discussions or chat groups (M = 0.18; SD = 0.24; α = 0.36).

Combined Study 1 and Study 2 Results

We begin by examining differences between those who do and do not read political blogs among those who otherwise use the Internet. Table 6.1 presents *t*-tests between blog readers and nonreaders on demographic and political variables for both studies. As we would expect from the diffusion literature, blog readers are more likely to have higher levels of formal education, at least in Study 1. However, age and gender, two other variables that the diffusion

Table 6.1 Differences Between Political Blog Readers and Nonreaders on Demographic and Political Variables

	Study 1: 2004 online panel		Study 2: 2004 Pew phone survey	
	Non- readers	Blog readers	Non- readers	Blog readers
Age		50.26	44.30	36.90[b]
Gender (female)	43%	36%	50%	34%[a]
Education	2.88	3.40[a]	3.11	3.27
Income	—	—	5.36	5.57
Political interest	7.58	8.64[b]	—	—
Political participation	0.33	0.53[b]	0.23	0.31[b]
General political knowledge	78.74	82.00	—	—
Political ideology	4.31	4.33	2.79	2.92
2004 presidential vote choice (Kerry)	38%	43%	43%	45%

[a] $p < .05$
[b] $p < .01$

literature suggests would correlate with the use of a new technology, do not differ by blog reading in Study 1 but do in Study 2.

In Study 2, the only study with a measure of income, there are no differences in income between readers and nonreaders. We suspect that any of these relationships is actually less about the diffusion of this technology and more about the nature of our samples (Internet users only and thus predictors of Internet access and use are in a sense "controlled") than about the political nature of our focal blog content.

Moving to the political variables, blog readers are more politically interested than nonreaders in Study 1, the only study in which this variable was present.[4] This is, of course, to be expected because use of any form of political media is likely to be correlated with interest in the political domain.

The strongest difference between blog readers and nonreaders on a political variable is for political participation. In both studies, participation was significantly higher among readers than nonreaders. However, blog reading was unrelated to political knowledge in Study 1. Also, despite the claims of prior research that blogs and blog readers are likely to be more conservative than average, our data from Study 1 and Study 2 suggest that blog readers and nonreaders are no different in political ideology or 2004 candidate choice.

Next, we examine differences between political blog readers and nonreaders in various forms of mediated and nonmediated communication (see Table 6.2). Here we find no evidence to support the hypothesis that reading blogs leads to a reduction in other forms of mediated or interpersonal com-

Table 6.2 Differences Between Political Blog Readers and Nonreaders on Other Forms of Communication

	Study 1: 2004 online panel		Study 2: 2004 Pew phone survey	
	Non-readers	Blog readers	Non-readers	Blog readers
Traditional news use	4.12	4.51	—	—
Newspaper use	—	—	0.81	0.93
Political discussion	4.29	5.40[a]	—	—
Talk radio listening	1.18	2.95[a]	—	—
Late-night comedy viewing	1.09	1.48	—	—
Cable news use	3.01	4.67[a]	—	—
Online news use	1.47	3.57[a]	0.39	1.01[a]
Online political discussion	0.88	2.80[a]	0.16	0.41[a]
Perceived news media bias	2.18	2.35	—	—

[a] $p < .01$.

munication. Quite the contrary—and consistent with our argument about symbiosis—those who read political blogs are also more likely to engage in most other forms of political communication. The exceptions are some offline forms of media use: Newspaper use (Study 2), traditional news media use and late-night comedy viewing (in Study 1) are all unrelated to blog reading. Blog readers are more likely than nonreaders to engage in political discussions, listen to talk radio, watch cable news, read news online and engage in online political discussion. The strongest of these relationships are those with online news use and discussion (in both studies) and with listening to talk radio (Study 1).

Finally, consistent with the common conception of political blogs as critical of the mainstream press, there is some evidence that those who read political blogs are also somewhat more likely to perceive traditional news media as biased against their views than nonreaders are (Study 1).

Although these bivariate relationships are instructive, it is also important to conduct multivariate tests of our hypotheses. Therefore, we begin by selecting variables we believe may be effects of blog reading and variables likely to stimulate blog reading. Among the variables that we expect may be effects of blog reading, political participation is the only one that appears to have even a zero-order relationship with blog reading, based on the bivariate analysis. Thus, we do not attempt multivariate analyses predicting political knowledge or vote choice.

We also identify predictors of blog reading, focusing primarily on demographic and communication variables. Table 6.3 presents the results of logistic

Table 6.3 Logistic Regression Predicting Political Blog Reading (Study 1)

	Odds ratio controlling current and prior blocks only	Odds ratio controlling all other variables
Age	.990	.977
Gender (female)	1.133	1.396
Education	.258	1.234
Interest	1.247[a]	.947
Ideology	.280[a]	.465
Ideology sq.	1.167[a]	1.104
Nagelkerke R^2	.121[b]	
Traditional news	.936	.912
Political discussion	1.219[a]	.935
Nagelkerke R^2 change	.027	
Talk radio	.218[a]	1.216[a]
Late-night comedy	1.071	1.007
Cable news	1.167	1.146
Nagelkerke R^2 change	.075[b]	
Online news	1.276[a]	1.273[a]
Online discussion	1.880[b]	1.866[b]
Nagelkerke R^2 change	.197[b]	
Perceived media bias	1.263	1.263
Nagelkerke R^2 change	.001	
Final Nagelkerke R^2	.421[b]	

[a] $p < .05$.
[b] $p < .01$.

regression models predicting the dichotomous blog reading variable in Study 1, and Table 6.4 presents results of similar models for Study 2. The first column in each of these tables provides results of a hierarchical model with coefficients controlling only current and prior blocks in the model. The second column in each table presents a model controlling all variables in the model simultaneously. We will address the findings of the column 1 first, then refer to differences between these analyses and the simultaneous model findings.

The first block tests the relationship between demographic and political variables and blog reading. None of the three demographic variables are related to blog reading once the two political variables are controlled in Study 1. However, without a control for political interest, Study 2 does reveal a significant relationship with age and gender, consistent with the bivariate analyses. In

Table 6.4 Logistic Regression Predicting Political Blog Reading (Study 2)

	Odds ratio controlling current and prior blocks only	Odds ratio controlling all other variables
Age	.965[b]	.981
Gender (female)	.535[a]	.611
Education	1.181	.776
Income	1.059	1.037
Ideology	1.085	.861
Ideology sq.	1.035	.902
Nagelkerke R²	.064[b]	
Newspaper use	1.486	.944
Nagelkerke R² change	.010	
Online news	8.497[b]	8.497[b]
Online discussion	9.746[b]	9.746[b]
Nagelkerke R² change	.251[b]	
Final Nagelkerke R²	.325[b]	

[a] $p < .05$.
[b] $p < .01$.

Study 1, political interest is positively related to blog reading, replicating the results of the bivariate tests.

The political ideology relationship merits closer consideration. Recall that, in the bivariate test, ideology was unrelated to blog reading in either study. In this model we test this linear relationship, but we also test for a quadratic relationship between ideology and blog reading. That is, we test for a possible curvilinear relationship and in fact do find one, at least in Study 1. The results of that study indicate that blog reading is greater among ideologues on both sides of the political fence, whereas political moderates are unlikely to read political blogs. Thus, instead of the finding of prior research that blog reading is biased in a conservative direction, we find that partisans—conservatives as well as liberals—are more likely to read political blogs than their moderate counterparts are (see Figure 6.1). However, this finding is not reproduced in Study 2, although a simple bivariate plot appears to suggest that the lowest levels of political blog reading are among moderates.

The next block of variables in the logistic regression models includes traditional news media use (or newspaper reading in Study 2) and political discussion (Study 1). As with the bivariate relationships, discussion is related to blog reading, but traditional news media use and newspaper reading are not.

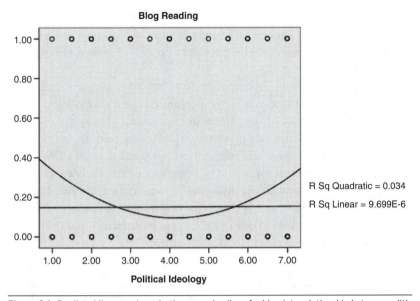

Figure 6.1 Predicted linear and quadratic regression lines for bivariate relationship between political ideology and political blog reading (Study 1).

The next block is available only in Study 1 and includes three "nontraditional" sources of political information: talk radio, late night comedy and cable news. Among these, only listening to talk radio is related to blog reading.

The next block of variables includes the two Internet variables, and both are related to blog reading. Those who read online news and those who engage in political discussions online are also more likely to read political blogs in both studies.

The last block for Study 1 adds perceived news media bias. Media bias perceptions, when all other variables are controlled, are unrelated to blog reading.

An examination of the coefficients after all variables are entered into the logistic model (column 2) reveals that only three variables remain significant predictors under simultaneous control in Study 1 and only two for Study 2. For Study 1, listening to talk radio, reading online news and engaging in political discussions online predict reading of political blogs. The same finding is replicated for Study 2, with the exception that the talk radio variable is not present in that study, so only online news use and online discussion remain significant predictors after all controls.

For Study 1, this model accounts for over 42% of the variance in blog reading; for Study 2, the full model accounts for almost 33% of variance (with five fewer variables). In Study 1 talk radio listening, online news reading and online discussion alone account for over 37% of the variance in blog reading among Internet users, without the need to include demographic, political or other communication variables. In Study 2, a model with only online news use and online discussion could account for over 29% of variance in political blog reading.

Table 6.5 (Study 1) and Table 6.6 (Study 2) present results of hierarchical (first column) and simultaneous (second column) regression models predicting political participation using various demographic, political and communication variables. Because our primary interest is blog reading, we focus on the last block of the hierarchical model. Here, we see that when all variables in the model with the exception of the other two Internet-related variables (online news reading and online discussion) are controlled, blog reading is a significant positive predictor of political participation in both studies. That is, above and beyond the impact of various demographic factors, political interest (Study 1 only) and ideology, political discussion (Study 1 only), traditional

Table 6.5 OLS Regression Predicting 2004 Political Participation (Study 1)

	Beta controlling prior blocks only	Beta controlling all other variables
Age	—	.05
Gender (female)	—	−.05
Education	—	.06
Interest	—	.16[a]
Ideology	—	−.01
Ideology sq.	—	.04
R²	.227[b]	
Traditional news	.14[a]	.14[a]
Political discussion	.23[b]	.13[a]
R² change	.058[b]	
Talk radio	.18[b]	.14[a]
Late-night comedy	.01	−.03
Cable news	.09	.01
R² change		.028[a]
Blog reading	.12[a]	.02
Online news	.09	.00
Online discussion	.28[b]	.27[b]
R² change	.058[b]	
Final R²		.371[b]

[a] $p < .05$.
[b] $p < .01$.

Table 6.6 OLS Regression Predicting 2004 Political Participation (Study 2)

	Beta controlling prior blocks only	Beta controlling all other variables
Age	—	.21[c]
Gender (female)	—	−.01
Education	—	.10[b]
Income		.05
Ideology	—	.02
Ideology sq.	—	.03
R²	.114[c]	
Newspaper use	.14[c]	.11[c]
R² change	.019[c]	
Blog reading	.14[c]	.03
Online news use	.21[c]	.08[a]
Online discussion	.35[c]	.31[c]
R² change	.116[c]	
Final R²		.249[c]

[a] $p < .10$.
[b] $p < .05$.
[c] $p < .01$.

news media use (or newspaper use in Study 2) and three forms of nontraditional political communication use (Study 1), those who read blogs are more likely to participate in politics.

However, adding the two strongest predictors of blog reading from Table 6.3 and Table 6.4 (online news use and online political discussion) as controls reduces the relationship between blog reading and participation to nonsignificance in both studies. Whether the reduction to nonsignificance represents a function of multicollinearity or spuriousness will be addressed in the discussion section.

In the final model controlling all variables, older and more highly educated individuals (Study 2), as well as those with higher levels of political interest (Study 1), traditional news media use (or newspaper use in Study 2), political discussion (Study 1), talk radio use (Study 1), online discussion and (marginally) online news use are more likely to participate in politics. The single strongest predictor of political participation in both of these studies was online discussion of politics. All variables combined accounted for over 37% of the variance in political participation in Study 1 and nearly 25% of variance in Study 2 (using four fewer variables).

Discussion

What are we to make of our findings, and how do they compare to the results of prior research and conjecture? We organize our results as we have the rest of this chapter by first addressing predictors of using political blogs and then the presumed effects of political blog use.

Users of Political Blogs

To begin, we should address issues of the diffusion of communication technology. Because political blogs are available on the "same" Internet as online news and discussion boards, there are no financial or technological barriers to the adoption of blog use by Internet users. It may be that the barriers to adoption of blogs by non-Internet users are not different from adoption of any other function of the Internet (e.g., online games, news sites, discussion boards). From the reader's perspective, it may be that blogs are really little different from any other website.

Thus, any demographic correlates of political blog reading among our samples of Internet users are probably more a function of the political content of this form of blog than a function of the diffusion of blogs as a communication technology more generally. Our findings are consistent with this interpretation. Among Internet users, there appear to be little if any demographic differences between political blog readers and nonreaders, and the differences that remain after statistical control are not consistent across the two studies. In the larger population, differences, if any, between those who do and do not read nonpolitical blogs are likely to be similar to differences between those with and without Internet access.

Moreover, prior conjecture and research suggesting that political blog readers are particularly conservative seems to have been inaccurate or, at best, a reflection of reality that has changed very quickly. Both of our studies suggest no linear relationship between reading political blogs and ideology *or* choice of presidential candidate in the 2004 election. However, there may be a nonlinear relationship such that those at the political extremes—liberals and conservatives—are drawn to political blogs. Although this finding disappeared in our full predictive model of blog reading in Study 1 and did not appear at all in Study 2, it is worth considering in future research.

This possible attraction from highly ideological segments of the population might serve as a valuable segue to another important predictor of political blog reading: talk radio use. In a perceptive observation, Johnson and Kaye (2004) argued that blogs resembled political talk radio in terms of their content and audiences. Although they used this analogy as support for a claim of a conservative tendency among blog readers for which we find no support in our data, the analogy may still be mostly correct. Talk radio and political blogs tend to espouse extreme views in one or another political direction;

thus, it makes sense that those who enjoy the highly opinion-based content and partisan rhetoric of talk radio would also be drawn to political blogs.

Johnson and Kaye (2004) also made another link in this reasoning. Talk radio and blogs have as a common theme some inadequacy or bias in mainstream media. This can help to explain our findings (at least at the bivariate level) that blog readers are somewhat more likely to perceive mainstream news media as biased against their own views than nonreaders would be.

Thus, our findings indicate that those who read political blogs are generally no different demographically or politically from other Internet users, but they are more likely to listen to talk radio. Most important, they are also heavy users of online news and opportunities for political discussion online. This finding is clearly replicated across both studies.

We believe that these links with other forms of Internet use are more than just a technology correlation. Instead, we think they are inherent in the symbiotic relationship of political blogs with online news and discussion. One of the most common forms of blog posts is to hyperlink to information available elsewhere online. Many of these links are to traditional online news sources. Thus, it is no surprise that those who read political blogs are also more likely to read online news because the blogs are often directing their readers to online news sources.

Moreover, one function incorporated into many blogs is the ability to post comments in response to a blog post. This function is essentially using online technology to engage in political discussion. Thus, once again, it should be no surprise that reading blogs is related to making political posts or sending politically related messages.

Although talk radio use and online news use and discussion predict blog reading, use of traditional and nontraditional political communication sources other than talk radio did not. Most important in this finding is the absence of a significant negative relationship between blog reading and traditional news media use. Blog readers are not abandoning traditional media sources; they simply are no more likely to use them than nonreaders are.

The Political Consequences of Blog Reading

Our data suggest that, at least at this early stage of blog development and adoption, political blog reading is unrelated to political knowledge. However, we should acknowledge that our measure of political knowledge is Delli Carpini and Keeter's (1993) measure of general political knowledge, which is not nearly as closely tied to the content of news and public discourse as we believe an ideal measure of political knowledge in communication research should be. Thus, it is entirely possible that this finding is a result of our operationalization of knowledge; a measure of candidate issue stance knowledge or knowledge of current events or prominent individuals in the news would likely have been a better choice.

The relationship of blog reading to political participation in this study is somewhat ambiguous. Bivariate analyses suggested a moderate relationship between blog reading and participation, and this relationship was statistically significant in both of our multivariate regression models until all but two final control variables were incorporated. Those two variables—online political discussion and online news use—were also the two strongest predictors of blog reading in both studies and have been shown to play an important role in participation in other research as well (e.g., Shah, Cho, Eveland & Kwak, 2005). As we have already discussed, in some ways these two variables are connected with political blog reading in a symbiotic relationship because blogs tend to direct their readers to online news sources and allow them to post their political comments in the blog.

We conducted a post-hoc analysis using the data from Study 1 to better understand where blog reading fit among the various measures of communication. We entered each indicator of communication described in the method section into a principal axis factor analysis with oblique rotation (see Table 6.7). The first factor included the three indicators of online discussion as primary loaders, plus blog reading as the weakest loader on this factor. The third factor included the two indicators of online news use as primary loaders. The second factor contained all other items and thus might be best thought of as offline communication.

The three factors were moderately correlated; the online discussion and online news use factors were most highly correlated ($r = .42$). Interestingly, although blog reading had its primary loading on the online discussion factor, it had an almost-as-strong secondary loading on the online news use factor. Therefore, just as we have conceptualized blog reading, it is a combination of online news use and online discussion, but does not fit very well with either of them compared to other indicators of these constructs. It is something different but, at the same time, inextricably intertwined with them. Given these findings, disentangling the political implications of these three closely interconnected, Internet-based variables must be left for future research. But, if nothing else, the relationship between blog reading and participation, if not direct, may be mediated through online discussion of politics.

Limitations and Suggestions for Future Research

All individual studies have limitations, and studies of the uses and effects of new communication technologies tend to share the same limitations. However, our approach of using data from two different studies using different sampling approaches tends to offset some of the limitations of either study alone. For Study 1, like most prior research on blog uses and effects, our study was unable to obtain a probability sample for which statistical generalization to the larger population is possible. We do believe that our approach of employing a sample of Internet users and comparing blog readers to nonreaders is a

Table 6.7 Principal Axis Factor Analysis of Communication Behaviors (Study 1)

	Online discussion	Offline communication	Online news use
E-mail political discussion	**.78**	.25	.34
Post to online discussion	**.68**	.21	.21
Read 'net political discussion	**.63**	.37	.47
Political blog reading	**.51**	.24	.43
Cable news use	.30	**.74**	.22
Network TV news use	.14	**.73**	.07
Discuss politics	.33	**.51**	.34
Political talk radio use	.30	**.43**	.25
Newspaper reading	.06	**.38**	.16
Late-night comedy use	.19	**.23**	.11
Online TV news site use	.37	.35	**.71**
Online newspaper use	.24	.14	**.64**

Note: Forced three-factor solution; four-factor solution differed with political talk radio use alone as a separate, fourth factor.

better alternative than sampling only blog readers. This is because, without a nonreading comparison group to blog readers sampled in the same manner as the blog readers were, it is impossible to make inferences about differences between blog readers and all others using the Internet. This is an issue of internal validity more so than one of generalizability (i.e., external validity). Our study better addresses the internal validity issue, but the external validity issue remains.

However, Study 2 minimized this problem by employing nationally representative survey data from Pew to address some of the same questions. Although many of the variables available in Study 1 were not available in Study 2 (in part because the Pew study employed a split-ballot approach for the key Internet-related questions), in cases where similar measures were available, findings were generally replicated, lending support to the findings from our original data collection.

In addition to our inability to reproduce all of the Study 1 variables in Study 2, the measurement in Study 2 appeared to be less reliable than in Study 1. A number of the key variables were not able to achieve typical standards of reliability. This is a problem with secondary analysis that we hope is offset by the measurement of most concepts in our original data collection in Study 1.

Moreover, although we technically have panel data available to us in Study 1, our panel study was not designed specifically to test causal hypotheses. Therefore, our measure of blog reading and most other measures for this chapter were gathered in the second wave of data collection. Thus, we were unable to take advantage of our panel design for the analyses presented here. Clearly, future research must address the causality question more clearly than we and other studies of blog users and effects have done.

Despite these limitations, our study suggests several interesting findings that future research should attempt to follow up. Most theoretically interesting of these is the symbiotic connection among blog reading, online news use and online political discussion. Understanding what, if any, causal connections exist among these three variables, as well as the extent to which one or all of them directly or indirectly influence political participation, should be at the top of the list of research goals for those interested in the phenomenon of political blogs.

References

Bar-Ilan, J. (2005). Information hub blogs. *Journal of Information Science, 31*, 297–307.

Bimber, B. (1999). The Internet and citizen communication with government: Does the medium matter? *Political Communication, 16*, 409–428.

Cai, X. (2005). An experimental examination of the computer's time displacement effects. *New Media & Society, 7*, 8–21.

Cantril, H., & Allport, G. W. (1935). *The psychology of radio*. New York: Harper & Brothers.

Charters, W. W. (1933). *Motion pictures and youth: A summary*. New York: Macmillan.

Cyberjournalist. (2005). J-Blogs: Ongoing. Retrieved December 20, 2005, from http://www.cyberjournalist.net/cyberjournalists.php#jblogs_ongoing.

D'Alessio, D. (1997). Use of the World Wide Web in the 1996 U.S. election. *Electoral Studies, 16*, 489–500.

Davis, R. (1997). Understanding broadcast political talk. *Political Communication, 14*, 323–332.

Dearstyne, B. (2005). Blogs: The new information revolution? *Information Management Journal, 39*(5), 38–44.

Delli Carpini, M. X., & Keeter, S. (1993). Measuring political knowledge: Putting first things first. *American Journal of Political Science, 37*, 1179–1206.

Euro RSCG Magnet. (2005). Eleventh Annual Euro RSCG Magnet and Columbia University Survey of the Media. Retrieved December 20, 2005, from http://www.magnet.com/index.php?s=_thought.

Eveland, W. P., Jr., & Dunwoody, S. (1998). Users and navigation patterns of a science World Wide Web site for the public. *Public Understanding of Science, 7*, 285–311.

Gruhl, D., Guha, R., Liben-Nowell, D. & Tomkins, A. (2004, May). *Information diffusion through blogspace*. Paper presented to the International World Wide Web Conference. Retrieved October 22, 2005, from http://www.www2004.org/proceedings/docs/1p491.pdf, 491–501.

Hofstetter, C. R., Donovan, M. C., Klauber, M. R., Cole, A., Huie, C. J. & Yuasa, T. (1994). Political talk radio: A stereotype reconsidered. *Political Research Quarterly, 47*, 467–479.

Jensen, M. (2003). A brief history of Weblogs. *Columbia Journalism Review, 42*(3), 22.

Johnson, T. J., & Kaye, B. K. (2004). Wag the blog: How reliance on traditional media and the Internet influence credibility perceptions of weblogs among blog users. *Journalism & Mass Communication Quarterly, 81*, 622–642.

Jones, D. A. (2004). Why Americans don't trust the media: A preliminary analysis. *Press/Politics, 9*(2), 60–75.

Kaye, B. K. (2005). It's a blog, blog, blog, blog world. *Atlantic Journal of Communication, 13*(2), 73–95.

MSNBC. (2005). The daily nightly. Retrieved December 20, 2005, from http://dailynightly.msnbc.com/.

Nisbett, R., & Ross, L. (1980). *Human inference: Strategies and shortcomings of social judgment*. Englewood Cliffs, NJ: Prentice Hall.

Norris, P. (2002). The bridging and bonding role of online communities. *Press/Politics*, 7(3), 3–13.

Pew Internet and American Life Project. (2005a). The Internet and Campaign 2004. Retrieved October 24, 2005, from http://www.pewInternet.org/pdfs/PIP_2004_Campaign.pdf.

Pew Internet and American Life Project. (2005b). The state of blogging. Retrieved October 22, 2005, from http://www.pewInternet.org/PPF/r/144/report_display.asp.

Reese, S., Rutigliano, L., Hyun, K. & Jeong, J. (2005, August). *Mapping the blogosphere: Citizen-based media in the global news arena*. Paper presented to the Association for Education in Journalism & Mass Communication, San Antonio, TX.

Robinson, J. P., Kestnbaum, M., Neustadtl, A. & Alvarez, A. (2000). Mass media use and social life among Internet users. *Social Science Computer Review, 18*, 490–501.

Rogers, E. M. (1986). *Communication technology: The new media in society*. New York: Free Press.

Scheufele, D. A., Nisbet, M. C., Brossard, D. & Nisbet, E. C. (2004). Social structure and citizenship: Examining impacts of social setting, network heterogeneity, and informational variables on political participation. *Political Communication, 21*, 315–338.

Shah, D. V., Cho, J., Eveland, W. P., Jr. & Kwak, N. (2005). Information and expression in a digital age: Modeling Internet effects on civic participation. *Communication Research, 32*, 531–565.

Stoll, C. (1996). *Silicon snake oil: Second thoughts on the information highway*. New York: Anchor Books.

Stromer–Galley, J. (2002). New voices in the public sphere: A comparative analysis of interpersonal and online political talk. *The Public, 9*(2), 23–42.

Sunstein, C. R. (2001). *Republic.com*. Princeton, NJ: Princeton University Press.

Technorati. Retrieved March 30, 2006, from http://www.technorati.com/.

The Washington Post. (2005). Achenblog. Retrieved December 20, 2005, from http://blogs.washingtonpost.com/achenblog/2005/12/the_annual_chri.html.

U.S. Department of Commerce. (2002). A nation online: How Americans are expanding their use of the Internet. Retrieved October 30, 2005, from http://www.ntia.doc.gov/ntiahome/dn/anationonline2.pdf.

Wall, M. (2005). Blogs of war. *Journalism, 6*(2), 153-172.

Notes

1. As Nisbett and Ross (1980, p. 10) write: "There is no assumption as critical to contemporary attribution theory (or to any theory that assumes the layperson's general adequacy as an intuitive scientist) as the assumption that people can detect covariation among events, estimate its magnitude from some satisfactory metric, and draw appropriate inferences based on such estimates. There is mounting evidence that people are extremely poor at performing such covariation assessment tasks. In particular, it appears that a priori theories or expectations may be more important to the perception of covariation than are the actually observed data configurations." Since requests for respondents to report whether their knowledge or participation had changed since engaging in some behavior is a request to assess covariation, this raises questions about the validity of such self-reports. Researchers interested in media effects should measure the outcome of interest directly instead of respondent perceptions of change in that outcome produced by the predictor of interest, unless, of course, the focus of the research is on the perceptions as in the case of work on third-person perceptions.

2. The Pew Internet and American Life Project bears no responsibility for the use or interpretation of their data reported here. We thank them for access to these data.

3. The blog reading question was not asked of those who did not use the Internet, so Internet nonusers are considered "missing" on this central variable anyhow. But, we could have chosen to consider all those who never use the Internet as having not used blogs and thus changed their "missing" values on this variable to 0. To make Study 1 and Study 2 as comparable as possible, we instead merely excluded non-Internet users because this was done as part of the Study 1 sampling design. All the following descriptive statistics for the sample reflect only those who reported using the Internet and who had completed form B of the split ballot study (maximum $N = 690$). The sample size for any given analysis varies due to missing values on specific items.

4. The Pew data do include an item that could be construed as interest, but the wording could also be taken as an overall measure of media attention. Given the ambiguity and mixed wording, we chose not to use it. The wording of that item is "Some people seem to follow what's going on in government and public affairs most of the time, whether there's an election or not. Others aren't that interested. Would you say you follow what's going on in government and public affairs…"

7
Blog Use Motivations: An Exploratory Study

BARBARA K. KAYE

Introduction

In the 1990s, uses and gratifications researchers began looking beyond traditional media to the Internet. Early examination concentrated on the Internet as a whole, but later, specific components such as the web, e-mail, bulletin boards and chat rooms were investigated. While there are many studies that have examined Internet users and uses (Charney & Greenberg, 2001; Eighmey, 1997; Ferguson & Perse, 2000; Johnson & Kaye, 2003a; Kaye, 1998; Kaye & Johnson, 2004; Lin, 2002; Papacharissi & Rubin, 2000), there is a dearth of academic research about why blog users use blogs. The few explanations of blog use available are generally based on casual observation and conversation among blog users, journalists and bloggers (Ashdown, 2003; Frauenfelder & Kelly, 2000; Kurtz, 2002; Leo, 2002; Morris, 2001; Rosenberg, 2002).

Blogs can be thought of as a gateway to vast sources of information and users may but are not required to respond to a blogger by sending comments and links to additional information; therefore, blog use gratifies many needs. The uses and gratifications approach is thus ideal for uncovering those needs.

Uses and gratifications studies of the Internet often employ preexisting scales of media use (Eighmey, 1997; Kang & Atkin, 1999; Kaye, 1998, 2005; Kippax & Murray, 1980; Lin, 2002: Perse & Dunn, 1998; Rubin & Rubin, 1982; Rubin & Step, 2000; Vincent & Basil, 1997). Although these scales have been found reliable and valid (Ruggiero, 2000), some researchers have found it necessary to employ open-ended responses to develop a motivational scale relevant to a particular medium or technology (Bellamy & Walker, 1990; Charney & Greenberg, 2001; Donohew, Palmgreen & Rayburn, 1987; James, Wotring & Forrest, 1995; Palmgreen, Cook, Harvill & Helm, 1988; Rubin & Bantz, 1989). Moreover, open-ended responses have often revealed motivations specific to a medium or technology that may not have been uncovered by adapting preexisting scales (Bellamy & Walker; Charney & Greenberg; James et al.).

This is one of few academic studies to focus on blog users defined as Internet users who access a blog. Rather than relying on preexisting scales, this study's motivational items are derived from open-ended responses from blog users who filled out an online survey. This is an exploratory, descriptive study that uncovers unique motivations for accessing blogs.

Why Study Blog Users?

For the most part, blogs were an obscure part of cyberspace until the 2001 terrorist attacks on the United States initiated a spike in the number of blogs and blog readers, who discovered these sites as a way to share their grief and get firsthand accounts of the events of the day (Jesdanun, 2001). Since then, blogs have become powerful voices for and against media and government and many other causes and issues.

In 1999 the 50 or so existing blogs were just a blip in cyberspace, but by the end of 2004 an estimated 8 million individuals had created a blog or web-based diary (Rainie, 2005). By early 2005, about 27% (32 million) of all Internet users accessed blogs and 12% had posted comments or links on these sites (Rainie, 2005; "The State of the News Media," 2005). Additionally, several studies report that blog users are young, well-educated, high-income males who are Internet veterans (Greenspan, 2003; Rainie, Fox & Fallows, 2003). More recent data, however, indicate that usage by women, minorities and individuals between 30 and 49 years of age is experiencing "greater than average growth" (Rainie, 2005).

But perhaps what sets blogs apart from other Internet resources is their growing power to mobilize citizens behind a cause and to bring about social and political change. Blog users rally around bloggers as self-styled watchdogs of the government and media. The extent of bloggers' power became apparent in late 2002, when traditional journalists overlooked Senate Majority Leader Trent Lott's assertion that the United States would be better off today if former Senator Strom Thurmond had won his 1948 segregationist bid for president. Bloggers led the outcry against Lott that eventually resulted in his resignation (Glaser, 2002; Ryan, 2003; Yousefzadeh, 2003). A subsequent headline on *Online Journalism Review* coined a term to describe the chain of events that led to Lott's downfall when it declared, "Trent Lott Gets Bloggered" (Glaser, 2002). Lott has not been the only public figure to get bloggered. Journalist Dan Rather resigned from CBS after bloggers claimed that documents used for a *60 Minutes II* segment asserting that President G. W. Bush got preferential treatment during his time with the Texas Air National Guard were fraudulent (Glaser, 2004; Kramer, 2004; Pein, 2005).

As blogs become more popular among the general population, their ability to bring about political and social change strengthens, bringing increased media attention and increased readership. But the question remains as to why Internet users are attracted to blogs.

Uses and Gratifications and the Internet

Uses and gratifications inquiry has been used for many years to gain an understanding of motivations for using media, and researchers advocated applying the approach to new communication technologies (Williams, Phillips & Lum, 1985) and specifically to the Internet (Morris & Ogan, 1996; Newhagen & Rafaeli, 1996). Over the last decade or so, Internet researchers have moved beyond simply examining online content and describing Internet users to explaining why users are attracted to the medium.

Uses and gratifications studies investigate how the audience uses the media rather than how the media use the audience (Blumler & Katz, 1974). Furthermore, the approach is based on the assumptions that individuals actively seek out media, media use is goal directed and media consumption satisfies a wide variety of needs. Uses and gratifications posits that individuals are aware of their reasons for using media and selecting specific content and that they use the media to gratify these needs (McLeod & Becker, 1981; Palmgreen, Wenner & Rosengren, 1985).

Some Internet studies have examined motivations for using the Internet as a whole; others have focused on the reasons for using the world wide web (Charney & Greenberg, 2001; Ferguson & Perse, 2000; Kang & Atkin, 1999; Kaye, 1998; Lin, 2002). As e-mail, bulletin boards and chat rooms became more popular, attention focused on why users turned to those interactive online resources (Fuentes, 2000; James et al., 1995; Kaye & Johnson, 2004; Papacharissi & Rubin, 2000).

The reasons for using a particular Internet resource vary according to how a resource functions and the types of interactions it allows. Although some webpages may contain interactive components, such as games or surveys, the web is largely a one-way source of information where a site creator posts information and the user is not expected to interact beyond accessing it. Most websites do not require user interaction or feedback to function.

On the other hand, on two-way sources, such as e-mail, bulletin boards, and chat rooms, users are expected to participate and interact with others for the resource to function as intended (Kaye & Johnson, 2004; Kaye & Medoff, 2001). These two-way sources are used for different purposes and serve needs different from those served by websites (James et al., 1995; Kaye & Johnson, 2004). Furthermore, asynchronous online resources, such as bulletin boards and electronic mailing lists, where users access and reply to messages at any time, satisfy needs different from synchronous modes of communication, such as chat rooms, where users "converse" in real time (Fuentes, 2000; James et al., 1995; Kaye & Johnson, 2004; Kaye & Medoff; Turkle, 1999).

Blogs are a combination website/bulletin board/e-mail and thus are used as one-way and two-way forms of communicating. Blog users may be as actively engaged as they wish. They may simply read what a blogger has posted, they may click on links, they may send the blogger their analyses and opinions along with links to additional information and they may engage in dialogue with the blogger and other blog readers. The amount of participation varies from session to session and blog to blog, but is determined by the user, not the technology. Because blogs are one- and two-way methods of communicating where users choose their level of participation, they may gratify entirely different needs from those met by than other Internet resources.

Motivations for Using the Internet and Blogs

Studies that have examined motivations for connecting to the Internet as a whole or to the world wide web specifically have found that individuals are motivated to connect online to satisfy entertainment, escape and social interaction needs and to pass the time (Charney & Greenberg, 2001; Eighmey, 1997; Ferguson & Perse, 2000; Kang & Atkin, 1999; Kaye, 1998; Korgaonkar & Wolin, 1999; Papacharissi & Rubin, 2000). Investigations of other Internet resources have found that electronic bulletin boards serve primarily information and socialization needs (James et al., 1995), political bulletin boards surveillance and curiosity (Garramone, Harris & Anderson, 1986) and entertainment/social utility needs (Kaye & Johnson, 2004). E-mail satisfies interpersonal needs (Stafford, Kline & Dimmick, 1999) and convenience (Papacharissi & Rubin, 2000), and chat rooms serve social contact (Fuentes, 2000), personal identity (Turkle, 1999) and guidance/information needs (Kaye & Johnson, 2004).

Research into the uses and users of blogs is scant. Casual observation by journalists yields several reasons why Internet users connect to blogs. Blogs seem to foster a sense of community, especially for those who think of themselves as online intellectuals who seek more in-depth analysis than what is available through traditional media and their online counterparts (Frauenfelder & Kelly, 2000; Wolcott, 2002). Moreover, blog content generally reflects the biases of the blogger, who tends to take one side of an issue, furthering a sense of belonging to a group of like-minded individuals (Levy, 2002a; Seipp, 2002; Rosenberg, 2002). Others offer convenience as a motivation for accessing blogs. Busy web users no longer need to click on many media sites and scan through a host of reports to find up-to-date news and information. Some blogs do the work for them by posting important items on one site (Blood, 2002; Hiler, 2000).

Information seeking is also commonly singled out as a reason for accessing blogs. Bloggers provide the latest news (some blogs are updated every 15 minutes) and analysis by experts and others with insider knowledge, some of which is glossed over or omitted by the traditional media (Hamilton, 2003; Hastings, 2003; Levy, 2002b; Palser, 2002; Ryan, 2003; Seipp, 2002). Blog users may also be attracted to blogs because bloggers tend to follow a story for a longer period of time than do the traditional media ("The State of the News

Media," 2005). Furthermore, one blog poll found that 60% of its readers log on every day ("Reader demographics," 2002), suggesting that blogs may be used out of habit.

While the uses and gratifications approach has been used to examine Internet uses and users, only one study could be found that specifically examined motivations for using blogs. Kaye (2005) analyzed 28 reasons for accessing blogs yielding six factors: Information Seeking/Media Check, Convenience, Personal Fulfillment, Political Surveillance, Social Surveillance and Expression/Affiliation. However, the motivational items were derived from previous studies (Johnson & Kaye, 2003a; Kaye, 1998; McLeod & Becker, 1974, 1981) and adapted to fit blog use, which may have missed many of the reasons why users access blogs.

Measuring Uses and Gratifications

Uses and gratifications studies of newer communication technologies often rely on preexisting scales that may or may not be adapted for the medium or technology under study (Eighmey, 1997; Kang & Atkin, 1999; Kaye, 1998; Kippax & Murray, 1980; Lin, 2002; Perse & Dunn, 1998; Rubin & Rubin, 1982; Rubin & Step, 2000; Vincent & Basil, 1997). For example, in their study of home computers, Perse and Dunn relied on motivation statements derived from examinations of television viewing. When Kaye investigated reasons for using the Internet, she adapted items constructed by Rubin (1981, 1983) for examining television-viewing motives. Other Internet uses and gratifications studies (Johnson & Kaye, 2003a, 2003b; Kaye & Johnson, 2002, 2004; Lin, 2002; Papacharissi & Rubin, 2000) combined motivation items from several sources and adapted them for the Internet, and Kaye and Johnson (2004) modified Internet motivation items for bulletin boards and chat rooms.

Other research studies assessed uses and gratifications through audience interviews (Donohew et al., 1987; Palmgreen et al., 1988; Rubin & Bantz, 1989; Stafford et al., 1999), a combination of interviews and items from existing uses and gratifications studies (Korgaonkar & Wolin, 1999) and interviews along with personal diaries and preexisting items (Massey, 1995). Some have used items derived from open-ended questions (Bellamy & Walker, 1990; Charney & Greenberg, 2001; Dimmick, Kline & Stafford; 2000; Garramone et al., 1986; James et al., 1995).

Open-ended questions may yield unique motivations that are tied to a particular medium. Although Charney and Greenberg's (2001) open-ended responses yielded some of the same motivations for using the Internet as were found in other studies of media use, they did identify several unique dimensions: aesthetic, fame, identity, future and peer pressure.

In their survey of electronic bulletin board users, James et al. (1995) employed open-ended questions to determine user preferences and behaviors. The researchers found five major categories of use, including "communication medium appeal" and "socializing," which were linked to the special quality of bulletin boards. Furthermore, they consider their work a benchmark for future analysis of bulletin boards. When Bellamy and Walker (1990) developed 12 gratification categories based on a prior survey that assessed motivations for using remote control devices (RCDs) through open-ended questions, selective avoidance emerged as a distinct motivation for using an RCD.

Using interviews and open-ended questions to develop survey items to assess motivations is crucial when working with a new technology or medium. Palmgreen et al. (1988) employed open-ended interviews to counter what they reported as weaknesses in uses and gratifications studies that used closed-ended scales that were not developed from qualitative examinations. Charney and Greenberg employed open-ended questions "so not to…influence the manner in which respondents thought about the subject of study" (2001, p. 384). Donohew et al. (1987) and Rubin and Bantz (1989) found their approach of developing a gratifications instrument from prior interviews necessary when no established scale for a medium exists.

Most scales developed to measure uses and gratifications have been found reliable and valid, and adaptable to various media and technologies. Although these scales should continue to be used and adapted (Ruggiero, 2000), further inquiry is needed to move toward a robust understanding of how consumers use new communication technologies and Internet resources such as blogs.

Research Question

Kaye and Johnson (Kaye, 2005) adapted 28 items used in prior Internet uses and gratifications studies to examine blog use. Although Kaye's factor analysis yielded six primary motivations, this study sets out to examine reasons for using blogs through open-ended inquiry to uncover additional motivations that may not be included on preexisting scales: RQ1: What are the primary reasons that blog users say they use blogs?

Method

A survey that specifically targeted blog users was posted online for one month in the spring of 2003. To reach the convenience sample, requests for announcements about the survey and a link to the survey URL were sent to a random selection of 239 bloggers identified by the author through Yahoo! and Google searches. The survey was linked from 131 blogs of diverse ideologies[1] and 14 blog-oriented bulletin boards/electronic mailing lists.[2] Additionally, a "snowball" technique was used that allowed respondents to forward the survey automatically to fellow blog readers (Babbie, 2001).

Blog Use Motivations

Motivations for using blogs were assessed with an open-ended question that asked respondents to list their reasons for connecting to blogs. Each respondent could list up to three separate reasons for blog use.

Coding Procedures

Using a procedure similar to one employed by James et al. (1995) in their pilot study of uses of bulletin boards, motivations for using blogs were coded and categorized. Using a multistep approach, the author first read and categorized each response. Responses were categorized based on the words and phrases used by each respondent to describe his or her reasons for accessing blogs. As with James et al., a unit of analysis "could be any grouping of words that express a meaning, and sometimes consisted of one word, but consisted of several sentences at other times" (p. 36).

Rather than fitting the responses into previously developed categories, the list of motivations was developed by grouping like responses together and then labeling each grouping as a motivational item. For example, "blogs are funny" and "I enjoy the humor on blogs" were counted as part of the humor/ mirth/absurdity motivational item. In cases where a response contained more than one reason, such as "I read blogs because they're funny, interesting, and I like the good writing," the response was coded as three separate motivations.

After each response was coded as a motivational item, the items were then grouped into broader motivational blocks. The items were grouped into the blocks based on similar meanings. For example, Anti-Traditional-Media Sentiment consists of five motivational items that all suggest that users are drawn to blogs because of some unfavorable characteristic of traditional media. The author repeated the process three times, further grouping and categorizing the responses.

Next, two assistant researchers followed the same protocol of categorizing the responses. As with Garramone et al. (1986), intercoder reliability was determined by calculating the simple percentage of agreement between each of the coders and the author. Intercoder agreement for the major motivational categories was 86.1% with the first coder and 92.5% with the second.

Results

The primary focus of this paper examines the reasons blog users say they use blogs. Overall, 3,747[3] respondents[4] filled out an online questionnaire that assessed blog use. Of the total number of respondents, 2,397 (63.9%) responded to an open-ended question that asked them their reasons for accessing blogs. This chapter presents the responses to that open-ended question. Many of the 2,397 respondents offered multiple reasons for accessing blogs; thus, 4,880 responses were gathered yielding 62 motivational items (Table 7.1).

Table 7.1 Motivations for Using Blogs

Count/Percentage	Motivation
821/16.8%	**Blog presentation/characteristics**
215	For links to more information/sources[a]
139	Depth of information/issues/viewpoints/coverage[a]
138	Commentary, insight, analysis about news[a]
118	For up-to-date information/immediate/timely/scoop others[a]
67	Nontraditional/different/unedited/unfiltered independence/no gatekeeping/censorship[a]
55	Admitted bias[a]
38	For unbiased viewpoints/fair/balanced presentation/both sides of an issue
34	Blogs are truthful/candor of opinion/credible[a]
17	Bloggers keep a story going[a]
788/16.1%	**Personal fulfillment**
366	Blogs are entertaining/fun/enjoy/exciting
187	Humor/mirth/absurdity/amusing[a]
90	Blogs are interesting[a]
56	Boredom/diversion/escape[a]
36	Curiosity/because they're new/novelty/voyeurism[a]
24	Addiction/news junkie/habit[a]
22	To be part of history/change in communication[a]
7	Because it helps me relax
745/15.3%	**Expression/affiliation with bloggers and blog users**
135	Communicating with friends who have blogs[a]
113	Interact with people/access news from around the world[a]
107	A personal accounting of information/human touch/blogger personality[a]
92	Sense of community/networking/social connection/sex/friendship
82	Follow and participate in dialogue between blogger and readers/interactivity[a]
80	To access a specific blog/blogger[a]
65	Contact with like-minded people
36	For personal information about others/gossip/human interest[a]
22	To express my opinions
8	For activism/grassroots/advocacy[a]
5	To find out about issues affecting people like myself[a]

Table 7.1 Motivations for Using Blogs (continued)

Count/Percentage	Motivation
720/14.7%	**Information seeking**
276	For specific information of interest
143	Wide variety of information/topics[a]
84	For scientific/technical information[a]
81	To keep up with the issues of the day/current events/general information
49	Research/work/school[a]
45	For information for my own blog[a]
29	Keep up with social issues/trends[a]
13	For accurate accounts of news and events[a]
497/10.2%	**Intellectual/aesthetic fulfillment**
162	Because of the good writing/writers[a]
160	Enlightening/to learn something new[a]
149	Intellectual discourse/debate/arguments/critical thinking skills[a]
26	Access to expert opinion/knowledge[a]
402/8.2%	**Anti-traditional-media sentiment**
243	For information I can't get from traditional media[a]
46	Avoid liberal media bias[a]
41	Lack of objectivity (nonspecified bias) of traditional media[a]
40	As an alternative to traditional media[a]
32	Don't trust/like traditional media[a]
375/7.8%	**Guidance/opinion seeking**
267	To get a wide variety of opinions
62	To see what the other side thinks
24	Make up my mind about important issues
22	For support for my opinions/validation/compare my opinions to others[a]

Table 7.1 Motivations for Using Blogs (continued)

Count/Percentage	Motivation
252/5.2%	**Convenience**
102	Filtering mechanism, blogger posts what's important, saves me time in looking[a]
69	Information is easy to obtain/convenient
58	Can get information quickly/fast
7	Free and less expensive than buying magazines/newspapers[a]
10	To access information at any time
3	To access information from work
3	Information can be copied and archived[a]
168/3.4%	**Political surveillance**
127	To keep up with politics/political issues
27	For specific political perspectives (i.e., conservative, libertarian, liberal)[a]
10	To keep up with election news[a]
4	To see how politicians stand on various issues
112/2.3%	**Fact checking**
72	To check on accuracy/verify/compare accounts of traditional media and bloggers
40	To expose others for wrong info/bias/fisking[a]

[a] Unique items revealed by open-ended responses in this study (not found by Kaye, 2005.)

Blog Use Motivational Blocks

For a better understanding of reasons for accessing blogs, the 62 motivational items were then grouped into 10 broader motivational blocks: Blog Presentation/Characteristics, Personal Fulfillment, Expression/Affiliation With Bloggers and Blog Users, Information Seeking, Intellectual/Aesthetic Fulfillment, Anti-Traditional-Media Sentiment, Guidance/Opinion Seeking, Convenience, Political Surveillance, and Fact Checking (Table 7.1).

Blog Presentation/Characteristics　These reasons for accessing blogs are specific to the nature of blogs. Users perceive blogs as having particular characteristics that cannot be found elsewhere or fulfilled by traditional media. Users view blogs as a refreshing alternative to other sources and as a place where information is presented in a way that is unique to blogs. For instance, readers are motivated to connect to blogs for the depth of information, for up-to-the-minute news, for commentary and analysis, for unfiltered information and to track a story over time. When commenting on how bloggers keep up with a story, one respondent said that blogs are "like reading an ongoing novel." Another respondent was drawn to blogs for the "most insightful analysis of important issues." Although some blog users claim that blogs are unbiased, others hail bloggers for revealing their biases. Readers appreciate accessing news that is not subject to traditional media gatekeeping and homogenizing. One respondent commented that, in general, "the disintermediation of the communication process creates opportunities for a wide variety of views."

Another blog characteristic that draws readers is the ability to link quickly to other sources. Blog users appreciate being able to "follow a thread through links to different blogs" and "link to news sites I would never go to." Links to other sources serve the purpose of "leading me to read more about a subject." Among the individual reasons that make up this motivational block, all but one—"for unbiased information"—emerged from the open-ended responses and were not found by Kaye (2005) (Table 7.1).

Personal Fulfillment Respondents are attracted to blogs for personal fulfillment reasons. Users find blogs entertaining, fun, relaxing and interesting. Blogs are also a novelty and offer an escape from boredom and work. Blogs fulfill an addiction to news and make users feel like they are part of history and a new way of communicating. One respondent turns to blogs because "I enjoy watching this form of communication develop" and another because "there is an almost voyeurism quality to reading blogs." The second most common personal fulfillment reason for accessing blogs is because they are humorous. When referring to a particular blogger, one respondent exclaimed, "Mean Mr. Mustard makes me fall out of my chair laughing." While most of the personal fulfillment items are similar to those found in other blog and Internet uses and gratifications studies, "to be part of history" and "for humor" are unique motivations that arose from the open-ended responses and were not found in other Internet uses and gratifications studies (Table 7.1).

Expression/Affiliation With Bloggers and Blog Users Blogs satisfy a need for affiliating with others and with specific bloggers. Users enjoy a blogger's personal touch and the way in which a blogger brings together like-minded people. Users express their opinions and read the opinions of others, keep up with social trends, network, develop a sense of community, make friends, mobilize behind a cause, find out about issues that affect people like them and keep in touch with their friends and family members who have blogs. One respondent exclaimed, "It's like being at a party with a bunch of intelligent, funny people." Others go on blogs to "find people who think like I do," to "promote my personal point of view" and to "ramble about anything and everything." Blogs also provide a means for users to participate as much as they choose; they can send in comments and links or they can simply read what others say. Users enjoy the "feedback loop in which the audience can immediately respond" and think of blogs as "the cyberspace version of the soapbox." One respondent commented that the "best part is that they're interactive." Expression/Affiliation goes beyond contacting like-minded people and expressing opinions, as found by Kaye (2005), and includes affinity with a particular blogger and following and participating in blogger/user dialogue (Table 7.1).

Information Seeking   Users look to blogs to access a wide variety of information for school or work, for their own blog, for personal reasons and to keep up with the issues of the day. This category is considered a more purposive activity where users look to blogs for specific information. Users turn to blogs for "availability and wide range of information." They also look for "information specific to my job," "to keep up with science and technology" and "to get information of special interest." Some of the respondents are motivated to access blogs as "fodder for my own blog" (Table 7.1).

Intellectual/Aesthetic Fulfillment   Users turn to blogs to learn something new, for intellectual discourse and debate, to sharpen their critical thinking skills, to learn from experts and because they are drawn to good writing. In general, blogs seem to gratify a need for intellectual stimulation. Individuals are motivated to connect to blogs for "the joy of encountering literacy," for "the great writing—some of the prose is just breathtaking," for "logical and intelligent handling of world affairs" and because "it sucks to be stupid—bloggers cure that." Others appreciate that blogs give them the opportunity to "learn something new," "expand my knowledge/horizons" and "exercise my own brain." This motivational block is unique to blogs and was revealed by this study's open-ended format (Table 7.1).

Anti-Traditional-Media Sentiment   Respondents are drawn to blogs because they do not like or trust the traditional media, which they consider biased to the right or to the left. Many respondents use blogs as an alternative to traditional media, but for others blogs supplement traditional media use. Overwhelmingly, respondents rely on these sites for "access to a broader spectrum of news than is available through traditional media outlets." Others turn to blogs because they "distrust and have disdain for traditional media" and are "sick of the mindless tripe." Others "loathe the left bias of traditional media," and some are escaping "Republican controlled corporate media lies." Another said, "Traditional newspapers and the three commercial networks are extremely slanted in coverage—I want news, not propaganda." Although Kaye (2005) included "for information not found in traditional media" as a reason for accessing blogs, this study found that blog users not only seek information they believe traditional media is withholding but also harbor negative attitudes towards the media, which may be what draws them to blogs (Table 7.1).

Guidance/Opinion Seeking   Respondents rely on blogs for support and validation of their opinions and to help them make up their minds about important issues. Blogs also afford users a way to access a wide variety of opinions and to see what the other side thinks. Mostly users are motivated to link to blogs for the "wide variety of opinions," the "numerous perspectives on issues" and for "keeping an eye on the enemy." Others look for guidance and "to help me sort out what I think about things" (Table 7.1).

Convenience   Blog users connect to blogs because they are easy to use, they can quickly access information and they can access information from almost anywhere. Respondents also mentioned that blogs are less expensive than buying a newspaper and that the information can be easily copied and archived. The open-ended responses also revealed that convenience means more than simply obtaining information quickly and easily as reported in other Internet studies. It also includes relying on bloggers to post important information. Bloggers save users time by gathering the important news of the day so that users need not spend time scanning through several sites. As one respondent said, "Blogs are like my own private news clipping service" (Table 7.1).

Political Surveillance   Blogs tend to fulfill the need for political surveillance and they specifically give users a way to track politicians and keep up with elections and political issues. Blogs also fulfill the need to connect to specific political perspectives, whether conservative, liberal, libertarian or other. One reader uses blogs to "follow day-to-day politics" and another to "keep up with politicians' doings." Blog readers trust blogs to tell them "what the government is really doing" (Table 7.1).

Fact Checking   Blogs gratify users' needs to quickly verify and compare accounts of news and information and check the accuracy of traditional media. Fact checking also involves "fisking," which is a point-by-point sarcastic and cutting refutation of a blog entry or news article. Fisking is so called for British journalist Robert Fisk, who was an early target of bloggers ("Blog Glossary," 2005); users are attracted to the process of fisking and eagerly follow the downfall of a public official or journalist. Several readers gleefully pointed out, "I love it when idiotarians get fisked," "I like the fisking of pompous/bias media people and hypocritical politicians" and "I thoroughly enjoyed watching Howell Raines squirming like a bug under the bloggers' scrutiny." Other reasons for accessing blogs range from "to insult stupid people and see their mistakes" and to go to sites that "dissect the misrepresentations of traditional media." Although Kaye (2005) included "to check the accuracy of media" and "to compare online accounts to traditional media" as motivational items, fisking was not included as a possible choice (Table 7.1).

Discussion

While the Internet has been studied extensively, the newest online resource, the blog, has received much less scholarly attention. Blogs are primarily the subject of journalistic reports that tend to focus on bloggers rather than on those who use blogs (Ashdown, 2003; Frauenfelder & Kelly, 2000; Kurtz, 2002; Leo, 2002; Morris, 2001; Rosenberg, 2002).

Many Internet uses and gratifications studies relied on preexisting motivational scales that were usually adapted to the Internet component under study (Eighmey, 1997; Johnson & Kaye, 2003a; Kang & Atkin, 1999; Kaye, 1998, 2005; Kaye & Johnson, 2002, 2004; Kippax & Murray, 1980; Lin, 2002; Perse & Dunn, 1998; Rubin & Rubin, 1982; Rubin & Step, 2000; Vincent & Basil, 1997). Other researchers, however, found it more appropriate to use open-ended responses to develop a motivational scale relevant to a particular medium or technology (Bellamy & Walker, 1990; Charney & Greenberg, 2001; Donohew et al., 1987; James et al., 1995; Palmgreen et al., 1988; Rubin & Bantz, 1989).

The purpose of this study was to examine open-ended responses to learn why blog users use blogs and to develop a scale for future quantitative analysis to test the motivations and broader motivational blocks to further understand what draws individuals to use blogs. The open-ended responses were gathered from a survey targeted to blog users and posted online for one month in the spring of 2003.

An open-ended question asked respondents to offer their reasons for connecting to blogs. A total of 62 unique reasons were culled out of a list of 4,880 responses given by 2,397 respondents. These reasons were then categorized into 10 broader motivational blocks: Blog Presentation/Characteristics, Personal Fulfillment, Expression/Affiliation With Bloggers and Blog Users, Information Seeking, Intellectual/Aesthetic Fulfillment, Anti-Traditional-Media Sentiment, Guidance/Opinion Seeking, Convenience, Political Surveillance and Fact Checking.

Although some of the blocks revealed by this study's open ended responses are similar to those found by Kaye (2005) in her study of blogs—Information Seeking/Media Check, Convenience, Personal Fulfillment, Political Surveillance, Social Surveillance and Expression/Affiliation—this study adds four motivational blocks not captured by Kaye, and 43 new motivational items not included in her original list of 28. Additionally, Kaye presented respondents with four reasons adapted from preexisting Internet use scales for accessing blogs that were not mentioned once by any of this study's respondents.

This study contributes to the understanding of the motivations for using blogs by uncovering the following four unique motivational blocks not found in other blog or Internet studies: Blog Presentation/Characteristics, Intellectual/Aesthetic Fulfillment, Anti-Traditional-Media Sentiment and Fact Checking.

This study found that blog users are primarily attracted to blogs because of the unique characteristics of blogs. Users perceive that bloggers present information in ways that cannot be found elsewhere. For example, users like blogs because bloggers keep a story going, they admit their bias up front, they out-scoop traditional media, they provide links to other sources, they provide in-depth and insightful commentary and analysis perceived to be absent from other media and they are not filtered or censored by traditional media gatekeepers.

This study also revealed that many respondents read blogs simply because they do not like or trust traditional media outlets. They do not totally shun traditional media, but rather, they are tired of what they perceive as biased, shallow news. They use blogs as an alternative to traditional media because they feel blogs print what the media omit or gloss over, but yet they cast a critical eye to what the media do report.

Furthermore, although Kaye (2005) listed "check the accuracy of media" and "to compare online accounts to traditional media" as motivational items, this study's open-ended responses found that fact checking contains the element of fisking. Respondents enjoy exposing others for wrong information, for biases and for illogical and inconsistent stances, and they like to make fun of others' opinions and attitudes.

These findings could signify that blog users find blogs useful precisely because they perceive them to have escaped the traditional media infrastructure. While they consider traditional media as adopting an objective posture, blog users celebrate the flexibility of the web and the immediacy with which bloggers can respond to breaking news. They perceive blogs as going behind the veneer of what the traditional media present— the backstory behind the story. Blog users are drawn to blogs not only because of the nature of the blog but also because of their sense of alienation from traditional media and their biases.

According to a 2002 poll conducted by the Pew Research Center, 59% of respondents believed that the traditional media are biased ("News Media's Improved Image," 2002). The respondents of this study mentioned that they consider blogs as an alternative to traditional media because of liberal and conservative biases. Perhaps it is not the particular slant, but rather the perception of a hidden slant that alienates consumers of news and information from traditional media. Blogs provide an outlet that is not associated with traditional journalism or media systems and does not conceal itself behind the guise of objectivity.

In addition to expanding the uses and gratifications framework, these findings could have implications for media substitution theory. Research suggests that when a new technology or medium, such as the computer and Internet, is introduced, individuals reallocate time previously spent with other media and establish new patterns of media use. Moreover, because people have a finite amount of time to devote to the media, when a new technology is viewed as more desirable they will reduce time spent with the older medium (Dimmick et al., 2000; Kang & Atkin, 1999; Lin, 2001a, 2001b; Vitalari, Venkatesh & Gronhaug, 1985).

The reasons blog users gave for using blogs could indicate that weblogs supplement rather than replace traditional media because blogs act as a foil (Gieryn, 1983) for traditional media. In other words, blogs are defined to a large extent by what they are not: traditional media. Traditional media provide the fodder with which blogs can take issue; thus, their content is perceived to be a commentary and a counterpoint to traditional media.

Using blogs for fisking perhaps best illustrates this point. If not for traditional media, there would be no axe to grind; therefore, fisking emerges as a reason for using blogs. By its nature fisking requires another medium whose content can be challenged and errors exposed—gleefully so because of the antagonistic attitudes towards it. Previous studies of media use derived from the very media that blogs challenge cannot possibly discern this uniquely adversarial aspect of blog use. Therefore, the use of preexisting scales to examine uses and gratifications of blogs would consistently miss what could be the essence of blog use.

Another motivational block that did not in emerge in Kaye (2005) is Intellectual Stimulation/Aesthetic Fulfillment. Blog users assert that they are eager to learn new information, that they want to be enlightened and hone their critical thinking skills and that they appreciate intelligent discourse and arguments. Unique to blogs, users say they enjoy reading blog material simply because of the excellent writing.

Information seeking is a commonly cited motive for radio, television and Internet use (Eighmey, 1997; Kaye & Johnson, 2002, 2004; Lin, 2002; Papacharissi & Rubin, 2000; Rubin, 1981, 1983) and was also indicated by this study's respondents. More important perhaps, the open-ended responses to this study revealed that blog users desire to learn about themselves rather than just about the external world. The notion that blog users are using information for its own sake is too limiting. Open-ended responses indicate that information seeking may be a more complex activity than previous uses and gratifications studies would suggest. The characteristics specific to blog use cannot be discerned easily by means of categories developed for studying other media. Therefore, it is doubtful that using preexisting scales of media and Internet use would reveal such motivations as "to learn about myself," "to access the excellent writing" and "to develop my own critical thinking skills" that are part of the Intellectual Stimulation/Aesthetic Fulfillment motivational block.

This study reinforces journalistic observations that found that blogs are popular because they provide a sense of community with like-minded people (Frauenfelder & Kelly, 2000; Levy, 2000a; Seipp, 2002; Rosenberg, 2002; Wolcott, 2002). Blog users like it when bloggers follow a story for a longer period of time than do the traditional media ("The State of the News Media," 2005) and when bloggers post the important news of the day (Blood, 2002; Hiler, 2000).

Also, as observed by journalists (Blood, 2002; Hiler, 2000) and found by Kaye (2005), blog users are motivated to seek out blogs for convenience and ease of use; they like to keep up with the issues of the day and they enjoy expressing their opinions.

This study also found that respondents are attracted to blogs for many of the same reasons as other Internet resources. Blogs fulfill entertainment, escape, relaxation and social interaction needs as does the Internet in general and the web specifically (Charney & Greenberg, 2001; Eighmey, 1997; Ferguson & Perse, 2000; Kang & Atkin, 1999; Kaye, 1998; Korgaonkar & Wolin, 1999; Papacharissi & Rubin, 2000). Additionally, blogs serve needs similar to those of bulletin boards, e-mail and chat rooms, which gratify information, social interaction, convenience and guidance needs (Fuentes, 2000; Garramone et al., 1986; James et al., 1995; Kaye & Johnson, 2004; Papacharissi & Rubin, 2000; Stafford et al., 1999; Turkle, 1999).

Limitations

This study is a qualitative examination of the reasons why blog users say they use blogs. The research method poses several limitations. First, the convenience sample limits the ability to generalize results. Even though respondents were solicited from a wide range of blogs, they were not randomly selected. Attempting to generate a random sample of blog users in 2003, a time when only a small percentage of Internet users were connecting to blogs, would yield a very high nonresponse rate due to nonqualification. Therefore, online postings of the survey URL and announcements were used.

This method follows the procedures used by others (Johnson & Kaye, 2003a, 2003b; Kaye & Johnson, 1999; Witte, Amoroso & Howard, 2000; Witte & Howard, 2002) and, though not ideal, such nonprobability sampling is an acceptable method when random sampling is not possible (Babbie, 1990). Although the results of this study are limited to a self-selected group of blog users, its demographic characteristics closely mirror those found by others at the time of data collection (Greenspan, 2003; Levy, 2002a; Rainie et al., 2003; Seipp, 2002).

Additionally, the construction of the motivational categories was subjective. Using open-ended responses, the author grouped like constructs into motivational blocks. Although intercoder agreement was 86.1 and 92.5%, the blocks cannot be tested for reliability. Additionally, the open-ended, fill-in-the-blank procedure does not allow for in-depth discussion, as do interviews, where the researcher can probe for deeper meaning and respondents can further explore their motivations for using blogs. That said, the purpose of this chapter is not to deliver a definitive list of blog use motivations or to test the findings statistically, but rather to offer a large number of reasons given by respondents as a benchmark for future studies. Rather than relying on motivations from preexisting scales that measure traditional media or Internet use that need to be adapted for blogs, researchers can begin further investigations using the list of 62 motivational items derived from the open-ended responses of this study.

Future Research

Continued examination into the uses and gratifications of blogs is necessary to understand the Internet and how its different components affect media consumption.

Future research could assess uses and gratifications through developing a scale where respondents mark their level of agreement with the 62 motivational items found in this study. Frequencies and mean scores could be calculated and a factor analysis and reliability testing could confirm strength of the motivational blocks and validity of the measures. Perhaps as more Internet users discover blogs, researchers could design a random sampling method where blog users could be identified and then solicited to complete a survey. Additionally, future research should examine the influence of activity on uses of blogs. Further research should address whether motivations for using blogs are content driven and dependent on larger social issues and current events.

In recent years, blogs have emerged as very important and influential forums for news and information. As they become more popular and as their power increases, it is likely that blogs may one day be as relied upon as the traditional media are today. Follow-up studies are crucial not only to assess the nature of blogs, but also to understand how they are used and what motivates individuals to connect to these sites.

References

Ashdown, P. (2003). *Letter from America: The online soapbox as a forum for public intellectuals.* Paper presented at the International American Studies Association, First World Congress. University of Leiden, the Netherlands, May 22.

Babbie. E. (1990). *Survey research methods.* Belmont: Wadsworth.

Babbie. E. (2001). *The basics of social research.* Belmont: Wadsworth.

Bellamy, R. V. & Walker, J. R. (1990). The use of television remote control devices: A transactional study. *News Computing Journal*, 6(1), 1–18.

Blog Glossary. (2005). *Samizdata.com.* Retrieved March 29, 2005, from http://www.samizdata.net/blog/glossary_archives/001961.html.

Blood, R. (2002). Weblogs: A history and perspective. In J. Rodzvilla (Ed.), *We've got blog* (pp. 7–16). Cambridge, MA: Perseus Publishing.

Blumler, J. G., & Katz, E. (1974). *The uses of mass communications: Current perspectives on gratifications research.* Beverly Hills, CA: Sage Publications.

Charney, T., & Greenberg, B. S. (2001). Uses and gratifications of the Internet. In C. A. Lin & D. J. Atkin (Eds.), *Communication technology and society: Audience adoption and uses of the new media* (pp. 379–407). Cresskill, NJ: Hampton.

Dimmick, J., Kline, S. & Stafford, L. (2000). The gratification niches of personal e-mail and the telephone. *Communication Research*, 27(2), 227–248.

Donohew, L., Palmgreen, P. & Rayburn, J. D., II. (1987). Social and psychological origins of media use: A lifestyle analysis. *Journal of Broadcasting and Electronic Media*, 31(3), 255–278.

Eighmey, J. (1997, June). Profiling user responses to commercial Web sites. *Journal of Advertising Research*, 37, 59–66.

Ferguson, D. A., & Perse, E. M. (2000). The World Wide Web as a functional alternative to television. *Journal of Broadcasting & Electronic Media, 44*, 155–174.

Frauenfelder, M., & Kelly, K. (2000). Blogging. *Whole Earth. Winter*, 52–54.

Fuentes, A. (2000, June). Won't you be my neighbor? *American Demographics, 22*, 60–62.

Garramone, G., Harris, A. & Anderson, R. (1986). Uses of political bulletin boards. *Journal of Broadcasting & Electronic Media, 30*, 325–339.

Gieryn, T. F. (1983). Boundary work and the demarcation of science from nonscience: Strains and interests in professional ideologies of scientists. *American Sociological Review, 48*, 781–795 .

Glaser, M. (2002, December 17). Trent Lott gets bloggered. *Online Journalism Review.* Retrieved February 17, 2005, from http://www.ojr.org/ojr/glaser/1040145065.php.

Glaser, M. (2004, December 21). Bloggers, citizen media and Rather's fall—Little people rise up in 2004. *Online Journalism Review.* Retrieved February 17, 2005, from http://www.ojr.org/ojr/stories/041221Glaser/index.cfm.

Greenspan, R. (2003). Blogging by the numbers. *CyberAtlas.* Retrieved July 24, 2003, from http://internetnews.com/stats/article/php/2238331.

Hamilton, A. (2003, April 7). Best of the war blogs, *Time, 161*, 91.

Hastings, M. (2003, April 7). Bloggers over Baghdad. *Newsweek, 141*, 48–49.

Hiler, J. (2000, October 31). Blogger's digest. *MicroContent News.* Retrieved June 8, 2003, from http://www.microcontentnews.com/articles/digests.htm.

James, M. L., Wotring, C. E. & Forrest, E. J. (1995). An exploratory study of the perceived benefits of electronic bulletin board use and the impact on other communication activities. *Journal of Broadcasting & Electronic Media, 39*, 30–50.

Jesdanun, A. (2001, October 14). In online logs, Web authors personalize attacks, retaliation. *The Florida Times-Union*, Retrieved June 24, 2003, from http://www.Jacksonville.com/tu-online/stories/101401/bus_7528493.html.

Johnson, T. J., & Kaye, B. K. (2003a). Around the World Wide Web in 80 ways: How motives for going online are linked to Internet activities among politically interested Internet users. *Social Science Computer Review, 21*(3), 304–325.

Johnson, T. J., & Kaye, B. K. (2003b, August). *The World Wide Web of sports: A path model examining how online gratifications and reliance predict credibility of online sports information.* Presented to the Association for Education in Journalism and Mass Communication, Kansas City, KS.

Kang, M., & Atkin, D. J. (1999). Exploring the role of media uses and gratifications in multimedia cable adoption. *Telematics and Informatics, 16*, 59–74.

Kaye, B. K. (1998). Uses and gratifications of the World Wide Web: From couch potato to Web potato. *New Jersey Journal of Communication, 6*, 21–40.

Kaye, B. K. (2005). It's a blog, blog, blog, blog world: Users and uses of Weblogs. *Atlantic Journal of Communication, 13*(2), 73–95.

Kaye, B. K., & Johnson, T. J. (1999). Taming the cyber frontier: Techniques for improving online surveys. *Social Science Computer Review, 17*(3), 323–337.

Kaye, B. K., & Johnson, T. J. (2002). Online and in the know: Uses and gratifications of the Web for political information. *Journal of Broadcasting and Electronic Media, 46*(1), 54–71.

Kaye, B. K., & Johnson, T. J. (2004). A Web for all reasons: Uses and gratifications of Internet resources for political information. *Telematics and Informatics, 21*(3), 197–223.

Kaye, B. K., & Medoff, N. J. (2001). *The World Wide Web: A mass communication perspective.* Mountain View, CA: Mayfield Publishing Company.

Kippax, S., & Murray, J. P. (1980). Using the mass media. *Communication Research, 7*(3), 335–360.

Korgaonkar, P. K., & Wolin, L. D. (1999). A multivariate analysis of Web usage. *Journal of Advertising Research, March/April*, 53–67.

Kramer, S. (2004, October 4). CBS scandal highlights tension between bloggers and news media. *Online Journalism Review.* Retrieved February 1, 2005, from http://www.ojr.org/ojr/workplace/1096589178.php.

Kurtz, H. (2002, July 31). How Weblogs keep the media honest. *Washington Post.* Retrieved June 8, 2003, from http://www.washingtonpost.com.

Leo, J. (2002, May 13). A blog's bark has a bite. *U.S. News & World Report*, 48.

Levy, M. R., & Windahl, S. (1985). The concept of audience activity. In K. E. Rosengren, L. A. Wenner & P. Palmgreen (Eds.), *Media gratifications research* (pp. 11–37). Beverly Hills, CA: Sage Publications.

Levy, S. (2002a, August 26). Living in the blogosphere. *Newsweek, 140,* 42–25.

Levy, S. (2002b, May 20). Will the blogs kill old media? *Newsweek, 139,* 52.

Lin, C. A. (2001a). Audience attributes, media supplementation, and likely online service adoption. *Mass Communication & Society, 4,* 19–38.

Lin, C. A. (2001b, August). *Online use activity and user gratification—Expectations.* Paper presented at the Association for Education in Journalism and Mass Communication, Washington, D.C.

Lin, C. A. (2002). Perceived gratifications of online media services among potential users. *Telematics and Informatics, 19,* 3–19.

Massey, K. B. (1995). Analyzing the uses and gratifications concept of audience activity with a qualitative approach: Media encounters during the 1989 Loma Prieta earthquake disaster. *Journal of Broadcasting & Electronic Media, 39*(3), 328–349.

McLeod, J. M., & Becker, L. B. (1974). Testing the validity of gratification measures through political effects analysis. In J. G. Blumler & E. Katz (Eds.), *The uses of mass communication: Current perspectives on gratifications research* (pp. 137–162). Beverly Hills, CA: Sage Publications.

McLeod, J. M., & Becker, L. B. (1981). The uses and gratifications approach. In D. D. Nimmo & K. R. Sanders (Eds.), *Handbook of political communication* (pp. 61–72). Beverly Hills, CA: Sage Publications.

Morris, H. J. (2001, January 15). Blogging burgeons as a form of web expression. *U.S. News & World Report,* 52.

Morris, M., & Ogan, C. L. (1996). The Internet as a mass medium. *Journal of Communication, 46*(1), 39–50.

Newhagen, J. E., & Rafaeli, S. (1996). Why communication researchers should study the Internet: A dialogue. *Journal of Communication, 46*(1), 4–13.

News media's improved image proves short-lived (2002, August 4). The Pew Research Center. Retrieved September 1, 2005, from http://people-press.org/reports/display.php3?ReportID=159http://www.cjr.org/issues/2005/1/pein-blog.asp.

Palmgreen, P., Cook, P. L., Harvill, J. G. & Helm, D. M. (1988). The motivational framework of moviegoing: Uses and avoidances of theatrical films. In B. A. Austin (Ed.), *Current research in film: Audiences, economics, and law* (pp. 1–23). Norwood, NJ: Ablex.

Palmgreen, P., Wenner, L. A. & Rosengren, K. E. (1985). Uses and gratifications research: The past ten years. In K. E. Rosengren, L. A. Wenner & P. Palmgreen (Eds.), *Media gratifications research* (pp. 11–37). Beverly Hills, CA: Sage Publications.

Palser, B. (2002). Journalistic blogging. *American Journalism Review, 24*(6), 58–59.

Papacharissi, Z., & Rubin, A. M. (2000). Predictors of Internet use. *Journal of Broadcasting & Electronic Media, 44,* 175–196.

Pein, C. (2005). Blog gate. *Columbia Journalism Review.* Retrieved February 18, 2005, from http://www.cjr.org/issues/2005/1/pein-blog.asp.

Perse, E. M., & Dunn, D. G. (1998). The utility of home computers and media use: Implications of multimedia and connectivity. *Journal of Broadcasting & Electronic Media, 42,* 435–456.

Rainie, L. (2005). The state of blogging. Pew Internet and American Life Project. Pew Research Center. Retrieved February 1, 2005, from http://www.pewinternet.org/.

Rainie, L., Fox, S. & Fallows, D. (2003). Pew Internet and American Life Project. Pew Research Center. Retrieved January 25, 2004, from http://www.pewinternet.org/.

Reader demographics. (2002, June 25). Andrewsullivan.com. Retrieved June 17, 2003, from http://www.andrewsullivan.com.

Rosenberg, S. (2002). Much ado about blogging. *Salon.* Retrieved February 13, 2003, from http://www.calon.com/tech/col/rose/2002/05/10/blogs.

Rubin, A. M. (1981). An examination of television viewing motives. *Communication Research, 8*(2), 141–165.

Rubin, A. M. (1983). Television uses and gratifications: The interactions of viewing patterns and motivations. *Journal of Broadcasting, 27*(1), 37–51.

Rubin, A. M., & Bantz, C. R. (1989). Uses and gratifications of videocassette recorders. In J. L. Salvaggio & J. Bryant (Eds.), *Media use in the information age: Emerging patterns of adoption and consumer use* (pp. 181–195). Hillsdale, NJ: Lawrence Erlbaum Associates.

Rubin, A. M., & Rubin, R. B. (1982). Older person's TV viewing patterns and motivations. *Communication Research, 9*(2), 287–313.

Rubin, A. M., & Step, M. M. (2000). Impact of motivation, attraction, and parasocial interaction on talk radio listening. *Journal of Broadcasting & Electronic Media, 44*(4), 635–654.

Ruggiero, T. E. (2000). Uses and gratifications theory in the 21st century. *Mass Communication & Society, 3*(1), 3–37.

Ryan, M. (2003, April 17). Blogs' rise stymies old media. *Chicago Tribune.* Retrieved April 17, 2003, from http://www.chicago.tribune.com.

Seipp, C. (2002). Online uprising. *American Journalism Review, 24*(5), 42.

Stafford, L., Kline, S. L. & Dimmick, J. (1999). Home e-mail: Relational maintenance and gratification opportunities. *Journal of Broadcasting & Electronic Media, 43*(4), 659–669.

The State of the News Media. (2005). An annual report on American journalism. Journalism. org. Retrieved March 15, 2005, from http://www.stateofthemedia.org/2005/narrative_ online_audience.asp?cat=3&media=3.

Turkle, S. (1999). Cyberspace and identity. *Contemporary Sociology, 28,* 643–648.

Vincent, R. C., & Basil, M. D. (1997). College students' news gratifications, media use, and current events knowledge. *Journal of Broadcasting & Electronic Media, 41*(3), 380–392.

Vitalari, N. P., Venkatesh, A. & Grohaug, K. (1985). Computing in the home: Shifts in the time allocation patterns of households. *Communications of the ACM, 28,* 512–522.

Williams, F., Phillips, A. F. & Lum, P. (1985). Gratifications associated with new communication technologies. In P. Palmgreen, L. A. Wenner, & K. E. Rosengren (Eds.), *Media gratifications research: Current perspectives* (pp. 241–252). Beverly Hills, CA: Sage Publications.

Witte, J., Amoroso, L. & Howard, P. E. N. (2000) Method and representation in Internet-based survey tools: Mobility, community, and cultural identity in Survey2000. *Social Science Computer Review, 18*(2), 179–195.

Witte, J., & Howard, P. E. N. (2002). The future of polling: Relational inference and the development of Internet survey instruments. In J. Manza, F. Lomax Cook & B. Page (Eds.), *Navigating public opinion: Polls, policy and the future of American democracy* (pp. 272–289). New York: Oxford University Press.

Wolcott, J. (2002, May). Blog nation. *Business2.com.* Retrieved February 13, 2003, from http://www.business2.com/articles/mag.

Yousefzadeh, P. (2003, February 7). Weasel words. *TechCentralStation.* Retrieved February 10, 2003, from http://www.techcentralstation.com/1051/.

Notes

1. Links to the survey were posted on the following blogs: 2020hindsight, Ackackackcom, Across Atlantic, Africapundit, Agonist, Alphecca, Altercation, Alternet, Amish Tech Support, Amishblogmo, AndrewOlmsted, AndrewSullivan, Apostablog, Atlanticblogcom, Atriosblogspotcom, Bag & Baggage, Balloon Juice, Baseball Musings, Behold, blogspot, Biasblogfodder, BlissfulKnowledge, Blogdex, Bloglogic, Blogosphere, Blogs Of War, Give Blogs4god, Blogtporg/K, Boingboingnet, BryonScott, Buck Stops Here, Cnn.com, Cold Fury, ComeOn, CoranteOnBlogging, Corantec, Corner On NRO, Counterrevolutionary, CraigsChamp, Crblogspot, Critical Mass, Cut On Bias, Daily Dish, Daily Pundit Daniel Drezner, Davespickscom, Daypopcom, Dead Parrot Society, Dean Esmay, Doc Searls, Docweblogs, DrudgeReport, Erablognet, Erin O'Connor, Ever Changing Select, Eyndenloo, Fark, Fat Guy, FreeRepublic, Geek-Chick, Glenn Reynolds, Goatsec, Greenfield, HanlonVision, Hierogrammate, HighClear, Hoder, HomelessGuy, Hoosier Review, HPANA, Hunnet, IdleType, Ihodercom, Instapundit, J.D. Lasica - New Media Musings, Jeff Cooper, Jessica'sWell, JoanneJacobs, JonahGoldberg, Josh Claybourne, Journalsp, Jsnotesblogs, Leftcoastblog, Leuschke, LGF, Light Of Reason, Like A Hooligan's, LA Livejournal, Lucianne, Matwyglesias.com, Mediaticblog, Melblogger, Metafilter, Metapop, Midwest Conservative, MouseMusings, MSNBC, National Review, Newsweek.com, No. 2. Pencil, Ogloboc, OnBias, Parduedur, Pattern Recognition, Popdex, Post-Atomic, Powerline, RachaelLucas, RealClearPolitics, Rebecca Blood, Resurrections, Ritingonwall, Rjwest. com, Sassafrass, Seaofkitt, Shellen.com, Silflay, Hraka, Slate, Slings and Arrows, SouthKnoxBubba, Suzanna Cornett, Tacitus, Tapped, Tim Blair, Uncorrelated.com, Unqualified Offering, Volokh Conspiracy, Warblogs, Winds Of Change, Zogbyblogspot.com.

2. Links to the survey were posted on the following bulletin boards/electronic mailing lists: Bloggingcommunity@Yahoo, Colorado Bloggers, Comp.Dcom.Telecom, Dfw-blogs, Lds-Poll@Yahoogroups.Com, Pinoybloggers, Salon Blogs Group, Telecomdigest, Theblosxom,Val-L, weblogdeveloperusergroup, weblogemailgroup, weblogusersgroup, Yahoogroups-Syndic8.

3. The survey's first question asked respondents to enter their e-mail addresses; 3,311 (88.4%) complied. The respondents' e-mail addresses together with their Internet Protocol (IP) addresses (programmed to appear on every completed survey) were used to delete duplicated surveys. Additionally, after a respondent sent the completed survey, a Web page would immediately appear thanking him or her for participating and verifying that the survey had been sent so that respondents would not retransmit the survey.

4. Respondents average 39 years of age, and just over three quarters (76.5%) are male. Almost nine out of ten (89.3%) are White, and just over one half (54.3%) earn between $25,001 and $65,000 per year. The respondents are a highly educated group with 92.6% reporting a college degree or higher. The demographic characteristics of the respondents closely mirrors that reported in other studies and through more casual observation at the time of data collection (Greenspan, R., 2003). *CyberAtlas,* retrieved July 24, 2003, from http://internetnews.com/stats/article/php/2238831; Levy, S. (2002, August 26). *Newsweek, 140,* 25–42; Rainie, L. et al. (2003). *Pew Internet and American Life Project.* Pew Research Center. Retrieved January 25, 2004 from http://www.pewinternet.org/; Seipp, C. (2002). *American Journalism Review, 24*(5), 42).

8

Credibility of Political Messages on the Internet: A Comparison of Blog Sources

LYNDA LEE KAID AND MONICA POSTELNICU

Rise of Blogs as Sources of Political Information

On any given day, 24 million Americans go to the Internet to look for political news or information. In 2004, about 97 million Americans visited government websites, 87 million got political news and updates on the presidential campaign, 38 million e-mailed government officials to try to influence policy decisions and 36 million became members of online support groups (Pew, 2005a). These numbers indicate that the world wide web has become an important channel for political communication and has the potential to enhance citizen involvement and participation, as many scholars have predicted (Corrado & Firestone, 1996; Milbank, 1999). The simplification of online-publishing technology and software allows citizens to become active contributors to the online political dialogue. On an average day, about 5 million Americans take advantage of content-creating applications and post their materials online (Pew, 2005a).

One of the easiest ways to publish content online is through blogs—defined as webpages organized as diaries, with dated entries arranged in reverse chronological order so that newer posts are at the top (Blood, 2002). Political blogs are specialized diaries, in the sense that they document the author's political views rather than his or her daily life (Pew, 2005b). Trammell (2003) notes that blogs are a very democratic medium with few entry barriers because one does not need specialized web design knowledge to create a blog. Therefore, every person with an Internet connection is potentially a person with a public voice.

There are currently about 8 million of these voices in the United States; 7% of Americans who use the Internet say that they have created a blog (Pew, 2005b). The readership of the blogosphere is 3 times as large, estimated at about 27% or 32 millions Americans who are most likely to be young, male, well-educated Internet veterans (Pew, 2005b). The constant, continuous, open and uninhibited flow of communication on blogs has been called a "soapbox" (Walker, 2005) and a "voice" for the people (Winer, 2003).

When the 2004 Democratic and Republican National Committees selected a handful of bloggers and accredited them to cover the parties' national conventions in the same way in which they accredited professional journalists (Trammell, 2005a, 2005b), blogs gained legitimacy as a channel for disseminating and obtaining political information. About 20 or so blogs known as the "A-list" have been called "a new force in national politics" (Pew, 2005b). Some bloggers perceive themselves as grassroots activists who "may sew [sic] the seeds for new forms of journalism, public discourse, interactivity and online community" (Lasica, 2001, online).

Numerous critics argue that the free and open nature of blogs for information distribution has a darker side as questions of responsibility, believability and credibility surface daily. The absence of a gatekeeping authority, combined with lack of formal journalistic education, can lead to postings of inaccurate content. For instance, errors normally filtered by the editorial process are sometimes not caught before being posted on the web, and entries can include all sorts of inaccuracies, from spelling to facts (Flanagin & Metzger, 2000). If such situations occur, bloggers are not bound by any legislation or editorial policy to publish retractions or corrections; many of them do not go back to correct a post (Fleishman, 2001).

Apart from the danger of inaccurate content, blogs may cause alterations in current communication values and journalistic practices. Trammell (2005a) reports that bloggers covering the 2004 national Democratic and Republican conventions sometimes published press releases with transcripts of candidates' speeches before the speeches were even made. Other concerns are related to bloggers' objectivity:

> Political bloggers chew over the news of the day frequently skewering journalists' coverage or spotlighting what they feel are uncovered stories. Objectivity is generally verboten in the blogosphere, although ideology tends to be less rigid than the partisan debates that play out so repetitiously in newspapers and on television (Smolkin, 2004, p. 39).

Bloggers responded to these accusations by arguing that fear of losing readers and compromising their reputation is enough incentive to keep them from publishing inaccurate information (Johnson & Kaye, 2004).

The political blogosphere is not limited to blogs authored by private individuals. In 2004, six of the ten Democratic candidates for the presidential nomination attached a blog to their campaign websites, making blogs an indispensable campaign communication tool. In addition to using their blogs to disseminate information and opinions, political candidates added new functions to blogs such as raising money, recruiting volunteers, republishing favorable media content and engaging in direct dialogue with supporters (Crumlich, 2004; Trippi, 2004). Howard Dean's success in raising millions of dollars through his blog inspired numerous other political entities—career or aspiring politicians, political issue groups, etc.—to start blogs. A rough estimate of the American political blogosphere is in the thousands of blogs (Ustinova, 2004).

Surveys show that blog readers tend to be young, well educated and Internet veterans (Pew, 2005c); thus, this chapter is concerned with whether young citizens find the political information posted on blogs credible enough to use it for decision making. Persuasion research stipulates that characteristics of the source have an impact on the degree of message credibility and the audience response to it. Our experiment tested how young people evaluate political messages created by different categories of bloggers (a career politician, an independent political group, and a celebrity).

Although celebrities do not have political blogs per se, their personal blogs sometimes include political content. Trammell (2004) analyzed 46 celebrity blogs and found that about 18% of the blog posts contained political statements, which were sometimes discussed by readers in the comment section of the blogs. During elections, celebrities are influential spokespersons for get-out-the-vote independent groups such as Rock the Vote. Therefore, it is important to test their credibility as sources of online political messages in comparison with more traditional sources.

Perceptions and Use of Online Sources of Information Among Young Citizens

Internet penetration among Americans aged 18 to 29 is about 84% (Pew, 2005e)—the highest connection rate of all segments of the population. College students in particular tend to rely heavily on the web for accessing general and academic information. About half of 356 undergraduate students surveyed by Metzger, Flanagin and Zwarun (2003) reported going online every day for a variety of purposes, from school-related research to communication with friends and family and from entertainment to news reading and other miscellaneous tasks. The Internet was the second most frequently used source of information; books were the number one source. However, 80% of the participants predicted that their reliance on the Internet will increase in the future.

The same study compared students' ratings of Internet credibility to a non-student population and discovered that students tend to perceive all media channels, the web included, as more credible than their nonstudent peers. They also tend to verify the accuracy of online content less often than other population groups. Johnson and Kaye (1998, 2000) confirmed that the more people rely on a source, the higher the credibility they attribute to it. Through surveys of consumers of online political information, these authors concluded that issue-oriented sites scored highest in credibility, while candidate-sponsored sites received the lowest trust. This finding suggests that people tend to believe an independent source rather than one whose intention to persuade is obvious.

Young citizens are also the main consumers of online news due to its convenience, accessibility, variety and zero cost compared to traditional media content (Pew, 2005d). Kiousis (2001) found that people tend to rate online news as more credible than television, but less credible than print newspapers. He also discovered positive correlations between the amount of interpersonal communication and the credibility attributed to online news. This was contrary to predictions that interpersonal communication undermines the credibility of a media channel (Chaffee, 1982). Also, a majority of people surveyed by the Pew Research Center (1999) reported no differences between the credibility of print newspapers and that of the news websites of those publications. Half of the participants expressed the belief that Internet news is more accurate than content produced by traditional media outlets.

Most of these findings refer strictly to news websites and ignore other online sources of political information. The scholarly research on how the audience—young people in particular—perceives political blogs has been limited. A majority of blog readers acknowledge that blogs are opinion oriented rather than fact based, but there is no indication of the impact of this awareness on the credibility of the source or the readers' attitude formation (Pew, 2005f). A recent survey of blog readers reported that these individuals rate blogs significantly higher than all other sources of information and that they are attracted to blogs due to their depth on information (Johnson & Kaye, 2004). However, readers felt that blog content is only moderately high with reference to fairness.

Highlights of Source Credibility Research

The early findings by Hovland and his associates at Yale, confirmed by numerous other studies, showed that a message's power to persuade is influenced by three categories of factors: the characteristics of the source, of the audience and of the message (Berlo, Lemert & Mertz, 1970; Hovland, Janis & Kelley, 1953; Hovland & Weiss, 1951–1952; Whitehead, 1968). Perloff (2003) lists authority, credibility and social attractiveness as the main attributes of a trustworthy source. Authority persuades because it makes people compliant by offering reward or punishment in exchange for the attitude change; credibility consists of expertise, trustworthiness and goodwill; and attractiveness plays into people's desire to model or associate with socially or physically appealing persons (Kelman, 1958; Perloff, 2003).

Bloggers are communicators whose potential to influence is derived from their credibility (i.e., expertise on a subject, or perception of being trustworthy, unbiased and independent) or their social attractiveness (famous, well-regarded individuals). Opinions are split about which type of message source is more persuasive because the effectiveness of the source is influenced by many variables, such as the audience characteristics; however, some studies have indicated that expert and trustworthy sources tend to be rated slightly higher than socially attractive sources. This leads to the first hypothesis of this study:

H1: Respondents will evaluate expert sources of blogs (such as career politicians) and trustworthy sources (such as independent groups) higher in credibility compared to socially attractive sources (such as celebrities).

Persuasiveness is also related to the perceived intentions of the communicator. Messages perceived as informational or educational have a higher acceptance rate than those overtly persuasive, such as advertising or propaganda (Hovland, Lumsdaine & Sheffield, 1949). Because blogs are hosted by all types of individuals and groups who may have no overt political agenda, it is possible for such sources to have a persuasion effect on blog readers and participants who do not take part in the conversation for political information, but rather for the chance to interact with a famous person or celebrity.

Studies on the credibility of celebrity endorsers in advertising discovered that celebrities tend to be viewed as more trustworthy than other categories of endorsers (Kahle & Homer, 1985). Atkin and Block (1983) found that younger people are more susceptible to influence by celebrities than older persons are.

With political content making up nearly one fifth of the content on celebrity blogs, Trammell (2004) suggested that these "stealth" political messages are very personalized and often related to the celebrity's life, giving them strong credibility for the reader. Based on these findings, the second hypothesis posits that:

H2: Respondents will be more likely to support the policy position expressed by the blog source with the least persuasive intentions (in this case, the celebrity) rather than the position of sources perceived as having persuasive intentions (a career politician or an independent issue group).

A better response to the celebrity blog is expected from young citizens for other reasons as well. The interaction between an individual and a celebrity can take the form of parasocial relationships—the illusion of friendship with the celebrity on the part of the individual (Rubin & McHugh, 1987). This makes individuals more likely to trust the celebrity and to perceive that celebrity as a "friend," rather than as a persuasive communicator.

When they read the blog of a "friend," it is possible that people are in a positive state of mind and, according to several scholars, the persuasive potential of the message is increased by positive moods and positive feelings towards the source (Janis, Kaye & Kirschner, 1965; Laird, 1974; McGuire, 1985). Also, people with low levels of involvement in the issue being promoted are more likely to become interested if the source of the message is a celebrity or an attractive person (Petty & Cacioppo, 1986; Petty, Cacioppo, Sedikides & Strathman, 1988).

Based on the same reasoning, it is possible that the credibility of a politician-sponsored blog is decreased by feelings of political cynicism that seem to characterize young citizens today. Several surveys revealed that distrust in government and politics is one of the top reasons for apathy among the younger generations of American voters (Declare Yourself, 2003; NASS, 1999).

Political cynicism is a negative emotion, and negative emotions can lead to resistance to persuasion (Petty et al., 1988). Therefore, we suggested that:

H3: Exposure to a blog by a political leader will cause respondents to express higher levels of political cynicism than will exposure to a blog authored by an independent group or a celebrity.

Mediating Factors in Blog Source Credibility

With research about political blogs still a new endeavor, very little is known about what types of factors may mediate the credibility of sources of the political information contained in a blog post. For instance, Trammell (2004) found significant differences between males and females in the motivations to access blogs. Researchers have also found that females are more likely to be persuaded by celebrity sources than males are (Petty, Cacioppo & Schumann, 1986).

Although researchers are beginning to identify some of the characteristics of those who access different kinds of political messages on the web, very little is known about the effects of these mediating characteristics (such as gender or partisanship) that affect the attitudes and opinions of blog readers. This leads to the following research question:

RQ1: Will respondent gender or partisan affiliation affect the credibility the respondents assign to the different blog sources?

Method

An experimental design was used to test the credibility ratings of different sources of political messages online. The experiment was also designed to determine whether the respondents' opinions on a given political topic would be influenced by the source and content of blogs. At the time at which this experiment was conducted, mass media, political and special interest groups and policy makers in and out of government were debating the possibility of reforming or privatizing Social Security. After reading blogs written by different sources on Social Security and related topics, we composed two blog posts and a series of four subsequent comments (two comments for each post) that we published on three different blogs. In each case the blog content (posts and comments) was the same, but the source of the blog was identified as different.

The first blog was attributed to a political expert, former Florida Senator Bob Graham, who was well known even outside the state of Florida because of his 2004 presidential primary campaign. The second blog was constructed as if it belonged to a celebrity, actor Ben Affleck, who was involved with Rock the Vote in 2004 and has been outspoken on a number of political issues. The third blog was attributed to the American Association of Retired Persons (AARP), an independent political group that the researchers felt would be believable as an interest group with a well-developed position on this issue.

All three blogs were identical in design: they visibly identified the owner through text and photos and featured two blog posts discussing Social Security signed by the owner of the blog and four pro and con arguments on Social Security attributed to blog visitors. The blog entries argued that privatizing Social Security is a risky policy reform that would lead to smaller retirement benefits for the current young generations of American workers.

A group of 169 undergraduate students from two large U.S. universities took part in the experiment in exchange for extra credit. The students were enrolled in large general education courses, had different majors, and were randomly assigned to one of the three conditions (Graham, Affleck or the AARP). Each student was instructed to fill out a pretest questionnaire posted online on a survey server. Then the students were asked to visit the blog assigned to them, read the post and comments on the blog, post their comments and then return to the survey server and fill out a post-test questionnaire.

The 169 students were distributed among the three experimental cells as follows: 51 in the Graham blog, 60 in the Affleck blog, and 58 in the AARP blog. The average age of these participants was 21 years; 33% were male and 67% were female. Their party identification was 33% Republican, 43% Democrat, and 24% independent/other. Chi square tests indicated that there was no difference in gender or partisan affiliation among the three groups, and a t-test confirmed that the mean ages were also essentially the same among the three groups.

The short pretest completed by all groups consisted of demographic questions (age, gender and partisan affiliation), as well as a series of questions about media habits and exposure, including questions about their use of the news media and the Internet for political information, and a series of eight items that made up a political cynicism scale.[1] These items were also used on the post-test questionnaire and achieved acceptable reliability when combined into an 8-item scale for cynicism (Cronbach's alpha of .64 in the pretest and .70 on the post-test). The pre- and post-test instruments also asked respondents to list in order of importance the five issues they felt were most important.

The post-test contained additional measures that asked respondents to rate Graham, Affleck and the AARP on a feeling thermometer (ranging from 0 for cool to 100 for warm).[2] Several other post-test questions asked the respondents to rate the fairness, ethicality, factual nature and other characteristics of the blogs. Respondents also indicated their level of support for the Social Security proposals mentioned in the blog and disclosed any emotional reactions they might have had to the blog post and comments.

Results

Differences in Information Received From Blog Sources

The first hypothesis suggested that respondents would evaluate expert sources (a career politician) and trustworthy sources (an independent group) higher in credibility compared to socially attractive sources (a celebrity). To test this hypothesis, participants were asked whether they thought that the information provided to them by blogs would help someone decide how to vote about privatizing Social Security. They were also asked to rate the blogs as factual, fair, misleading and ethical on scales of 7 (strongly agree) to 1 (strongly disagree).

In regard to the usefulness of the blogs, readers of Graham's blog (the expert source) said that the information in the blog was significantly more likely to help them decide how to vote on the Social Security reform proposal discussed in the blogs (M = 4.29; SD = 1.6) than readers of celebrity blog (M = 3.18; SD = 1.3) or the independent group blog (M = 3.59; SD = 1.7; F(2) = 3.88; p = .02).

While the results were in the predicted direction, showing a slight preference for the expert source compared to the celebrity or the independent source, ANOVA tests revealed no significant differences between respondents' ratings of each blog on the factual, fair, misleading and ethical scales (see Table 8.1). Respondents who were exposed to Senator Bob Graham's blog rated the content as factual with a mean of 4.04, which was not significantly different from the mean score of 3.80 given to Ben Affleck's blog or the 3.90 rating for the AARP blog. Similar patterns are apparent for the judgments of blog information fairness, ethicality and misleading nature. Overall, then, the first hypothesis was not confirmed.

Effect of Blog Source on Decision-Making

The second hypothesis predicted that readers would be more likely to support a policy position expressed by a source with no obvious persuasion intentions, such as a celebrity, rather than by sources with a visible agenda, such as a politician or an advocacy group. This hypothesis was also not supported. The blog entries argued that young people should vote against Social Security reforms, but this position did not obtain the readers' support. Only 24% of all study

Table 8.1 Effect of Blog Source on Information Judgments

	Graham (n = 51)		Affleck (n = 60)		AARP (n = 58)	
	Mean	SD	Mean	SD	Mean	SD
Based on facts	4.04	1.2	3.80	1.5	3.90	1.6
Fair	4.04	1.5	3.90	1.6	4.09	1.6
Misleading	3.2	1.5	3.43	1.6	3.23	1.6
Ethical	4.37	1.5	4.33	1.5	4.43	1.3
Help decide[a]	4.29	1.6	3.51	1.6	3.59	1.7
Learned about issue	3.35	1.4	3.18	1.3	3.16	1.5

[a] ANOVA analysis indicates difference at $p \leq .05$. Tukey's HSD test indicates that Graham is superior to Affleck at $p = .03$ and to the AARP at $p = .05$, but no significant difference is present between Affleck and the AARP.

Table 8.2 Levels of Cynicism Before and After Exposure to Blogs

	Pre	SD	Post	SD	Significance
Graham	26.5	4.4	26.7	4.9	n.s.*
Affleck	26.0	4.6	25.9	4.9	n.s.
AARP	27.5	4.5	27.1	4.8	n.s.

*n.s. means no significance.

participants said they were likely to vote no on privatizing Social Security; 36% said they would favor the reform and 39% declared that they were undecided. Students exposed to the expert source blog were more negative about the reform (31%) in comparison with readers of the celebrity blog (20%) or independent source blog (23%), which is contrary to our prediction. However, a chi square test indicated no statistically significant differences among the three blog sources ($\chi^2 = 3.601$; df $= 4$; $p > .05$).

Political Cynicism and Blog Sources

The third hypothesis was also not supported. This hypothesis expected that exposure to a blog sponsored by a politician would increase readers' levels of political cynicism more than exposure to an independent or a celebrity-sponsored blog. There was no difference among the three groups in the level of political cynicism of their readers after exposure; none of the blog sources caused readers to become more cynical, as shown in Table 8.2.

Gender and Partisan Differences in Blog Source Credibility

The research question asked whether there might be any differences in responses to the three blogs based on the gender or partisan affiliation of the respondents. In this area, the most interesting results related to the gender of the respondents. However, it is important to note that there were no significant differences by gender in how the respondents rated the information value of the blog sources. Regardless of the blog source, male and female respondents rated the factual basis, fairness, ethicality, misleading nature and vote helpfulness of the blogs the same.

Another comparison was made to look at the possibility that gender might directly affect the ratings of the blog sources. The feeling thermometer that asked for evaluations of the three blog sources in each blog did reveal that male and female respondents rated the blog sources differently. Table 8.3 shows these ratings broken down by blog source. It should be noted, however, that regardless of gender, there are clear differences in the ratings of these blog sources. Readers of Graham's blog, for instance, rated Graham significantly lower (20.49)[3] than Affleck (49.12) or the AARP (32.72), neither of which appears or is mentioned in Graham's blog. This pattern is consistent across

Table 8.3 Ratings of the Blog Sources and Gender Ratings

	Graham blog (n = 51)		Affleck blog (n = 60)		AARP blog (n = 58)	
	Mean	SD	Mean	SD	Mean	SD
Graham	20.49	31.7[a,c]	20.32	28.8[a,c]	23.14	29.9[c]
Male (n = 20)	24.75	33.26	24.71	33.0	25.59	30.5
Female (n = 31)	17.7	31.3	18.58	27.1	22.10	30.1
Affleck	49.12	26.6[b,c]	51.5	27.5[b,c]	43.7	28.3[b,c]
Male (n = 17)	37.85	26.7	36.29	30.8	31.18	30.3
Female (n = 43)	56.39[d]	24.3	57.47[d]	23.8	49.03[d]	25.9
AARP	32.73	30.9[a,b]	31.75	31.2[a,b]	29.82	33.5[b]
Male (n = 17)	38.65	28.6	40.18	29.3	21.47	32.4
Female (n = 40)	28.90	32.2	28.42	31.6	33.38	33.7

[a] t-test between AARP and Graham $< .05$.
[b] t-test between AARP and Affleck $< .05$.
[c] t-test between Affleck and Graham $<.05$.
[d] t-test difference between males and females is significant at $p < .05$.

the blogs; that is, the political leader is rated lower than the actor or the independent group, even in blogs in which the political leader does not appear.

There were also significant differences between male and female respondents' ratings of the blog sources. Table 8.3 shows that these differences occur only in regard to ratings of actor Ben Affleck. Female respondents consistently rated him significantly higher than did male respondents, regardless of the source of the blog to which they were reacting.

Partisan affiliation of the respondents made no difference in how they evaluated the blog sources. Even though Bob Graham represented the Democratic Party when he was a U.S. senator and in his unsuccessful bid for the presidential nomination, respondents who identified themselves as Democrats did not rate him any more favorably than they did Affleck or the AARP. The same was true for Republicans and those who said they were independents or belonged to another political party. Political party affiliation also made no difference in how respondents evaluated information in the blogs or in their decisions to support the Social Security reform after exposure to any of the blogs.

Discussion

Overall, this experiment uncovered concerning trends regarding young people's belief of information retrieved from the Internet. Regardless of whether the message came from a political expert, an independent group or a celebrity, respondents tended to rate each source as believable as the others. The young citizens who participated in this study seemed equally likely to form or change political attitudes based on the information provided to them by the blogs without questioning the source of the information.

Participants were asked to join the political dialogue about Social Security reforms and comment on the entries written by the blog owners. Only a handful of people questioned the validity of the blog content and the authority and expertise of the source to make comments about Social Security. In particular, a few participants doubted the credibility of the celebrity source. A 20-year-old male with independent party affiliation questioned the expertise of an actor about political topics: "Why should I care what Ben Affleck has to say? People are so celebrity crazy that now they are listening to Ben Affleck for political news." A 20-year-female with Republican Party affiliation shared the same point of view and wrote that "I'm just wondering how Ben Affleck knows this much and why he's posting a blog."

The credibility of the celebrity source was also compromised by perceptions of incongruity between the celebrity's financial status and the financial status of people most affected by a possible Social Security reform. A 21-year-old male who classified himself as politically apathetic and not affiliated with any party wrote:

> Why is Ben Affleck, a multimillionaire with present and future financial security ensured, voicing an opinion that will have little or no effect on his life? I think I would take a comment from a politician more seriously than that of a celebrity.

A 20-year-old female student with Democratic Party affiliation expressed similar skepticism about politicians: I would never trust someone urging the privatization of social security who is a multimillionaire (and most politicians are). It's the working class people who work so hard to get social security and who need it the most.

However, except for the four participants quoted previously, all the other young people in the study accepted the information provided to them by the blog entries to express or construct their views of the issue, without questioning the credibility of the information. This is consistent with existing theory about persuasion through peripheral cues such as the attractiveness of the source. Individuals with low levels of involvement and low knowledge about an issue are more likely to be influenced by persuasive messages and are more likely to rely on heuristic cues (Petty & Cacioppo, 1986; Popkin, 1991).

The participants in our experiment fit the definition of low involved publics because their score of political information efficacy was only slightly above the average ($M = 12.8$; $SD = 4.05$; the maximum possible score was 20). Also, Ben Affleck (whose celebrity status is a peripheral/heuristic cue) received the highest ratings from all participants on the thermometer scale; his score was $M = 48.12$; $SD = 27.52$. The politician obtained the lowest score ($M = 21.33$; SD

= 29.94) and the independent political group was rated somewhere between the two (M = 31.39; SD = 31.72).

The lack of statistical significance between the credibility of the various sources of political information can also be related to participants' media consumption. The Internet was the top source of information for people in our sample, followed by interpersonal communication with family and friends, national television and the campus newspaper. Johnson and Kaye (2000) argued that "using is believing" and that the more people rely on a source of information, the more they tend to trust that source and accept its validity.

Exposure to the blog sponsored by the politician did not lead to increased levels in political cynicism among the participants, regardless of Bob Graham's low likability on the thermometer measure. This is, in fact, an encouraging finding. Previous research indicates that mass media coverage of political affairs that focuses on scandal and horse-race frames in presenting political events, as well as negative messages from politicians (such as negative advertising during campaigns), gives the public the impression that politics is corrupt and leads to feelings of political cynicism and apathy (Ansolabehere & Iyengar, 1995; Cappella & Jamieson, 1997). It seems that the online communication initiated by political entities has the potential of alleviating these skeptical attitudes due to the Internet's potential for direct interaction between the parties.

Visiting the websites of political actors (candidates, government, etc.) may prompt positive attitudes toward the site owner if the website offers interactive tools for communication (Stromer–Galley & Foot, 2002). Sundar, Hesser, Kalyanaraman and Brown (1998) discovered that exposure to a campaign website with a moderate to high degree of interactivity resulted in higher ratings of the candidate, who was perceived as more responsive, trustworthy or charismatic by politically apathetic users. Therefore, politicians can be efficient in lessening political cynicism among the electorate and gaining people's trust by setting up interactive blogs.

The differences between men and women in evaluation of source credibility also raises interesting issues. Of course, it would not strike readers as surprising that female participants rated movie actor Ben Affeck more positively than males did, particularly because this was true even in the blogs sponsored by other sources and in which Affleck was not even mentioned. There were no differences between male and female participants in their judgments about the information in the blogs. However, we identified other differences in reactions based on the emotions generated by the blogs. We asked each participant to tell us how he or she rated his or her emotional responses to the blog information. Table 8.4 shows that after reading the blogs, male participants said they were significantly more "optimistic," "confident" and "secure" than female participants were. Female participants, on the other hand, were more likely

Table 8.4 Emotions Generated by Blogs by Gender

	Males (n = 55)		Females (n = 114)	
	Mean	**SD**	**Mean**	**SD**
Optimism[a]	1.07	1.09	.78	.99
Confidence[a]	1.04	1.14	.75	1.03
Anxious	1.29	1.10	1.44	1.04
Excited	.65	1.01	.52	.90
Secure[a]	.85	1.08	.56	.95
Fearful[a]	1.30	1.08	1.71	.96
Bored	1.42	1.08	1.38	1.04
Patriotic	.67	1.04	.81	1.03
Concerned	2.27	.80	2.42	.55
Angry	1.49	1.15	1.53	1.07

[a] t-test indicates difference between males and females is significant at $p \leq .05$.

to experience a negative emotional reaction, indicating that they were significantly more likely than males to feel "fearful" after exposure to the blogs.

There are some limitations to the study reported here. Of course, it is important to determine whether the results found here are unique to the particular topic or particular sources used. The study needs to be replicated with additional issues beyond Social Security and with various source types to determine whether source credibility findings are limited to the particular sources or types of sources used here. One particularly interesting concern is the potential evaluation of the AARP group. As a group with a particular affiliation to older Americans, the AARP might be perceived by young citizens as representing points of view very different from their views. Blog source credibility for a wider variety of independent and expert sources should be investigated.

Overall, these findings suggest the need for more research on source credibility of blog messages. Blogs may be an important and underappreciated source of political messages in the Wild, Wild West of the modern web. As increasing numbers of groups and celebrities use their blogs to discuss political policy issues and to express points of view that may be accepted uncritically by supporters or fans, these communication sources create a type of "stealth" political communication that may be able to reach and persuade the less interested, less informed and less involved citizen.

In conclusion, this study confirmed prior findings that heavy Internet users like the young people in our sample tend to rate online information as credible. The data failed to reveal a clear preference for one type of source over others, and all sources—the expert, the trustworthy, and the celebrity—were rated similarly as information sources. However, the participants attributed more credibility to the celebrity source, which is not surprising for a low involved public.

The finding that most young people trust political information online, even when the source does not have political expertise (the case with Ben Affleck), is equally important. Blogs are presently a popular online destination for millions of people; placing stealth political messages on nonpolitical blogs could become a persuasion strategy for campaign managers and other political entities, similar to product placement in advertising.

References

Ansolabehere, S., & Iyengar, S. (1995). *Going negative: How attack ads shrink and polarize the electorate.* New York: The Free Press.

Atkin, C., & Block, M. (1983). An experiment revealed the effectiveness of celebrity endorsers. *Journal of Advertising Research, 23*(1), 57–61.

Berlo, D. K., Lemert, J. B. & Mertz, R. J. (1970). Dimensions for evaluating the acceptability of message sources. *Public Opinion Quarterly, 33,* 563–576.

Blood, R. (2002). The Weblog handbook: Practical advice on creating and maintaining your blog. Cambridge, MA: Perseus Publishing.

Cappella, J. N., & Jamieson, K. H. (1997). *Spiral of cynicism: The press and the public good.* New York: Oxford University Press.

Chaffee, S. H. (1982). The interpersonal context of mass communication. In F. G. Kline & P. J. Tichenor (Eds.), *Current perspectives in mass communication research* (pp. 95–120). Beverly Hills, CA: Sage Publications.

Corrado, A. C., & Firestone, C. (1996). *Elections in cyberspace: Toward a new era in American politics.* Washington, DC: Aspen Institute.

Crumlich, C. (2004). The power of the many. How the living Web is transforming politics, business, and everyday life. Alameda, CA: Sybex.

Declare Yourself (2003, November 13). Major national survey shows increased promise, new strategies for increasing youth vote. Youth vote 2004 survey shows narrow window of opportunity to engage young voters; points to "political incompetence" as major barrier to voting. Retrieved June 20, 2005, from http://www.declareyourself.org/press/pressroom.htm.

Flanagin, A. J., & Metzger M. J. (2000). Perceptions of Internet information credibility. *Journalism & Mass Communication Quarterly, 77,* 515–540.

Fleishman, G. (2001). Been "blogging"? Web discourse hits higher level. *The Seattle Times,* Business & Technology. Retrieved April 10, 2004, from http://seattletimes.nwsource.com/html/home/.

Hovland, C. I., Janis, I. L. & Kelley, H. H. (1953). *Communication and persuasion.* New Haven, CT.: Yale University Press.

Hovland, C. I., Lumsdaine, A. & Sheffield, F. (1949). *Experiments on mass communication.* Princeton, NJ: Princeton University Press.

Hovland, C. I., & Weiss, W. (1951–1952, Winter). The influence of source credibility on communication effectiveness. *The Public Opinion Quarterly, 15*(4), 635–650.

Janis, L. K., Kaye, D. & Kirschner, P. (1965). Facilitating effects of "eating while reading" on responsiveness to persuasive communications. *Journal of Personality and Social Psychology, 1,* 181–186.

Johnson, T. J., & Kaye, B. K. (1998). Cruising is believing? Comparing the Internet and traditional sources on media credibility measures. *Journalism & Mass Communication Quarterly, 75,* 325–340.

Johnson, T. J., & Kaye, B. K. (2000). Using is believing: The influence of reliance on the credibility of online political information among politically interested Internet users. *Journalism & Mass Communication Quarterly, 77*(4), 865–879.

Johnson, T. J., & Kaye, B. K. (2004). Wag the blog: How reliance on traditional media and the Internet influence credibility perceptions of Weblogs among blog users. *Journalism & Mass Communication Quarterly, 81*(3), 622–642.

Kahle, L. R., & Homer, P. M. (1985). Physical attractiveness of the celebrity endorser: A social adaptation perspective. *The Journal of Consumer Research, 11*(4), 945–961.

Kaid, L. L., McKinney, M. S. & Tedesco, J. C. (2000). *Civic dialogue in the 1996 presidential campaign: Candidate, media, and public voices.* Cresskill, NJ: Hampton Press.

Kelman, H. C. (1958). Compliance, identification, and internalization: Three processes of attitude change. *Journal of Conflict Resolution, 2,* 51–60.

Kiousis, S. (2001). Public trust or mistrust? Perceptions of media credibility in the information age. *Mass Communication & Society, 4*(4), 381–403.

Laird, J. D. (1974). Self-attribution of emotion. The effects of expressive behavior on the quality of emotional experience. *Journal of Personality and Social Psychology, 29,* 475–486.

Lasica, J. D. (2001). Blogging as a form of journalism. *Online Journalism Review.* Retrieved April 14, 2004, from http://www.ojr.org/ojr/workplace/p1017958873.php.

McGuire, W. J. (1985). Attitudes and attitude change. In G. Lindsey and E. Aronson (Eds.), *The handbook of social psychology* (3rd ed., Vol. 2). New York: Randon House.

Metzger, M., Flanagin, A. J. & Zwarun, L. (2003). College student Web use, perceptions of information credibility, and verification behavior. *Computers & Education, 41,* 271–290.

Milbank, D. (1999, July 5). Virtual politics, *The New Republic,* 22–27.

NASS (National Association of Secretaries of State) (1999). New millennium survey: American youth attitudes on politics, citizenship, government and voting. Retrieved on October 11, 2005, from http://www.stateofthevote.org/survey/.

Perloff, R. M. (2003). *The dynamics of persuasion. Communication and attitudes in the 21st century* (2nd ed.). Mahwah, NJ: Lawrence Erlbaum Associates.

Petty, R. E., & Cacioppo, J. T. (1986). *The elaboration likelihood model of persuasion.* New York: Academic Press.

Petty, R. E., Cacioppo, J. T. & Schumann, D. (1986). Central and peripheral routes to advertising effectiveness: The moderating role of involvement. *The Journal of Consumer Research, 10*(2), 135–146.

Petty, R. E., Cacciopo, J. T., Sedikides, C. & Strathman, A. J. (1988). Affect and persuasion: A contemporary perspective. *American Behavioral Scientist, 31*(3), 355–371.

Pew Research Center (1999). Online news consumption: The Internet news audience goes ordinary. Retrieved December 10, 2005, from http://people-press.org/reports/display.php3?PageID=337.

Pew Research Center (2005a). The Internet: The mainstreaming of online life. Retrieved January 20, 2006, from http://pewresearch.org/publications/trends/trends2005-internet.pdf.

Pew Internet and American Life Project (2005b). Buzz, blogs, and beyond: The Internet and the national discourse in the fall of 2004. Retrieved on June 10, 2005, from http://www.pewinternet.org/.

Pew Internet and American Life Project (2005c). Data memo: The state of blogging. Retrieved on June 10, 2005, from http://www.pewinternet.org/.

Pew Research Center (2005d, June 26). Public more critical of press, but goodwill persists. Online newspaper readership countering print losses. Retrieved December 10, 2005, from http://people-press.org/reports/pdf/248.pdf.

Pew Internet and American Life Project (2005e). Who's online. Retrieved January 10, 2006, from http://www.pewinternet.org/trends/User_Demo_12.05.05.htm.

Pew Research Center (2005f). Media: More voices, less credibility. Retrieved January 15, 2006, from http://pewresearch.org/publications/trends/trends2005-media.pdf.

Popkin, S. L. (1991). *The reasoning voter: Communication and persuasion in presidential campaigns.* Chicago, IL: University of Chicago Press.

Rosenstone, S. J., Kinder, D. R., Miller, W. E. & the National Election Studies (1997). American national election study, 1996: Pre- and post-election survey [Computer file]. Ann Arbor, MI: University of Michigan, Center for Political Studies [producer], 1997. Ann Arbor, MI: Interuniversity Consortium for Political and Social Research [distributor].

Rubin, R. B., & McHugh, M. P. (1987). Development of parasocial interaction relationships. *Journal of Broadcasting and Electronic Media, 31*(3), 279–292.

Smolkin, R. (2004, June/July). The expanding blogosphere. *American Journalism Review,* 38–43.

Stromer–Galley, J., & Foot, K. A. (2002). Citizens perceptions of online interactivity and implications for political campaign communication. *Journal of Computer-Mediated Communication,* 8(1). Retrieved January 15, 2006, from http://jcmc.indiana.edu/vol8/issue1/stromerandfoot.html.

Sundar, S. S., Hesser, K. M., Kalyanaraman, S., & Brown, J. (1998, July). *The effect of Website interactivity on political persuasion.* Paper presented to the Social Psychology Division at the 21st General Assembly & Scientific Conference of the International Association for Media and Communication Research, Glasgow, U.K.

Trammell, K. D. (2003). *Impact of source credibility in accessing online health messages based on culture.* Paper presented to the Association of Internet Researchers annual conference, Toronto, Ontario, Canada.

Trammell, K. D. (2004). *Celebrity blogs: Investigation in the persuasive nature of two-way communication regarding politics.* Unpublished doctoral dissertation. Gainesville: University of Florida.

Trammell, K. D. (2005a, November). *Blog bias: Reports, inferences, and judgments of credentialed bloggers at the 2004 nominating conventions.* Paper presented to the Political Communication Division, National Communication Association annual conference, Boston, MA.

Trammell, K. D. (2005b, November). *Frame analysis of credentialed blogs covering the 2004 national political party conventions.* Paper presented to the Political Communication Division, National Communication Association annual conference, Boston, MA.

Trippi, J. (2004, July 1). The revolution will not be televised. Democracy, the Internet, and the overthrow of everything. New York: Regan Books.

Ustinova, A. (2004, July 18). Political blogs catching on. Web fundraising, commentary rise. *Chicago Tribune.* http://www.chicagotribune.com/news/specials/elections/chi-04071801 89jul18,1,4681798.story?coll=chi-elections-utl.

Walker, J. (2005). Weblog (definition). In D. Herman, M. Jahn & M.-L. Ryan (Eds.), *Routledge encyclopedia of narrative theory.* London: Routledge.

Whitehead, J. L. (1968). Factors of source credibility. *Quarterly Journal of Speech, 54,* 59–63.

Winer, D. (2003, May 23). What makes a Weblog a Weblog? Retrieved December 10, 2005, from http://blogs.law.harvard.edu/whatMakesAWeblogAWeblog.

Notes

1. These eight items consisted of 5-point scales asking for agreement/disagreement with a series of scales that have been frequently used to measure political trust, political cynicism, political efficacy and political alienation. These scales were (1) Whether I vote or not has no influence on what politicians do; (2) One never really knows what politicians think; (3) People like me don't have any say about what the government does; (4) Sometimes politics and government seem so complicated that a person like me can't really understand what's going on; (5) One can be confident that politicians will always do the right thing (reversed when scored); (6) Politicians often quickly forget their election promises after a political campaign is over; (7) Politicians are more interested in power than in what the people think; and (8) One cannot always trust what politicians say. Several of these items were adapted from the American National Election Studies (ANES) questions on political trust and efficacy (Rosenstone, Kinder, Miller & the National Election Studies, 1997), and they were also used as a scale to measure cynicism in the same format as used here by Kaid, McKinney and Tedesco (2000).

2. This feeling thermometer was the same as that used by the ANES (Rosenstone et al., 1997) to measure feeling toward political candidates.

3. Surprisingly, a large number of participants indicated that they were not familiar with Bob Graham and could not give him an informed rating. This resulted in a large number of "0" ratings for Graham, which may have artificially depressed his rating scores.

Blog Readers: Predictors of Reliance on War Blogs

THOMAS JOHNSON AND BARBARA K. KAYE

The first Gulf War popularized newsgroups as a way for people to maintain contact as well as to share news and personal information (Ashley, 1992). The most recent Iraq war boosted the popularity of blogs[1] as a way to find out about war news as well as for soldiers to remain connected with their families (Smolkin, 2004; Palser, 2002; Seipp, 2002).

Although Pew Research suggested that only 4% of Internet users turned to blogs during the Iraq war (Fallows & Rainie, 2004),[2] they are important to study because their influence exceeds their readership. Indeed, one British journalist blamed blogs for increasing the division between the United States and Europe over Iraq (Crabtree, 2002). The military also censored or shut down several "milblogs"—blogs posted by soldiers in Iraq—because of fear that they could contradict the military's official version of events or breach operational security (Schulman, 2005).

Internet users who relied on blogs visited them often because they provided more thoughtful analysis of the war than the traditional media, as well as on a more frequent, consistent basis (Ryan, 2003). Therefore, blogs are being touted, even by the traditional media, as a genuine alternative source to mainstream news outlets (Grossman, Hamilton, Buechner & Whitaker, 2004). For instance, Sean-Paul Kelley's site, Agonist.com, reported 130,000 unique hits per day during the Iraq war (Bedell, 2003). Traditional media depended heavily on blogs, especially warblogs (a blog that focuses on war and the political and diplomatic circumstances surrounding the war) such as The Command Post, and on milblogs for news and analysis they did not see elsewhere (Reynolds, 2004).

Blogs became a common topic of embedded journalists' posts. The most written about journalist during the War did not work for a 24-hour news outlet or a major news magazine. Rather, he was a 29-year-old Iraqi architect who called himself Salam Pax and created the warblog, "Where is Raed?" (Snyder, 2003). Finally, many journalistic organizations started blog sites (Rosenberg, 2002; Yousefzadeh, 2003), and many journalists created blogs on which they voiced their thoughts and opinions about the war and their experiences in Iraq (Hamdy & Mobarak, 2004; Palser, 2003).

This study surveyed blog users online to find out the degree to which they relied on blogs for information about the war and how reliance on blogs compared to that on traditional and other online media. Finally, this study examines the demographics and political variables that predict reliance on blogs for information about the Iraq war.

Reliance on Blogs

Blogs gained a boost in popularity during the days after September 11, 2001 (Jesdanun, 2001), and have emerged as an important source of news for a core of Internet users since the Iraq war began (Hamilton, 2003; Hastings, 2003; Simon, 2003). In fact, some observers suggest that blogs came of age during the war (Hastings). Analysts suggest that blogs gained popularity during the Iraq war for several reasons:

> Several blogs, such as L.T. Smash and Stryker's Morning Briefing, were written from the war zone by soldiers who could provide more insights into the war than the journalists covering it could (Bedell, 2003).
> Similarly, because blog postings "bypassed the sanitizing Cuisinart of big-media news editing," (Levy, 2003), they reported a more personal side of the war. For instance, in his web postings, Salam Pax described the columns of smoke rising from the burning oil-filled trenches in Baghdad set afire by bombs (Andrews, 2003).
> Although most media feature one-way communication, most blogs provide links to other sites, and they allow blog readers to respond to the postings, fostering a healthy debate about the progress and purpose of the war (Hastings, 2003). Similarly, people visited blogs to find out what other Americans were thinking and to gain a sense of community by communicating with like-minded individuals (Carver, 2003; Katz, 2002; Thompson, 2003; Papacharissi, 2004).
> Blogs often present more up-to-date news than traditional news sources. Many sites provide new information every 15 minutes (Ryan, 2003).
> Critics claim that traditional media present a narrow perspective, but blogs feature writers from many regions of the world whose varied political perspectives brought insights on the war different from those of the largely American traditional media (Hamilton, 2003; Hastings, 2003; Reynolds, 2004).
> Because bloggers do not operate by the same standards as traditional journalists and are not subject to the same advertising pressures as mainstream media (Blood, 2002; Delwiche, 2004), they interject their views as well as show images that U.S. media refuse to carry,

such as photographs of American POWs (Wall, 2005; Sydell, 2003; Fallows & Rainie, 2004).

Indeed, Kaye and Johnson (2004) found that when almost a thousand blog readers were asked why they relied on blogs for information about the Iraq war, they praised blogs as an alternative source of news and information not filtered by the traditional media. Blog users argued that blogs provided more accurate, in-depth and often firsthand accounts of the war from individuals more knowledgeable about the realties of war than the traditional journalists. Blogs also provided thoughtful war analysis, which users felt was lacking from traditional media.

Furthermore, bloggers include links to traditional media sites that allowed readers to compare accounts of the war easily. Similarly, blog uses and gratifications during the Iraq war (Kaye, 2005a) and during the 2004 presidential election (Chapter 7; Kaye & Johnson, 2006) suggest users were finding information not available from traditional news, checking the accuracy of traditional media and keeping up with major issues of the day. Heavy users also touted blogs for their convenience: because information could be accessed at any time and because information was easy to obtain.

Blogs as Substitutes for Other Media

Although only 4% of Internet users relied on blogs for information during the Iraq war (Rainie, 2005), studies suggest loyal blog users reduced the time they spent with broadcast news. However, blog use spurred increases in personal discussion and online newspaper use.

Kaye and Johnson (2004) found that nearly half of blog users during the Iraq war reduced the time spent with online television news—which they did not deem a credible source of news and information about the war (Kaye & Johnson, 2004). On the other hand, more than half said they increased the time spent discussing the war (Kaye & Johnson). Presumably, blogs sparked increased interest in the Iraq war and spurred readers to share what they learned on blog sites with others. More than four in ten said that they increased their time spent with online newspapers. The interactive nature of blogs allowed readers to compare the information they received there with other online sources. Also, blogs relied heavily on online newspapers for their postings and provided links to the original articles, allowing users to read the online newspaper stories for additional information.

Eveland and Dylko (2006) discovered that political discussion, listening to talk radio, cable news use, online news use and online political discussion positively correlated with political blog use during the 2004 presidential campaign. However, only talk radio, online news and online discussion remained significant after controlling for other factors.

Blogs and Political Attitudes

Blogs have been described as the cyber version of talk radio (Crabtree, 2002). Blogs are places where conservatives gather to find information that supports their views as well as to spout their opinions on stories posted to the site. Although some blogs are hosted by liberals, the blogosphere at the time of this survey was predominantly right of center, whether conservative or libertarian (Leo, 2002; Levy, Figueroa, Campo–Flores, Lin & Gossard, 2002). Not surprisingly, conservative blogs attract a conservative audience. When he surveyed readers of his conservative blog andrewsullivan.com, Andrew Sullivan found that 31.7% identified themselves as conservative and another 29.6% claimed to be right of center. Only 6% characterized themselves as liberals. Because most bloggers and blog readers were conservative, blogs—particularly warblogs—largely supported the government's war efforts (Thompson, 2003; Crabtree, 2002; Kaye & Johnson, 2004).

Bloggers and blog readers harbor a distrust of institutions, particularly the media, which they contend are dominated by an Eastern Establishment liberal bias (Seipp, 2002). Commentators suggest that the rising popularity of blogs coincided with a growing distrust and dislike of the traditional media (Amis, 2002; Lasica, 2002). Several blog sites are specifically devoted to critiquing media coverage, and bloggers and blog readers take particular glee in pointing out errors in traditional media accounts (Reynolds, 2002; Kurtz, 2002). Scholars suggest that one source of political distrust of traditional media is that Internet users did not feel that corporate-controlled media delivered the entire story about events such as the Iraq war, but blogs connected to news sources around the world and ran stories that were unavailable or ignored by the mainstream media (Wall, 2005).

Blog users are politically active, and politics is the second most common theme of blogs (Whelan, 2003). One of the leading bloggers, Glenn Reynolds of Instapundit, claims that the independent, unedited, opinionated and personal style of blogs makes them addictive (Ryan, 2003). Indeed, Andrew Sullivan found that almost two thirds of his readers visited his site daily and 12% visited it more than once a day.

However, politically active readers do not limit themselves to blogs. Blog users tend to be political junkies who rely on several sources for political information. Kaye and Johnson (2004) discovered that blog use increased time spent with face-to-face discussion, cable television news and reading online newspapers. The blog reader, then, is a politically interested and politically knowledgeable individual who relies on blogs as well as some of the traditional media for information about the war and other political topics.

Blog readers may also feel high levels of political efficacy (the ability to bring about political change). Howard Dean relied heavily on blogs to raise money early in his campaign and, based on his Internet fund-raising, became the early front runner (Kornblum, 2003). Blogs sometimes take on issues ignored by traditional media and, through the persistence of their coverage, get the issue on the media agenda. For instance, CNN Chief News Executive Eason Jordan resigned from his position less than 2 weeks after the blog of an economic forum quoted him saying that the U.S. military had targeted and killed a dozen journalists. Jordan's comments were picked up by blogs around the world, and CNN was buried under a blizzard of complaints about Jordan's comments (Potter, 2005). Blogs may be places where ordinary Internet users, as recipients as well as providers of news and commentary, have a heightened sense of power to bring about political and social change.

Eveland and Dylko (2006) specifically examined the influence of political variables on political blog reading during the 2004 election campaign. They found that political interest and participation correlated with blog reading, although political knowledge and ideology did not. However, in regression analysis, interest did not predict blog reading and blog reading failed to influence political participation after controlling for other measures.

Blogs and Demographics

Evidence suggests that the average blog reader resembles the veteran Internet user as well as the average Internet user for war information: young, White, affluent and well-educated males (Kaye & Johnson, 2004; Rainie, 2005; Rainie, Fox, & Fallows, 2003). For instance, Rainie discovered that 57% of blog creators are male and nearly half (48%) are under the age of 30. More than 40% live in households earning more than $50,000 and 39% have college or graduate degrees.

Studies have found little connection between web reliance and demographics as the Internet audience became more mainstream (Johnson & Kaye, 2004). Because studies have found that heavy blog users were more likely to be male, younger and to hold a graduate degree than other Internet users, Johnson and Kaye (2004) predicted that demographics would have a greater influence on blog reliance than general Internet use. However, they found that demographic measures were a weak predictor of trusting blog information with no demographic variable predicting blog credibility (Johnson & Kaye, 2004). Similarly, Eveland and Dylko (2006) found that only education positively related with blog use and that relationship became insignificant after controlling for other factors.

Research Questions

This study examines how much blog readers rely on blogs for war information and the degree to which reliance on blogs is predicted by demographic and political variables. More specifically, it will address the following questions:

- How does reliance on blogs compare to reliance on more mainstream traditional and online news sources?
- To what degree is reliance on blogs predicted by demographic (gender, age, education and income) and political variables (political involvement, political knowledge, general news knowledge, knowledge about the Iraq war, political interest, general news interest, interest in the Iraq war, political efficacy and political trust)?

Method

This study examines reliance on blogs for information about the Iraq war through a survey that was posted online from April 23 to May 22, 2003—a period that spanned the end of the formal ground war and the beginnings of efforts to maintain peace in Iraq. The purpose of the survey was to gather demographic and attitudinal information about blog readers and to determine how much they relied on blogs to learn about the Iraqi invasion. To target blog readers, announcements about the survey were sent to bloggers who posted the survey URL on their blog[3] and to blog-oriented chat rooms and bulletin boards/lists.[4] The survey was linked from 131 blogs of diverse ideologies and from 14 blog-oriented bulletin boards/electronic mailing lists. Additionally, a "snowball" technique, in which respondents could automatically forward the survey to fellow blog readers, was used (Babbie, 1990).

Although this study relies on a convenience sample, the method used was appropriate for specifically reaching a narrow group of Internet users: blog readers. Attempting to generate a random sample of this small, but influential, group would result in a large nonqualification rate because only a small percentage of Internet users access blogs (Greenspan, 2003; Rainie, 2005). Therefore, the best way to find blog readers was to post announcements of the survey on blogs and other online resources that blog readers tend to access.

Source Reliance

Reliance on blogs and on other traditional and online sources for information about the Iraqi war was assessed using a 5-point scale ranging from "heavily rely on" to "don't rely on at all." Respondents were asked their levels of reliance on blogs, online sources (broadcast television news sites, cable television news sites, newspaper sites, radio news sites and news magazines sites), traditional media (broadcast television news, cable television news, newspapers, radio news, talk radio and news magazines) and face-to-face discussion.

Attitudes, Involvement, Interest and Knowledge

Trust, Self-Efficacy and Involvement   Trust in the government and self-efficacy were measured as a summated index made up of the following items from the National Election Studies conducted by the University of Michigan: "Most of our leaders are devoted to service," "Politicians never tell us what they really think" and "I don't think public officials care much about what people like me think." Self-efficacy was measured by the following statements: "People like me don't have any say about what the government does" and "Every vote counts in an election, including yours and mine." The response options for each attitude index ranged from "strongly disagree" (1) to "strongly agree" (5). The polarity was reversed on the second and third statements of the trust index and the first efficacy item. The reliability for the trust index is .75, and .58 for the efficacy index.[5] Respondents were also asked whether blog use has influenced their level of political involvement ("greatly increased," "increased," "stayed the same," "decreased" or "greatly decreased").

Interest and Knowledge About Politics, General News and the Iraq War   Respondents indicated their degree of interest in the war, in general news and in politics in general on a 0 (no interest) to 10 (extremely interested) scale. Respondents were asked whether their knowledge about politics, general news and the Iraqi war "greatly increased," "increased," "stayed the same," "decreased" or "greatly decreased" since they first started using blogs.

Demographics

Respondents indicated whether they are male or female and entered their age as of their last birthday. Respondents selected their highest level of education from among seven options that ranged from "less than high school" to "Ph. D. degree" and "other." Respondents estimated their 2003 income from one of seven categories ranging from less than $10,000 to more than $95,000.

Data Analyses

Frequencies were run on the reliance variables, political attitudes, knowledge and interest variables and demographics. Paired *t*-tests were employed to compare reliance on blogs to reliance on other traditional and online sources. Hierarchical regression determined whether the independent variables predicted reliance on blogs. The predictors were entered as blocks. Demographic variables (age, income, gender and education) were entered first, followed by attitude measures (trust in the government; self-efficacy; political involvement since becoming a blog user; knowledge about politics, general news and the Iraqi war; and interest in politics, general news and the Iraqi war). Reliance on online sources (broadcast television news sites, cable television news sites, newspaper sites, radio news sites and news magazines sites), traditional media (broadcast television news, cable television news, newspapers, radio news, talk radio and news magazines) and face-to-face discussion were entered last.

Results

Respondent Profile

The demographic characteristics of 3,747 respondents[6] who completed the survey were similar to the profiles of blog readers reported by others done at the time of this survey (Greenspan, 2003; Rainie et al., 2003; Whelan, 2003). Just over three quarters (76.5%) of the respondents were male and almost nine out of ten were White (89.3%). The respondents were highly educated, with 92.6% reporting some college or higher. Additionally, four out of ten (41.8%) earned more than $65,001 per year. However, those who relied on blogs for war information were older than had been suggested in earlier studies; the average age was close to 40 (Table 9.1).

The respondents were knowledgeable about politics, general news and the war. Almost nine out of ten (87.3%) reported they knew more about politics and about general news and current events (88.7%) since they had begun using blogs. Just over eight out of ten (82.7%) asserted that using blogs increased their knowledge about the war.

The respondents were also very interested in world events. Just over three quarters (76.1%) were highly interested in the Iraqi war, 67.8% reported high interest in general news and current events and 64.9% were very interested in politics. Additionally, about one third (32.3%) credited blogs as a catalyst to greater political involvement (Table 9.1).

Although the respondents were a politically involved, knowledgeable and interested group that largely supported the Iraqi war and believed that they had the power to bring about political change, they were only moderately trusting of the government. Three quarters of the respondents were "very supportive" or "supportive" of the war. Slightly more than three quarters (76.5%) claimed high levels of self-efficacy, and only 7.4% believed that they were politically powerless. While almost one half (47.0%) of blog readers indicated high to very high levels of trust in the government, 30.9% reported that they were moderately trustful and 22.1% claimed low to very low degrees of trust. Additionally, almost one half (48.0%) were affiliated with the Republican Party and 14.5% considered themselves Democrats; the remaining 37.5% were independents or others (Table 9.1).

Reliance on Blogs, Traditional Media and Online Sources

While only a small percentage of Internet users relied on blogs for news on the war, results suggest that these users leaned heavily on blogs for news and information. Just over three quarters (76.8%) of the respondents relied heavily on blogs as a source of information about the Iraqi war. Cable television news was the next most relied on source, but less than half (47.3%) claimed heavy reliance. Traditionally delivered newspapers were heavily relied on by 40.1% of respondents. Online cable television news and online newspapers were

Table 9.1 Profile of Respondents

<table>
<tr><td colspan="2" align="center">Demographics</td></tr>
<tr><td>Female: 23.5%</td><td>College degree or higher: 92.6%</td></tr>
<tr><td>Male: 76.5%</td><td>White: 89.3%</td></tr>
<tr><td>Average Age: 38.9</td><td>Black: 0.9%</td></tr>
</table>

Political attitudes

General news knowledge	Interest in general news
Increased/greatly increased: 88.7%	High/very high: 67.8%
Stayed the same: 10.8%	Moderate: 29.3%
Decreased/greatly decreased: 0.5%	Low/very low: 2.9%

Political knowledge	Interest in politics
Increased/greatly increased: 87.3%	High/very high: 64.9%
Stayed the same: 12.2%	Moderate: 30.3%
Decreased/greatly decreased: 0.5%	Low/very low: 4.8%

Knowledge about the war	Interest in the war
Increased/greatly increased: 82.7%	High/very high: 76.1%
Stayed the same: 16.7%	Moderate: 19.6%
Decreased/greatly decreased: 0.6%	Low/very low: 0.4.3%

Trust in government	Self-efficacy
High/very high: 47%	High/very high: 76.5%
Moderate: 30.9%	Moderate: 16.1%
Low to very low: 22.1%	Low to very low: 7.4%

Political involvement	Political ideology
Increased/greatly increased: 32.3%	Republican: 48.0%
Stayed the same: 65.5%	Democrat: 14.5%
Decreased/greatly decreased: 1.7%	Independent: 21.4%
	Other: 16.1%

Support of the Iraq war

Very supportive/supportive: 75.0%

Somewhat supportive: 7.9%

Not supportive at all/not very supportive: 17.1%

the two online sources heavily relied on by slightly fewer that four out of ten respondents, but almost as many reported that they "rarely" or "do not at all" rely on these sources. Face-to-face discussion was more heavily relied on by a greater percentage of respondents (34.5%) than any of the other traditional or online sources (Table 9.2).

Table 9.2 Media Reliance for War Information

	Heavily rely on for war info.	Somewhat rely on for war info.	Rarely/do not rely on for war info.
Reliance on: Blogs	76.8	13.7	9.5
Cable TV news	47.3	22.9	29.8
Newspapers	40.1	28.4	31.5
Online cable news	38.1	27.4	34.5
Online newspapers	37.9	29.3	32.8
Face-to-face discussion	34.5	38.7	26.8
Broadcast radio news	27.7	26.4	45.9
Broadcast talk radio	23.9	18.1	58.0
News magazine	20.6	25.9	53.5
Broadcast TV news	14.9	20.6	64.5
Online magazines	14.1	26.3	59.6
Online broadcast TV news	12.5	22.3	65.2
Bulletin boards/ electronic mailing lists	6.5	11.1	82.4
Chat rooms	2.7	6.8	90.5

Reliance on Blogs Versus Traditional Media and Online Sources The first research question compares reliance on blogs to reliance on other online and traditional sources for information concerning the war on Iraq. The findings from paired sample *t*-tests show that blogs were relied on significantly more than any of the traditional media, online sources and face-to-face discussion (Table 9.3).

Predictors of Reliance on Blogs The second research question examined which independent variables predicted reliance on blogs as a source of information regarding the invasion of Iraq. After controlling for demographics, knowledge about the war as a result of using blogs was the strongest predictor ($b = .33$; $p < .001$) of reliance on blogs, followed by interest in the war ($b = .17$; $p < .001$). Knowledge about politics, knowledge about general news and trust in the government were also positive but weaker predictors. Respondents who felt that blog content increased their knowledge about politics, general news and the war, as well as those with a greater interest in the war and more trusting of the government, were more likely to rely on blogs when seeking information about the war (Table 9.4). Interest in general news was a significant but negative predictor ($b = -.07$; $p < .001$) of blog reliance. Respondents who were not

Table 9.3 Reliance on Blogs Versus Online and Traditional Media for Information About the War on Iraq

Paired sample t-scores:	Reliance on Mean Scores	Reliance on: Mean Scores	
Blogs	4.1	Blogs	4.1
Online TV news	2.1	TV news	2.2
t-score	76.8[a]	*t-score*	69.9[a]
blogs	4.1	Blogs	4.1
Online cable TV news	3.0	Cable TV news	3.2
t-score	42.0[a]	*t-score*	32.9[a]
Blogs	4.1	Blogs	4.1
Online newspapers	3.0	Newspapers	3.1
t-score	40.9[a]	*t-score*	36.7[a]
Blogs	4.1	Blogs	4.1
Online radio	1.6	Radio news	2.6
t-score	108.2[a]	*t-score*	52.7[a]
Blogs	4.1	Blogs	4.1
Online news magazines	2.2	Talk radio	2.3
t-score	73.9[a]	*t-score*	65.2[a]
Blogs	4.1	Blogs	4.1
Bulletin board/electronic mailing lists	1.6	News magazines	2.4
t-score	103.9[a]	*t-score*	63.15[a]
Blogs	4.1	Blogs	4.1
Chat rooms	1.4	Face-to-face discussion	2.9
t-score	124.8[a]	*t-score*	48.17[a]

[a] <.025, two-tailed.

as interested in general news and current events were more likely to turn to blogs to read about the war (Table 9.4).

Overall, Table 9.4 shows that six of the nine measures of attitude, involvement, knowledge and interest were significant, and the variables explain 49.6% of the variance of reliance on blogs. These measures are stronger predictors of blog reliance than is reliance on traditional and online sources.

Reliance on traditional media, online sources and face-to-face discussion only accounts for 1.5% of the variance for reliance on blogs. After controlling for demographics and attitude measures, reliance on online newspapers and reliance on face-to-face discussion were the only positive predictors of reli-

Table 9.4 Predictors of Reliance on Blogs

Gender	−.04[a]
Age	.03
Education	.04[a]
Income	−.02
R2	.092 (.09%)
Political involvement	.02
Knowledge about politics	.12[c]
Knowledge about general news	.08[c]
Knowledge about the war	.33[c]
Interest in politics	.03
Interest in general news	−.07[c]
Interest in the war	.17[c]
Trust in government	.07[c]
Self-efficacy	−.00
R2	.588 (49.6%)
Reliance on:	
Online broadcast television news	.01
Online cable television news	.02
Online newspapers	.05[b]
Online radio	−.05[b]
Online magazines	.00
Bulletin boards/electronic mailing lists	.03
Online chat	.02
Broadcast television	−.10[c]
Cable television	.03*
Printed newspapers	−.04[a]
Broadcast radio news	.01
Broadcast talk radio	.02
Printed news magazines	.01
Face-to-face discussion	.06[c]
R2	.603 (1.5%)
R2	.603
Adjusted R	.363
Significance	.000

[a] $p < .05$.
[b] $p < .01$.
[c] $p < .001$.

ance on blogs. Respondents who relied on online newspapers and discussion with friends and family about the war also relied on blogs for war information. Broadcast television news, printed newspapers and online radio news were also significant, but negative, predictors of reliance on blogs. Respondents less likely to rely on broadcast television, ($b = -.10$; $p < .001$), traditionally delivered newspapers ($b = -.04$; $p < .05$) and online radio news ($b = -.05$; $p < .01$) turned to blogs to learn about the war (Table 9.4).

Gender and education also predicted reliance on blogs. Educated males were most likely to rely on blogs for war information. This finding closely matches other research that found that educated males are the typical blog users (Greenspan, 2003; Rainie et al., 2004; Rainie, 2005).

Generally, respondents most likely to rely on blogs for information about the war on Iraq were educated males who trusted the government, were interested in the war, but not very interested in general news and claimed that blogs increased their knowledge about politics, general news and the war. Furthermore, for war information, they relied on online newspapers and face-to-face discussion but not on online radio or broadcast television.

Discussion

This study employed an online survey of blog users to find out how much they relied on blogs for information about the Iraqi war and how blog reliance compared to reliance on traditional and other online media sources. The study also examined the degree to which demographics and political variables predicted reliance on blogs for war information. Observers suggest that, since the Iraq war, blogs have become an important source of news for a core of Internet users (Hamilton, 2003; Hastings, 2003) and that traditional journalists depend on blogs, particularly warblogs, for news and analysis ("Surfing the Warblogs," 2003).

Political observers suggest that, although only about 4% of Internet users relied on blogs during the Iraq war (Rainie et al., 2004), this core of loyal blog users visited the blogs frequently because they provided a genuine alternative to traditional and other online sources (Ryan, 2003). Users have praised blogs for providing more accurate, in-depth and personal accounts of the war than traditional media did (Levy, 2003; Ryan, 2003; Kaye & Johnson, 2004). Also, blogs often provided firsthand accounts of the war by soldiers and other individuals more knowledgeable than traditional journalists (Bedell, 2003).

Users also contend that blogs provide more thoughtful analysis as well as perspectives not offered by traditional and other online media sources (Wall, 2005; Hamilton, 2003; Hastings, 2003). Indeed, this study suggests that more than three quarters of blog users relied heavily on blogs as a source of information about the war—significantly more than any other source of war information. The next highest source of information, cable television news, was only heavily used by 47% of the respondents.

Users may rely more on blogs than on other sources because they perceive blog content to be superior to that of traditional and other online media; however, characteristics of the blog users may explain part of the disparity between reliance on blogs and other sources. This study supports previous research suggesting that blog users hardly resemble mainstream America in terms of ideology (Leo, 2002; Levy et al., 2002; Thompson, 2003; Crabtree, 2002) and background characteristics (Whelan, 2003; Rainie, 2005). The war on Iraq was supported or strongly supported by three quarters of the respondents, and almost half are affiliated with the Republican Party as compared to 14% who consider themselves Democrats.

Not surprisingly these conservative blog users are much more likely (64.5%) to seek information from what they consider conservative or very conservative blogs as opposed to liberal or very liberal blogs (16.3%). Although traditional media strive to present both sides of the issue, bloggers are under no such pressure. Blogs reflect the bias of their creators and conservative users are attracted to such blogs to read and to share views with like-minded individuals.

Demographically, blog users in this study represent an elite group: They are affluent, well-educated, White males, much like users during the early days of the Internet. The demographic profile of blog users may help explain their high reliance on traditional newspapers as well as blogs. Studies show that newspapers are read by those of high socioeconomic status more than those with lower incomes and less education, in part because they are a high-effort medium: Newspapers tend to present more in-depth information than broadcast news and require active attention while television permits passive viewing (Chew, 1994; Chaffee & Frank, 1996; Chaffee & Schleuder, 1986).

Blogs may be an even higher effort medium than newspapers. Most political and warblogs are simply paragraphs of text without images in which the reader can click on a link to get detailed stories on a topic. Furthermore, blogs often allow readers to comment about stories posted. Therefore, to read a blog story completely, one typically reads the blogger's commentary on a subject and the story upon which the blogger is expounding, as well as comments posted by blog users. Demographics, however, were a weak predictor of blog reliance, explaining less than 1% of the variance. Educated males were more likely to rely on blogs for war information; age and income had no influence. This supports studies of blog credibility that found demographics had little influence on how much one trusts the medium (Johnson & Kaye, 2004).

Blog users are highly critical of traditional media, which they contend are run by a liberal elite (Seipp, 2002). Indeed, some suggest that the popularity of blogs coincided with a growing distrust of and disgust for traditional media (Amis, 2002; Lasica, 2002). Studies suggest that trust in a medium is strongly linked to how much one relies on it (Austin & Dong, 1994; Wanta & Hu, 1994; Johnson & Kaye, 1998, 2000). If this is the case, then bloggers' dislike of traditional media is not a blanket condemnation, but rather one aimed largely at broadcast news. More than eight out of ten said they rarely or did not rely on broadcast and online broadcast television news for war information and almost three quarters said they rarely or did not rely on broadcast radio sites. Furthermore, the regression equations suggested that the less people relied on broadcast television news and broadcast radio sites, the more they used blogs for war information.

Blog users, do, however, rely more heavily on online and traditional newspapers and online and traditional cable news. Some cable television news outlets, particularly FoxNews, are known for their conservative news slant (Johnson, 2002), so it is not surprising that blog users look to cable television news to support their positions. Political observers suggest a paradoxical relationship between newspapers and blogs. Although blogs such as talking-points.com are specifically devoted to critiquing media—particularly large newspapers such as the *New York Times* (Reynolds, 2002; Kurtz, 2002), bloggers rely heavily on newspapers for information and they routinely link to online newspaper stories (Rosenberg, 2002).

This paradox is reflected in this study. Reliance on traditional and online newspapers posted the third and fifth highest scores, respectively, for information about the Iraq war. Also, the more people rely on online newspapers, the more they rely on blogs for war information. Blogs, then, supplement information they receive from online newspapers. Although blog users rely on traditional newspapers, the medium is a negative predictor of accessing blogs: Those less likely to rely on traditional newspapers were most likely to visit blogs to get war information. Presumably, it is easy for blog users to compare blog accounts of events to online newspaper stories that they can quickly scan through newspapers from all over the world. These results parallel those of Eveland and Dylko (2006), who discovered that online news, but not traditional news use, predicted blog reading.

Finally, those more likely to discuss the war with others rely more heavily on blogs for war information. Several observers suggest that one of the strengths of blogs is that they allow people to read information that supports their worldview and to share views with like-minded individuals (Thompson, 2003). Presumably, discussing the war with like-minded individuals sparks interest in the war, provokes thought and stimulates people to visit blogs that share their views on the Iraq war. Although they did not specifically examine blogs, these results also support Hardy and Scheufele (2005), who found evidence of a differential gains model in which those who rely more on face-to-face and online discussion relied more on news sources and were able to extract more meaningful information from them.

Political attitudes proved the strongest predictors of blog reliance, accounting for almost half of the variance. In particular, knowledge of and interest in the war predicted reliance on blogs for war information. Knowledge about politics and general news was a weaker, though significant, predictor of blog use. Most mass communication researchers examine the influence of media use on political variables such as knowledge and interest. However, this study supports other research that suggests that the relationship between media use and knowledge and interest is reciprocal (Weaver, 1996). Those more interested and knowledgeable about the war visit blogs for in-depth, analytical information about the war, which, in turn, boosts their interest and knowledge about the war.

Previous research suggests content exposure is a stronger predictor of political variables than general exposure measures (Johnson et al., 2000; McLeod & McDonald, 1985). This study takes that research one step further by noting that knowledge and interest in a particular content, in this case the Iraq war, strongly predicts reliance on a medium, in this case blogs, for information about that topic.

Trust in government also positively predicted reliance on blogs for war information despite relatively low political trust among blog users. Perhaps the positive relationship between trust and blog use reflects the fact that this conservative group of blog users trusts the conservative Bush administration—particularly on the handling of the war—and this trust translates into visiting blog sites supporting the war effort.

Limitations

The study was designed to examine how much people relied on blogs for information about the war and the factors that predicted their blog use for war information. However, only about 4% of Internet users visited blogs for war information. Therefore, results from this study cannot be generalized to Internet users in general. Also, because this study relied on a convenience sample of blog users, the degree to which these findings can be generalized to all blog users is uncertain. Reaching this small population of Internet users is difficult, if not impossible, because traditional methods of data collection do not readily apply to the Internet. The Internet does not have a mechanism for random sampling of the Internet population, much less blog users; therefore, nonprobability sampling is appropriate and commonly used when posting an online survey (Babbie, 2001).

The Internet is conducive to purposive sampling because subsets within the larger population can be identified and solicited through announcements posted on message boards and sent out to special mailing lists, and through hyperlinks posted on key online sites, as was done in this study (Kaye & Johnson, 1999). Careful use of purposive sampling generates results that may be representative of a specific subset of Internet users, but may not be representative of the larger population (Babbie, 2001). However, the demographic profile of blog users who responded to this study closely mirrors the characteristics of blog readers reported by others done at about the time of this survey (Greenspan, 2003; Rainie et al., 2004; Whelan, 2003), suggesting this survey was representative of blog users then.

This study found that blog users relied considerably more on blogs than on other information sources for war information and that knowledge of and interest in the war were the strongest predictors of visiting blogs for information on the Iraq war. Thus, this study examined blog use in a particular context—the Iraq war—during a time at the end of the ground war and the beginnings of efforts to establish peace in the region. Future studies should explore blog use in general and see how blog reliance compares to use of traditional and online sources.

The exponential growth of blog use after the war caused some bloggers to predict giddily that blog use would soon replace traditional media (Reynolds, 2002; Seipp, 2002). It appears doubtful that this prediction will come to pass. However, it would be interesting to study blog users in the future to see whether, like Internet users in general, blog readers became more demographically mainstream as blogs become more popular.

References

Amis, D. (2002, Sept. 21). Web logs: Online navel gazing. [Online]. http://www.netfreedom.org.

Andrews, P. (2003). Is blogging journalism? *Nieman Reports*, (57)3, 63–64.

Ashley, C. (1992). Internet groups allow for productive information gathering. *Online Review*, 16, 157–159.

Austin E. W., & Dong O. (1994). Source v. content effects of judgments of news believability. *Journalism Quarterly* 91 (winter: 973-83.

Babbie, E. R. (1990). *Survey research methods*. Belmont, CA: Wadsworth.

Bedell, D. (2003, April 7). War blogs add personal edge to news. *The Dallas Morning News*. [Online]. http://www.dallasnews.com.

Blood, R. (2002). Blogs: A history and perspective. In J. Rodzvilla (Ed.), *We've got blog: How blogs are changing our culture* (pp. 7–16). Cambridge, MA: Perseus Publishing.

Carver, B. (2003). What would Dewey do? Librarians grapple with Internet. *Library Journal*, 128, 30–32.

Chew, F. (1994). The relationship of information needs to issue relevance and media use. *Journalism Quarterly*, 71, 676–688.

Chaffee, S. H., & Frank, S. (1996). How Americans get political information: Print versus broadcast news. *The Annals of the American Academy of Political and Social Sciences*, 546, 48–58.

Chaffee, S. H., & Schleuder J. (1986). Measurement and effects of attention to media news. *Human Communication Research*, 13, 76–107.

Crabtree, J. (2002, September 30). Bloggers of the Left, unite! *New Statesman*, 36.

Delwiche, A. (2004, May). *Agenda-setting, opinion leadership, and the world of Web logs*. Paper presented at the International Communication Annual Convention, New Orleans, LA.

Eveland, W. P., Jr., & Dylko, I. (2006). Chapter 6, this volume.

Fallows, D., & Rainie, L. (2004). The Internet as unique news source: Millions go online for news and images not covered in the mainstream press. http://www.pewinternet.org, July 8, 2004.

Greenspan, R. (2003). Blogging by the numbers. Cyberatlas [Online]. http://cyberatlas.internet.com/ bigpicture/applications.

Grossman, L., Hamilton, A., Buechner, M. M., & Whitaker, L. (2004). Meet Joe blog. *Time*. [Online]. http://www.time.com/archive.

Hamilton, A. (2003, April 7). Best of the war blogs. *Time*, 161, 91.

Hamdy, N., & Mobarak, R. (2004). Iraq war ushers in Web-based era. In R. D. Berenger (Ed.), *Global media goes to war: Role of news and entertainment media during the 2003 Iraq war* (pp. 245–254). Spokane, WA: Marquette Books.

Hardy, B. W., & Scheufele, D. A. (2005). Examining differential gains of Internet use: Comparing the moderating role of talk and online interactions. *Journal of Communication, 55*(1), 71–84.

Hastings, M. (2003, April 7). Bloggers over Baghdad. *Newsweek, 141,* 48–49.

Jesdanun, A. (2001, October 14). In online logs, Web authors personalize attacks, retaliation. *The Florida Times-Union,* Retrieved June 24, 2003, from http://www.Jacksonville.com/tu-online/stories/101401/bus_7528493.html.

Johnson, P. (2002). Fox News enjoys new view—From the top. *USA Today.* pp. 1A–2A.

Johnson, T. J., & Kaye, B. K. (1998). Cruising is believing? Comparing Internet and traditional sources on media credibility measures. *Journalism & Mass Communication Quarterly, 75,* 325–340.

Johnson, T. J., & Kaye, B. K. (2000). Using is believing: The influence of reliance on the credibility of online political information among politically interested Internet users. *Journalism & Mass Communication Quarterly, 77,* 865–879.

Johnson, T. J., & Kaye, B. K. (2004). Wag the blog: How reliance on traditional media and the Internet influence credibility perceptions of blogs among blog users. *Journalism & Mass Communication Quarterly, 81*(3), 622–642.

Katz, J. (2002). Here come the blogs. In J. Rodzvilla (Ed.), *We've got blog: How blogs are changing our culture* (pp. 17–24). Cambridge, MA: Perseus Publishing.

Kaye, B. K. (2005a). It's a blog, blog, blog, blog world: Users and uses of blogs. *Atlantic Journal of Communication, 13,* 73–95.

Kaye, B. K., & Johnson, T. J. (1999). Taming the cyber frontier: Techniques for improving online surveys. *Social Science Computer Review, 17,* 323–337.

Kaye, B. K., & Johnson, T. J. (2004). Blogs as a source of information about the war in Iraq. In R. D. Berenger (Ed.), *Global media go to war* (pp. 291–301). Spokane, WA: Marquette Books.

Kaye, B. K., & Johnson, T. J. (2006). The age of reasons: Motives for using different components of the Internet for political information. In A. P. Williams & J. C. Tedesco (Eds.), *The Internet election: Perspectives on the Web's role in Campaign 2004.* (pp. 147–167). Lanham, MD: Rowman & Littlefield Publishers, Inc.

Kaye, B. K., & Johnson, T. J. (1999). Taming the cyber frontier: Techniques for improving online surveys. *Social Science Computer Review, 17,* 323–337.

Kornblum, J. (2003). Web logs convey "raw stuff" of Iraq war. *USA Today.* Available at http://www.usatoday.com/tech, March 24.

Kurtz, H. (2002). How blogs keep the media honest. [Online]. http://www.washingtonpost.com.

Lasica, J. D. (2002). Blogging as a form of journalism: Blogs offer a vital, creative outlet for alternative voices. In J. Rodzvilla (Ed.), *We've got blog: How blogs are changing our culture* (pp. 163–170). Cambridge, MA: Perseus Publishing.

Lenhart, A., Fallows, D. & Horrigan, D. (2004). Content creation online: 44% of U.S. Internet users have contributed their thoughts and their files to the online world. [Online] http://www.pewinternet.org/reports.

Leo, J. (2002, May 13). A blog's bark has a bite. *U.S. News & World Report,* 48.

Levy, S. (2003, March 29).Bloggers' Delight, MSNBC.com [Online]. http://www.MSNBC.com,

Levy, S., Figueroa, A., Campo-Flores, A., Lin, J. & Gossard, M. H. (2002, August 26). Living in the blogosphere. *Newsweek,* 42–45.

McLeod, J., & McDonald, D. G. (1985). Beyond simple exposure: Media orientations and their impact on political processes. *Communication Research, 12,* 3–34.

Palser, B. (2002, July/August). Journalistic blogging. *American Journalism Review, 24,* 58.

Palser, B. (2003). Free to blog? *American Journalism Review,* (June/July), 62.

Papacharissi, Z. (2004, May). *The blogger revolution? Audiences as media producers.* Presented at the annual meeting of the International Communication Association, New Orleans: May 2004.

Potter, D. (2005, April/May). A victim of arrogance. *American Journalism Review, 27,* 72.

Rainie, L. (2005). The state of blogging. [Online]. http://pewinternet.org/reports.

Rainie, L., Fox, S. & Fallows, D. (2003). The Internet and the Iraq war: How online Americans have used the Internet to learn war news, understand events, and promote their views. [Online]. http://www.pewinternet.org/reports.

Reynolds, G. (2002). A technological reformation. [Online]. http://www.techcentralstation.com.

Reynolds, G. H. (2004). The blogs of war. *National Interest, 75*, 59–64.

Rosenberg, S. (2002). Much ado about blogging. [Online]. http://www. Salon.com/tech/col/rose/.

Ryan, M. (2003). Blogs' rise stymies old media. *Chicago Tribune.* [Online]. http://www.chicago.tribune.com, April 17.

Schulman, D. (2005, Sept./Oct.). Their war. *Columbia Journalism Review, 44,* 13.

Seipp, C. (2002, June). Online uprising. *American Journalism Review, 24,* 42–47.

Simon, S. (2003, March 29). Analysis: Web logs the newest way to convey war information. National Public Radio. [Online]. http://www.npr.org.

Smolkin, R. (2004). The expanding blogsphere. *American Journalism Review, 26,* 38–43.

Surfing the warblogs for news from the front (2003, April 7). Maclean's, [Online]. http://www.macleans.ca/topstories/article.jsp?content=57745#.

Sydell, L. (2003). Web logs the newest way to convey war information. Weekend Edition, National Public Radio. [Online]. http://www.npr.org.

Thompson, G. (2003). Blogs, warblogs, the public sphere, and bubbles. *Transformations.* [Online]. http://transformations.cqu.edu.au/journal/issue_07/article_02.shtml.

Wall, M. A. (2005). Blogs of war: Warblogs as news. *Journalism, 6,* 153–172.

Wanta, W., & Hu, Y. (1994). The effects of credibility, reliance and exposure on media agenda-setting: A path analysis model. *Journalism Quarterly, 71,* 90–98.

Weaver, D. (1996). What voters learn from media. *The Annals of the American Academy of Political and Social Science, 556,* 34–47.

Whelan, D. (2003). In a fog about blogs. *American Demographics, 25,* 22.

Yousefzadeh, P. (2003). Weasel words. [Online]. http://www.techstation.com.

Notes

1. This study asked respondents about their use of blogs for information about the war. This includes blogs that discussed war issues as well as blogs specifically devoted to the war (warblogs). Although the study focuses on blogs containing news and political opinions, this constitutes only a portion of the blogging universe. Indeed, the most popular blogs are personal diaries of an individual's life (Whelan, 2003).

2. A follow-up study by Pew Research in early 2004 suggested that the number of those who had visited blogs had increased to 11% of the Internet population (Lenhart, Fallows & Horrigan, 2004) and to 27% by the end of 2005 (Rainie, 2005). However, the Rainie study also suggested that only 6 in 10 Internet users (62%) knew what a blog was.

3. Blogs: 2020hindsight, Ackackackcom, Across Atlantic, Africapundit, Agonist, Alphecca, Altercation, Alternet, Amish Tech Support, Amishblogmo, AndrewOlmsted, Andrew-Sullivan, Apostablog, Atlanticblogcom, Atriosblogspotcom, Bag & Baggage, Balloon Juice, Baseball Musings, Behold, blogspot, Biasblogfodder, BlissfulKnowledge, blogdex, bloglogic, blogosphere, blogs Of War, Give blogs4god, blogtporg/K, Boingboingnet, BryonScott, Buck Stops Here, Cnn.com, Cold Fury, ComeOn, CoranteOnblogging, Corantec, Corner On NRO, Counterrevolutionary, CraigsChamp, Crblogspot, Critical Mass, Cut On Bias, Daily Dish, Daily Pundit, Daniel Drezner, Davespickscom, Daypopcom, Dead Parrot Society, Dean Esmay, Doc Searls, Docblogs, DrudgeReport, Erablognet, Erin O'Connor, Ever Changing Select, Eyndenloo, Fark, Fat Guy, FreeRepublic, Geek-Chick, Glenn Reynolds, Goatsec, Greenfield, HanlonVision, Hierogrammate, HighClear, Hoder, HomelessGuy, Hoosier Review, HPANA, Hunnet, IdleType, Ihodercom, Instapundit, JdLasica, JD New Media Musings, Jeff Cooper, Jessica'sWell, JoanneJacobs, JonahGoldberg, Josh Claybourne, Journalsp, Jsnotesblogs, Leftcoastblog, Leuschke, LGF, Light Of Reason, Like A Hooligan's, LA Livejournal, Lucianne, Matwyglesias.com, Mediaticblog, Melblogger, Metafilter, Metapop, Midwest Conservative, MouseMusings, MSNBC, National Review, Newsweek.com, No. 2. Pencil, Ogloboc, OnBias, Parduedur, Pattern Recognition, Popdex, Post-Atomic, Powerline, RachaelLucas, RealClearPolitics, Rebecca Blood, Resurrections, Ritingonwall, Rjwest.com, Sassafrass, Seaofkitt, Shellen.com, Silflay, Hraka, Slate, Slings and Arrows, SouthKnoxBubba, Suzanna Cornett, Tacitus, Tapped, Tim Blair, Uncorrelated.com, Unqualified Offering, Volokh Conspiracy, warblogs, Winds Of Change and Zogbyblogspot.com.

4. Bulletin boards/electronic mailing lists: bloggingcommunity@Yahoo, Colorado bloggers, Comp.Dcom.Telecom, Dfwblogs, Lds-Poll@Yahoogroups.Com, Pinoybloggers, Salon blogs Group, Telecomdigest, Theblosxom,Val-L, blogdeveloperusergroup, blogemailgroup, blogusersgroup andYahoogroups-Syndic8.
5. The efficacy index is below the normal .70 standard for internal reliability. However, low reliability scores are not unusual for an index of only two items. One of the main ways to ensure reliability is to use measures proven reliable in previous research (Babbie, 2001). Therefore, the authors combined the two items into an index because these items from the National Election Studies have proven reliable in past studies.
6. The survey's first question asked respondents to enter their e-mail addresses; 3,311 (88.4%) complied. The respondents' e-mail addresses together with their Internet Protocol (IP) addresses (programmed to appear on every completed survey) were used to delete duplicated surveys. Additionally, after sending the completed survey, a Web page would immediately appear thanking the respondents for their participation and verifying that the survey had been sent so that respondents would not retransmit the survey.

Part Three
The Future of Media: Examining the
Impact of Blogging on Journalism

10

Press Protection in the Blogosphere: Applying a Functional Definition of "Press" to News Web Logs

LAURA HENDRICKSON

Since the Supreme Court first acknowledged constitutional protection for "the lonely pamphleteer," (*Branzburg v. Hayes*, 1972), the lines between who does and does not receive deference under the First Amendment as members of the press have been blurry. The dominant position with respect to First Amendment protections—in theory if not in practicality—is that the press does not receive any privileges that individuals do not receive. Still, "the press" is often singled out to be accommodated at public events and protective legal doctrines are sometimes casually referred to with reference to "the press" (*New York Times v. United States*, 1971; *Near v. Minnesota*, 1931)[1] without necessarily any explicit insistence that the doctrines may apply more broadly. Add to the existing ambiguity a potentially new form of press—the blog—and who qualifies as "the press" may be as much open to debate as whether the press in any form deserves special protections.

This chapter examines whether bloggers may be our contemporary pamphleteers and whether, in using a functional definition of press, bloggers should qualify for the same privileges—most obviously, the journalistic privilege or shield laws—offered to more traditionally defined journalists. In asking this question, the chapter also must confront whether the press in any form is entitled to special protections or privileges. The question is more important than ever as individual citizens take to their keyboards to produce blogs about the major, and sometimes minor, issues of the day. On occasion, bloggers even take pride in adopting the role of watchdogs of the more mainstream, established news media (Power Line, 2004; Little Green Footballs, 2004).[2] Should these not-so-lonely "blogeteers" have weaker protections than the major news outlets so readily recognized by the average person? If so, why?

The chapter begins with a brief discussion of the blogging phenomenon and how it requires a new way of thinking about the dissemination of news and commentary, then moves to a discussion of the Press Clause of the U.S. Constitution[3] and the sources of privileges enjoyed by the press—most obviously, the right to be shielded from subpoenas for notes and for the names of confidential news sources. However, because granting any special protections to the press requires a delineation of who qualifies for that protection—that is, who is the press—the chapter then discusses the potential of moving to a functional definition of the press to make that determination, addressing potential components of such a definition and pointing out that this is likely to require the inclusion of at least some blogs.

The Bloggers

Blogging in many ways has returned to individuals and small groups the power to affect public discourse. Blogs have the advantages of old and new: They are relatively inexpensive to produce and have the power to reach large audiences quickly in a way more traditionally associated with the large, complex news organizations that were considered essential for disseminating messages under the traditional definition of "mass communication" (Severin & Tankard, 2000). The traditional model included newspaper delivery and prescheduled broadcasts filled with a wide variety of information about government, lifestyles, science, crime, and so on. It required general assignment and beat reporters, photographers, graphic artists, editors, managers, press operators, ad sales people and others. Each had an individualized set of skills and each was a required component of the whole. Shoemaker and Reese (1996) point to the varying natures of these organizations as being significant enough to have an important effect on media content.

Because establishing such an organization requires substantial investments of time, money, effort and risk, the entry costs have been prohibitive to most average citizens. As a result, producing the news has become a relatively exclusive domain. It is not so surprising that many late 20th century news establishments initially resisted the web's significance as a viable news outlet, largely because of the ease and economy with which individuals could make use of the new medium. News blogs in some cases were resisted and criticized by mainstream journalists as they emerged, with some even publishing complaints with titles such as "Matt Drudge is not my colleague" (Borger, 1998). Some traditional journalists also objected to the rapidity with which information was posted without any checking mechanisms, perceiving the practice as error prone and reckless.

This chapter defines "blog" somewhat generally, given the ambiguity in the term's use and the lack of consensus as to its precise meaning. At least one writer has called blogs "something [we] can no more easily define than a Rorschach splotch" (Conniff, 2005). Nevertheless, some defining characteristics should be identified if analysis is to be of any use. Blogs could be identified by the structure of their websites, by their function or by their components. Winer (2003) has said that the unedited voice of a person is the "essential element of Weblog writing," while Jason Calcanis has indicated that important defining characteristics include postings in reverse chronological order, unfiltered content, a space for reader comments and the presence of hyperlinks to other web content (Calcanis, cited in Conniff, 2005).

For purposes of this chapter, we mostly exclude from our definition of blogs the online content provided by news outlets already established in other forms, such as television networks and newspapers. However, the blogs that remain include a wide variety—some with known or notable authors and others that are more anonymous; some that use flip, informal styles and others with more serious tones; some that engage in journalistic newsgathering and others that focus more on commentary with links to other news sources; some written by one individual and others produced cooperatively by two, three or four contributing writers. Most are updated regularly and include an interactive element that allows readers to respond with comments. Not all of the news sites used as examples here would necessarily describe themselves as blogs.

In fact, on the frontier of Internet news, sites that purport to be news oriented vary in style and content, and some are noticeably partisan. Some of these sites act more as conduits, or news digests, providing space for citizens to post links to separate online news sources, while not producing much original news content. Two politically conservative news sites that emerged early on the web are Free Republic and Lucianne, where individuals post links to stories from other online news sites and anonymously discuss their reactions to them. These sites would not be blogs according to the narrowest use of the term.

However, other sites are dedicated to producing their own content, much of it opinion and commentary. Many of those who engage in partisan blogging see themselves as a counterbalance to an institutional press they perceive as biased.[4] Today bloggers emerge from a variety of political ideologies when they express an ideology at all. Instapundit is generally considered conservative or libertarian, while a blog known as DailyKos[5] is a major space on the web for liberal political debate. What many of these sites primarily produce is public discussion about the news of the day, and some have established rules by which that discourse will take place (see TalkLeft's Comment Policy, 2006; Captain's Quarters Comment Moderation Policy, 2004).[6]

Many bloggers also engage in activities traditionally associated with the practice of journalism. They lurk in the halls of government, conduct background research, carry cameras (or camera phones) and adopt engaging, informal writing styles. For example, a Texas blog on criminal justice issues openly discusses the writer's attempts to obtain information through the state's Public Information Act (Henson, 2005).

In addition, some bloggers acquired press passes to the national political conventions during the 2004 presidential campaign. Among them were TalkLeft, which defines its mission as "liberal coverage of crime-related political and injustice news." There was also OxBlog, run by a couple of former Oxford graduate students, boasting complimentary quotes on its front page from more traditional journalists Fareed Zakaria ("a great read") and Michael Barone ("I enjoy oxblog very much"). PressThink, NYU journalism professor Jay Rosen's blog, has described itself as the "ghost of democracy in the media machine."

In addition to providing news, some blogs provide space for the public to weigh in anonymously. It is a regular town square—but is it journalism and are the participants "the press"? Is Matt Drudge a journalist's colleague after all, and why does it matter? From a legal perspective, it matters primarily in those cases where the press receives privileges or protections not otherwise available to average citizens. While the dominant First Amendment doctrine suggests that the press and individuals should be treated similarly, as a practical matter the press does receive privileges such as press passes that allow them entry into legislative chambers or courtroom trials, while excluding others; fee waivers for Freedom of Information Act requests as well as postal subsidies; and, significantly, statutory protection in many states from having to respond to subpoenas for their notes or for the names of their sources.

The Meaning of the Press Clause

Those who believe the press as an institution should receive protections not granted to individual citizens often point to the presence in the First Amendment of a Speech Clause and a Press Clause. The importance of the distinction, of course, is that if the Press Clause did not represent a separate set of rights it would be a superfluous part of the First Amendment; in the words of U.S. Supreme Court Justice Potter Stewart (1975), it would be a "constitutional redundancy" (p. 633). First Amendment scholar David Anderson (2002), who previously had discussed whether the framers intended an independent role for the Press Clause (1983), points out the "reluctance" of the Supreme Court "to confront directly the meaning of the Press Clause" (2002, p. 452). But Justice Stewart (1975) was at least one person who tried to confront it, making the argument that the press performs a special function in a democratic society, specifically as "an additional check on the three official branches" (p. 634).

Some have carefully parsed the language of the First Amendment to find an answer. Ugland points out:

> The use of a comma and "or" suggests, however subtly, that there was a deliberate separation of these two words. The use of the word "the" could even be significant. By referring to "the press," the framers appear to refer to a distinct institution (2003).

Frederick Schauer (2000) has said that "the distinctions between freedom of speech, largely the right of individuals and associations...and freedom of the press, largely the right of the institutionalized media, are important" (n. 3). He goes on, however, to treat the clauses interchangeably, arguing that "the conflation accurately reflects American First Amendment doctrine, in which the press receives no rights under the Press Clause that all speakers, including the press, don't get under the Speech Clause."

As Schauer points out, some have used the Speech Clause to apply to individuals and the Press Clause to apply to the institutional or corporate press. It probably was always a dubious exercise in line drawing, but contemporary communication technology shows us even more clearly that it simply no longer holds up under scrutiny. Many websites and bloggers today perform functions the same as or similar to the institutional press, although blogs are organized differently and usually generated by individuals or small groups rather than large organizations.

It also seems plausible that the two relevant clauses of the First Amendment, the speech and press clauses, exist to distinguish by medium and not by messenger—to make clear that the Constitution protects spoken and written expression, as well as any future means of communication provided by new technology, regardless of the source (Ugland, 2003).

It could also be argued that the Press Clause, if it was intended to protect an institution, was targeting the function of that institution more than its structure and organization. Even before the popular use of the world wide web, legal analysts called for recognizing a functional dimension to the Press Clause. In the 1980s, Shiffrin (1980) suggested that "many of the objections to a separate privilege for the press could be overcome if the press clause were regarded as protecting a function—the countervoice to government—rather than an institution or private business" (p. 618). Some contemporary bloggers might also add a desire to see blogs as a countervoice to the mainstream media, which, regardless of their ideology, many of them tend to perceive as biased and powerful.

Whether the Press Clause of the First Amendment is explicitly invoked or not, its existence probably has contributed to a general sentiment that some entity known as "the press" is valued in a democratic society and is protected because it is named in the Constitution. Today, so-called citizen journalists are able to perform much the same function as the institutional press, reaching large audiences from the privacy of their homes but without a large staff to produce and distribute their content. In fact, bloggers share characteristics with the early American press. All of this raises the question: What, if anything, about the institutional press as it evolved in the 20th century would make it uniquely eligible for certain legal protections not granted to individual citizens performing essentially the same functions?

Sources of Press Protection

As at least one writer has pointed out, we could take three potential legal approaches to treatment of the press: (a) no special press privileges or protections; (b) privileges or protections granted by sources other than the First Amendment; or (c) Press Clause-based privileges or protections (Anderson,

2002, p. 435). The question of whether the Press Clause, as a matter of constitutional law, offers more expansive protections to newspapers, magazines and television networks than it does to everyday citizens is not fully resolved, and a number of laws intended to protect journalists remain ambiguous as a matter of constitutional law. However, the privileges granted the press often come by way of state or administrative law, through statutes and rules; while they are not clearly or explicitly guaranteed by current First Amendment doctrine, neither have they been constitutionally voided.

The focus of statutes and rules that protect the press tends not to be on material that is published or broadcast, which is fairly universally accepted as protected by the First Amendment under the Speech Clause, but on newsgathering, where the significance of the Press Clause, as well, could be invoked most directly. Legal press protection, including for newsgathering, can be viewed as shield and sword. Some "sword" laws ensure access to information or places, while "shield" laws protect journalists from being charged for certain activities in the newsgathering process.

The press is protected through such statutes as the federal Freedom of Information Act (1967) and the various state open records and open meetings (or "sunshine") laws, which provide access to meetings and government records. These broadly drafted laws generally are considered to apply to individuals and to the press. However, as a practical matter, the use of press passes that limit access to important events, as well as the fee waivers that established journalists receive in requesting information under the FOIA, suggests the press does enjoy special administrative privileges that most individuals do not.

In addition, limited space at public events or in public spaces, such as in courtrooms and legislative chambers, requires that access be limited to a certain number of people. With the perception that the press acts as a surrogate for the public, the limiting parameters of who gets access usually require that the press be defined in some way. The U.S. Senate requires the committee making these determinations to limit access in certain cases to "bone fide correspondents of repute in their profession." Those who qualify for access to the periodicals press gallery would be those whose "principal income is obtained from news correspondence intended for publication in newspapers entitled to second-class mailing privileges" (Rules Governing Press Galleries, 2006).

However, in addition to the laws that ensure press access to information (for which limited space at any given event perhaps suggests some practical rationale, for example, for limiting press passes), we also have the so-called shield laws that protect journalists from having to identify anonymous sources or turn over confidential information to law enforcement. These laws vary from state to state and have been constitutionally ambiguous for some time. Periodically, when authorities have attempted to subpoena reporters' notes or cite journalists for contempt for refusing to testify, the issue has been spotlighted in the press (Liptak, 2004).[7]

Shield laws are sometimes also referred to as "journalistic privilege." Privileges granted at common law historically were granted to people such as spouses, doctors and clergy to encourage people to speak openly with each other without losing the incentive for communication provided by confidentiality. Journalism shield laws, by contrast, typically are state statutes intended to protect reporters from having to identify news sources to whom they have promised confidentiality and from having to turn over notes they have taken in the course of newsgathering, whether those notes ever saw the light of publication or not. Thus far, the Supreme Court has declined to acknowledge constitutional protection for such a privilege. While several federal bills sponsored by lawmakers from both parties were introduced as recently as 2005 (Free Flow of Information Act, 2005; Free Speech Protection Act, 2005), the U.S. Congress has thus far declined to pass such a law. As a result, the protection journalists receive from these laws varies from state to state.

The rationale for such laws is straightforward. If journalists are forced to turn over information, especially when they have promised confidentiality to their sources, a chilling effect will follow. Sources no longer will be willing to give information to journalists if those sources know that a promise of confidentiality will not protect them when the reporter is subpoenaed. As Linda L. Berger (2003) has pointed out, shield laws exist to protect the free flow of information, not to protect individual sources and reporters. When sources stop speaking to reporters, the rationale suggests, the public loses because information will become scarcer. Protecting journalists in this way presumably also keeps them from being used as an investigative arm of the government.

Because this privilege's protection under the First Amendment is ambiguous at best, it is not clear whether the Speech Clause or the Press Clause would more appropriately be applied to it. The relevance of the Speech Clause to shield laws probably depends on whether one believes the press would be chilled—that is, their freedom of expression curtailed—in the absence of a law to protect the way in which they gather the news. The definitive Supreme Court case on shield law protection, *Branzburg v. Hayes* (1972, p. 704), has been used in support of and in opposition to constitutional protection for shield laws. In a narrow majority in *Branzburg*, the Court ruled against journalists who had argued for a constitutional privilege to protect their sources. However, many since then have borrowed from the concurrence as well to conclude that some First Amendment protection may still remain for news gathering, the extent of which is anything but clear.

Should the Press Receive Special Protections?

Because newsgathering has traditionally been perceived as a unique function of the press, and expression is more universal, the Press Clause is more typically invoked, along with the other potential sources of press privilege, to protect the rights to newsgathering. However, establishing constitutional protection for newsgathering has been far more problematic than establishing protection for expression.

Some case law challenges the notion that the institutional press is constitutionally unique when it gathers the news. The U.S. Supreme Court said, in *Cohen v. Cowles Media* (1991), that "[g]enerally applicable laws do not offend the First Amendment simply because their enforcement against the press has incidental effects." When journalists make promises of confidentiality, the Court said, they are subject to legal principles of promissory estoppel just like any other citizen. This suggests that if journalists issue promises on which other parties reasonably rely, then they are liable to the promisee for those promises. This creates some tension with the notion that journalists must then respond to subpoenas to reveal their sources, but enough nuances distinguish these situations for the two theories to have existed side by side for a while.

However, one writer (Dyk, 1992) has called it "both appropriate and desirable that the press enjoy a special constitutional right of access in newsgathering" (p. 929) to counteract the emergence of a more powerful government since World War II. He says the press "must be given a *broader* right of access than that enjoyed by the general public" (emphasis in original) (p. 929) and argues that the press serves interests "that public presence promotes only remotely, if at all" (p. 935). He also points out that the presence of the public at important news events like crimes, disasters and military operations may create more danger of disruption and the press can perform a "sifting" function (p.935) with information that the individual citizen cannot.

While Justice Powell, in his concurring opinion in *Branzburg,* said that the Court "does not hold that newsmen, subpoenaed to testify before a grand jury, are without constitutional rights with respect to the gathering of news or in safeguarding their sources," there is scant historical evidence for the notion that the framers intended the First Amendment explicitly to provide unique protections to the press for newsgathering. As one writer points out, "How the framers felt about the right to gather news is more difficult to calculate because newsgathering practices had not yet evolved into the sophisticated set of techniques and standards that we are familiar with today" (Ugland, 2003).

It was perhaps inevitable that, as citizens—many of whom previously had used blogs largely to rant—increasingly moved into the realm of newsgathering, they would seek the same protections for their activity that the press often claims. This issue arose recently in the case of some websites that, with the help of the Electronic Frontier Foundation, claimed a journalistic privilege when faced with a subpoena in a civil case. In *Apple v. Does* (2005), a subpoena demanded that the web operators' Internet service provider turn over information that might identify the source who had provided the websites with information about a new Apple product. A judge ruled in March 2005 that Apple had the right to subpoena the names of sources in that case, despite the existence of a California shield law on which the website operators had tried to rely.[8]

While this case is often interpreted as addressing whether shield laws apply to bloggers, the opinion provides little guidance in that area because the court did not reach that question. As occurs with many such cases involving bloggers or web journalism, the court based its decision on other grounds—specifically, in this case, the disclosure of trade secrets—also saying that the journalist privilege claim was "overstated." Carefully avoiding the prickly questions of whether bloggers are "the press" or whether shield laws apply to bloggers, the court simply declared: "The California Legislature has not carved out any exception to these statutes [on trade secrets] for journalists, bloggers, or anyone else."

It is not only shield laws to which bloggers may be turning for legal protections. They also are seeking access to news events. However, while bloggers such as those who were credentialed for the 2004 major political conventions increasingly may have access to important events, it still is easier to get a press pass if a blogger can attach his or her name to a large media organization. In fact, during the 2005 legislative session, a blog on Texas politics, known as In the Pink Texas (Bloggers are People, Too, 2005),[9] showed this entry:

> I'm outside the House chamber, waiting to grab a state rep to take a picture of him for a freelance story. See, I'm OUTSIDE the House chamber with all the lobsters because I can't get credentialed. The MSM is passing by and LAUGHING at poor, poor pitiful me.

The denial of a press pass clearly cannot always be blamed on a writer's status as a blogger, but bloggers' status as outside the mainstream is, in fact, a favorite topic for them. Their focus on their outsider status may be in part because they do not receive the recognition that established media organizations do, and it may be in part because more politically oriented blogs seem to emerge as alternative voices to the dominant tone of the domains they cover.[10]

The organization of news outlets as complex organizations is a means to an end and, for a long time, was probably the only means to that end if publishers wanted to reach large audiences. But this is no longer so. The Internet, a worldwide network, gives individuals the capacity to reach audiences around the globe, free of the natural limits of the airwaves, the constraints of paper delivery or the related need to be affiliated with a recognized media organization. The fear of the traditional media may well be summed up in the thought that "if it really is impossible to distinguish the protected from the unprotected, no privilege can be justified" (Berger, 2003, pp. 1373–1374).

The rationale for protecting and privileging the press stems from our desire to encourage informed public discourse on the important issues of the day. Without protection, the press will not assert itself, society believes, and our national conversation will be that much poorer. Laws protecting the press rest on a rationale that suggests the press performs a valuable societal function distinct from the functions performed by other institutions and individuals.

One suggestion is that the news media provide a countervoice. Another is that the news media serve as a surrogate for the public at important news events (*Richmond Newspapers v. Virginia*, 1980) or as the public's "eyes and ears" (*Houchins v. KQED*, 1978). However, the application of these rationales to a unique institution, when truly scrutinized, appears to depend on a set of assumptions, which, while once justifiable, is increasingly questioned. Rarely do we see the rationale for privileging the press explicitly spelled out, and yet it is not difficult to speculate on what the components of such a rationale might be:

The institutional press is essentially credible and trustworthy.
The institutional press is motivated by a goal of informing the public.
The institutional press does the best job of gathering, confirming and disseminating information on behalf of and to the public.
The institutional press has the means to reach large audiences and is accountable to and will be corrected by the public when it makes mistakes.

Without taking a position on the validity of unique protections for the press, the next part of this chapter addresses how, other than the traditional way, we could go about making a distinction as to who qualifies for press protections.

A Functional Definition of Press

When the institutional press was the only entity recognized as "the press," any exceptions to our traditional understanding of what that entity was, such as investigative book authors or freelance writers, could adequately be dealt with by determining whether in those exceptions the individuals involved were functioning as the press according to some "functional definition" of press applied by the court. The courts would pull the exceptions into the protected group by way of the definition or would decide against them on other grounds, usually unrelated to whether they were press or not.[11]

The most common functional definition used by the courts, when it has been necessary to apply one, may be the one set forth in *Von Bulow v. Von Bulow* (1987). That definition required that the person invoking a press privilege have, at the time at which the person gathered information that he or she sought to keep confidential, the intent to disseminate that information to the public. This definition seems to have worked for some of the exceptions to traditional media that have claimed the privilege since then. It has allowed the courts to protect, for example, authors of investigative books (*Shoen v. Shoen*, 1993) and to exclude from the protected group a professional wrestling commentator (*In re Madden*, 1998).

But the increasing influence of blogs may preclude us from considering blogs to be exceptions. It was probably always conceptually dubious to talk about book authors as exceptions. However, as long as the numbers of people outside institutional media claiming a privilege remained small, it was manageable for the courts to dispense with those cases by using a functional definition invoked only for those cases and then neatly put away until the next exception emerged.

The most common functional definition also kept the number of people claiming shield protection under it relatively small. It required an *intent* to disseminate information at the time it was gathered. However, it is difficult to form the intent to disseminate without the *means* to do so. Those who had the means were likely to be well-funded organizations with access to the appropriate equipment or those with contracts to publish their work. As long as relatively few people had the means to distribute the information that they gathered, few people were in a position to form the intent necessary to qualify for press status. However, as the web increases the number of people with the means to distribute widely any thought on their minds or any information they acquire, the people falling within the functional definition are likely to increase in number and broaden in scope.

With more people potentially qualifying as "press" and with a broader application of a functional definition, the courts may well be forced to examine more closely what the protected function is and whether the *von Bulow* definition will hold up under new circumstances. David Anderson (2002), who has referred to the concept of the press as "largely a creation of law" (p. 430), argues for a functional definition that will hold up as media forms and technology change (p. 435), pointing out that, when the press has been legally defined at all, it has been more by form than by function (p. 436). Anderson also has compared the concept of press to the function of journalism (pp. 445–452), whereby value is added to information through some editorial effort, while acknowledging that there is not really an historical basis for this potentially problematic comparison (p. 446).

We can also look to a variety of state shield laws for statutory definitions of the press. Berger (2003) suggests we define the function not by the person performing it or by the content that results, but by the work process involved. "When individuals are engaged in this protected journalism work process," she says, "they should be eligible for the privilege no matter who they are, in what medium they publish, or, within limits, what kind of content results" (pp. 1375–1376).

Federal journalism shield bills that illustrate the difficulty with defining the group to whom such laws would apply have been introduced in Congress. An analysis by the Reporters Committee for Freedom of the Press suggests that one Senate bill (Free Flow of Information Act, 2005) would cover freelancers, but only those with contracts to produce their work, and that it would not cover those who publish solely on the web. By contrast, another bill (Free Speech Protection Act, 2005) would cover "electronic means of disseminating news or information to the public," which would seem to include web-only news sites.

Perhaps a foundation for a functional definition can be found in the rationale, discussed earlier, for providing special privileges to the press in the first place. One such rationale includes the presumption that the press, as a representative of the public, contributes to the public discourse by providing a uniquely high-quality form of information on important public issues while remaining credible and accountable to its audience. While distinguishing by content is potentially constitutionally problematic, the distinction is already inherent in many of our assumptions about who the press is.

Thus, a functional definition of press might draw from the rationale for protecting the press in the first place. How does the press contribute to the public discourse? They do so by gathering and disseminating information, two elements that could become part of a functional definition. However, they do not gather and disseminate just any information, but information of public importance or concern. Some have raised concerns about the content neutrality of specially protecting issues of public concern in other contexts (Smolla, p. 1151). Still, any number of examples are available where the legal standard of public concern could provide guidance in determining who does and who does not deal in that kind of information.

The press also does not disseminate information to just anyone; they disseminate it to "the public." Therefore, a functional definition would require at least minimal indicators for who that is. Clearly, it is not just the disseminator's immediate family, but a group that is substantial and, to some degree, anonymous—providing yet another element for a potential definition. Finally, the press is accountable to the public in some form, giving us reassurance that if mistakes are made, they will be corrected. For a press that reaches large audiences, the audience can be counted on to provide that accountability through direct feedback, letters to the editor and, as a last resort, lawsuits. Accordingly, a functional definition might include similar factors: (a) gathering information and adding value to it for dissemination to an audience; (b) disseminating that information to a substantial, partially anonymous audience, with a mechanism for feedback; and (c) dealing primarily in issues of public importance or concern.

However, the down side is that, taking the preceding factors into account, we could be dealing not only with a person-by-person analysis but also with a story-by-story analysis to determine when someone was functioning as "the press." Also, many of the concepts remain quite vague, but to specify them further would narrow immediately the group that would qualify. The very term "press" is one whose meaning we have come to expand but that, in its general use, is something of an artifact of the past—a term that applied to mass-produced copies of the printed word or to the machine that produced them. However, one of the more significant differences between the press of 200 years ago and the blogs of today may be merely the ink and the paper. If that is the case, then it is worth questioning whether that is enough of a difference to justify a separate standard of legal protection.

Applying a Functional Definition of "Press" in the Blogosphere

The problem with any functional definition for legal purposes is that it is cumbersome. It requires us to apply the definition on a case-by-case basis and often to do individual analyses after a problem arises. This after-the-fact application of a functional definition also creates substantial problems of uncertainty. If parties do not know whether they qualify for press status, will their efforts be chilled? This approach raises significant First Amendment questions.

However, if a functional definition were to be the standard for identifying who qualified for press privileges and that functional definition were applied on a story-by-story basis, the traditional news organizations may need to be subject to the same story-by-story analysis. If the increasing influence of blogs forces us to use a functional definition to determine whether a blog is protected by a shield law, there seems to be little basis for *not* requiring us to use a functional definition to determine whether, for example, the *New York Times* or a television news broadcast is so protected.

However, a functional definition of press need not disadvantage the traditional, institutional press. Characteristics of the traditional press might qualify them almost automatically for privileges, in most cases, under a functional definition. They have substantial, anonymous audiences and trained staffs that add value by gathering data with a presumed intent to disseminate it, making the data comprehensible, organizing it, editing it and sometimes visually presenting it. They usually still deal in issues of public concern, and journalists are stationed at local, state and federal government centers.

Any functional definition of press consistent with our traditional understandings of the institution is going to disadvantage bloggers to a degree. Large, well-funded organizations are likely to be at more of an advantage in proving they meet the functional definition than will an individual with a home office, a computer and a limited budget. In addition, many bloggers, who rely strongly on their reputations for being irreverent and must compete for attention in an increasingly crowded, wildly free-market blogosphere, often veer off into gossip, innuendo, ridicule and vacuous sarcasm—like adolescents trying to get attention—as much as they cover "the news." To the extent to which they do this, they may continue to function as entertainment vehicles with all the warranted protections for expression that involves, but they may not be taken seriously as purveyors of information and commentary on "issues of public concern."

If we return to our assumptions about why the press is sometimes privileged in the first place, as well as to a functional definition of press, we have to ask whether the mainstream press continues exclusively to serve the function traditionally attributed to it. Anderson (2002) has recently pointed out that which even most casual observers can discern: "Mainstream journalism seems to be edging away from the public-interest ideal," with more coverage of celebrity issues and sharper "economic imperatives" (p. 477). He points to "fundamental changes in the news business, which seem to undermine arguments that the media are different from other businesses" (p. 433).

Political commentator Hugh Hewitt (2006), who has a blog, has indicated that citizens are now bypassing the presumed media surrogates and independently seeking information. Hewitt says bluntly,

> There is simply too much expertise, all of it almost instantly available now, for the traditional idea of journalism to last much longer. In the past, almost every bit of information was difficult and expensive to acquire and was therefore mediated by journalists whom readers and viewers were usually in no position to second-guess (p. 2).

At the very least, we have to ask whether all of the mainstream institutional press necessarily serves its traditional function—the one that is supposed to be the subject of press protection—better than some of the best news weblogs can or do. Because that traditional function appears to be the basis for the privileges granted to the press, it does indeed matter whether they are serving it. Many bloggers, motivated as they sometimes are by partisan or even by nonpartisan but highly specialized interests, truly see themselves as watchdogs promoting the public good, in many cases checking facts and investigating rumors more fervently than would many reporters for mainstream news organizations. The idea of bloggers acting as watchdogs of the mainstream press does give us pause to wonder whether the large media organization or the blogger on a mission is the less economically motivated and more public-spirited actor.

The role of bloggers in public discourse can no longer be the subject of novelty conversations and must be absorbed as a significant and potentially positive factor in the interplay of news and commentary. However, still today, much of the natural advantage in newsgathering and production remains with traditional news organizations if they choose to use it to its full advantage. In a free market of information, journalists will compete for audiences with the quality of their product. As large, complex organizations with comparatively large budgets, highly skilled staffs and built-in checking mechanisms, the mainstream media (or "MSM" as the bloggers refer to them) retain the potential to be the best producers of the best news content available from any source. The web should not and likely will not be the future's only medium for news. However, traditional news organizations should perhaps no longer take their status for granted; it appears to be time to invite all of those who serve the protected function, regardless of medium or organizational makeup, into the community of "the press."

A more widely applied functional definition of press seems inevitably to be on the horizon and already exists to some degree when legislators attempt to bracket who will be covered by their state shield laws. The much more difficult and important question for the future will be how any functional definition would be applied in the courts, as well as how press status could possibly be determined enough in advance to provide assurance to those who seek to take advantage—through energetic pursuit of the news—of any privileges membership in "the press" might offer, if, in the long run, we decide it warrants any particular privileges at all.

References

Anderson, D. A. (1983). The origins of the press clause. *UCLA Law Review, 30*, 455, 533–535.

Anderson, D. A. (2002). Freedom of the press. *Texas Law Review, 80*, 429, 452.

Apple v. Does, No. 1-04-CV-032178 (Cal. Super. Ct. 2005).

Berger, L. L. (2003). Shielding the Unmedia: Using the process of journalism to protect the journalists' privilege in an infinite universe of publication, *Houston Law Review, 39*, 1371–1414.

Bloggers are people, too (2005, March 23). In The Pink Texas. Retrieved Sept. 10, 2006, from http://www.inthepinktexas.com/2005/03/23/bloggers-are-people-too.

Borger, G. (1998). Interview with Marvin Kalb. Matt Drudge is not my colleague. *Harvard International Journal of Press/Politics, 3*, 132–137.

Branzburg v. Hayes, 408 U.S. 665, 704 (1972).

Captain's Quarters Comment Moderation Policy. Retrieved Feb. 2, 2006, from http://www.captainsquartersblog.com/mt/archives/001902.php.

Cohen v. Cowles Media, 501 U.S. 663, 669 (1991).

Conniff, M. (2005). Just what is a blog anyway? *USC Annenberg Online Journalism Review*. Retrieved Feb. 1, 2006, from http://www.ojr.org/ojr/stories/050929/.

Dyk, T. B. (1992). Newsgathering, press access, and the First Amendment. *Stanford Law Review, 44*, 927, 929.

Free Flow of Information Act, S.1419 (2005).

Free Flow of Information Act, H.R. 3233 (2005).

Free Speech Protection Act, S. 369 (2005).

Henson, S. (2005). Does Tarrant County need a public defender? Grits for Breakfast. Retrieved Jan. 30, 2006, from http://www.gritsforbreakfast.blogspot.com/2005/09/does-tarrant-county-need-public.html.

Hewitt, H. (2006, Nov. 30). The media's ancien régime. Columbia Journalism School tries to save the old order. *The Weekly Standard*.

Houchins v. KQED, 438 U.S. 1 (1978).

Little Green Footballs. Retrieved from http://www.littlegreenfootballs.com.

Liptak, A. (2004, Aug.13). *Times* reporter is subpoenaed in leak case. *The New York Times*, A14.

In re Madden, 151 F.3d 125,131 (3d Cir., 1998).

Near v. Minnesota, 283 U.S. 697 (1931).

New York Times v. United States, 403, U.S. 713, 717 (1971) (Black, J., concurring).

OxBlog. Retrieved Feb. 1, 2006, from http://www.oxblog.blogspot.com.

PowerLine. Retrieved Feb. 2, 2006, from http://www.powerlineblog.com.

PressThink. Retrieved Feb. 1, 2006, from http://journalism.nyu.edu/pubzone/weblogs/pressthink.

Reporter ordered jailed, fined again, in Plame investigation (2004), News Media Update, Reporters Committee for Freedom of the Press. Retrieved Feb. 1, 2006, from http://www.rcfp.org/news/2004/1014inresp.html.

Richmond Newspapers, Inc. v. Virginia, 448 U.S. 555 (1980).

Rules Governing Press Galleries, United States Senate. Retrieved July 3, 2006, from http://www.senate.gov/galleries/daily/rules.htm.

Schauer, F. (2000). *Free speech and the social construction of privacy, the Joan Shorenstein Center on the Press, Politics and Public Policy*. Presented to the Social Research Conference on Privacy, New School University, New York, and Medill School of Journalism of Northwestern University. Retrieved Dec. 31, 2005, from http://www.ksg.harvard.edu/presspol/Research_Publications/FirstAmendmentSeries/freespeechprivacy.PDF, n.3.

Severin, W., & Tankard, J. W. (2000). *Communication theories: Origins, methods, uses in the mass media* (5th ed.). White Plains, NY: Longman.

Shiffrin, S. H. (1980). Government speech. *UCLA Law Review, 27*, 565–655.

Shoemaker, P.J., & Reese, S. D. (1996). *Mediating the message: Theories of influences on mass media content* (2nd ed.). White Plains, NY: Longman.

Shoen v. Shoen, 5 F.3d 1289 (9th Cir. 1993).

Smolla, R. A. Information as contraband: The First Amendment and liability for trafficking in speech. *Northwestern University Law Review, 96*, 1099.

Stewart, P. (1975). Or of the press, *Hastings Law Journal, 26*, 631–637.

Swope, C. (2005, July). Instant influence—a new generation of web scribes is shaking up state capitol politics, *Governing*, 20–25. Retrieved July 3, 2006, from http://66.23.131.98/archive/2005/jul/blosgs.txt.

TalkLeft. Retrieved Feb. 1, 2006, from http://www.talkleft.com.

TalkLeft's Comment Policy. Retrieved Feb. 1, 2006, from http://talkleft.com/new_archives/009862.html.

Ugland, E. F. (2003). *Newsgathering and the First Amendment: Toward a progressionist theory of constitutional interpretation*. Paper presented to the law division, Association for Education in Journalism and Mass Communication annual conference, Kansas City, MO. Retrieved Dec. 31, 2004, from http://list.msu.edu/cgi-bin/wa?A2=ind0309d&L=aejmc&F=&S=&P=9947.

Von Bulow v. Von Bulow, 811 F.2d 136 (2d Cir., 1987).

Winer, D. (2003). What makes a Weblog a Weblog? Weblogs at Harvard Law, Berkman Center for Internet and Society. Retrieved Feb. 1, 2006, from http://blogs.law.harvard.edu/whatMakesaWeblogAWeblog.

Notes

1. For example, in *Near v. Minnesota*, the Court said "… that the liberty of the press may be abused by miscreant purveyors of scandal does not make any less necessary the immunity of the press from previous restraint in dealing with official misconduct"; in *New York Times v. United States*, Justice Black's concurrence told us that "the press was to serve the governed, not the governors."

2. One example of this is the initiative of the blogs Power Line and Little Green Footballs to demonstrate that documents relied on by CBS in a story about President George W. Bush's National Guard service might be fraudulent.

3. The First Amendment to the U.S. Constitution contains speech and press clauses. Specifically, it says, "Congress shall make no law…abridging the freedom of speech, or of the press.…"

4. Politically conservative columnist Mark Steyn, discussing the Power Line blog, has written bluntly, "Everything that's wrong with American newspapers is summed up by the fact that these guys [the bloggers] do it for free and their disparager, the pompous windbag editor at the *Minneapolis Star-Tribune*, gets paid for it."

5. The blog is named for the last syllable in the first name of its writer, Markos Moulitsas Zúniga.

6. For example, TalkLeft has a policy that says it "reserves the right to edit all e-mail and posted comments for content, clarity, and length.… Comments that are abusive, offensive, contain profane or racist material…will be removed.… TalkLeft will limit commenters to four comments a day if, in its sole discretion, the commenter is a 'chatterer'…" At Captain's Quarters, the blogger writes in the comment moderation section, "I can ban abusive users immediately, and spammers can't access my comments at all. Most CQ readers know that I never ban people for disagreeing with me—heck, I love debate, and some of my best readers hardly ever agree with what I write."

7. One of the most recent examples involved journalists cited for contempt for refusing to disclose information about confidential sources for an investigation into who revealed the name of a CIA employee to the press.

8. In May 2006, a California state appeals court ruled in favor of a petition filed by the Electronic Frontier Foundation on behalf of the online writers, finding that the subpoena was inconsistent with the federal Stored Communications Act and the California shield law. The Court's opinion said of the shield law claim: "We decline to embroil ourselves in questions of what constitutes 'legitimate journalism.' ... We can think of no workable test that would distinguish 'legitimate' from 'illegitimate' news."

9. It is reportedly named for the pinkish tone of the granite in the Texas Capitol building.

10. The national blogosphere is widely regarded as having been dominated by conservative ideology in its early days in the 1990s, whereas in Texas, the political blogs that were the earliest to receive attention tended to satirize and criticize the more conservative governing majority in that state, a phenomenon discussed in an issue of *Governing* magazine (Swope, 2005).

11. As just one example, in the case of Vanessa Leggett, a Houston teacher whose notes from interviews about a notorious Houston crime were sought by law enforcement, the question of whether she was functioning as a journalist for the book she said she intended to write was not central to the court's decision. The court seemed to suggest that even if Leggett were a journalist, she would be required to provide information to a grand jury under the circumstances of that criminal case.

11

Blogs Without Borders: International Legal Jurisdiction Issues Facing Bloggers

BRIAN CARROLL AND BOB FRANK

Internet communication transcends geographic boundaries and normally that is a good thing. For bloggers, however, the transborder nature of the media format in particular and Internet communication in general could mean that local laws everywhere, from Australia to Zimbabwe, apply to them. Several international Internet communication court cases suggest, for example, that where a blog post is downloaded and read can be more important than where it is published or uploaded, which makes online writers and publishers potentially subject to the laws of 190 countries. Not surprisingly, the result is dizzying jurisdictional complexity. With no international consensus to guide how or even where jurisdictional disputes should be resolved, bloggers should beware.

The purpose of this chapter is to outline the legal risks faced by blogging journalists, including student journalists, due to the nature of Internet communication, which does not recognize national sovereignty or international borders. Because there have been few court cases involving bloggers per se, this chapter looks to litigation in the broader area of Internet communication to find guidance from the world's courts.

The gravest dangers to bloggers concern legal challenges in the areas of libel, prior restraint and, to a lesser extent, copyright. These are areas of the law relevant to online communication and publication in which international courts have spoken. Even in these areas, however, there is much confusion. Beyond the scope of this article are issues and legal questions related to trademark and patent law, personal privacy, criminal behavior and patently illicit and, therefore, unprotected speech, such as pornography.[1]

After examining the key court challenges to free expression online, this chapter will seek to provide a framework for understanding, anticipating and mitigating the risks. Included in this discussion will be problems in enforceability, another area in which little judicial or legislative clarity exists. Finally, potential remedies and solutions are proposed that include international cooperation and legislation written to give courts in common-law nations greater freedom to adjudicate than common law typically affords. The proposed remedies strive to balance the rights of citizens of all nations with the goals of a free press and freedom of expression.

Review of Libel Case Law

Calls to unify international defamation and libel law predate the Internet. Personal jurisdiction questions alone make libel a potentially treacherous area of law for any court being petitioned by a foreign plaintiff or considering action against a defendant in a foreign land. The advent and subsequent popularity of Internet communication have added another dimension of complexity to what were already confusing legal questions, and the paucity of decided cases on these questions belies their importance. Collectively, even the handful of cases that does exist could set limits on the global dissemination of speech. Absent court decisions in cases specifically involving bloggers, the following libel suits were selected because they concern content published online and because in each instance a U.S. publisher was haled into a foreign court.[2]

In *Yousef Jameel v. Dow Jones & Co.* (2005), a British citizen claimed in a London court that a March 2003 article in the *Wall Street Journal*'s online edition linked him with Osama bin Laden. The published article contained a hyperlink to a document Yousef Jameel said referred to him. The English court affirmed jurisdiction and required Dow Jones & Co. to appear in a British court. In February 2005, an appeals court threw out the libel action because, according to court documents, only five people in England could be shown to have read the report, a number that included Jameel's solicitor and two of the plaintiff's business associates (Soames, 2005).

Importantly, the English court ruled that media companies could not be sued in England unless there had been a substantial publication in the country. According to the judgment, written by Lord Phillips, "It would be an abuse of process to continue to commit the resources of the English court, including substantial judge and possibly jury time, to an action where so little is now seen to be at stake" (McCollam, 2003, p. 10). The solicitor for Dow Jones, Mark Stephens, told London's *Guardian* newspaper that the ruling was "a significant decision for Internet publishers. It started to inject into the world of online publications some much needed clarity" (Dyer, 2005).

In important ways, the outcome of the *Jameel* case quieted at least some of U.S. publishers' concerns that stemmed from a well-known case in Australia, *Gutnick v. Dow Jones & Co.* (2004), particularly when the *Jameel* ruling is paired with another English case, *Harrods v. Dow Jones & Co.* (2003). In *Gutnick*, simply by claiming jurisdiction, Australia's High Court shook the journalism and online publishing firmaments in the United States (Sandburg, 2002).

The suit centered on an October 30, 2000, article, "Unholy Gains," in *Barron's Online* that described Melbourne businessman "Diamond" Joe Gutnick as having had an improper relationship with an Australian businessman jailed for tax evasion and money laundering. Gutnick sued for defamation. Dow

Jones appealed to Australia's High Court in December 2002, claiming that the Victoria court could not have jurisdiction over a company in the United States publishing (or uploading) on servers in the United States (New Jersey).

The High Court ruled against Dow Jones, declaring that Victoria indeed had jurisdiction in the defamation case and that the New York City-based news organization would have to defend itself in Australia (Grant, 2002). Dow Jones settled with Gutnick in early November 2004, agreeing to pay him between $400,000 and $580,000 in compensation and legal costs.[3] The settlement ended 4 years of litigation and perhaps prevented the world from learning the lengths Australian judges are willing to go to avoid U.S. legal hegemony over online publishing, which was at least one of the judges' stated goals in the case (*Gutnick v. Dow Jones & Co.*, 2004).

Just as Dow Jones was defending itself in Australia, *Harrods v. Dow Jones & Co.* (2003) sprung in England from a parodic press release issued on April Fool's Day 2003 by London's Harrods department store. The release detailed plans by the merchant to float stock in the company. Apparently fooled by the press release, *The Wall Street Journal* published a follow-up article calling Harrods "the Enron of Britain," a story that was published in the print edition as well as on the *Journal's* website. Claiming damage to reputation and libel, Harrods sued in Britain, where libel laws are much less protective of speech and, therefore, more protective of individual and corporate reputation than in the United States.[4]

As was the case in *Gutnick* and *Jameel*, Dow Jones claimed in *Harrods* a relatively small number of online readers in the United Kingdom and, therefore, only minimum contacts with British readers and consumers. For that reason, the media company petitioned England's High Court to reject the case on jurisdictional grounds.[5] The High Court found that England was in fact an appropriate place to hear the dispute and refused to stay the proceedings. Ominously for bloggers, the High Court cited the jurisdiction decision in *Gutnick*, among others, in holding that an article online should be considered as having been published where Internet users download, read and comprehend the article rather than, as publication is determined in the United States, where the story is uploaded or hosted.

Harrods v. Dow Jones went forward and the U.S. media company claimed that the offending article was "intended to be tongue-in-cheek," not unlike the Harrods press release (Naik, 2004, p. B8).[6] A jury required roughly 2 hours to agree with Dow Jones, determining the article not to be libelous (Tait, 2004). Harrods also was ordered to pay Dow Jones' costs of defending itself. The media company nevertheless lamented "that so much time and effort [had] been expended on such a trivial matter" (Naik).[7]

Discussion of Libel Decisions

The *Jameel*, *Harrods* and *Gutnick* cases as a triumvirate are a mixed blessing. *Gutnick* threatened to chill speech worldwide because Australian courts held that publication occurs where actionable content is downloaded, or received and read. This interpretation would saddle U.S. publishers, including individual bloggers, with liability in countries that similarly interpret libel's effects and potential effects, particularly in common-law countries that do not recognize the single publication rule.[8] Single publication generally has been interpreted to mean that there can be only one cause of action and that the statute of limitations begins upon the first general publication or broadcast of a statement that is potentially libelous, regardless of how many copies of the publication are distributed or how many people hear or see the broadcast.[9]

The United States has a 1-year statute of limitations on Internet publication, and in 2002, the New York Court of Appeals applied the single publication rule to online communication in determining that the statute of limitations for an online defamation action begins on the date the allegedly defamatory statements are posted. The action is not retriggered each time the posting is accessed.[10] The United Kingdom also has a 1-year statute of limitations, which is articulated in the Defamation Act of 1996.

U.S. courts would have rejected the case on purely jurisdictional grounds because the principle of minimum contacts is one of the primary factors in determining interstate and international jurisdiction in the United States. In U.S. law, personal jurisdiction requires "a sufficient connection between the defendant and the forum state" (Riou, 1995, p. 741). For actions against foreign defendants, this connection has been interpreted in U.S. law to mean continuous and systematic contacts (Riou).[11] Courts in other common-law countries, however, including Australia and England, traditionally have not considered the number of real or potential contacts between a publisher and a claimant in determining jurisdiction.

A more recent common law-based case, *Bangoura v. Washington Post*, which went to court in Ontario, Canada, in March 2005, hinges on the notion of substantial publication and minimum contacts. Cheickh Bangoura, a former United Nations employee, was the subject of two stories in the *Post* in January 1997. Bangoura sued the newspaper and three of its reporters in Ontario's Superior Court, claiming $9 million in damages (Tyler, 2005). The *Post* is claiming that the case has no "real or substantial connection" to Ontario, that Bangoura has no reputation in Ontario, and that the *Post* had only seven paid subscribers in Ontario in January 1997. In spite of the absence of significant contacts, the Ontario court has claimed jurisdiction, citing *Gutnick* in its opinion (*Bangoura v. Washington Post*).

The *Jameel* and *Harrods* cases demonstrated that one of the countries where liability is greatest is England. Dow Jones & Co.'s victories there, however, signal changes in English jurisprudence, particularly in regards to the consideration of minimum contacts. In the *Jameel* decision, the English court rejected the libel claims as an abuse of process because only five people were determined to have read or even accessed the potentially libelous content, a number that included three agents or associates of Yousef Jameel (Riou, 1995).[12] Such "insignificant publication," wrote Lord Justice Phillips, failed to justify further proceedings (Riou, p. 742). This ruling, therefore, reduces the risk of liability in England and, by extension, in other common law-based countries.

The cases also reveal key differences in U.S. libel law and common law-based libel actions. The United States Constitution's First Amendment and a series of legal precedents bolstering press freedoms, beginning with the landmark 1964 Supreme Court decision *Times v. Sullivan*, have created a tradition in U.S. jurisprudence that makes it extremely difficult for plaintiffs to win libel suits.[13] Chief among these differences is burden of proof. Australia and England do not recognize categories or levels of fault, for example, and therefore do not expect a higher burden of proof from public figures or government officials in libel actions brought against publishers. In these common-law countries, the burden of proof rests on the defendant rather than on the plaintiff.[14] In *Gutnick*, Dow Jones would have had to prove its statements true to win the case.

Review of Prior-Restraint Case Law

The scarcity of international jurisdiction cases involving prior restraint, however encouraging, does not mean that bloggers should feel safe. Just because Saudi Arabia has not thus far tried to prosecute a U.S. blogger for violating its restrictive laws regarding commentary on and coverage of political or moral topics does not mean that it will not do so in the future. A few cases should illustrate the potential risks.

In 2000, the Superior Court of Paris claimed jurisdiction in *LICRA v. Yahoo!* (2000), a suit brought by two French organizations against the U.S.-based Internet company. The plaintiffs argued that the U.S. Yahoo! auction site, accessible to French citizens, violated French laws prohibiting the sale of Nazi memorabilia or anti-Semitic documents, such as Protocols of the Elders of Zion and Adolf Hitler's *Mein Kampf.* Although Yahoo! immediately removed the auction items from its Yahoo! France website, the items remained on its U.S. site, which was accessible to French citizens. The French court ordered Yahoo! to remove the items from its U.S. website or face financial sanctions.

Fined $15 million by the Paris court, Yahoo! petitioned U.S. courts to block enforcement of the French ruling (Dawson, 2004). The Ninth Circuit Court of Appeals in California ruled in early 2006, however, that Yahoo!'s free-speech rights likely had not been violated by the French, but it emphasized again doubts that the judgment by the Paris court could be enforced.[15]

In Germany in late 2000, the German Supreme Court claimed jurisdiction in a case involving hate speech uploaded to the web from servers in Australia. In Germany, actionable hate speech has included denying the Holocaust and disseminating pro-Nazi propaganda. Though the opinions of Frederick Toben, including his view that the Holocaust did not occur, were disseminated via a server based in Australia, he was found guilty of violating Germany's hate speech laws.[16] For the verdict to be enforced, Toben would first have to step foot on German soil.

Other prior-restraint cases in Germany simply have not risen to the level of court decisions. For example, Google voluntarily removed from its searches and findings 65 sites in Germany that deny the Holocaust or promote White supremacy, in order to avoid legal liability (Jones, 2002). In another case, Felix Somm, a Swiss national, was convicted by a German court for distributing pornography over the Internet in Germany. Somm maintained residence in Germany and was head of CompuServe's wholly owned German subsidiary (August, 2002).

The *Bernard Connolly v. Commission of the European Communities* case, admittedly, is not a genuine international jurisdiction case, in the sense that it was resolved within European borders. In this 2001 suit, British economist Bernard Connolly was convicted by the European Court of Justice for his vigorous criticism of European monetary integration and the establishment of the euro in his 1995 book, *The Rotten Heart of Europe*. The court determined that Connolly's work was not protected speech and was essentially blasphemous ("E.U. and free speech," 2001).

The preceding cases point to two problems in the realm of prior restraint on an international level that confront journalists who blog. First, a U.S. blogger who violates prior-restraint codes of foreign nations might find his or her postings deemed actionable and under jurisdiction in the courts of those nations. Second, foreign courts subscribe to notions of jurisdiction that radically differ from jurisdiction law in the United States. These courts are more concerned with the effects of blog content than the intent of the author or publisher. While much of U.S. jurisdictional law is tied to *International Shoe v. Washington* (1945), in which the court determined that a litigant must establish minimum contacts within an area to warrant jurisdiction, a foreign court is more apt to consider the effects of a communication within its forum, including potential effects, regardless of the actual number of contacts that might prove intent.

Moreover, foreign courts are more likely to reject any form of *sliding scale* analysis popular with U.S. courts. In such cases, U.S. courts try to determine whether the Internet site (or blog) is merely passive, accessible everywhere, but not targeted at any particular jurisdiction. A site that clearly targets or is published in a certain jurisdiction is one that produces evidence of numerous, solicited interactions with residents of that jurisdiction. In such cases, the courts try to determine appropriate jurisdiction according to location on this scale of Internet availment.

Review of Copyright Case Law

Although instances involving legal requests to take down infringing Internet postings are numerous, there is still no settled case law regarding copyright infringement between the United States and other foreign countries. Most recently, in late March 2005, Agence France-Presse (AFP) sued Google for copyright violations. AFP sued in the United States and in France, claiming that Google had infringed its copyrights since 2002 by posting thousands of headlines, story leads and photographs (Johnson, 2005). While this case is obviously in the early stages of litigation, one earlier case points to the complexity of copyright issues in a borderless internet.

In 1989 the Second Circuit Court of Appeals resolved a case in which Russian journalists sued a New York Russian-language newspaper for copying newspaper and magazine articles originally written and published in Russia (*Itar-Tass Russian News Agency v. Russian Kurier, Inc.*, 1998). Ruling in favor of the Russian authors, the court determined that the U.S. newspaper had infringed upon the Russians' copyright. In arriving at its decision, the court relied on Russian law, to determine ownership of the copyright, and U.S. law, to determine infringement via distribution of the copied works in the United States.

The facts of these two cases belie their potential complexity. The Russian journalists only sued in U.S. courts; AFP sued in U.S. and French courts. The Russians very well could have sued in Russia and in the United States; AFP could have sued in every country where Google News Service operates. The principal guide to resolution of international copyright disputes continues to be the Berne Convention (Xalabarder, 2002).[17] Although Berne does not spell out jurisdictional protocols for copyright infringements, it does require signatory nations to honor the copyright rights of authors in other member countries in the same manner in which each nation protects the works of its authors under the principle of national treatment (Yu, 2001).

Bloggers, particularly noncommercial bloggers, may take some comfort in the fact that they are at the mercy of the divergent copyright laws of some 190 countries. Given the costs of translations, attorneys' fees and compilation and verification of national copyright laws, few foreign authors would bother to pursue a lone U.S. blogger who innocently infringed on a copyright. If the foreign author sued in his or her national court, the blogger need not appear in court. To the extent that the alleged infringement did not violate U.S. copyright law, U.S. courts would likely decline to enforce the default judgment, as the Yahoo! cases indicate.

Framework for Gauging Legal Risks

Communication literature contains a number of categorical schemas for analyzing cultural approaches to communication regulation. Most notably, Siebert, Peterson and Schramm articulated the classic four theories of the press: libertarian, social responsibility, authoritarian and soviet–communist (1972). Eko deftly adapted the Schramm rubric for the Internet era in dividing the nations of the world according to the nature of their Internet regulation policies: internationalist, neomercantilist, culturalist, gateway and developmentalist (2001).

For purposes of clarity, relying primarily on Eko's taxonomy, this chapter synthesizes and simplifies some of the differing cultural, political and historical approaches to render five loosely bound categories, arranged by the degree of control exercised by the nation states over Internet content, from the least to the greatest:

1. Libertarian countries are best if not solely exemplified by the U.S. approach toward the Internet and legal issues relating to prior restraint and libel.

2. Common-law countries' cultural histories have placed a premium on respect for the dignity of the individual. This emphasis has resulted in libel laws that heavily favor the plaintiff. Examples of these countries are the United Kingdom, Australia, New Zealand and Canada.

3. Civil-code countries are heavily bound by prior-restraint codes that forbid certain types of speech deemed offensive to the culture and historical memory of these countries. Exemplary among the civil-code countries are France, Germany and most of the non-English members of the European Community.

4. Developing countries seek to capitalize on the benefits of e-commerce, but at the same time restrict Internet speech that interferes with establishing cultural identity or political or economic stability. These nations include most of the African, South American and Southeast Asian nations.

5. Authoritarian countries are at the far end of the spectrum. These countries include China, North Korea and Singapore. In a perverse sense, these nations are the least worrisome to bloggers. The approach, distilled, is simply to shut down or otherwise block Internet sites deemed to obstruct economic, cultural or political objectives in any way.

The purpose of this categorization, while risking clarity in its blending and blurring of political, legal and economic regimes, is to provide bloggers a useful guide to the legal risks incurred when communications reach the entire world. To that end, the regimes and structures looked to are those seen as dominant in defining the risks of publishing online. Bloggers and educators who employ blogs cannot be expected to understand the regulatory mechanisms unique to each of the world's nations, so this analytic framework summarizes the historical and cultural roots of the most important regulations facing bloggers.

Libertarian Model

Paradigmatic of the libertarian model is the United States. The 45-word First Amendment, as interpreted by the U.S. Supreme Court since the amendment's ratification in 1791, guarantees "freedom of speech" and "of the press." The Court's many interpretations and the First Amendment's enforcement make the United States unique among the 190+ nations of the world, even among those with similar constitutional verbiage. Since the Supreme Court began aggressively combating prior restraint in *Near v. Minnesota* in 1931, U.S. courts have systematically narrowed the range of unprotected speech and, therefore, have consistently expanded the sphere of protected speech.

The guiding philosophy for this system of unfettered free speech is John Milton's notion of a "marketplace of ideas," in which a free competition of ideas furthers the search for truth. "Who ever knew Truth put to the worse, in a free and open encounter?" Milton wrote in his 1644 essay, "Aeropagitica." In the marketplace of ideas, then, the response to *bad speech* is not regulation; it is more *good speech* (1644). This same principle has largely directed development of the technological architecture of the Internet, constructed mostly by U.S. technicians using U.S. codes and software, U.S. protocols and the English language. The very design of the Internet was to promote a free exchange of ideas (Fagin, 2003).

The most noteworthy safeguards the libertarian model affords bloggers are (a) protection from recrimination from expressions commonly regarded as hate speech; (b) a greater degree of protection for defendants in libel cases than one finds in the rest of the world (Sutton, 2004); and (c) substantial freedom from copyright infringement charges as found in the "fair use" provisions of U.S. copyright law.

Common-Law Countries

Dow Jones' concerns in the *Jameel*, *Gutnick* and *Harrods* cases are bloggers' concerns: Through rulings like the jurisdictional decisions in these cases, a kind of "tyranny of the lowest common denominator" could chill speech around the globe and stifle debate (Garnett, 2004, p. 76). Though Dow Jones emerged victorious in two of the three cases, it expended a great deal of time and money fighting each claim. For bloggers in particular, defamation is evolving from being an issue that historically has affected only media concerns to one that, in one writer's words, jeopardizes "all those who publish on the Internet" (Edwards, 1997, p. 183). Defamation cases are of particular concern in common-law countries because of the priority placed in these countries on the rights of the individual citizens over protections of unfettered expression.

Common-law countries—Australia, Canada, New Zealand and many African nation states that formerly were English colonies—depart from U.S. legal tradition by locating jurisdiction where the sting of the claimed libel is felt rather than where the content is published. Other distinctions that favor the plaintiff include a presumption that any defamatory material published is false and that a statement need only be potentially defamatory to defame the plaintiff, who therefore would not need to prove that any one person actually lowered his or her opinion of the plaintiff as a result of the disputed statement (Australian Press Council, 2004).

Even within a common-law nation, determining what might be interpreted as libelous is difficult. The existence of eight separate defamation laws in Australia, for example, fueled efforts at reform and at harmonizing the laws. In summer 2004, however, reform proposals stalled, leading the Australian Press Council to decry "the present roller-coaster of excessive and unpredictable litigation" (2004). Until reform is achieved, blogging journalists should be wary of common-law courts called on to balance the reputations of petitioners against freedom of the press, including the foreign press, and demonstrating a predisposition toward citizen petitioners.

The *Gutnick* case, in particular, likely would have hinged on how the Victorian court interpreted a 156-year-old publication rule and applied it to publishing on the Internet. The English publication rule established in *Duke of Brunswick v. Harmer* in 1849 states that there is a separate publication and therefore a separate cause for action for each delivered *copy* of the publication and every observation of a defamatory statement.[18] While Dow Jones claimed 55,000 online subscribers for *Barron's* globally, only 1,700 had paid using credit cards issued in Australia (Grant, 2002). The English publication rule suggests 1,700 potential causes of action, an interpretation at variance with U.S. law, which in 1977 rejected multiple-publication interpretations nationally in favor of a single-publication application.

If common law countries could be convinced also to reject this rule, actions like *Gutnick* could be avoided on jurisdictional grounds because the place of publication generally would be determined to be where the online expression is uploaded. The pattern in the Australian courts of mechanically interpreting common law, however, makes a single-publication interpretation unlikely, as does their unwillingness or, considering the limits of common-law interpretations, inability to recognize fundamental differences between Internet and print publishing (Garnett, 2004).

Perhaps the most troubling aspect of the *Gutnick* case, one related to presumed damage, is the Australian court's refusal to consider the intentionality of publication. Dow Jones claimed no more than 1,700 *Barron's* subscribers in the whole of Australia. Though it is accessible throughout Australia, a country that gets roughly 95% of its web content from the United States, *Barron's Online* publishes in the United States for a predominantly U.S. readership (Grant, 2002). Its writers, editors and servers are in the United States. The High Court decided, however, that the availability of *Barron's Online* in Australia was enough for Australian libel law to apply, which puts U.S.-based bloggers in jeopardy. Garnett pointed out that Australia is the only country willing to assert jurisdiction in such circumstances; in the United States such an assertion likely would be deemed a violation of due process (2004). The out-of-court settlement denied online publishers, including bloggers, an indication of whether Australian courts were prepared to rationalize its libel laws.

Gutnick, Jameel and *Harrods* are important for blogging journalists everywhere because these precedents likely will be followed in other common-law countries. Garnett wrote in his analysis of *Gutnick* that other common-law countries may find that their precedents, like Australia's, leave them no choice but to reach similar findings in similar cases (2004).[19] Even before *Gutnick* was settled, a New Zealand court in August 2004 used the Australia High Court's jurisdictional decision in *Gutnick* to justify proceeding with a defamation suit in New Zealand against, ironically, an Australian newspaper (Bell, 2004).[20] *Gutnick* also was cited as precedent in *Dow Jones & Co. v. Harrods* in determining that England indeed had jurisdiction in the dispute.

In short, bloggers accustomed to First Amendment-level protections of expression should note that the rest of the world could view those protections as less valuable and, therefore, trumped by other claims and concerns. A justice in the *Gutnick* decision, for example, wrote that Australia "does not share the American, as others see it, obsession with free speech" (*Dow Jones & Co. v. Gutnick*).[21] What the High Court justice sees as a fixation many U.S. judges would describe as a necessary underpinning of a free society and a vibrant, participative democracy.

Copyright cases in common law countries (as well as civil code counties) also place a premium on the integrity of the individual. In these European countries, copyright codes are grounded in the principle of *moral right* or *droit moral*. Accordingly, the work of an author is part and parcel of the author's integrity as a human being; infringing on a person's copyright is, therefore, a moral affront (Jackson, 2003). The European *moral right* justification for copyright contrasts vividly with the economic principle of property right employed in the United States.

Civil-Code Countries

Although this category certainly overlaps with others, such as libertarian and common law, the defining characteristic of developed countries is widely regarded as a democratic regime that has adopted a civil code forbidding certain kinds of speech. To be sure, nearly all nations generally forbid child pornography and most instances of gross pornography (obscenity). What are defined here as civil-code countries, however, comprise sovereignties whose civil codes go at least one step further: They prohibit hate speech or *anticulturalist* speech or both. Although hate-speech codes are generally anathema in the United States, they are commonplace in Europe and in other parts of the world. Most countries of Europe, for example, forbid speech that puts Nazi propaganda or Nazi ideas in a favorable light (Fagin, 2003).

The historical roots of such codes would seem obvious. European nations emerged from World War II with bitter memories of the savagery and destruction wrought by the Nazis. That racist and anti-Semitic Nazi propaganda was allowed to thrive in prewar Germany is seen as a contributing cause to the rise of Nazism. Today, Germany, France and the entire European community have enacted human rights codes that emphasize the dignity of the individual, as well as *group dignity* (Fagin, 2003). In the name of these human rights, the same countries have erected a panoply of hate-speech laws. As Spector observed, in Germany the idea of human dignity "effectively trumps the freedom of speech, allowing Germany to regulate hate speech" (2002, p. 155).

Some nations (France most notably) are deeply concerned about preservation of national culture in face of an Internet dominated by U.S. content providers and about the blurring of cultural distinctions. The French have written laws to protect the French national identity, language and culture. For example, France legally requires that webpages hosted in France have at least a portion of French language content (Eko, 2001).

Developing Countries

This group comprises by far the largest number of the 190+ nations of the world. These nations include most African, South American, and Southeast Asian nations, a few Middle Eastern nations and many East European nations. The goals of these countries regarding Internet regulation are essentially threefold: Maximize economic development, promote cultural identity and minimize political dissidence. If a website or blog advances the nation's economic interests, it will not only be allowed, but it will be promoted (Kalathil, 2003). Websites and blogs that detract from the unique cultural identity of a nation will be subject to lawsuits, blocked using filters or simply shut down. Websites that promote former colonial values also could be prohibited. Finally, the governments of developing nations generally are fragile. Not surprisingly, they seek to promote political stability. To the extent that Internet sites and blogs encourage political dissent, the governments of developing nations will attempt to shut them down or to block access to them (Eko, 2001).

Admittedly, there is a fine line of distinction between developing nations and authoritarian nations. One vital distinction is the degree of commitment to economic development. Although developing nations are deeply concerned with issues of political stability and cultural preservation, they tend to yield in complex situations that cross all three boundaries (political, cultural and economic) to policies that advance their economic objectives. Authoritarian countries tend to prefer political stability first, then cultural preservation and economic advancement last.

There is little to worry bloggers in this category in terms of law or regulations that can affect them. Most of these nations lack the resources to purchase and maintain blocking technology. They similarly lack the resources to pursue lawsuits against bloggers who offend their laws. Those who can afford filtering technologies have little interest in suing bloggers because they have already silenced bloggers' voices using technology.

Once on the soil of one of these nations, however, bloggers should of course beware. In 2002, prosecutors in Zimbabwe brought charges against an American reporter for the British newspaper, *The Guardian*, for "publishing a falsehood" ("Court Challenge," 2002, p. 12). The story, which linked the political party of Zimbabwean president Robert Mugabe to suspected murderers, was available in the African nation only on the Internet. Though the reporter, Andrew Meldrum, ultimately was acquitted, the case, as well as the press-gag law upon which it was based, provides alarming evidence that foreign countries will claim jurisdiction purely on the basis of online publication and, therefore, will prosecute foreign journalists within their borders.[22]

Authoritarian Countries

Authoritarian countries, or, as Eko describes them, nations for which political culture, history or traditions give little or no room for freedom of speech or of the press, pose little legal risk to blogging journalists in the United States (2001). These gateway countries, which grant or deny Internet access in the name of national security, culture, morality or some other government interest, are perhaps best represented by China. Blogging journalists likely will not face legal challenges from these countries' governments or citizens because their work likely will not be read by citizens in those countries.

China's government, which serves as Internet regulator *and* operator, has, for example, banned access to publications such as *The Wall Street Journal*, *The New York Times* and *The Washington Post* (Gauthier, 2001).[23] These news organizations can publish whatever they want, but their content is blocked by the Chinese government, which, according to the Berkman Center for Internet and Society, blocks about 10% of all websites throughout the world.[24] According to one writer, China's communist government has stepped up efforts to control Internet use, going so far as to block access to Google for 1 month in 2002 (Mooney, 2004).[25] In 2003 and early 2004, Beijing shut down four blogging services—Blogspot, Blogbus, Typepad and Blogcn—and the government has invested millions of dollars in blocking technology, most of it ironically from the United States and U.S. companies such as Microsoft and Sun Microsystems (Sham–Shackleton, 2004).

Saudi Arabia, Singapore, Malaysia and Brazil are other countries whose governments have assumed the role of information gatekeeper. According to Eko, these governments believe the Internet to be "an electronic conveyor belt for Western decadence and debauchery, which, if allowed into certain countries unimpeded, would infect their religions, political systems, cultures and ways of life" (2001, p. 475). Eko cites a report by Reporters Sans Frontieres that indicates as many as 45 countries of the world restrict access to the Internet, or roughly 20% of the world.[26]

Fortunately for U.S. bloggers, the overlapping interests of developing nations and authoritarian countries offer at least one protection: minimal adherence to copyright conventions cherished by Western nations. Developing nations value more the revenues generated by sales of copyrighted foreign works (Engle, 2002). Authoritarian nations like China tend to eschew notions of private property and promote instead wide access to the common heritage of their societies (Jackson, 2003). Treaties like TRIPS may require copyright legislation in these countries, but they offer little recourse in regard to enforcement.[27] Thus, bloggers face a scant likelihood of infringement suits originating in these countries.

Solutions

The Toben case in Germany and Yahoo! cases in France point to the difficulties of enforcement in those instances where a member of the foreign media is found guilty. Toben has particular relevance for blogging journalists because the defendant, an Australian citizen publishing via the web in Australia, is, like most bloggers, a private citizen and not a member of a large, global media organization (Anti-Defamation League, 2000). Though Toben was found guilty by a German court, enforcing the judgment has thus far proven problematic.[28] The defendant lives in Adelaide, Australia, and continues to operate his website. [29] Should Toben step onto German soil, however, he likely would be arrested.

The problem of enforcement is in a way a boon to bloggers, making victory for a plaintiff in a transborder action a Pyrrhic one. U.S. courts thus far have been more than reluctant to enforce in the United States rulings made by courts abroad, particularly when the actions involve First Amendment protection claims. Edwards reasoned that many countries choose not to recognize a judgment, while others lack the mechanism to recognize the action (1997). If a legal judgment depends upon a legal basis or upon principles alien to or in conflict with the values of the defendant country's laws, such recognition and therefore enforcement are unlikely.

In *Yahoo! v. LICRA* (2001), for instance, the Ninth Circuit Court demonstrated its unwillingness to abide by foreign court rulings that abridge First Amendment protections. Those rulings, therefore, are not enforceable in the United States. Individual bloggers in this country should, therefore, have few worries about violating foreign laws concerning defamation, prior restraint and copyright (Fagin, 2003). Where bloggers have assets in a foreign country, however, they could risk losing those assets if that country's courts rule against them.

To harmonize international communication law, a number of scholars have proposed international agreements and treaties. One such proposal suggests the notion of limited liability. Sutton, for example, predicts an agreement that "would simply state that no country will subject content providers who are not nationals or citizens of that country to more stringent liability than the content providers would face under their own country's laws" (2004, p. 432). Another plan is to get nations to agree "that speech and other expression over the Internet will be regulated by authorities in its place of origin" (Okoniewski, 2002, p. 295). Such a plan would resolve many if not most jurisdictional disputes.

Advances in filtering technology, including geo-location software, may assist bloggers in the future to minimize liability on the borderless Internet. ISPs in the United States might use filters to keep messages from reaching certain countries that would find them offensive. More practicably, foreign nations can and do use filtering devices to screen out messages that transgress their laws. Some experts have great faith in the efficacy and accuracy of such filters (August, 2002). Others, like Van Houweling, are less sanguine. She wrote of her belief that current geo-location filters, especially those designed to filter illegal speech, are too easily circumvented by computer users (2003). Thus, if a nation like France supports a policy of *zero tolerance* of Internet hate speech, faulty filters will not offer journalistic bloggers predictable protection.

In libel law, nations have long attempted consensus, and they have failed. The Hague Convention on Jurisdiction and the Recognition and Enforcement of Foreign Civil Judgments, for example, concluded in 2001 that consensus in this area, among other tort actions, was too problematic. The convention chose instead to focus on areas where consensus was more likely, such as international business-to-business contract issues (Standeford, 2003). Nonetheless, some form and level of international cooperation is necessary. Until and unless nations offer guidelines on at least who should resolve jurisdictional conflicts, if not how, international libel, defamation and copyright law will remain quagmires. Writers and publishers might restrict their expression to conform to the law of the most restrictive jurisdiction in which their online content is downloaded and read.

Common-law countries, in particular, must acknowledge the inadequacy of their judicial systems in reckoning with a communication medium that recognizes no borders. It is incumbent on these nations' legislatures to write new law giving their judiciaries latitude, unchaining them from centuries-old law and a time that knew no mass media. Specifically, these nations must act to prevent forum shopping—the practice of searching jurisdictions for the one in which the plaintiff believes he or she can succeed in bringing an action. Some recognition of intentionality and/or number of contacts, too, would offer remedy in cases of potential libel. Garnett, for example, called on the Australian Parliament to adopt a jurisdictional rule to protect Internet speakers that do not aim their speech at Australia, which would give that country's court system an alternative to the restrictions of historical precedent, nearly all of which involves pre-Internet media (2004).

Conclusions

Many bloggers and most journalists are proud of their editorial independence, and that is as it should be. In the United States, the First Amendment and a string of landmark Supreme Court cases affirm and protect that independence.[30] But, as English poet John Donne realized almost four centuries ago, "no man is an island entire of itself" (1624). The laws of many nations might apply. Any one journalist's loss in a foreign court is a loss for all journalists, including—perhaps especially—those who blog. In another echo of Donne, "Any man's death diminishes me because I am involved in mankind; and therefore never send to know for whom the bell tolls; it tolls for thee" (1624).

For journalists who blog for large media organizations, awareness of potential legal challenges internationally could prevent legal actions that threaten to hale the employer organization into a foreign court. For most lone, untethered bloggers without the benefit (and bane) of large, constituent legal departments, the lack of significant material assets abroad and relative anonymity likely provide ample protection against lawsuits.

References

Anti-Defamation League (2000). Combating extremism in cyberspace: The legal issues affecting Internet hate speech. [Online]. Available at http://www.adl.org/Civil_Rights/newcyber.pdf.

August, R. (2002, Summer). International cyber-jurisdiction: A comparative analysis. *American Business Law Journal*, 39 [Online], 531–539. Available at LexisNexis Academic.

Australian Press Council. (2004). *Press law in Australia*. [Online]. Available at http://www.presscouncil.org.au/pcsite/apcnews/aug04/defo.html and http://www.presscouncil.org.au/pcsite/fop/auspres.html#defam.

Bangoura v. Washington Post (2005), 235 D.L.R. (4th) 564.

Bell, S. (2004, August 28). Offshore Website publisher can be sued for defamation in New Zealand, judge finds. *Computerworld* [Online]. Available at http://computerworld.co.nz/news/nsf/0/5E45574D0B649922CC256EFD001E1760?OpenDocument&pub=Computerworld.

Bernard Connolly v. Commission, E.C.R. (1999). Case 273/99 & 274-99. [Online]. Available at ECJ CELEX LexisNexis Academic 6619; 2001 ECR I-1611.

Cameron, M. (2004, November 18). "Sore losers" take a swipe at Aussie libel laws. *The Australian*, 17.

Court challenge: Journalists contest "unfair" law. (2002, July 23). *The Guardian* [Online], 12. Available at LexisNexis Academic.

Dawson, C. (2004, Winter). Creating borders on the Internet: Free speech, the United States, and international jurisdiction. *Virginia Journal of International Law*, 44 [Online], 637–663. Available at LexisNexis Academic.

Defamation Act of 1996 (United Kingdom). Available at http://www.opsi.gov.uk/acts/acts1996/1996031.htm.

de Freitas, I. (2004, December 12). There are hard lessons in store for Internet publishers. *New Media Age*, 18.

Donne, J. (1624). Devotions upon Emergent Occasions. *Meditation 17* [Online]. Available at http://www.imaginary.com/~borg/Literature/Poems/Meditation17.html.

Dow Jones & Co., Inc. v. Gutnick, Case No. (2002) H.C.A 56 [Online]. Available at http://www.austlii.edu.au/au/other/hca/transcripts/2002/M3/2.html.

Dow Jones & Co. v. Harrods, Ltd., 237 F. Supp. 2d 394, 2002 U.S. Dist. [S.D.N.Y. 2002].

Dow Jones & Co. Inc. v. Yousef Jameel (2005). EWCA Civ 75. Case No: A2/2004/1540 [Online]. Available at http://www.bailii.org/ew/cases/EWCA/Civ/2005/75.html.

Duke of Brunswick v. Harmer, 14 Q.B. 185, 188–89 [1849].

Dyer, C. (2005, February 4). *Wall Street Journal*'s online libel win brings "much-needed clarity." *The Guardian* [Online]. Available at http:// guardian.co.uk/business/story/0,,1405498,00.html.

Edwards, L. (1997). Defamation and the Internet. In L. Edwards & C. Waelde (Eds.), *Law and the Internet: Regulating cyberspace* (p. 183). Oxford, England: Hart.

Eko, L. (2001, Summer). Many spiders, one worldwide web: Towards a typology of Internet regulation. *Communication Law & Policy, 6* [Online]. 461–482. Available at LexisNexis Academic.

Engle, E. A. (2002, Spring). When is fair use fair? A comparison of E.U. and U.S. intellectual property law. *Transnational Lawyer, 15*, 187–189.

E.U. and free speech. [Staff editorial]. (2001, March 14). *University Wire* [Online]. Available at http://www.mndaily.com/daily/2001/03/14/editorial_opinions/ee0314/.

Fagin, M. (2003, Spring). Regulating speech across borders: Technology vs. values. *Michigan Telecommunications & Technology Law Review, 9* [Online]. 395–455. Available at LexisNexis Academic.

Garnett, N. W. (2004). *Dow Jones & Co. v. Gutnick*: Will Australia's long jurisdictional reach chill Internet speech worldwide? *Pacific Rim Law and Policy Journal, 13*, 77–85.

Gauthier, A. (2001, Winter). World-wide worry. *The News Media & The Law*, 12.

Grant, D. (2002). Defamation and the Internet: Principles for a unified Australian (and world) online defamation law. *Journalism Studies, 3*, 115–132.

Gutnick v Dow Jones & Co., Inc. (2001) V.S.C 305 [Online]. Available at http://www.austlii.edu.au/au/cases/vic/VSC/2001/305.html and http://www.4law.co.il/582.htm.

Harrods v. Dow Jones & Co., Inc. [2003] EWHC 1162 (Q.B.).

International Shoe Co. v. Washington, 326 U.S. 310, 316, 90 L. Ed. 95, 102, 66 S. Ct. 154, 158 (1945).

Itar-Tass Russian News Agency v. Russian Kurier, Inc., 153 F. Supp. 3d 82 [2d Cir. 1998].

Jackson, M. (2003). Harmony or discord? The pressure toward conformity in international copyright. *Idea, The Journal of Law and Technology, 43*, 607.

Johnson, A. (2005, March 23). News service sues Google over content; Drudge, other Web sites at risk. *The Washington Times* [Online]. Available at http://washingtontimes.com/business/20050323-120718-4353r.htm.

Jones, K. (2002, November). Web means more work for lawyers. *St. Louis Journalism Review*, 9.

Kalathil, S. (2003, March 1). Dot com for dictators, Internet use to challenge authoritarianism. *Carnegie Endowment for International Peace Foreign Policy*, 43.

McCollam, D. (2003, May/June). Dateline everywhere? How the Web may make us vulnerable to long-distance libel. *Columbia Journalism Review*, 10.

Milton, J. (1644). Aeropagitica, speech for the liberty of unlicensed printing to the Parliament of England.

Mooney, P. (2004, September 20). China's government shuts down online bulletin board based at Peking U. *The Chronicle of Higher Education* [Online]. Available at http://chronicle.com/temp/email.php?id=2mbs0je20g0lvk5xvly33vohprlwtlyq.

Naik, G. (2004, February 18). Harrods loses libel suit against the *Journal*. *Wall Street Journal*, B8.

Near v. Minnesota, 283 U.S. 697 (1931).

New York Times Co. v. Sullivan, 376 U.S. 254 (1964).

Okoniewski, E. (2002). *Yahoo!, Inc. v. LICRA*: The French challenge to free expression on the Internet. *American University International Law Review, 18*, 295–301.

Restatement (Second) of Torts § 577 (1977).

Restatement (Second) of Torts § 613 (1977).

Riou, P. (1995). General jurisdiction over foreign corporations: All that glitters is not gold issue mining. *Review Litigation, 14*, 742–743.

Sandburg, B. (2002, December 11). Australian court ruling could extend reach of libel law. *The Recorder, 126*. Available at LexisNexis Academic.

Sham–Shackleton, Y. (2004, May 12). Born and banned in China. *PopMatters.com* [Online]. Available at http://www.popmatters.com/columns/sham-shackleton/040512.shtml.

Siebert, F. S., Peterson, T. & Schramm, W. (1972). *Four theories of the press*. Champaign: University of Illinois Press.

Soames, M. (2005, February 7). Media: Don't rely on Reynolds. *The Guardian*, 14.

Spector, J. (2002, Fall). Hate speech on the Internet: Spreading angst or promoting free expression? *Miami International & Computer Law Review, 10* [Online], 155–156. Available at LexisNexis Academic.

Standeford, D. (2003, June 17). U.S. to decide whether to pursue Hague talks as concerns linger. *Washington Internet Daily, 4* [Online]. Available at http://www.inta.org/press/news2003_14.html.

Sutton, M. F. (2004, March 1). Legislation the Tower of Babel: International restrictions on Internet content and the marketplace of ideas. *Federal Communications Law Journal, 56*, 421–422.

Tait, N. (2004, February 18). Harrods loses case against U.S. publisher. *Finland Times*, 4.

Tannenbaum, W. (2003, Winter). Questions of internet jurisdiction spin web of confusion for online publishers. *The News Media & The Law*, 35.

Tyler, T. (2005, March 8). Libel case chills world's papers. *Toronto Star* [Online]. Available at http://www.thestar.com/NASApp/cs/ContentServer?pagename=thestar/Layout/Article_Type1&call_pageid=971358637177&c=Article&cid=1110235812206.

UEJF et LICRA v. Yahoo!, Inc., T.G.I. Paris, Nov. 20, 2000, No. RG: 00/05308 [Online]. Available at http://www.cdt.org//speech/international/001120yahoofrance.pdf.

Unger, C. (2004). *House of Bush, house of Saud: The secret relationship between the world's two most powerful dynasties*. New York: Scribner.

Van Houweling, M. S. (2003, Spring). Cyberage conflicts law: Enforcement of foreign judgments, the First Amendment, and Internet speech: Notes for the next *Yahoo! V. LICRA. Michigan Journal of International Law, 24*, 697–703.

Xalabarder, R. (2002, Spring). Copyright: Choice of law and jurisdiction in the digital age. *Annual Survey of International Law, 8*, 80–81.

Yahoo! Inc. v. La Ligue Contre Le Racisme et L'Antisemitisme, 169 F. Supp. 2d 1181, 1189–91 [N.D. Cal. 2001].

Yahoo! Inc. v. La Ligue Contre Le Racisme et L'Antisemitisme, No. 01-17424, D.C. No. CV-00-21275-JF [N.D. Cal. 2005].

Yu, P. K. (2001, April). Conflict of laws issues in international copyright cases. *Gigalaw.com* [Online]. Available at http://www.gigilaw.com/articles/2001-all/yu-2001-04-all.html.

Notes

1. To date, there are five general categories of unprotected speech in the United States: obscenity (and broadcast indecency as regulated by the Federal Communications Commission), fighting words, incitements to lawlessness, bias-motivated conduct (including speech) and false or misleading commercial speech (also regulated, by the Federal Trade Commission).

2. There has been libel litigation involving bloggers, but like libel cases involving traditional media, it typically is settled out of court. One of the more prominent examples is *Blumenthal v. Drudge and AOL* (1998) Civil Action No. 97-1968. Available at http://www.epic.org/free_speech/blumenthal_v_drudge.html. Very common are cease-and-desist letters, which seek to quiet or silence bloggers by threatening legal action.

3. Accounts of the settlement amount vary. *The Australian*'s Michael Cameron reported the amount at $580,000 (2004). An attorney in London, Ian de Freitas (2004), put the total instead at $400,000.

4. See Unger (2004). The author examines how litigation is used around the world to repress free speech freedoms and intimidate publishers.

5. Dow Jones claimed only two dozen readers of its online *Wall Street Journal* in the United Kingdom. The company also has a European edition of the *Journal*, but the article in question was not published in or on that edition (Naik, 2004). Dow Jones also petitioned a U.S. federal court in October 2002, asking for the application of the Declaratory Judgment Act to stop Harrods, and by extension other foreign parties, from suing Dow Jones abroad. The media company's case was dismissed by a lower court, a decision affirmed in October 2003 by the U.S. Court of Appeals (see *Dow Jones & Co. v. Harrods Ltd*).

6. The offending article, "The Enron of Britain," from the April 5, 2003, *Wall Street Journal*, has been deleted from Dow Jones' article databases.

7. Estimates put the publisher's legal bills at about 500,000 pounds, or approximately $900,000.

8. See Restatement of [Second] Torts § 577 (1977).

9. See *The Traditional Cat Assn., Inc. v. Laura Gilbreath*, D041421, 118 Cal. App. 4th 392; 13 Cal. Rptr. 3d 353; 2004 Cal. App.; 32 Media L. Rep. 1998; 2004 Cal. Daily Op. Service 3899.

10. See *Firth v. State*, No. 87, N.Y. Ct. App., July 2, 2002.

11. Riou cites *Perkins v. Benguet Consol. Mining Co.*, 342 U.S. 437, 438 (1952).

12. It should be noted that Dow Jones removed the article Jameel objected to from its Web site and from its archive.

13. In a unanimous decision, the *Times* case established that public officials must prove a fault level of "actual malice" to win a libel suit based on defamatory allegations. The court extended the actual malice rule to plaintiffs considered public figures (see *Curtis Publishing Co. v. Butts*, 388 U.S. 130 [1967] and *Associated Press v. Walker*, 389 US 28 [1967]). In *Gertz v. Robert Welch*, 418 U.S. 323 (1974), the court established another fault category, that for limited public figures.

14. Restatement of Torts § 613 puts the burden of proof on the plaintiff for establishing "the defamatory character of the communication," "publication by the defendant," "application to the plaintiff," "recipient's understanding of its defamatory meaning," "special harm resulting to plaintiff from its publication," and "negligence, reckless disregard or knowledge regarding the truth or falsity and the defamatory character of the communication."

15. For the court's opinion, see *Yahoo! Inc. v. La Ligue Contre Le Racisme Et L'Antisemitisme* (2005). Available at http://www.ca9.uscourts.gov/ca9/newopinions.nsf/3DF703F416DC0608882570F40006DDCF/$file/0117424.pdf.

16. The Executive Council of Australian Jewry also brought a suit against Toben in Australia seeking the enforcement of a Human Rights and Equal Opportunities Commission. The commission, a government body, ordered Toben in October 2001 to remove Holocaust revision material from his Adelaide Institute Web site. He refused to do so (see Australian faces trial for holocaust denial [2000, December 14]. *Reuters*; see also *Jones v. Toben* [2002] F.C.A. 1150 [Sept. 17, 2002] [Online]). Available at http://www.austlii.edu.au/au/cases/cth/federal_ct/2002/1150.html).

17. Two additional international legal structures governing intellectual property, the World Intellectual Property Organization and Trade-Related Aspects of Intellectual Property Rights, are more generally concerned with disputes involving commercial copyright matters.

18. The Duke sent one of his servants to buy a magazine 17 years after it had been published, then claimed damages resulting from one of his servants reading the publication. The court held that the content was actionable and that damage could, therefore, be presumed.

19. See also Tannenbaum (2003).

20. The newspaper is *The Australian*, owned by Nationwide News. Newlands University brought the suit after the newspaper described it as a "wannabe university" and "degree mill." Nationwide News does not have a physical presence in New Zealand.

21. Quote from Transcript of Oral Argument in *Dow Jones & Co. v. Gutnick*.

22. Meldrum was the first journalist tried under Zimbabwe's Access to Information and Protection of Privacy Act.

23. In September 2004 China shut down one of its most popular online bulletin boards, Peking University's YTHT, which claimed more than 700 discussion forums and more than 300,000 registered users. Access is blocked using keyword filters. See Mooney (2004).

24. The Berkman Center is available at http://cyber.law.harvard.edu/home.
25. The government relented under widespread protest from business people, scholars and scientists.
26. Other examples include Cuba, Iran, Libya and Tunisia.
27. TRIPS refers to the Agreement on Trade-Related Aspects of Intellectual Property Rights, which was signed in 1993 as a constituting document of the World Trade Organization. It sets minimal rules for national intellectual property law in order to prevent member nations from using intellectual property as a hidden trade barrier against other nations.
28. Toben's Web site is located at http://www.adelaideinstitute.org. See also August (2002).
29. See http://www.adelaideinstitute.org/Australia/025.htm.
30. Landmark decisions at the U.S. Supreme Court level protecting free speech include *New York Times v. Sullivan*, 376 U.S. 254 (1964); *Gertz v. Robert Welch*, 418 U.S. 323 (1974); and *Philadelphia Newspapers v. Hepps*, 475 U.S. 767 (1986). As Garnett notes, no common-law countries other than the United States have followed the Sullivan decision in ruling that the constitutional protections against abridgement of speech apply to the law of defamation (*supra* note 21, 71).

12
Emergent Communication Networks as Civic Journalism

LOU RUTIGLIANO

Introduction

Although the term has fallen into disfavor, it is possible that the concept of civic journalism is of renewed importance amid the shrinking audiences (Meyer, 2004; Mindich, 2005) and damaged credibility presently facing the traditional news media. In this environment, civic journalism's ultimate mission—to use the news to revive democracy and, at the same time, revive the importance of the news in the daily life of citizens—should resonate with many in the journalism business today.

Recent research has placed the civic journalist's burden upon the blog. Initial attempts to inject civic journalism's ideals into the mass media had mixed results, often facing criticism or outright resistance because of the clash between the proactive, engaged civic journalist approach and journalism's traditional standards of objectivity and distance. Blogs are civic journalism on steroids: Civic journalism sought to use the news media to encourage participation and debate among the public (Rosen, 1999), but blogs are interested in bringing public participation and debate into the everyday practice of journalism.

Blogs have evolved significantly since their birth in 1999 and now encompass a variety of formats. The spectrum of interactivity in the medium ranges from tightly controlled formats with little audience participation to versions that are mostly built from the bottom up through the participation of their audience.

Community blogs are the most overt example of this. They intend to apply the blog software popularized by the more well-known individual bloggers to a specific geographic area and allow the residents of that area to create and maintain their own news organization. Through this sort of online experimentation, public journalism is becoming "the public's journalism" (Witt, 2004).

To compare the reality of blogs to their hype, it is pivotal to consider them in the context of network and complexity theory. Recent applications of this theory to other areas of social science—political campaigning, business organization, urban planning—apply here as well. Understanding the two can help clarify the limits and potential of blogs for those attempting to build a democratic public sphere.

By applying these theories to an analysis of several community blogs, this chapter also hopes to show that the current experimentation with online participatory public journalism has opened a window for media researchers for a new line of research. The natural laws of chaos and complexity are rarely used in communication research (Gunaratne, 2003). However, for many of the research questions generated by community blogs, these laws will be indispensable.

The laws of network and complexity theory have much to add to this discussion. The former reveals the obstacles facing individual blogs in the blogosphere if they want to realize the levels of interactivity and openness of which blog proponents boast. The latter provides hope that a decentralized group of individuals acting without direction can still produce content that achieves the goals of civic journalism. Consideration of networks and the self-organizing behavior of complex systems helps in structuring the blog to avoid certain pitfalls. For example, if fully open systems favor the powerful, what structure can counteract that? This chapter looks at three community blogs with different structures to show how these theories, born from math and physics, can help in the creation of civic journalism.

Civic Journalism and the Public Sphere

Habermas's public sphere is useful to conceptualize civic journalism's goal of creating a space where citizens can debate public issues. Despite valid criticisms (Fraser, 1993) that questioned Habermas's assumption that the public sphere was ever democratic, Habermas's overall argument that the public sphere exists in the mass media and that the mass news media do not facilitate a democratic and participatory public sphere was echoed by the civic journalism movement. Habermas argued that to make such democratic public discourse a reality, all of the large-scale institutions within society had to become more democratic, piece by piece. In the case of the media, more democratic structures were needed to increase public access and counteract the concentration of ownership and the growth of media conglomerates (Calhoun, 1993).

Such reform of national and international media models requires what Downing calls "radical media activism" (2000, p. 28). This umbrella term incorporates media literacy, the improvement of the practice of journalism and the creation of alternative versions of print and broadcast media. Downing refers to Dewey's belief that the media can provide the information and communication possibilities required for democratic discourse (p. 42). However, he then draws upon the theories of Raymond Williams, who argued that media must disconnect from private or state ownership and be open to mass participation by the public.

The civic journalism media reform movement also believed in the existence of this public ability. Rather than demand such a complete dismantling of the news media, civic journalism tried to encourage the news media to incorporate the public (and a wider swath of it) into its work. Advocates furthermore argued that it was the media's responsibility to help reconnect citizens to society, revive public life and facilitate civic action (Burd, 2001, 2002).

> The readers and viewers would create, collect and communicate news from their own perspective using the new electronic technologies, thereby making the journalists less dependent on experts and government as sources...any loss of press objectivity by its organizing civic action, it is argued, would be offset by serving the public good (Burd, 2002, pp. 9–10, citing Rosen 1991, 1993, and Rosen & Merritt, 1994).

However, the various experiments at newspapers throughout the country met with mixed results. Rosen notes that citizens did not always respond to civic journalism, and although some initiatives had an impact on the community they were trying to reach, "there were others that passed with little effect" (1999, p. 274). In a more recent article, Witt (2004) cites the conclusion of Massey and Haas (2002) that civic journalism did not have a significant effect on journalists or citizens.

But Witt also notes that many in the civic journalism movement have shifted their efforts from the newsroom to the Internet. In particular, the blog has given many of these advocates renewed hope by providing a new vehicle by which to involve the public in the news. There are many echoes of the goals of civic journalists in discussions of the benefits of blogs. Traits such as the conversational, informal and opinionated writing; the ability to share locally specific news; the networking capability that mobilizes action and more are common ground for bloggers and civic journalists. Although it is not explicitly acknowledged, blogging has once again placed civic journalism's agenda on the media radar (Scott, 2004).

Blogging proponents claim that a low barrier to participation is an inherent benefit of their craft and that blogs have blurred the lines between producers and users. They have stated that blogging software has "given millions of people the equivalent of a printing press on their desks" (Blood, 2003, p. 61), that blogging can lead journalism to "expand from a centralized, top-down, one-way publication process to the many-hands, perpetual feedback loop of online communications" (Andrews, 2003, p. 64), that blogs are an egalitarian "informal conversation" (Lasica, 2003, p. 71) because "the readers want to be a part of the news process" (Lasica, p. 74) and that blogs "break down many of the existing barriers between journalists and the public" (Grabowicz, 2003, p. 74).

Many of these claims are untested (Witt, 2004). Indeed there are already signs that the blogosphere is becoming less interactive and open to participation. In addition to the steep drop-off in traffic from the most popular blogs to the majority of blogs, Clay Shirky (2003) predicted in a March 2003 essay that as a blog's audience grew, the blog would not be able to link to everyone seeking its attention and would not be able to respond to incoming mail or comments. Thus, it would become "a broadcast outlet, distributing material without participating in conversations about it."

There are two popular responses among blogs to these trends: putting up walls to reduce the flood of feedback and adding ways to allow audience members to interact with each other as a self-regulating community. One thing is certain: As the audience for individual bloggers grows, it becomes more difficult to manage the audience and control its feedback. In August 2004, Shirky confirmed this and observed that the most popular blogs had obtained such high levels of traffic that they had little choice but to function like broadcast media with low levels of interactivity. On October 28, 2004, a guest blogger on Instapundit offhandedly acknowledged this when he said that "Instapundit doesn't have comments, but it does have email. I can't even read it all, let alone answer it" (Instapundit).

Emergent Communication Networks

Blogs can potentially accommodate mass participation and remain open and competitive, thereby providing the more democratic public sphere that civic journalists and blog enthusiasts desire. But they first need to surrender part of their operation to the laws of emergence.

Emergent, "bottom-up" systems rely on the work of many simple parts to solve problems, thereby forming a far more complex and adaptive system that does not require the guidance of a single member to make it function (Kelly, 1994, pp. 22–25). The laws of such self-organization are at play in anthills, the human brain and urban development. They are distinguished by the absence of a central authority, autonomy and freedom of each unit within the whole, a high level of connectivity among these units and the ability of one unit to influence another (Kelly). Such flexibility allows emergent systems to adapt, evolve, expand and survive, but also makes them inefficient (it takes greater lengths of time for an emergent system to gain complexity and functionality) and difficult, if not impossible, to control, predict and understand (Kelly).

But now, as Steven Johnson observes in his analysis of the website Slashdot, systems are designed to mimic this emergent behavior intentionally and realize that simplistic behavior changes when a group reaches a certain level of members; many simple elements can join together to create sophisticated behavior where complicated elements would fail; and it is important to allow random interactions instead of manipulating or ordering behavior (Johnson, 2001, pp. 77–79). Johnson notes that to manage the growth of Slashdot's audience while maintaining its open and participatory structure, Slashdot relied on emergent behavior, allowing decentralized control and interactions between the audience without the interference of the site's creator (Johnson, p. 154).

The result is "the closest thing to a genuinely self-organizing community that the web has yet produced" (Johnson, 2001, p. 152). But even that accomplishment, which places debate fully in the hands of the public, must answer Johnson's question of how to avoid the tyranny of the majority (Johnson, pp. 160–161)—another way to describe the power laws of network theory.

The science of networks has provided a way to explain and predict groups that once seemed far more random. The underlying features of networks of individual parts—from social groups of people to neurons in the brain—have become apparent through research advances in mathematics during the past 10 to 15 years. The most relevant law of networks for this discussion is the power law, which states that there are many small members in a network, in terms of significance, alongside a few large members (Barabasi, 2002, p. 67). Power laws are "nature's unmistakable sign that chaos is departing in favor of order" and "the patent signatures of self-organization in complex systems" (Barabasi, p. 77). This law implies an uneven distribution of power and seems to contradict the argument that blogs give everyone a voice.

An additional trait of networks—preferential attachment—would only worsen this imbalance. Preferential attachment dictates that individual nodes in a network are more likely to link to well-connected network hubs. This behavior "helps the more connected nodes grab a disproportionately large number of links at the expense of the latecomers" (Barabasi, 2002, p. 88). The blogosphere's apparent destiny overall is instead to provide a platform for only a few to reach many and for many to reach only a few. If a community blog is designed as a miniature blogosphere, a completely open and self-regulating system might meet the same fate.

Research Questions and Methods

Therefore, a self-organized approach might not be the best solution. Adding decentralized emergent crowd behavior to a blog adds the benefits described in the previous section. But an emergent system completely left to its own devices, with absolute freedom for the individuals within the system, would only lead to another network with a handful of hubs attracting all the attention and dominating the discourse. This chapter considers this dynamic in order to determine the appropriate balance between central control and self-organized behavior on a community blog.

This study works from a definition of community blogs as websites that invite participation from residents of a particular geographic area and allow the public to assume responsibility for media production. These websites apply the blog software popularized by more well-known individual bloggers to a specific geographic area and allow the residents of that area to create and maintain their own news organization. They generally permit high levels of feedback and interactivity, a relatively decentralized work process and low barriers to entry.

Community blogs are often included in lists of online "citizens' media" efforts. Cyberjournalist.net has a running list of these projects that at the time of writing included 68 websites.[1] While all these sites strive for higher reader participation and interactivity, they are not all based on a particular local geographic community. Some are structured more like a discussion forum, blog aggregator or online magazine with a fixed number of contributors; some are focused on particular topics rather than general news; some still have a rate of production too limited to be studied yet (10 articles a month or less in some cases). This leaves less than a dozen known websites, all of which fall into one of three categories defined by the degree of editorial freedom they allow their users to exercise:

Controlled: The bulk of the blog's content is provided by one writer, typically the founder and maintainer of the site. Contributions from the public are accepted and posted to the site's home page, but there is more centralized editorial control of the content in an effort to adhere more to standard journalistic norms of objectivity and writing structure.

Hybrid: A blog uses a small, centralized part-time or volunteer staff, typically one to two people, who generate content and moderate content provided by citizens. Although posts are reviewed by these moderators, they are generally moved to the site's home page untouched. The staff will occasionally contribute posts and comments, but here the relationship found in the controlled model is reversed: In the controlled model, the staff seems to contribute 75% and users 25%; in the hybrid, the staff contributes 25% and users 75%.

Open: A blog has an administrator and an advisory board, but a very small degree of obvious direction or intervention. The staff or volunteers in this case may simply approve posts and comments, but rarely contribute them. There is therefore little visible involvement of the site's owners or moderators in the site's daily content. The high degree of member ownership of the site that results from this reduced guidance makes this version the most self-organized of the three models.

One representative community blog from each of these three categories was included in the study. Coverage of the topic in the Online Journalism Review and the Institute for Interactive Journalism's "New Voices" program also helped to determine which sites had already earned some attention and recognition for their efforts. This led to the selection of WestportNow.com (controlled), iBrattleboro.com (hybrid) and LiveFromArlington.com (open). The report then reviewed the posts (brief articles added throughout the day by a blog's contributors) generated on these three blogs during 2 months (March and December 2005) to get a sense of who contributed, what type of posts they wrote, and what they wrote about.

The analysis was primarily qualitative, although a category scheme was devised and basic quantitative comparisons were used to show general patterns of behavior. This period of time was chosen because, at the time of the study (the first week of April 2005), going back a month allowed time for the comment discussion on each post to unfold and end (theoretically providing time for the feedback necessary for self-organization and providing further material for analysis of the sites) while not going so far back in time as to make links inactive and therefore the context of each post difficult to distinguish. The gap in time also provided an opportunity to see whether any trends detected in March had intensified by December, as network theory's preferential attachment law would seem to suggest.

Because of varying levels of activity on each site, the results were tallied and presented as percentages of the overall activity on each individual site. A number of posts that did not fit into the main categories also existed. These posts are accounted for in the result tables as "other," but discussed in further detail in the results section. Three main factors were considered: the type of post, the subject of the post and the source of the post. The type of post was an announcement (describing an upcoming event), reporting (generating news through observation or other firsthand research) or commentary (opinions about news generated from another source). The subject of the post was government, community organization/nonprofit, businesses/for-profit or an individual (all "local" versions). The source of the post was a public official, a spokesperson/professional or an individual citizen (all "local" versions).

These criteria will help to show when a community blog has produced not only journalism, but also civic journalism (with a high degree of involvement from the "community," i.e., the users). If the ideal is to create a news media where individual citizens can create their own news about issues relevant to the rest of the public (the activities of government vs. activities of family), then the most effective of the three structures will reflect this.

Results

The "type" of post category was meant to distinguish between journalism, where the post provided original news and opinion, and content that basically amounted to press releases, with no additional information. The former would highlight an issue covered elsewhere and generate revealing public discussion about that issue or generate news through first-hand observations and research. The latter would include basic dates, times and information about an event in a format that appeared to be sent by a spokesperson to every possible media outlet (Table 12.1).

Compare the discussion of a Westport teen buying his own home, which led readers to comment: "This is so quintessentially Westport that it's repulsive"[2]

Table 12.1 Type

	March 2005			December 2005			Total		
	C	H	O	C	H	O	C	H	O
Announcement	15%	30%	78%	15%	38%	68%	15%	34%	75%
Reporting	58%	40%	12%	47%	19%	16%	53%	30%	13%
Commentary	1%	18%	5%	1%	19%	16%	1%	18%	8%
Other	26%	12%	5%	37%	24%	0%	31%	18%	4%

to the posting of a fund-raising dinner in Arlington for a youth-based charity with a few sentences about speakers and honorees and the address of the event.[3] The reporting and commentary found in the former example contain much more depth in comparison to the latter, which is more of a calendar listing.

The controlled and hybrid models were therefore more effective at producing journalism, while the open model was dominated by announcements of events at churches, museums and charities. However, the differences between the controlled and hybrid models' level of journalism are complex. The "other" category in the case of WestportNow is mostly posts of photos of weather or holiday scenes, with little additional information. For iBrattleboro, "other" included posts that began as simple links to press releases, but were followed by several public comments. For example, an initial post on iBrattleboro of a link to an article about the sale of a local telecommunications company to a larger conglomerate led to discussion in the comments about the loss of "local autonomy."[4]

The "subject" category compared the content of posts on the three sites to see whether posts were discussing issues typically considered to have news value: local politics, economics and culture. Postings centered on individuals accounted for content that was more focused on private matters—a common criticism of community websites allegedly full of photos of family pets. Table 12.2 shows that, to different degrees, each of the three sites had content that discussed figures found in the public sphere, such as LiveFromArlington's

Table 12.2 Subject

	March 2005			December 2005			Total		
	C	H	O	C	H	O	C	H	O
Government	11%	23%	24%	13%	17%	5%	12%	20%	18%
Nonprofit	12%	18%	49%	13%	15%	37%	13%	16%	45%
Business	3%	10%	12%	2%	19%	32%	2%	15%	18%
Individual	11%	9%	0%	8%	9%	21%	10%	9%	7%
Other	63%	40%	15%	64%	40%	5%	63%	40%	12%

review of local political candidates[5] (a rare instance when the site administrator provided content) and iBrattleboro's staff and reader dissection of local government procedures for filling vacancies in town offices.[6]

However, in some cases the fact that the subject of the post is a local business or nonprofit does not mean that the post contains similarly weighty content. This is an important distinction that requires considering the "subject" category in the context of the "type" and "source" categories. For instance, LiveFromArlington has posts with local businesses as "subject," but these are announcements provided by the businesses.[7] On the other hand, posts on iBrattleboro dealing with local businesses as "subject" are more often contributed by readers with more revealing details, such as a post about the fate of a low-powered local radio station.[8]

The "source" category looked at who provided content to the three sites and which of the three models effectively provided citizen-generated content. Table 12.3 shows that although the open model contained some citizen content, it was most likely to have "professional" content contributed by spokespeople for organizations—for example, a post from an Arlington electric company announcing its new website, followed by a comment (from the same contributor) that compliments the site. The controlled site and hybrid site were able to gather citizen-contributed content.

But again this citizen content varies widely, from a photo of a sunset on WestportNow[9] to entries posted by an iBrattleboro member from Cairo, Egypt, about a peace conference.[10] The relationship between a site's staff and its readers is important to consider as well and worthy of future study. Although WestportNow has more staff-generated posts, these can trigger public comments, such as how an initially staff-written story on a government investigation into a local resident's charity develops into a public discussion on oversight of nonprofits.[11]

Discussion

Although the always evolving nature of the Internet and the small sample of qualifying websites make generalizations difficult at this time, several trends emerged in this initial comparison. Community blogs are meant to be a way for

Table 12.3 Source

	March 2005			December 2005			Total		
	C	H	O	C	H	O	C	H	O
Public officeholder	0%	1%	5%	0%	2%	0%	0%	2%	3%
Spokesperson	15%	15%	51%	21%	25%	68%	18%	20%	57%
Citizen	42%	56%	37%	51%	54%	11%	46%	55%	28%
Other	43%	28%	7%	28%	19%	21%	36%	23%	12%

individual citizens to provide news about their community, so the ideal output would not be posting information provided by a spokesperson for an institution. Posts that seemed to contain almost identical information and content as a press release were considered to be "announcements" rather than individually provided reporting or commentary written in a more personal voice.

Table 12.1 shows how the controlled model delivered the highest percentage of "reporting" as defined by journalistic norms. In interviews, the site's founder, a former professional reporter for several media organizations including the *New York Times* and CBS News, has stated his daily involvement in writing, editing and recruiting volunteers to contribute to the site.[12]

WestportNow's professed high degree of staff involvement is reflected in the "other" category in Table 12.3 (staff submissions, in each case), for which the controlled model had the highest percentage. This percentage is also understated considering the large number of posts contributed by one female volunteer reporter in December. Future studies should examine the distribution of submissions to determine the diversity of the pool of contributors in comparison to the community. Even though they are volunteers, if six individuals do almost all the work, is that truly "community" media?

It is interesting to compare the output of the hybrid model to that of the controlled model. Although the two residents who started iBrattleboro participate in the blog (with far less frequency), their guidance is more indirect. The posting of information about the actions of local government by the iBrattleboro staff seems to shift the discourse when it veers into less important topics, such as the posting of animals for adoption. Such occasional interference steers the far more self-organized community back on course.

The hybrid has the highest percentage of citizen participation, as well as the most coverage of government, and its percentage of "reporting" (information provided by individuals on topics of relevance to the community) is just slightly less than the controlled version: 48% for iBrattleboro and 54% for WestportNow, despite the significant difference between the two in the degree of guidance and "staff" work: (23% for iBrattleboro and 36% for WestportNow).

If that provides some evidence of the possibilities of self-organized journalism, the open system suggests the problems found when there is almost no visible guidance or editorial interference. There is little sense on LiveFrom Arlington that the site's founder or advisory board participates in the site on a daily basis. It functions far more like the mailing list that preceded it: as a place where anyone can post anything, with little resistance from a central figure to serve as a corrective or even motivating force. This led the open system to relative disinterest of individual residents (best reflected by the steep drop-off in total number of posts from 41 in March (compared to 220 on WestportNow and 97 on iBrattleboro) to 19 in December (217 on WestportNow and 100 on iBrattleboro).

Instead, the discourse is dominated by announcements and press releases provided by local institutions, such as basic calendar information for upcoming events at a nonprofit fund-raiser. The distinction between simple announcements and citizen reporting is critical and is illustrated by comparison to a sequence of posts on iBrattleboro: After a local farm posted an invitation to the community to attend a holiday party at its headquarters, an individual posted allegations that the event was intended as a recruitment event for a local religious organization.

Institutional competitive strengths that exist offline, such as the resources of time and money, transfer to the community blog under this format, as if the hubs of the offline network have transplanted the advantages of their offline power to this online arena. Institutions are better equipped to contribute compared to most citizens with little experience or inclination to participate. Therefore, these groups set the tone for the community blog's content by contributing the bulk of it.

The open model contained 75% announcements, with 57% of the content contributed by representatives from government, business, or organizations such as churches and nonprofits. The subject matter on the blog was therefore predominantly about the activities of these institutions, whereas WestportNow and iBrattleboro contained a mix of stories on other topics, such as crime, real estate and culture.

Conclusions

This preliminary analysis of community blogs shows how a mostly self-organized network of individuals can produce content that corresponds to the goals of the blog's central administrators without direct guidance. This would seem to be good news for advocates of civic journalism and its current incarnations because the widespread participation of the public does not necessarily mean chaos.

However, the laws of networks raise questions about the equation of democracy with complete freedom. Eventually, a completely free and self-organized network will settle into an orderly structure that conforms to a power law. A community blog that is a completely open system will merely become a smaller version of the wider blogosphere, with certain elements dominating others. The most unregulated of the three community blogs studied here hints at such a system, in which the hubs of the offline network outside the blog— institutions from the public and private sector rather than individuals—have become the hubs of the online network inside the blog.

This raises interesting questions about the role of the journalist in a more participatory era. Ironically, emergent journalism does not render *journalists* obsolete. In fact, it creates a new role for a journalist: managing complexity— in this case, complex systems. The journalist becomes a monitor of the public, tending to a complex system and saving it from its worst natural instincts, because a democratic public sphere is not a necessary product of a self-organized public.

Just who constitutes that public is of course an issue as well. Questions of access, power and demographics are also relevant here. This study made a simple distinction between individuals and institutions to focus attention on the mere presence of citizens—but which citizens and what are they writing about? Further analysis of the content is necessary and provides an additional level of depth to this discussion.

The application of complexity theory and network theory to communication research is only beginning. However, as news media fragment and online experiments explore different ways of reassembling the splintered audience, the time will come to explore theories outside the boundaries of traditional communication research.

References

Andrews, P. (2003). Is blogging journalism? *Nieman Reports, 57*(3), 63–65.

Barabasi, A.-L. (2002). *Linked: The new science of networks.* Cambridge, MA: Perseus Publishing.

Blood, R. (2003). Weblogs and journalism: Do they connect? *Nieman Reports, 57*(3), 61–63.

Burd, G. (2001). *The convergence of new urbanism and civic journalism.* Paper presented to Urban Affairs Association, Detroit, MI, April 25–29, 2001.

Burd, G. (2002). *Public affairs and civic journalism: A "marriage proposal" for educators.* Paper presented at Southwest Education Council for Journalism and Mass Communication, Nov. 1–2, 2002.

Calhoun, C. (Ed.) (1993). *Habermas and the public sphere (studies in contemporary German social thought).* Cambridge, MA: MIT Press.

Downing, J. (2000). *Radical media: Rebellious communication and social movements.* Thousand Oaks, CA: Sage Publications.

Fraser, N. (1993). Rethinking the public sphere: A contribution to the critique of actually existing democracy. In B. Robbins (Ed.), *The phantom public sphere.* Minneapolis: University of Minnesota Press.

Grabowicz, P. (2003). Weblogs bring journalism into a larger community. *Nieman Reports, 57*(3), 74–76.

Gunaratne, S. A. (2003). Thank you Newton, welcome Prigogine: "Unthinking" old paradigms and embracing new directions. Part 1: Theoretical distinctions. *Communications, 28,* 435–455.

Instapundit: http://instapundit.com/archives/018738.php.

Johnson, S. (2001). *Emergence: The connected lives of ants, brains, cities, and software.* New York: Scribner.

Kelly, K. (1994). *Out of control: The rise of the neo-biological civilization.* Reading, MA: Addison–Wesley Publishing Company.

Lasica, J. D. (2003). Blogs and journalism need each other. *Nieman Reports, 57*(3), 70–74.

Massey, B. L., & Hass, T. (2002). Does making journalism more public make a difference? A critical review of evaluative research on public journalism. *Journalism and Mass Communication Quarterly, 79,* 559–586.

Meyer, P. (2004). *The vanishing newspaper: Saving journalism in the information age.* Columbia: University of Missouri Press.

Mindich, D. T. Z. (2005). *Tuned out: Why Americans under 40 don't follow the news.* New York: Oxford University Press.

Rosen, J. (1991). Making journalism more public. *Communication, 12,* 267–284.

Rosen, J. (1993). *Community connectedness—Passwords for public journalism.* St. Petersburg, FL: The Poynter Institute.

Rosen, J. (1999). *What are journalists for?* New Haven, CT: Yale University Press.

Rosen, J., & Merritt, D., Jr. (1994). *Public journalism: Theory and practice.* New York: Kettering Foundation.

Scott, Lori Cooke (2004). Deliberative Communities Online: Towards a Model of Civic Journalism Based on the Blog. (Paper submitted to Association of Educators in Journalism and Mass Communication, June 30, 2004).

Shirky, C. (2003): http://shirky.com/writings/powerlaw_weblog.html.

Shirky, C. (2004). Why Oprah will never talk to you. Ever. *Wired Magazine, August,* 052–053.

Witt, L. (2004). Is public journalism morphing into the public's journalism? *National Civic Review, Fall,* 49–57.

Notes

1. http://www.cyberjournalist.net/news/002226.php.
2. http://www.westportnow.com/index.php?/v2/comments/westport_teen_with_her_own_home_suite_featured_in_ny_times/.
3. http://www.livefromarlington.com/article.php?story=20050317092729388.
4. http://www.ibrattleboro.com/article.php?story=20051222101608905#comments.
5. http://www.livefromarlington.com/article.php?story=2005032614185396.
6. http://www.ibrattleboro.com/article.php?story=20050325155446781.
7. http://www.livefromarlington.com/article/php?story=20051203105948967.
8. http://www.ibrattleboro.com/article.php?story=20050323132855476.
9. http://www.westportnow.com/index.php?/v2/comments/days_end/.
10. http://www.ibrattleboro.com/article.php?story=2005032111352493.
11. http://www.westportnow.com/index.php?/v2/comments/don_imus_we_have_a_30_million_estate_on_the_water_in_westport_conn/.

13
Citizen Journalism: A Case Study

CLYDE BENTLEY, BRIAN HAMMAN, JEREMY LITTAU,
HANS MEYER, BRENDAN WATSON AND BETH WELSH

Introduction

If necessity is the mother of invention, panic may be the mother of journalistic innovation. The newspaper industry has been awash with panic for two decades. Daily circulation in the United States is falling even as population is rising. Advertising revenues are attacked by free-circulation shoppers, broadcast, cable, billboards and now the Internet. Even the credibility of professional journalists was cast in doubt by a series of reporting scandals at major publications.

This case study describes the philosophy and theory behind MyMissourian.com, an academic attempt to address these issues through what has come to be called *open source* or *citizen* journalism. The study documents the effects of this type of Internet site on journalism education and on a community.

A high-technology attack on the traditional newspaper industry led to the MyMissourian project. In 1999, frustration with the "one-way journalism of the 20th century and the haughty attitude common in the Korean media" led to inspiration for one young Korean journalist. Unable to make an impact on the conservative Korean media and political landscape through traditional means, Oh Yeon-Ho (2004) launched a media revolution based on five words: "Every citizen is a journalist." The result, launched February 22, 2000, was OhMyNews, an Internet-based publication for which 727 "citizen reporters" volunteered to supply news and commentary from their own perspectives. Four years later, OhMyNews had more than 32,000 citizen reporters and worldwide respect.

"The citizens of the Republic of Korea had long been preparing for a grand revolution in the culture of news production and consumption," Oh explained. "All I did was raise the flag" (2004).

That battle flag, proclaiming that titles and training grant no monopoly on reporting, caught the eyes of journalists worldwide. In the United States, Mary Lou Fulton—a former AP, *Los Angeles Times*, washingtonpost.com and AOL journalist—saw it as a call to action. "News coverage has become dominated by bad news and event-driven news," Fulton told Cyberjournalist. net. She continued:

> When readers try to tell journalists about things that don't fit the formula, they hear lots of rules explaining why what's important to them is unworthy of attention. We need to find more ways to bring the accomplishments and concerns of ordinary people into the spotlight (Dube, 2005).

Rather than "find" an answer, she "founded" it: The Northwest Voice, a combination website and community newspaper in suburban Bakersfield, California. The Northwest Voice used Oh's concept of citizen journalists, but with less political tone than OhMyNews. A key difference in The Northwest Voice approach was a link to the free-distribution, total market coverage (TMC) arm of its parent newspaper, the *Bakersfield Californian*. Fulton used the Northwest Voice to gather content that could then be published in the free print shopper, thus tapping into a proven revenue stream and the resources of an established publication.

News of Fulton's venture lit up online bulletin boards and journalism professional publications in 2004. At the Missouri School of Journalism, the concept was discussed on faculty e-mail lists. In May 2004, Associate Professor Clyde Bentley and Columbia Missourian Online Editor Curt Wohleber proposed a trial citizen journalism site as part of an existing class. The reaction of the dean of school, Dean Mills, was enthusiastic support.

That summer, Bentley and a team of graduate students outlined the procedures and technology needed to launch a site. By fall, undergraduate students in the online journalism class were contacting local community sources for content. By October 1, MyMissourian.com was online. A year later, it launched a print edition and reversed the print-to-web publishing paradigm. Within 18 months, this journalistic toddler was dealing with the challenges of mass media maturity.

Review of the Literature

Citizen Journalism Defined

"Citizen journalism" is a popular label used to describe a form of media that involves moderated reader participation. Citizen-based media generally starts as web-based publications, but one of the long-term strategies is to develop a "best of" print edition that ultimately serves as the publication's revenue source. *The Northwest Voice*, which is the citizen journalism arm of the *Bakersfield Californian*, used material from the web edition to revive its shopper edition (Terdiman, 2004). The paper's institutional research showed that readership of its regular shopper edition was low, and this was not pleasing to advertisers. Mary Lou Fulton, drawing upon an idea pioneered at OhMyNews in South Korea, guided the start of a community website that was run solely on story and photo submissions from the community (Bentley et al., 2005). As content increased, the material eventually replaced the stale material that often stocked the shopper editions (Glaser, 2004).

Whereas OhMyNews was intended to compete directly with existing media, the first incarnation of citizen journalism in America was an attempt at synergy. *The Northwest Voice* used the citizen journalism content to revive an existing product; thus, it was not intended to be in direct competition with the parent product. This is the "umbrella" model of citizen journalism, which sees this medium as a way to enhance the company's products rather than compete with them. MyMissourian made use of this umbrella model, although it did take some time for this notion to sink in with the management at *The Missourian*.

But beyond the popular definition and the benefits in rebuilding sagging publications, what is citizen journalism? In point of fact, citizen journalism reverses the sender–receiver process of traditional journalism. Whereas newspaper, television and web media use the journalist as a gatekeeper in the process of selecting and presenting news, in the citizen journalism format the journalist is a "shepherd" in the process (Glaser, 2004). This means that the journalist's role is to seek out community voices and encourage submissions; the only editing role is in making sure that copy is readable and does not open the publication to legal problems such as libel or defamation. Then he or she makes selections as to what goes on the main pages of the website.

It is worth noting that "citizen journalism" is just the latest name for this type of medium, but it is the one with the most popular appeal. In its beginnings it was referred to as "participatory journalism" or "open source journalism", but it also has been referred to as "grassroots journalism" (Gillmor, 2004).

Citizen journalism is going to force a reshaping of current theories about online journalism. One work theorizes four types of online journalism that are deployed along an axis (Deuze, 2003): mainstream news sites, index and category sites, meta and comment sites and sites for sharing and discussion. The horizontal axis, which ranges from left to right, goes from an emphasis on editorial content to an emphasis on public interaction. The vertical axis, from top to bottom, goes from an emphasis on moderated participatory communication to unmoderated participatory communication.

Mainstream news sites offer originated (original copy produced for the web medium) or aggregated (taken from the parent medium and replicated for the web, sometimes called "shovelware") content with very little participation from users; most online newspaper sites, Deuze (2003) notes, fall into this category. Index and category sites do not produce original content, but rather link to it; examples would include portal sites such as Yahoo! or the Drudge report, but some blogs also fit into this category. Meta and comment sites are sites about journalism, written by journalists and often containing comment about how the news is produced rather than comments about the news. Share and discussion sites offer places for users to connect with one another and exchange ideas in an open forum. Group (or community) blogs or discussion sites such as Slashdot are good examples of this type of online journalism (Deuze, 2003).

Citizen journalism exhibits characteristics of share and discussion sites for the most part, because the emphasis is on participation and exchange of ideas. But unlike sites such as Slashdot, a popular weblog, those building citizen journalism websites often are seeking out people in the community to write. Citizen journalism is partly built on the personal nature of blog writing. It can be written in first person or third person. If a person decides to weave opinion with fact, that is considered acceptable; the basic tenet is that community members are not trained to think or write in the artificial standard of media objectivity, and thus they often are not forced to adopt that standard. In addition, citizen journalism is more like a community blog in the sense that there are multiple authors; however, unlike a typical community blog, there are no limits placed on who is allowed to submit to the site (Glaser, 2004).

The notion that citizen journalism is moderated is what separates citizen journalism from a typical community blog and, in fact, is what elevates the posting format into a news format. The editor running the site often determines what is placed on the front page, and thus the gatekeeper role still happens to a limited a degree (Glaser, 2004). Citizen journalism sites are usually designed like a news site, not a blog, and thus there are layered pages containing a main front page and several topic categories. Still, the gatekeeper role is greatly diminished from what it would be at a typical news site because the editor would determine what makes the front page and what stories make it onto the site. Unless the stories violate standards for submission, citizen journalism sites tend to publish anything submitted.

Design tends to be a big concern in terms of gatekeeping; photos that would grab attention tend to make the front pages, as do more dramatic stories (Glaser, 2004). Also, many sites incorporated the use of statistical software in their design. The result is that modules within the site software can move the most popular stories to the front page, giving the site's readers more of a choice in what goes on the front.

Because it offers more interactivity than traditional news outlets, one can use a citizen journalism site in one of three ways: as a reader, as a writer or as both (Ananny & Strohecker, 2002). One last point about citizen journalism worth highlighting is that there have been surprising results in submissions. Political copy submission rates have been lower than expected at some sites, whereas story topics considered "softer" in some newspaper circles, such as gardening, food, and religion, were areas with greater rates of submission.

Technology

One of the first challenges faced by the MyMissourian team was the selection or creation of software that could support a citizen journalism website. The software needed to be affordable enough for the smallest community newspaper, yet powerful enough to be managed by one or two editors and flexible enough to be adapted to future needs of citizen journalism. The rapid launch schedule—about a month—also meant the software had to be simple to set up. These restrictions left MyMissourian without a software model. The abbreviated development schedule meant there would be no time to develop software similar to that used by OhMyNews, and the cost of the commercial software of the Northwest Voice was too expensive to be adopted by small papers (Coyle, 2004). Instead, the editors chose to launch the site using a freely available open-source content management system called Mambo. Mambo is an award-winning, mature, content-management system with an active development community (Mambo Project Team, 2005). On October 1, 2004, MyMissourian launched using one of the templates available on the Mambo System and a logo developed by the editors (see Figure 13.1).

While Mambo included more features than most free content-management software, it was still far from the ideal platform for hosting a citizen journalism publication. In particular, the built-in submission form did not allow for the attachment of photos, so photos had to be e-mailed to the editors. Within a few months of launching, the editors designed a custom submissions page, called the "Easy Form," which gave citizen reporters the ability to meet that

Figure 13.1 The home page.

need (Figure 13.2). Immediately following the creation of the form, the rate of photo submissions to the site tripled. In its first year, approximately one quarter of all submissions to Mymissourian included photographs.

The influx of photo submissions made it necessary to redesign the website. The new design reserved an entire column to highlight photographs, which are consistently the most popular items on the site. We also made it possible for editors to control the position of stories included on the front page (Figure 13.3).

Finally, in order to support this more complex homepage, graduate student Brian Hamman created the Easy Editor content management system that allowed more control in the editing and layout of MyMissourian. The system consolidated many of Mambo's aspects and created new tools so that editors could manage all the content for MyMissourian from a single location, including exporting the content for the print publication (Figure 13.4).

Despite these improvements, the editors still were limited by a heavily customized version of free software. Many of the citizen journalists had difficulty with the technology to capture, size and upload a digital image through the online form and instead chose to send the photos through e-mail or not at all. To allow multiple photo submissions, the editors turned to a third-party

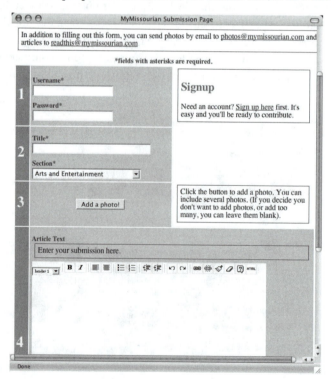

Figure 13.2 The Easy Form submission page.

Figure 13.3 The new home page.

site, Flickr, with links to MyMissourian. The editors tried accepting photos directly from camera phones, but this proved challenging. Without installing expensive software on the server, photos could only be submitted to MyMissourian using an e-mail address, which seemed unfamiliar to most phone users. MyMissourian received only a handful of photo phone submissions despite a concerted effort to solicit them.

As MyMissourian continues to grow in complexity, the editors are looking to new technologies to run the site. After months of working with the current site, however, it is clear that the system chosen to run a citizen journalism website will need to be flexible and extendable in order to accommodate the changes necessary to keep up with the changing needs of citizen reporters and editors.

Policies and Procedures

The most immediate concern of the team assigned to establish MyMissourian was to ensure a level of credibility for the site. The Missouri School of Journalism has a long history of traditional journalism values. Its founder, Walter Williams, is the author of the widely quoted "Journalist's Creed" (Williams, 1908).

It was obvious that the normal credibility procedures found in a newsroom would not easily transfer to an open-source journalism project. Fact checking was harder because the authors were not staff members and were not always immediately available. As expected, biased stories from the public were the

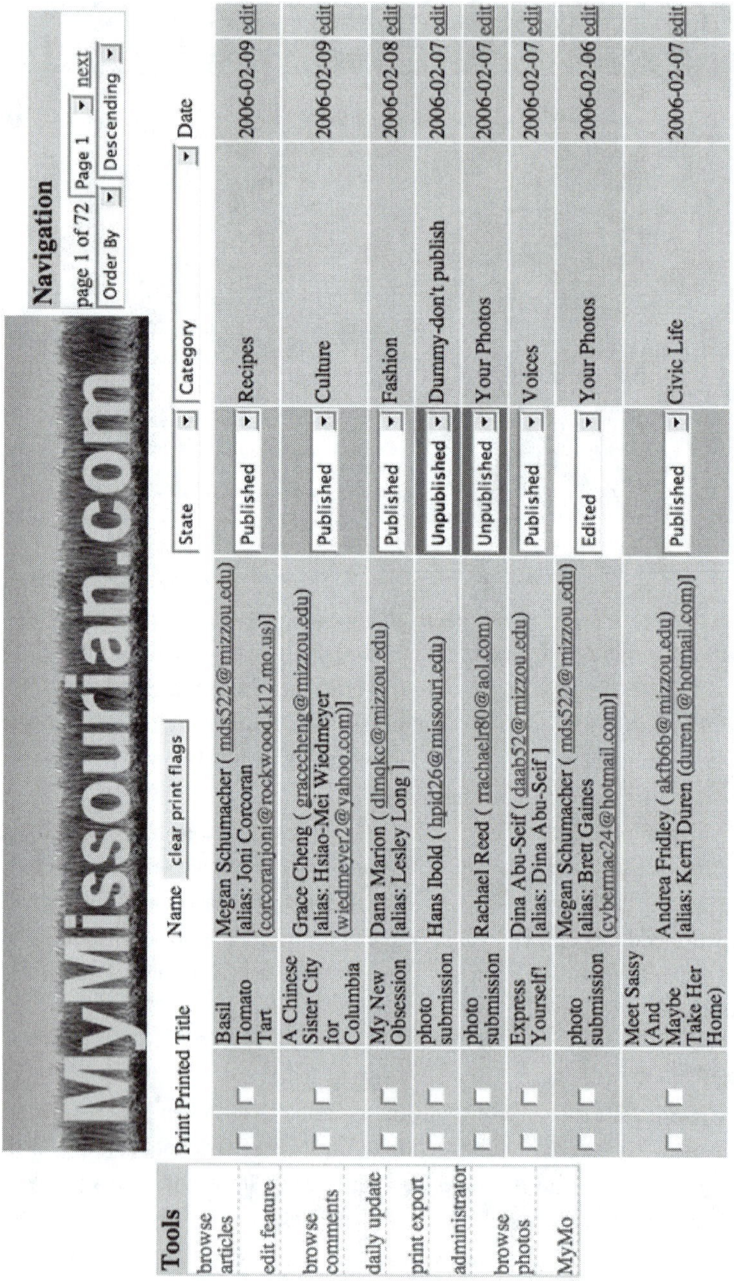

MyMissourian.com

Tools

- browse articles
- edit feature
- browse comments
- daily update
- print export
- administrator
- browse photos
- MyMo

Navigation

page 1 of 72   next

Order By   Page 1   Descending

Print	Printed Title	Name clear print flags	State	Category	Date
☐	Basil Tomato Tart	Megan Schumacher (mds522@mizzou.edu) [alias: Joni Corcoran (corcoranjoni@rockwood.k12.mo.us)]	Published	Recipes	2006-02-09 edit
☐	A Chinese Sister City for Columbia	Grace Cheng (gracecheng@mizzou.edu) [alias: Hsiao-Mei Wiedmeyer (wiedmeyer2@yahoo.com)]	Published	Culture	2006-02-09 edit
☐	My New Obsession	Dana Marion (dlmqkc@mizzou.edu) [alias: Lesley Long]	Published	Fashion	2006-02-08 edit
☐	photo submission	Hans Ibold (hpid26@missouri.edu)	Unpublished	Dummy-don't publish	2006-02-07 edit
☐	photo submission	Rachael Reed (rrachaelrf80@aol.com)	Unpublished	Your Photos	2006-02-07 edit
☐	Express Yourself!	Dina Abu-Seif (daab52@mizzou.edu) [alias: Dina Abu-Seif]	Published	Voices	2006-02-07 edit
☐	photo submission	Megan Schumacher (mds522@mizzou.edu) [alias: Brett Gaines (cybermac24@hotmail.com)]	Edited	Your Photos	2006-02-06 edit
☐	Meet Sassy (And Maybe Take Her Home)	Andrea Fridley (akfb6b@mizzou.edu) [alias: Kerri Duren (duren1@hotmail.com)]	Published	Civic Life	2006-02-07 edit

Figure 13.4 The Easy Editor.

norm. There was neither a management system to discipline a writer nor a professional code of conduct that writers were obligated to follow.

The editors decided to approach the issue with a simplified set of rules and procedures. The goal was to establish rules specific enough to prevent most credibility challenges, but broad enough to allow for flexibility and nonprofessional writing style. Bentley launched the discussion with a memo asking the student editors to consider four areas:

- "decency" (use of language, content topics, etc.)
- "commercialism" (promotion of a business, organization, religion, etc.)
- "literacy" (How much editing and rewriting should we do?)
- "banalism" (Is anything just too stupid to appear on the site? If so, how dumb is dumb?)

The discussion raged for days and reflected the traditional training and concern for professionalism of the editors. In the end, however, the group made the following decisions:

- MyMissourian was part of a family-oriented newspaper and openly available to children. Therefore, the profanity and nudity common on some weblogs were not appropriate.
- Although MyMissourian was designed to be commercially viable, the connection between livelihood and living was too close to bar any reference to commerce from the postings. The editors would use their journalistic skills to rein blatantly commercial writers.
- The *AP Stylebook* is a standard for journalists, but does not always match the rules of writing taught in most high schools. Rather than follow a strict style guide, the staff would just edit submissions to enhance readability.
- The question of banality produced the longest discussions. Eventually, however, the group decided journalists really have little to stand on when they attempt to judge what is silly and what is not. Instead of making that call, the editors decided to reserve an "Oddities" section where the weird and less fathomable could be posted. To date, that section has never been employed.

The next question was how to translate that discussion into a set of rules that members of the public would quickly and easily understand. A group discussion again ensued, leading to just four simple statements of what material was banned from the site:

no nudity
no profanity
no personal attacks
no attacks on race, religion, national origin, gender or sexual orientation

Beyond that, the editors agreed to use their training to work with the writers. This required a logistical rule that all submitters had to give their real name and contact information before their material would be posted. Minor additional procedures were worked out in staff meetings as the site developed, but the emphasis was on simplicity and flexibility.

The editors' gamble that simple procedures could protect credibility was put to the test in March 2005 when a reader submitted a commentary on the deportation of Canadian Ernest Zundel, who has denied the Holocaust. The essay met the four basic rules of MyMissourian, but the subject was controversial to several readers.

Some respondents to the original post stepped over the rules about "attacks" by making anti-Jewish statements. Those submissions were not posted to the site. Then MyMissourian received an e-mail that the original post contained material taken directly from a syndicated column. The original post was quickly pulled from the site and a notice was published explaining why and warning against plagiarism.

There were no further complaints and other political discussions continued. The "self-correcting" nature of citizen journalism seemed to work. To make the concept clearer to readers, the editors later added a tagline to posts urging readers to submit all corrections, complaints or comments about articles promptly.

The simple submission rules were meant to bring an air of civility to the content, but not to control the volume of content, as in many print papers. Rather than restricting content, MyMissourian channels and moderates it through a system of content sections and coaching from trained journalists.

Content Sections

Researchers found that websites that rely on user-submitted content have higher levels of participation when information is well organized and easily browsed by readers (Tedjamulia, Olsen, Dean & Albrecht, 2005). MyMissourian did this by developing content categories familiar to readers. The editors drew on the organization of traditional media and websites and a front-page category index to help readers quickly find information. The assumption was that journalists are best equipped to guide the public to information topics.

What editors quickly learned is how often these sections must adapt. In its first 18 months, MyMissourian used more than 20 sections. Twelve original sections—Gardening, Arts and Entertainment, Business, Celebrations, Photos, Civic Life, Schools, Science/Technology, Spiritual Life, Sports, Recipes and Voices—were developed through discussion among the site's editors. At the start of 2006, seven of these original sections remained but nearly all were significantly changed. They also shared the site with six new sections—Your Photos, Fashion, Culture, History, Health & Science and Local Blogs—that reflect increased contributor influence.

The editors found that the most popular sections are not those that borrow heavily from traditional media, but those that receive less coverage, such as religion and recipes. The initial designers misunderstood this premise and launched the website on a model that mimicked a traditional newspaper.

To be fair, timing influenced the site's launch under a somewhat traditional model. In October 2004, the Internet was playing a major role in the presidential election. By the end of that election, 29% of the general population and 52% of all Internet users had turned to the web for political information (Rainie, Homqan & Cornfield, 2005). Politics seemed an obvious concentration for MyMissourian and became the focus of the editors' content efforts. The editors aggressively promoted this section, attending festivals where politicians were campaigning for local, state and national offices and attending major political events.

Despite these efforts, there were few contributions to the politics section at any time during the campaign season. There were several contributions on the topic of why young people should vote and a contribution from a student discussing her experiences as an intern during a congressman's campaign. The site's editors, however, wrote the majority of the section's content, hoping to "seed" other submissions.

Shortly after the election, the politics section was folded into "Civic Life"— a new section where Columbia residents could discuss important local issues affecting the community. The section sparked interest with stories on local marijuana laws, a proposal to ban smoking in local restaurants and reflections on the shooting death of a Columbia police officer. Her death spurred enough interest among the community that MyMissourian created a temporary special section in her memory. That section received more than 10 contributions in 2 days, which at that early stage in the site's development was the site's greatest number of contributions in that short a time. It also drew the most page visits in the first year of MyMissourian. An article titled "National Thoughts and Prayers for Officer Bowden" received more than 542 page views.

The Civic Life section also made inroads in communities underserved by the mainstream media. Early contributors included an African-American university student writing about issues in her ethnic community. Another lived in a city-owned residence for elderly and disabled adults.

A lesson the editors learned from success of the "Civic Life" section (and the lack of success of the "Politics" section) is that readers and potential contributors are not interested in a rehash of events and issues already covered by the city's other news media. Rather, they are interested in issues largely ignored on the front page. The successes of the "Spiritual Life" section illustrated this. There are more than 300 places of worship in Columbia, yet these organizations receive relatively little coverage in the city's mainstream media. The Internet, however, has been a natural gathering place for religious groups and individuals (Larson, 2004). The "Spiritual Life" section recorded the most sustained number of contributions to MyMissourian.

The needs of Columbia's young families are particularly underrepresented in traditional media. The 2000 Census said the average age of Columbia residents is 26.8 years old. More than 50% of the residents are currently married or have been married and the average household has 2.26 people. MyMissourian appealed to this demographic group with a very successful "Recipes" section, featuring everything from family recipes to commentary on "The Great American Meal" to nutrition tips for the holiday season. The section has such a reliable base of submissions that the print edition features a new recipe in the right-hand column every week and a web-only cookbook is under consideration.

Not all "young family" themes worked, however. The "Schools" failed to take off as predicted despite the traditional media's dearth of day-to-day coverage of elementary or high school classroom activities.

The MyMissourian editors, however, realized their initial work-through-the-principals approach may have contributed to the problem when they received an unsolicited submission from a high school teacher about a rock music-themed student end-of-finals celebration. The teacher heard about the site from one of the school's journalism instructors and simply navigated through the submission system alone. It quickly became apparent that an enthusiastic teacher and a handful of curious students could make a difference. Editors gave the teacher's students disposable cameras to document the party. The site then presented a photo gallery that included 41 photos. The students eventually contributed music reviews and other stories nearly every week.

Despite the popularity of youth soccer and baseball in Columbia, "Sports" was a troubled section. Editors trained at a traditional journalism school had trouble transforming moving their focus beyond football, baseball, basketball and hockey. The graduate student managers of the site had difficulty getting the undergraduate sports editor to contact youth coaches until the site received a set of unsolicited stories and photos from a volleyball player and a wrestler and his family wrote of his struggle for champion status.

The biggest sports success was not a team sport at all, but a photo series on deer hunting. Members of the sister *The Columbia Missourian*'s advertising staff suggested a sponsored contest allowing hunters to post photographs of the deer they bagged. The traditional newspaper had long refused to publish "dead deer" photos despite hunting's popularity in mid-Missouri. Even theMyMissourian editors were hesitant, worried the photos would be too graphic. However, the submissions were tasteful and plentiful. MyMissourian received more than a dozen hunting photographs in just a few days; most included smiling and obviously proud hunters from the community. The popularity of the site was amazing. One of the first photos (the contest's eventual winner) received more than 500 views. It was the most visited submission on the site for more than a month. This contest generated the kind of chain reaction that editors always thought was possible and gave a participant community a chance to come together.

Experience has taught the editors how to reach some groups, but it has not solved all their concerns. Demographically, an important group to MyMissourian is college students, but maintaining their interest has proved a challenge. While there are three campuses in Columbia—the University of Missouri-Columbia, Columbia College and Stephens College—with a combined enrollment of more than 30,000 students, MyMissourian made a conscious decision not to focus heavily on students. To ensure it was self-sustaining, the site focused on Columbia's stable resident population. But the need for a student audience and student editors became obvious in December 2005, when the three schools went on holiday break. Submissions dropped so precipitously that the editors took down the entertainment section. It was clear that an entertainment-oriented section required intensive shepherding as well as an attentive audience.

Another section was similarly challenged by traditional journalism assumptions. MyMissourian editors established a "Science/Technology" section thinking the college audience would fill it with high-technology stories. They overlooked the five major medical treatment facilities in Columbia and the University of Missouri's medical school and a large life science research center. Health stories quickly outstripped science and technology submissions and struck a chord with the city's Baby Boomers. The section was renamed "Health & Science" and embraced by the medical community. The healthcare profession used it effectively not just to disseminate health information but also to promote some of its causes. A university surgeon's article on a holiday CD he recorded remained one of the most popular articles well after Christmas. An arthritis rehabilitation center also produced a widely read article aimed at adults.

The key to nearly all of these sections is active editor involvement. Two of the most visited new sections derived directly from editors seizing upon existing information to create a community interest. MyMissourian started the "Fashion" section after the instructor of one of the university's fashion marketing courses approached Professor Bentley. Dr. Jana Hawley wanted to give her students a real-world application of their coursework, so she sent them into the community to find ways to market local stores and fashion trends. They produced a well-read and researched examination of fashion trends, as well as business expansions and opportunities. The intensely local focus and effective use of photographs to illustrate points made this section one of the most popular during the 2005 winter semester.

Editors tried to capitalize on the blogging phenomenon with a collection of links to local blogs. Bentley at first created this section to teach his online journalism students the techniques of "staff blogging," but editors quickly realized blogs' ability to generate interest and contributions. While the students' blogs still dominate the section, a number of local bloggers contacted the site and asked to be included. Before a blog is listed in MyMissourian, the author must sign a statement agreeing to the site's four rules and acknowledging the editors' right to delete the link at any time.

The MyMissourian "Local Blogs" section not only provides links to participating blogs but also pulls individual items and photos from blogs, edits them into freestanding stories and then links back to the original blogs. The tactic highlights blog contents for readers who would not otherwise cruise the blogosphere.

Photography

The one section MyMissourian editors thought would remain in much the same form as they envisioned it was "Photography." The digital camera that has become nearly ubiquitous with its inclusion on cell phones should have made digital photo submission painless. However, photography on MyMissourian posed a challenge on the technological and personal fronts from the onset. The first issue was Mambo. The open-source software lacked photo-uploading functionality and MyMissourian contributors were initially limited to using e-mail to contribute photos. While this method was adequate for stand-alone photo contributions, the lack of a photo-uploading function in the site's online contribution form confused users who wanted to upload photos with textual contributions. Not until January 2005—3 months after the site launched—was a better photo-uploading solution implemented.

This update did not make the submission of more than one photo practical. MyMissourian's photo submissions did not take off until the site adopted the secondary use of Flickr, a photo-sharing website owned by Yahoo!. Flickr allows users to post a nearly unlimited number of photos to their personal sites. MyMissourian purchased a professional account upgrade (which costs $20 a year) that allows the user to post as many galleries as he or she would like. Instead of requiring submitters to create their own Flickr accounts, MyMissourian receives the submissions, and editors upload the photos to Flickr. One or two of the best photos are posted directly on the MyMissourian site, creating a story that contains the link to the Flickr gallery. The result was a simple and inexpensive, off-the-shelf photo submission system.

Providing photo galleries made photo submissions skyrocket. The revamped "Your Photos" receives more submissions than any other site. MyMissourian now boasts several roving photographers who snap digital pictures while they are out and upload them for all to see. The most popular "rover" has even accepted assignments to shoot photos for other people's submissions.

The expansion of the "Photos" section has allowed editors to confront another challenge. The ubiquity of camera ownership makes identifying likely groups to approach for photo contributions difficult. Other MyMissourian content sections could readily identify interest groups, such as soccer leagues for "Sports" and the local Democrats for "Politics," but photography was meant to permeate the site, not to be limited to one section. One way to do this was to emphasize the importance of requesting photo contributions with all textual contributions. Another was to identify general-interest groups, such as 4-H, whose activities include photography.

Taking a cue from the Northwest Voice, MyMissourian launched a photo contest in November 2004 to encourage photo contributions. A local photography store sponsored the contest and became the site's first commercial sponsorship. Even the lure of $25 gift certificates did not increase photo contributions, and the sponsorship ended after 3 months. This first attempt at a photo contest lacked the best solution thus far to attract photo contributions: Narrow the focus to a specific group of citizens and solicit that group for photos related to its interests.

In March 2005, a renewed effort at generating photo contributions via a contest paid off handsomely. The "Cutest Critter Contest" was deliberately crafted to tap into a likely source of *existing* photographs, rather than requiring entrants to find and photograph something new, thereby lessening one important barrier to participation. The other factor contributing to this contest's success was a focused marketing effort. Two MyMissourian photo editors visited, talked with and posted flyers at a number of local pet-related businesses. While no direct evidence is yet available to verify the impact of the promotion on contest participation, common sense suggests that targeting pet-related locations led to greater participation than generalized marketing. The loss of the contest's sponsor restricted the zero-budget effort to a more modest prize—publication of the winner's name and photo in the printed *Columbia Missourian*; however, this shortcoming did not appear to inhibit contest participation.

MyMissourian has since launched four more photo contests, most without sponsors. The most successful, by far, was the "Big Bucks" photo contest with at least a dozen entries and hundreds of visits. The winner of that contest received a $25 gift certificate to Wal-Mart. However, the "Fall Photos" contest received more than 30 entries without a sponsor. The rewards now include $15 digital cameras in addition to publication of their photos.

Buoyed by these successes, MyMissourian launched a holiday-themed contest to encourage cell phone camera contributions. Cingular Wireless eagerly latched on and donated a $250 black Razr phone as a prize. By every measure, the contest was a failure. Large promotional ads were placed in the print edition and teasers were placed on the website. After 2 months of promotion, the contest had received less than five entries, and several of those were from journalism school staff.

The lack of interest in the cell phone contest—despite its substantial prize— is the subject of ongoing research. However, one of the biggest concerns is the difficulty users have uploading photos. The common way to use photo cell phones, which cellular companies promote, is to send a picture to another cell phone using a telephone number. Inexpensive systems that allow a phone number to send photos to a computer network were unavailable. The alternative was to have the users e-mail the photos from their phone. While this is actually quite easy, it is such an unfamiliar technique that many users do not use it.

Another effort to publish photos of New Year kisses also failed to drum up reader interest and shows that a photo contest needs more than promotion or a fancy prize to succeed. To make photo contributions work, citizen journalism needs to tap a topic that people are actively discussing. At MyMissourian, editors could see no better example of that than the Big Bucks contest; the hunting-themed contest gave a community underserved by the traditional media a place to interact and assemble. But the New Year kisses contest was the product of wishful thinking by journalists rather than an indication of desire by the public.

Future photo initiatives need to focus on real public desire and not just on encouraging people to use their digital cameras. The MyMissourian photo section must remain a place for people who have an active interest in sharing their photos and no other place to do it. Citizen journalism must remain open to all photo contributions, but actively seek those that relate to something people are talking about.

Finding Readers and Writers

The key to a successful marketing plan, business experts agree, is targeting a specific audience and catering all promotion efforts to them. With MyMissourian.com, however, the editors had to create a site that appealed to nearly everyone because, as author Dan Gillmor explained, open source/citizen journalism must include all:

> It all boils down to something simple: readers (or viewers or listeners) collectively know more than media professionals do. This is true by definition: They are many, and we are often just one. We need to recognize and, in the best sense of the word, use their knowledge. If we don't, our former audience will bolt when they realize they don't have to settle for half-baked coverage; they can come into the kitchen themselves (Gillmor, 2004).

To succeed, MyMissourian had to attract the widest variety of submissions and readers possible because mass appeal, in this case, does not mean publishing something everyone will like. It means creating a place where everyone feels welcome and free to share.

From its inception, MyMissourian was designed to be more than a community blog. While it is open to all opinions, it is meant to provide news and information, especially content that has otherwise been unavailable in or rejected by the community newspaper or local TV news report. The first impression some have is that the site is designed only for people to submit opinions or, as one person said, to "rant and rave." Others, on the other hand, have pushed the editors to make the site an unedited, freewheeling forum. The answer lies somewhere between the two.

Just visiting the site was convincing enough for one long-time Columbia resident. John, a 20-year-old student who grew up in Columbia, said, "I must admit, before seeing the site, I thought it was blog-like, but after seeing it, I would not put it on the same level as a blog. It's much more professional" (Spratt, 2005). The central message of nearly every community presentation since is to encourage people to visit the site. Presentations to civic groups have included projected screen captures of the homepage and several of the section pages as well as submissions to show people how easy it is to submit and what kinds of articles others have submitted.

Another important tactic to dispel the blog reputation was stressing editor involvement. Submissions to MyMissourian are not posted to the site immediately. One or more editors read every submission first. While the major guidelines the editors follow are the four submission rules and an order to fix common grammatical and spelling errors, they also use their journalism training to question ethical, libel and factual "red flags." When questionable content is noted, the editor working with the submission contacts the author for clarification. This extra step adds to the site's credibility with readers and writers. Readers still want a journalist to guide the news dissemination process. Preliminary qualitative interviews indicated readers want better ordering of submissions and ways to search for the news that relates to them quickly and easily. Others added that a weekly, printed "best-of" edition would enhance their reading and submission experience because it would provide examples of what editors thought were effective submissions.

Stressing editor involvement also helps to dispel two other common myths. First, many citizens think they are not good enough writers to meet journalism's high standards. They seem to know that someone will scan their submissions for grammatical and spelling errors before it is posted. Others, especially those in the sports community who were asked to submit their game reports and scores, said they preferred to see journalists do the work of journalism. The editors made personal contact with these critics, however, to frame the work as a partnership that resulted in stories that otherwise would not see public light,

Another recruitment technique that paid off was to connect editors with the existing Internet community in the area. Editors use e-mail extensively and scan blogs, bulletin boards and list servers for contacts. A post to the Columbia section of FreeCycle.com was particularly successful. The website has nearly 2,500 Columbia members and allows people to post "ads" for items they want to give away rather than sell. Bentley posted a note on FreeCycle that produced six semiregular columnists. The language of the post shows how the editors boiled down the site's mass approach to reach specific target audiences while keeping the door open for diverse content:

"MyMissourian's role is to fill the gaps between the traditional media and the rumor mill. We are looking for information you won't find elsewhere in Columbia," it says. It spells out the benefits in terms regular Internet users understand. "As with FreeCycle, this is not a money-making offer. You get paid in the adoration of your readers." Possible column topics ranged from the best FreeCycle finds to weather forecasts based on trick knees and sore elbows to the cricket game report.

From Web to Print

From the beginning, the site's developers planned to follow the example of the Northwest Voice and offer a weekly printed edition. This was less of an editorial notion than a business proposal. Although newspaper websites are often profitable, they bring in a much smaller portion of the paper's revenue than the print operation.

A key to smaller newspapers' profitability is their "TMC" or total market coverage editions. These often weekly editions are distributed free to nonsubscribers and, in combination with the paper's paid circulation, they provide advertisers with blanket coverage. The *Columbia Missourian*, like many newspapers, filled its TMC products with old stories previously published in the daily edition. Also like many newspapers, the *Missourian* suffered from "driveway rot": papers left in the driveway unread because their recipients did not feel they were worth picking up.

MyMissourian capitalized on the experience of the Northwest Voice to use citizen journalism as a way to give TMC readers compelling content that was not duplicated by the daily paper. In theory, such a product should have greater appeal and less chance of neglect by householders.

Before jumping headlong into this endeavor, however, the editors wanted to ensure they had enough reliable content. MyMissourian reached the reliability plateau within 6 months, but Bentley and the *Missourian*'s management decided to wait until after the university's 2005 summer break to launch a print product. This allowed MyMissourian to demonstrate it could maintain a flow of content when student readers and student editors were in short supply. A single graduate student assistant maintained the site during the summer and kept a good flow of new stories.

Once the flow was assured, Bentley, Potter and *Columbia Missourian* Executive Editor Tom Warhover determined the logistics of the print edition. The Columbia Missourian publishes two TMC editions, one on Wednesday and one on Saturday. The three chose to put citizen journalism content in the Saturday edition, largely because the *Columbia Missourian* does not publish a normal daily edition that day.

With fall at hand, the editing team chose to launch the print edition on the first anniversary of MyMissourian. *Missourian* designers worked with the online staff to create a print product that emulated the homespun, nontraditional feel of MyMissourian's web edition. The new product carried the same "Saturday Weekly" flag it had for years, but added a MyMissourian logo and the tag line "You write it. We print it."

The Mambo-based core program of MyMissourian was modified so that editors could mark stories and photos for potential use in the print edition. Once weekly, another software feature allows editors to "sweep" the marked content into a standard text file, which is then exported to the *Columbia Missourian*'s print editing system. The daily's copy desk then produces the print edition.

Response to the new print product was phenomenal. While site registration is not necessary to read MyMissourian online, it does indicate interest because one must register to write for the site. In the web-only first 12 months of MyMissourian, the site attracted 441 registered authors. In October 2005—the first month of weekly print edition, 130 authors registered. By the end of the calendar year, author registration was up to 682. Page views showed similar gains.

The potential for the hybrid web/print MyMissourian is high. Print display advertisers are happy because community comment about the product bearing their ads is high. Ad lineage continues to grow and costs remain extremely low. Because MyMissourian used free open-source software and existing faculty and staff, the out-of-pocket expense for the web edition was only the few hundred dollars required to register the URL. There was no extra cost in producing the print edition because the *Columbia Missourian* had edited and printed a TMC for years.

Similar returns on investment were realized by *Bakersfield Californian*'s Northwest Voice, which first developed the format. Northwest Voice has operated with a staff of just three people. Although MyMissourian uses nearly two dozen students in its production, that number is primarily a reflection of its teaching function. The use of just one editor to produce the section over the summer and the university's winter break demonstrated that a similar product could be successful with minimal staff.

Conclusion

While MyMissourian was inspired by pioneering citizen journalism sites such as Northwest Voice and OhMyNews, its editors believe it has paved new ground in the online world. The site successfully fills three important roles: It is a successful commercial venture, it is a potent research platform and it is an attractive teaching instrument for 21st century journalism skills.

The site has demonstrated that citizen journalism works in small communities without a huge financial commitment from the newspaper sponsor. But it returns to that newspaper sponsor revenue and important social functions.

By eliminating the newsroom "no," citizen journalism units become valuable safety valves for traditional newspapers. They allow the umbrella media organization to guarantee a place for almost any story, almost any photograph and almost any content.

Citizen journalism sites also feed the public hunger for what the Readership Institute calls "intensely local, people-centered news" (2001). MyMissourian also provides an unlimited news hole and communication between reporter and reader seen only as promises in the first "New News" seminar at the Poynter Institute 10 years ago (Paul, 2005).

Because of its affiliation with the Missouri School of Journalism, MyMissourian has operated not just with open-source software but also as an open source for research and experimentation. Those within the industry have noticed the site and its potential influence. Since its inception, more than 20 publications, including Online Journalism Review, Editor and Publisher, Northwestern University's New Media Hack and the Newspaper Association of America, have reviewed the site.

But the most telling review came from a citizen journalism site in Lafayette, Colorado, iLafayette.net. The site's author lists MyMissourian as one of his main influences. In fact, he claims he pilfered the idea from MyMissourian (iLafayette.org, 2005). To the editors of MyMissourian, the iLafayette.net incident had the same impact as a reporter finding her feature story stuck to a neighbor's refrigerator: clear evidence someone is listening.

The general concept is also finding popularity with the newspaper industry. Morris Communications heralded the launch of its free daily newspaper in Bluffton, South Carolina, with an open-source website that debuted April 1, 2005, as a "grand experiment in citizen journalism" (Yelvington, 2005).

On the academic side, qualitative and quantitative research based on MyMissourian continues. The site is the subject of at least six master's theses and is in the review process for several doctoral dissertations. It has been the subject of several academic papers as well as academic and professional presentations, including one at the OhMyNews International Citizen Reporter's Forum in Seoul.

The teaching benefits were an underestimated bonus by Bentley. Students commented that the focus on developing new sources without being allowed to write the story sharpened their reporting skills. The reputation of MyMissourian to highlight the interests of readers has become so well known at the University of Missouri that reporters at the school's other publications regularly read it for leads.

The Missouri School of Journalism's experiment, started in October 2004, is already paying off. How far it will take journalism depends not just on the communications professionals at newspapers and universities who have been involved in the site, but also on the readers who have relabeled themselves "citizen journalists."

References

Ananny, M., & Strohecker, C. (2002). *Situated citizen photojournalism and a look at dilemmatic thinking.* Association for the Advancement of Computing in Education's E-Learn Conference. Montreal, Canada.

Bentley, C., Littau, J., Hamman, B., Meyer, H., Welsh, B. & Watson, B. (2005). *The citizen journalism movement: Mymissourian as a case study.* Association for Education in Journalism and Mass Communication. San Antonio, TX.

Coyle, D. (2004). Readers drive "open source journalism" (Vol. 2006): inlandpress.org.

Deuze, M. (2003). The Web and its journalisms: Considering the consequences of different types of news media online. *New Media and Society, 5*(2), 203–230.

Dube, J. (2005). Northwest voice: Behind the scenes, Cyberjournalist.com, *2005,* Website, American Press Institute.

Gillmor, D. (2004). *We the media: Grassroots journalism by the people, for the people.* Sebastopol, CA: O'Reilly Media.

Glaser, M. (2004). The new voices: Hyperlocal citizen media sites want you (to write)! *Online Journalism Review,* University of Southern California. Available from http://www.ojr.org/ojr/glaser/1098833871.php.

iLayfaette.org. (2005). About ilafayette.org. From http://www.ilafayette.org.

Larson, E. (2004). Deeper understanding, deeper ties: Taking faith online. In P. Howard and S. Jones (Ed.). *The Internet in Context.* Thousand Oaks, CA: Sage Publications.

Mambo Project Team. (2005). Mambo: Power in simplicity. Retrieved March 28, 2005, from http://www.mamboserver.com.

Oh, Y.H. (2004). *OhMyNews Story.* Retrieved from: http://english.ohmynews.com/articleview/article_view. asp?article_class=8&no=181975&rel_no=1.

Paul, N. (2005). "New news" retrospective: Is online news reaching its potential? *Online Journalism Review,* March 24, 2005. University of Southern California. Available from: http://www.ojr.org/ojr/stories/050324paul/.

Rainie, L., Homqan, J. & Cornfield, M. (2005). The Internet and Campaign 2004. Pew Internet & American Life Project. Retrieved March 15, 2005, from http://www.pewinternet.org/PPF/r/150/report_display.asp.

Readership Institute. (2001). An analysis of U.S. daily newspaper content: What makes readers more satisfied. June 2001. From http://www.readership.org/content/content_analysis/summary_report.htm.

Spratt, A. (2005). *Interview analysis: Mymissourian.com and open source journalism.* (unpublished report for undergraduate research project). Columbia, MO: Missouri School of Journalism.

Tedjamulia, S. J. J., Olsen, D. R., Dean, D. L. & Albrecht, C. C. (2005). *Motivating content contributions to online communities: Toward a more comprehensive theory.* Paper presented at the 38th Hawaii International Conference on System Sciences, Hawaii.

Terdiman, D. (2004). Open arms for open-source news. Wired News, http://www.wired.com/news/culture/0,1284,64285,00.html?tw=wn_tophead_4, Downloaded February 28, 2005.

Williams, W. (1908). The journalist's creed. Retrieved from http://www.journalism.missouri.edu/about/creed.html.

Yelvington, S. (2005). No fooling! We flip the newspaper site model upside down. Retrieved April 1, 2005, from http://www.yelvington.com/item.php?id=988.

14
Harnessing the Active Audience: Synthesizing Blog Research and Lessons for the Future of Media

MARK TREMAYNE

We are experiencing an unprecedented era of information expansion. Pre-existing work is moving online, but it is new content that fuels the explosion. The blogosphere is a part of that. Individuals who had ideas but no convenient platform to reach a wider audience now have the opportunity and are taking advantage of it by the millions. There are two primary ways for legacy media to cope with the massive influx of new content producers. One is to denigrate the content and its authors and hope the mass audience ignores it. This, pre-dictably, was the dominant approach of mainstream media in the early 2000s. Blog content was depicted as trivial, mostly navel-gazing, and when serious topics were addressed, the writing was amateurish, filled with errors and not credible. Blog writers were seen as relatively unsophisticated people sitting at their computers in their underwear.

To some degree, the depictions were accurate. But the blogosphere is a very large place and generalizations are difficult to make. The research in this volume and work published previously provide a more accurate representation of this sphere. One goal of this chapter is to provide a synthesis of this research and leave the reader with a more nuanced picture of the blogosphere, why it is read and what consequences this use may have, as well as to suggest areas of research still needed.

A second approach that traditional media could take towards the nascent phenomenon is to view it as an opportunity. The most common types of links found in blog posts are links to mainstream news websites (Cornfield, Carson, Kalis & Simon, 2005; Halavais, 2002; Reese, Rutigliano, Hyun, & Jeong, 2005). Bloggers are news readers—often very active readers. The links they create are paths that lead, in many cases, directly to mainstream news sites. The more paths to one's site that exist on the web, the more traffic one can expect.

Nevertheless, news organizations such as *National Public Radio*, the *Dallas Morning News* and the *Chicago Sun Times* at one time had policies prohibit-ing the practice of so-called "deep linking" (Tremayne, 2005). They wanted user traffic to come to the site through the main page, not through the stories posted there. While most online news outlets have discontinued this practice, the effect of pay-only or registered user-only sites is the same: They serve as roadblocks on a path that would otherwise lead to mainstream news. In doing this, news organizations inadvertently tell potential readers, "Stay out."

For a medium where revenue is increasingly advertising dependent, this is an odd choice. But at mid-decade there is evidence that some editors are beginning to see the importance of and value in what bloggers do (Jarvis, 2005). Beyond lowering the barriers to site entrance, some forward-looking news executives are considering ways to incorporate citizens into the news-gathering process. The second major goal of this chapter is to catalog some of the ways in which journalism is already changing and suggest further changes that may be coming in the near future.

What Research Says About Blogs and Blog Readers

Myths and Realities of the Blogosphere

A reading of popular press and the earliest published research on the blogosphere reveals some contradictions. The blogosphere is described as a forum for political discussion or, alternately, a collection of electronic diaries written by adolescents. It is described as a virtual public sphere and a place for spreading rumors. It is described as highly interactive and not. It is described as a hangout for young, educated, technically savvy and conservative men and also as egalitarian. It is described as a worldwide phenomenon and as dominated by the United States.

Some of these contradictions are explained by the nature of networks (see the Introduction). The hubs of any network have special qualities—characteristics that cause them to attract a disproportionate number of ties (Barabasi, 2002; Barabasi & Albert, 1999). In the blogosphere, those who write about issues that affect large numbers of people are more likely to attract links than those who write about personal matters. Certainly quality of writing and other characteristics of blog authors will be factors as well. Therefore, descriptions of the blogosphere or of blog readers and writers are dependent on whether one wishes to characterize the majority or only the central actors in the network. In the following sections, we examine some of the contradictions and provide some answers from the research literature on blogging.

Is It Journalism or Something Else?

Blogging can be, in the opinion of some, a form of journalism (Gillmor, 2003; Lasica, 2003). Lasica, senior editor for the *Online Journalism Review* and former editor at the *Sacramento Bee*, described bloggers' activities: "They take part in the editorial function of selecting newsworthy and interesting topics, they add analysis, insight and commentary, and they occasionally provide a first-person report about an event, a trend, a subject" (p. 73). Gillmor, a former columnist for the San Jose *Mercury News*, calls it "participatory journalism," a practice whereby citizens "are combining powerful technological tools and innovative ideas that are fundamentally altering the nature of journalism in this century" (p. 79).

In this book, Rutigliano describes three variants on what he and others are calling "citizen journalism" and Hendrickson argues for an expansion of legal protections for bloggers who are functioning as journalists. Deuze (2003) describes four forms of online journalism and lists blogging as belonging to the last: "share and discussion sites" (p. 210). He cites a defining feature of journalism from Kovach and Rosenstiel's *The Elements of Journalism* (2001): to provide citizens with the information they need to be free and self-governing (p. 17).

Witt (2004) argues that blogging and examples of citizen journalism like South Korea's *OhmyNews* are creating something he calls the "public's journalism." O'Brien (2004) defends the bloggers-as-journalists notion not only by highlighting examples of journalistic work but also by pointing out the poor job that mainstream media has been doing, particularly television coverage of political campaigns.

Most researchers have been less willing to define blogging as journalism. Johnson and Kaye (2004) did find that blog *readers* consider it journalism that is, in many ways, better than traditional media. Dissatisfaction with mainstream media was one motivation for blog use (see also Kaye, chapter 7). But content analyses of the blogosphere have been less supportive of the notion that most bloggers are doing journalism.

Papacharissi (chapter 2) found just 5 blogs in her sample of 260 that were devoted to discussion of news. Another 15% had occasional links to news items. These blogs were not necessarily engaged in original reporting, just discussion or comment on the news. By far the most common blog type was the personal journal. Likewise, Herring, Scheidt, Bonus and Wright (2005 and chapter 1) found approximately 70% of blogs to be this type. They both conclude that the representation of blogs as journalistic is exaggerated.

If few scholars find original reporting in blogs, many find evidence of political discussion (Adamic & Glance, 2005; Drezner & Farrell, 2004). In two studies on the political blogosphere, Drezner and Farrell and Adamic and Glance make the same point: In their discussion of politics and current events, bloggers function as frame setters. Even if individual blogs contain only a percentage of political content, collectively they can generate lively debate. Cornfield et al. (2005) says blogs create buzz that ultimately affects mainstream news coverage of politics.

While political blogs have received considerable attention from scholars, dozens of other content categories exist, including "war blogs" (see Johnson & Kaye, chapter 9), "tech blogs," "sports blogs," "entertainment blogs" and "health blogs." Each can be divided into subcategories, such as the 47 blogs about mental health studied by Sundar, Edwards, Hu and Stavrositu (chapter 5). If these niche blogs are not journalistic by traditional definitions, they at least convey information previously found in other media. They represent competition for traditional journalism.

Are Blogs Credible?

A primary criticism of the blogosphere (from traditional media and defenders of it) is that the information within it lacks credibility. Not surprisingly, blog readers seem to disagree (Johnson & Kaye, 2004). Johnson and Kaye found that most blog readers (74%) considered the information to be moderately or very credible, but that many also acknowledged that blogs are not fair. Johnson and Kaye explained the apparent contradiction this way: Some blog users see a virtue in up-front bias. They know the information is one sided, but they agree with that side and appreciate the frankness of the writer.

Johnson and Kaye draw a parallel between blog use and talk radio use: Both audiences find value in partisan political debate. Their data suggest partial support for this: "The more blog readers use talk radio, the more credible they view weblogs, even though blog users did not rate talk radio as highly credible" (p. 634). Eveland and Dylko (chapter 6) also found support for a connection between talk radio use and blog use. In addition to online news and discussion forum use, they found that listening to talk radio was a statistically significant predictor of blog use.

Neither Johnson and Kaye (2004) nor Eveland and Dylko (chapter 6) suggest that blog use is causing a decline in support for traditional media. The former found that, while blog users find blogs credible, most also rate mainstream media as somewhat to very credible. The latter found no evidence to suggest that traditional media use is negatively affected by blog use. Evidence from content analyses of blog-linking patterns suggests that political blogs are heavily dependent on mainstream media for the content of their commentaries (Cornfield et al., 2005; Halavais, 2002).

Kaid and Postelnicu (chapter 8) conducted an experiment on blog credibility by using a variety of sources—a politician, a celebrity and an interest group—to present the same information about Social Security privatization via blog to study participants. The resulting credibility scores were not significantly different amongst the three sources. Overall, study participants rated their site (random assignment to one condition) as credible. The clear implication is that blog users are not discriminating between sources with significant expertise and those with little. The authors correctly point out, however, that the characteristics of the study participants (college students) and the issue (Social Security) limit the ability to generalize the results.

An important issue for credibility researchers to consider concerns the unique structure of the blogosphere that makes comparisons between blogs and other media difficult. An individual blog, without the staff or resources of a mainstream news operation, is likely to suffer in a one-to-one comparison when it comes to accuracy, fairness and comprehensiveness of reporting. Even comparing an average blog or a collection of average blogs with mainstream media may not be the best comparison.

Because of its network structure, the power of the blogosphere comes in its collective reporting power and its informal peer-review process. The clearest example is the one touched on by a number of authors in this book and elsewhere: the Dan Rather debacle over forged documents regarding George Bush's military record. No single blog presented an in-depth, even-handed exposé on the problems with the *60 Minutes* story. But the collective effort was devastating in its speed and, ultimately, its credibility. As one would expect on this story, Bush defenders did most of the work. But liberal bloggers worked hard, at first, to provide counterevidence for every point made by conservative bloggers. In the end, however, most liberal bloggers, such as Dailykos.com, conceded that conservative bloggers had proved their point: The memos were forgeries.

By its structure, the blogosphere is supportive of argument and counterargument, but that does not mean that careful deliberation is the norm (see also Meraz, chapter 4). Nevertheless, the collective efforts of bloggers engaged in citizen reporting can provide a useful function (see Rutigliano, chapter 12). When mechanisms are available that, in essence, allow the collective to peer review the work so that the best pieces are highlighted, a group-bestowed credibility can be the result.

In the blogosphere as a whole, the mechanism is the hyperlink. By using their blog rolls or providing links in posts, bloggers collectively decide whose work is most important and most credible. It is not a perfect system. On some of the busier group blogs, different mechanisms are used, including the ability to "score" a post after one reads it. The posts that achieve the highest scores are highlighted on the main page while others can only be accessed on subsidiary pages.

Another blog study found that original reporting about the war in Iraq, although rare, was a significant predictor of incoming links (Tremayne, Zheng, Lee, & Jeong, 2006). This result serves as another indicator that quality work is rewarded in this sphere and that original content, not just hearsay and opinion, may play a larger role in the blogosphere of the future.

Who Reads Blogs, Why and to What Effect?

At the beginning of the new millennium, those reading blogs were early adopters, mostly male, more highly educated than average and with above-average incomes. In one of the first published studies of political blog use, Johnson and Kaye (2004) posted a survey on the web and recruited volunteers at 131 blogs and 14 other forums and listservs. Their sample of 3,747 blog users was 89% White, 77% male and 93% with at least some college education.

Shortly after this period, blog use rose dramatically. The Pew Internet and American Life Project documented a 58% rise in readership of blogs during 2004 (Rainie, 2005). Among Internet users, 27% of American adults, or 32 million people—about 40% the size of the talk radio audience and 20% that of newspapers—reported reading blogs. By then, some of the divides were narrowing. For example, 66% of men and 61% of women reported using the Internet (Pew Internet and American Life Project: May–June 2004 tracking survey, 2004). Another study found that blog authors were more likely to be male (57%) but by a narrower margin than some expected (Rainie, 2005).

One of two studies reported by Eveland and Dylko (chapter 6) found that just 34% of female Internet users access blogs compared to 50% of men—a statistically significant difference (Study 2). Their other study had a statistically insignificant difference. Study 2 also showed blog users to be younger than other Internet users. Both studies found a significant bivariate relationship between blog use and political participation. Unlike Johnson and Kaye (2004), whose earlier study found blog users to skew conservative, Eveland and Dylko identified a more even mix of conservatives and liberals, but also found evidence of political extremism. That is, like the talk radio audience, there are few blog users who describe themselves as moderate on the political spectrum.

A desire for political commentary is one motivation identified by Kaye (chapter 7) for blog reading. The most common motivation blocks she identified were blog characteristics (use of links, depth, timeliness, etc.), personal fulfillment (entertainment, diversion, etc.), expression/affiliation (communicating with friends) and information seeking. She also found evidence that some blog users hold anti-mainstream media attitudes and are looking for expressions of opinion.

Other blog users may be more calculated in their activities. Blogs can be used to spread ideas beneficial to a person or a group. For example, the political campaigns of those running for office have a stake in monitoring blog talk and actively using blogs to "spin" for their candidate and generate buzz (Williams, Trammell, Postelnicu, Landreville & Martin, 2005). The consequences of blog use have only recently come under examination. Eveland and Dylko (chapter 6) reached several conclusions from the two surveys they presented.

First, they found no evidence that blog use was associated with a decrease in use of mainstream media. Second, in neither study was blog use associated with political knowledge. The authors suggest the operationalization of political knowledge may have been inadequate and that knowledge of current events, candidates and their issue stances might have changed the results. This is a potential area for further study. Third, both studies identified a relationship between blog use and political participation. The authors suggest, however, that this association may be mediated through online political discussion (at news sites, etc.). A similar hypothesis is proposed by Hardy and Scheufele (2005). Their examination of political participation and Internet use found evidence that political chat moderates the effects of online news consumption on political participation.

Blog Research Frontiers

The chapters in this volume and prior research on the blog phenomenon provide some clues concerning the role blogging plays, and may increasingly play, in American life. But many questions remain. Who are the top bloggers? We know that, at least during the 2004 election cycle, they were predominantly male (Harp & Tremayne, 2006). Many blogs, such as AndrewSullivan.com, TalkingPointsMemo.com and KausFiles.com, are written by journalists or former journalists. Others, such as Instapundit.com and DanielDrezner.com, are written by academics.

Do the pedigrees of these authors, the quality of their writing, the quality of their ideas or their linking practices predict their success in the blogosphere? The hubs in a network form through a process of preferred attachment unique for each network (Barabasi, 2002; Tremayne, 2004). What are the causes of preferred attachment in the blogosphere? The answers may also explain prior media success (why did some newspapers beat all local competitors in a city?) and future media success.

Can a blog community function as a journalistic entity? Rutigliano (chapter 12) examines some of the interesting media experiments now playing out on the web. Will the success and commercialization of such entities destroy the unique atmosphere they currently enjoy?

Will increasing blog use result in decreased or increased use of mainstream news? Will mainstream news providers adopt blog methods (and buy out the top bloggers) in order to maintain their market shares? How will the citizenry be affected by increased blog use or changes to prior practices of traditional media? Will such a media environment increase partisanship? Is blog use an indicator of political participation, a cause of it, or both (see Eveland & Dylko, chapter 6)? Can the increased voter turnout in the 2000 and 2004 presidential elections be attributed, in part, to a media culture that is increasingly partisan or is it entirely explainable by other factors? Do blog readers really make no discriminations about the credibility of the sources they read (Kaid and Postelnicu, chapter 8) or is that true only of younger readers?

Perhaps broader cultural, economic and legal forces will reign in bloggers and restore power to the professionals. If the courts do not expand legal protections to bloggers (as Hendrickson surmises in chapter 10), they may be unable to gain access to the same information that professional journalists can access. Without expensive lawyers, some may be quickly quieted or put out of business altogether (see Carroll and Frank, chapter 11). The more successful bloggers are already beginning to look like the mainstream media they once ridiculed. Their sites carry extensive advertising. Some of the interactivity they once supported has been eliminated because of high traffic and the cost of site maintenance. Some are no longer independent but have joined a corporate-owned site.

Each of these areas has just begun to be explored. More work is needed. The results of that work will provide further answers about what lies ahead and may even help shape a more beneficial media environment.

The Future of Media

Blogging, at least in its current incarnation, will not replace the functions of traditional journalism. There is very little original reporting within the blogo-sphere (Reese et al., 2005; Tremayne et al., 2006). Unless bloggers begin cover-ing school board and city council meetings, major and not so major crimes, serious and not so serious accidents and fires, weather, issues of importance to the few and to the many and issues of little interest to themselves—all this on a daily basis—they will not provide the services now covered by the main-stream press.

However, to the extent that they do some of these things and that newspa-per readership continues to fall and television use to decline (UCLA Center for Communications Policy, 2001), they will have an impact. They already have the media barons' attention. How can traditional journalism change and how might we expect it to change in this environment? Based on the professional and scholarly literature on blogging and online news, I suggest five broad areas of change: microlocal journalism, managed citizen journalism, prob-lem-based journalism, database journalism and better quality journalism.

Microlocal Journalism

There is already some evidence that online journalism is more locally focused than printed newspapers (Singer, 2001). But now, when it comes to target audi-ences, it is time to think even smaller. Mark Potts, a former reporter for the *Washington Post,* serves as an example of this concept (Kurtz, 2004). He and a partner started Backfence.com, a venture into neighborhood-based jour-nalism. The site provides the kind of news currently not available, such as reporting on little-league games, school plays and local events and issues. In the past, larger neighborhoods might have been served by a small community paper but the cost of production forces these papers to reach a big enough audience to offset the fixed costs of publishing. With production costs now minimal, the means exists to satisfy a demand that has probably always been there. People care about what is going on in their immediate proximity.

Another facet of the web medium may play a role as well. At one's fin-gertips one can now access the *New York Times, The Washington Post, CNN.com* and dozens of other publications that are national in scope. *Google News* and *Yahoo! News* do an adequate job of drawing from all of these sources, as do some bloggers. Simply stated, national outlets have little room for growth except in the untapped potential of small regions not currently covered on a daily or even weekly basis.

Where will the content come from? Most of it will come from the audience. Another key to journalism's future is in the role of the citizen journalist.

Managed Citizen Journalism

The Backfence.com operation relies on ordinary citizens who work for free. It is an experiment in "open-source" journalism much like the one described by Bentley et al. in this volume (chapter 13) and that blogs such as Dailykos.com follow. Empower the readers to become producers. There are two primary benefits. The obvious one is cost and the other is the proximity the writers have to the subject matter; they know the neighborhood better than an outside journalist will.

The drawback is the lack of training the writers will bring to the task. This is where careful management is required. As Bentley et al. describe, the jobs of editors are magnified in this environment. Editors' roles will skew heavily toward the teaching or coaching aspect of the job.

Some mainstream news sites have experimented with citizen journalism. The websites of BBC and MSNBC solicited content from Londoners who witnessed the terrorist bombings in 2005. They ran first-person accounts and digital photos taken by the submitters. This type of effort is likely to grow as a way of responding to the changing expectations of the audience and of generating relatively cheap (and sometimes compelling) content.

Problem-Based Journalism

The London bombings afforded event-based citizen journalism; other issues call for problem-based journalism. Deuze (2003) emphasizes the growing importance of connectivity over content-focused journalism. This idea relates to citizen journalism as well as problem-based journalism. What the blogosphere has demonstrated is the power of a collective to tackle and quickly bring to bear the resources of interested citizens to a particular issue or problem. Glenn Reynolds, author of top-ranked blog Instapundit.com and law professor at the University of Tennessee, calls this phenomenon "the army of Davids" (2006). This potential on the web has been hailed as a possible rebirth of public journalism (Witt, 2004) because it makes affordable and easy what was logistically difficult and expensive: town meetings. On an issue-by-issue basis, local online news sites could mobilize efforts to collect information, share conversation and work toward solutions. Another example of this phenomenon comes from columnist Michael Kinsley. Kinsley had an idea for a column on flaws he observed regarding President Bush's Social Security privatization plan. Before writing the column he emailed his proposal to several experts he was acquainted with and to several blog authors. He received little or no response from his usual sources but a flood of e-mail from blog readers, many of whom provided detailed and compelling critiques of his ideas: "What floored me was not just the volume and speed of the feedback but its seriousness and sophistication" (Kinsley, 2004). In addition to e-mailing Kinsley, the blog authors and readers were busy posting their thoughts on numerous blogs so that ideas could be shared and arguments refined. The ideals of civic journalism are embodied in this example. Rather than merely observing this activity amongst blog users, online journalism organizations have an opportunity to foster it and benefit from it.

Database Journalism

This term has been associated with computer-assisted reporting (Garrison, 1995) but has taken on new meaning in the last decade. In the past, news organizations accessed databases of, typically, government-created information to find specific information or to look for trends. Now, instead of using preexisting databases to write stories, news outlets could generate their own databases of news content. For example, every item from the police blotter, every high school sports score, every neighborhood issue, etc. could be categorized by zip code, type of news and other criteria. From this database one could generate highly personalized news products that could be delivered online or via other digital devices or printed as a section of a local newspaper. This is the model Google and other online information providers are using to reach disparate audiences. This method of organization, coupled with a citizen workforce feeding information via an online entry system, may be one direction in which journalism is headed.

Better Quality Journalism

While some news organizations are shedding staff and resources in response to a shrinking audience, the opposite may be needed: a recommitment to quality. One place to go to improve quality is the audience. It may be counterintuitive to some, but the blogosphere has proven a capable entity for fact-checking. Wikipedia, the "open source encyclopedia," can be applied to news as well, if news organizations are willing to cede some control and make a leap of faith. Experiments in this direction by mainstream media are certainly warranted.

To some degree, bloggers are the watchdogs of the watchdogs (Witt, 2004; Cooper, 2006; Scott, chapter 3). Their efforts can be harnessed and put to the task of improving news product at little financial, but apparently great emotional, cost. For now, bloggers remain at the margins, but everyone is beginning to recognize the changes that are coming:

> We journalists are no longer the gatekeepers in the marketplace of ideas. The doors have been flung wide open by the egalitarian nature of the Internet and when you look at the big picture you see—chaos. You see

a medium in its infancy, howling and kicking against the limitations of the world into which it was born (McBride, 2004).

How the mainstream media responds to the howling and kicking blogosphere remains to be determined. But the old model of mass communication, which allowed relatively little voice for the audience, is changing. Thriving in the new media environment will require adapting to this new reality.

References

Adamic, L., & Glance, N. (2005). The political blogosphere and the 2004 U.S. election: Divided they blog. Retrieved April 27, 2005, from http://www.blogpulse.com/papers/2005/Adamic GlanceBlogWWW.pdf.

Barabasi, A.-L. (2002). *Linked: The new science of networks.* Cambridge, MA: Perseus Publishing.

Barabasi, A.-L., & Albert, R. (1999). Emergence of scaling in random networks. *Science, 286,* 509–512.

Cooper, S. D. (2006). *Watching the watchdog.* Spokane, WA: Marquette Books.

Cornfield, M., Carson, J., Kalis, A. & Simon, E. (2005). Buzz, blogs, and beyond. From http:// pew.org.

Deuze, M. (2003). The Web and its journalisms: Considering the consequences of different types of newsmedia online. *New Media & Society, 5*(2), 203–230.

Drezner, D., & Farrell, H. (2004). *The power and politics of blogs.* Paper presented at the American Political Science Association, Chicago.

Garrison, B. (1995). Online services as reporting tools: Daily newspaper use of commercial databases in 1994. *Newspaper Research Journal, 16*(4), 74–86.

Gillmor, D. (2003). Moving toward participatory journalism. *Nieman Reports, 57*(3), 79–80. Available from http://www.nieman.harvard.edu/reports/03-73NRfall/V57N73.pdf.

Halavais, A. (2002, October). *Blogs and the social weather.* Paper presented at the Internet Research 3.0 meeting, Maastricht, The Netherlands.

Hardy, B. W., & Scheufele, D. A. (2005). Examining differential gains from Internet use: Comparing the moderating role of talk and online interactions. *Journal of Communication, 55*(1), 71–84.

Harp, D., & Tremayne, M. (2006). The gendered blogosphere: Examining inequality using network and feminist theory. *Journalism and Mass Communication Quarterly, 83*(2), 247–264.

Herring, S., Scheidt, L. A., Bonus, S. & Wright, E. (2005). Weblogs as a bridging genre. *Information, Technology and People, 18*(2), 142–171.

Jarvis, J. (2005). And when will there be a museum of blogging? *Buzz Machine.* Available from: http://www.buzzmachine.com/index.php/2005/09/30/museum/.

Johnson, T., & Kaye, B. (2004). Wag the blog: How reliance on traditional media and the Internet influence credibility perceptions of Weblogs among blog users. *Journalism & Mass Communication Quarterly, 81*(3), 622–642.

Kinsley, M. (2004, December 19). Blogged down. *Washington Post,* pp. B07, available: http:// www.washingtonpost.com/wp-dyn/articles/A9270-2004Dec9217.html.

Kovach, B., & Rosenstiel, T. (2001). The elements of journalism: What newspeople should know and the public should expect. New York: Crown Publishers.

Kurtz, H. (2004, December 13). This just in, from the guy next door. *Washington Post,* p. C01.

Lasica, J. D. (2003). Blogs and journalism need each other. *Nieman Reports, 57*(3), 70–74. Available from http://www.nieman.harvard.edu/reports/03-73NRfall/V57N73.pdf.

McBride, K. (2004, Sept. 16). Journalism in the age of blogs. Poynteronline, available at http:// www.poynter.org/column.asp?id=53&aid=71447.

O'Brien, B. (2004). *Blogging America: Political discourse in a digital nation.* Wilsonville, OR: William James & Co.

Pew Internet and American Life Project: May–June 2004 tracking survey. (2004). From http:// www.pewInternet.org/trends/DemographicsofInternetUsers.htm.

Rainie, L. (2005). The state of blogging. From http://www.pewinternet.org/pdfs/PIP_blogging_ data.pdf.

Reese, S. D., Rutigliano, L., Hyun, K., & Jeong, J. (2005). Mapping the blogosphere: Professional and citizen-based media in the global news arena. Paper presented at the Association for Education in Journalism and Mass Communication, San Antonio.

Reynolds, G. (2006). *Army of Davids*. Nashville, TN: Nelson Current.

Singer, J. B. (2001). The metro wide Web: Changes in newspapers' gatekeeping role online. *Journalism & Mass Communication Quarterly, 78*(1), 65–80.

Tremayne, M. (2004). The Web of context: Applying network theory to the use of hyperlinks in journalism on the Web. *Journalism & Mass Communication Quarterly, 81*(2), 237–253.

Tremayne, M. (2005). News Websites as gated cybercommunities. *Convergence: The Journal of Research into New Media Technologies, 11*(3), 28–29.

Tremayne, M., Zheng, N., Lee, J. K., & Jeong, J. (2006). Issue Publics on the Web: Applying Network Theory to the War Blogosphere. *Journal of Computer-Mediated Communication, 12*(1), available http://jcmc.indiana.edu.

UCLA Center for Communications Policy. (2001). Surveying the digital future. From http://ccp.ucla.edu/pages/InternetStudy.asp.

Williams, A. P., Trammell, K. D., Postelnicu, M., Landreville, K. & Martin, J. D. (2005). Blogging and hyperlinking: Use of the Web to enhance viability during the 2004 U.S. campaign. *Journalism Studies, 6*(2), 177–186.

Witt, L. (2004). Is public journalism morphing into the public's journalism? *National Civic Review, 93*(3), 49–57.

Editor

Mark Tremayne is an assistant professor in the School of Journalism at the University of Texas at Austin. His work focuses on the changing role of the audience in modern mass communication and the impact of this on journalistic content. His work has been published in academic journals such as *Journalism & Mass Communication Quarterly*, *Convergence* and the *Journal of Computer-Mediated Communication*.

Contributors

Clyde Bentley was a newspaper editor, advertising manager and general manager for two decades before becoming an associate professor at the Missouri School of Journalism. He is the founder and supervisor of MyMissourian.com.

Brian Carroll is an assistant professor at Berry College in Mt. Berry, Georgia. His research interests include communication technology, law and policy and media convergence.

Ivan Dylko is a graduate student in the School of Communication at Ohio State University. He is primarily interested in the role played by political opinion leaders in shaping public opinion and implications of political blogs for the sociology of news.

Heidi Hatfield Edwards is an assistant professor of communication at the Florida Institute of Technology. Her research focuses on communication and social issues, with special emphasis in two areas: corporate involvement in social issues and the cultural and societal implications of communication regarding social issues, particularly health.

William P. Eveland, Jr., is associate professor of communication and political science and director of graduate studies for the School of Communication at Ohio State University. His interests center on the role of traditional mass media, new media technologies and interpersonal communication in producing an informed and participatory citizenry.

Bob Frank is an associate professor and chair of communication at Berry College in Mt. Berry, Georgia.

Brian Hamman is a graduate student at the Missouri School of Journalism with a background in computer technology.

Laura Hendrickson specializes in media and communications law. She holds a J.D. from the Georgetown University Law Center and a Ph.D. from the University of Texas at Austin School of Journalism.

Susan C. Herring is professor of information science and linguistics at Indiana University, Bloomington, and editor of the *Journal of Computer-Mediated Communication*. She founded and directs the Blog Research on Genre (BROG) project.

Yifeng Hu is a senior doctoral candidate in the College of Communications at Pennsylvania State University. Her research focuses on the role of new communication technologies in health communication.

Thomas Johnson is the Marshall and Sharleen Formby Regents Professor in the College of Mass Communications at Texas Tech University. He is the author of two books and numerous research articles.

Lynda Lee Kaid is professor of telecommunication in the College of Journalism and Communications at the University of Florida. She is the author or editor of more than 20 books, including *The Handbook of Political Communication Research* and *Videostyle in Presidential Campaigns*.

Barbara K. Kaye is an associate professor in the School of Journalism and Electronic Media at the University of Tennessee, Knoxville.

Inna Kouper is a doctoral student in the School of Library and Information Science at Indiana University, Bloomington. She is interested in cultural and social aspects of computer-mediated communication and information seeking. She has been a member of the BROG project since September 2003.

Jeremy Littau is a former newspaper reporter and editor who is a doctoral student at the Missouri School of Journalism. His research examines citizen journalism as a means of generating social capital.

Sharon Meraz is a doctoral student at the University of Texas at Austin. She researches emerging web technologies and repercussions for the mass media ecosystem.

Hans Meyer is a doctoral student at the Missouri School of Journalism. Before returning to school, he was the general manager of a small daily newspaper in Southern California and launched several weekly newspapers.

Zizi Papacharissi is assistant professor and director of graduate studies in the School of Communications and Theater at Temple University, Philadelphia. Her research interests include emerging technologies and political communication.

Monica Postelnicu is an assistant professor in the Manship School of Mass Communication at Louisiana State University. Her research focuses on the implications of the Internet and new media for political communication.

Lou Rutigliano is a doctoral student at the University of Texas at Austin. His research interests include participatory media, digital community networks, the digital divide and media sociology.

Lois Ann Scheidt is a doctoral student specializing in computer-mediated communication at the School of Library and Information Science at Indiana University, Bloomington. She is a founding member of the BROG project.

D. Travers Scott is a doctoral student at the University of Southern California Annenberg School for Communication. He is editor of *Strategic Sex: Why They Won't Keep It in the Bedroom* and author of two novels.

Carmen Stavrositu is a senior doctoral student in the College of Communications at Pennsylvania State University.

S. Shyam Sundar is an associate professor and codirector of the Media Effects Research Laboratory in the College of Communications at Pennsylvania State University. His research investigates psychological effects of technological elements unique to mass communication.

Brendan Watson is an online editor with the *St. Petersburg Times* and a graduate student at the Missouri School of Journalism.

Beth Welsh is the coordinator of Community Faces, the citizen-journalism photography section of KansasCity.com. She holds a master's degree from the Missouri School of Journalism.

Elijah Wright is a doctoral student in the School of Library and Information Science at Indiana University, Bloomington. His research interests span social software, social network analysis, blogs and scientometrics. He is a founding member of the BROG project.

Index

A

Adamic, L. A., 64, 65, 263,
Afghanistan, 6
Albrecht, C. C., 248
A-list blogs, 3, 6, 37, 150
Allport, G. W., 105
Alvarez, A., 108
Amis, D., 168, 178
Amoroso, L., 143
Ananny, M., 242
Anderson, D. A., 190–191, 197, 200
Anderson, R., 130
Andrews, P., 6, 40, 166, 227
Anonymity, 10, 89, 108, 220
Ansolabehere, S., 160
AOL, 23, 62, 87, 239
Argument repertoire, 62
Ashdown, P., 127, 140
Ashley, C., 48, 165
Aspden, P., 21
Atkin, D. J., 127, 129–131, 140–143, 153
Atrios, 64
Attitude change, 152
August, R., 210, 219
Austin, E. W., 178

B

Babbie, E., 132, 143, 170, 180, 184
Ballard, C., xvi
Bandow, Doug, 48
Bandwagon effect, 84–86
Bantz, C. R., 29, 127, 131–132, 140
Baoill, A., 60, 63, 67
Barabasi, A.-L., xi, 229, 262, 267
Barber, B., 60, 67
Bargh, J. A., 85, 89–90
Bar–Ilan, J., xii, 106
Bass, S. B., 89
Bates, M. J., 8, 11
Bauer, M. W., 8
Becker, L. B., 129, 131,

Bedell, D., 165, 166, 177
Bell, S., 215
Bellamy, R. V., 127, 131–132, 140
Benhabib, S., 60–61, 67
Bennett, W. L., 51, 54
Bentley, C., xviii, 240–241, 247, 251,
    255–256, 258, 269
Berger, L. L., 193, 195, 197
Berkman, L. F., 87, 217, 224
Berlo, D. K., 152
Bimber, B., 107
Blades, M., 47, 54
Blanchard, A., 88
Block, M., 153
Blog topics
    alternative news, 31, 47, 50, 59
    art and entertainment, 31, 263
    health and medical, 28, 31, 40,
        83–101, 251, 264
    natural disasters, xiii, 3
    politics, vii, x, xii, 3, 39–54, 64,
        87–88, 98, 105–124, 149–154,
        167–169, 263–265
    technology, vii, x, 31, 138, 263
    war, xii–xiii, xvii, 3, 6, 16–17, 45,
        165–181, 263, 265
Blogdex, 64,
Bloggers as opinion leaders, 3, 275
Bloggers as public intellectuals, 3
Blogosphere
    buzz, xiii, xv, xvi
    credibility, 52–53, 64, 264–265
    defined, vii
    gender and, 87, 267
    growth of, vii, xiii, 3–5, 45, 53, 106,
        245, 257
    mainstream media and, xiv, 41–42
    size of, vii, 149, 151
    spread of information through,
        ix–xii, 262
Blood, R., vii, 3–5, 9, 14, 130, 142–143,
    149, 166, 227
Bloom, J., 4–6

Blumler, J. G., 129
Boberg, E. W., 89
Bohman, J. F., 60, 61, 67
Bolter, J. D., 50, 54
Bonus, S., 3, 263
Borger, G., 188
Bortree, D., 90
Boyd, S., 89
Broder, David, 50
Brossard, D., 63, 110
Brown, J., 40, 160
Browning, G., 59
Buchanan, Pat, 59
Bumiller, E., xiv
Burd, G., 227
Burkhalter, S., 60
Burleson, B. R., 91
Bush, George W., 4, 40, 44–49, 60, 72,
    110, 112, 128, 180, 265, 269

C

Cable news, 110, 114–115, 118, 123
Cacioppo, J. T., 61, 153, 154, 159
Cai, X., 107
Calhoun, C., 226
Calvert, S. L., 90
Campbell, K., 66
Cantril, H., 105
Capella, J. H., 62–64
Cappella, J. N., 160
Carey, J. W., 90
Carson, J., x, 261
Carter, B., 41
Carver, B., 166
Cavanaugh, T., 6
CBS, xiv, 40–41, 44–45, 47, 49, 52, 128,
    234; see also Memogate
Celebrity, 37, 151–162, 200, 264
Chaffee, S. H., 63, 76, 152, 178
Charney, T., 127, 129–132, 140, 143
Charters, W. W., 105
Cheney, Dick, 46, 47
Chesher, C., 6
Chew, F., 178
China, 212, 217, 218, 223

Citizen journalism, 15, 49, 239–258, 263,
    268–269
Citizen journalists, 3, 39, 40, 191, 240,
    244, 258
Civic journalism, 225–227, 229, 231, 233,
    235
Clark, Wesley, 60
Clift, Eleanor, 50
Clinton–Lewinsky scandal, 53
Cohen, I., 60–61, 67, 194
Collective reporting, 265
Community formation, 60
Connectedness, 22, 26–27, 88, 94–95, 97
Connectivity, 9, 23, 228, 269
Conniff, M., 188, 189
Content analysis, 3, 4, 6–9, 17, 22–25,
    28–29, 35, 39, 67, 91–94, 105
Conventions, political, 40, 45, 46, 49,
    150, 189, 195, 211, 218
Conversation, 21, 59–67, 73–74, 77–78,
    127, 153, 195, 227, 269
Conyers, John, 60
Cook, J. M., 62
Cook, P. L., 127
Cook, T., 6
Cooper, S. D., 270
Copyright, 205, 211, 213, 215, 218, 219,
    223
Cornell, D., 61
Cornfield, M., x, 249, 261, 263, 264
Corrado, A. C., 149
Correlation, function of mass media, 41,
    42, 44, 49, 50
Coyle, D., 243
Creativity, 23, 32, 34–36
Credibility
    blogs, xvi, 53–54, 264
    citizen journalism, 245, 247–248, 255
    experiments, xvii, 149–162, 267
    mainstream media, 108, 225, 239
    perceived, 61
    power of the collective, 265
    predictors of, 169, 178
Crumlich, C., 150
Customization, 23, 85
Cynicism, 153–155, 157, 160

D

D'Alessio, D., 59, 105
DailyKos, xiii–xv, 42, 44–46, 48, 53, 189, 265, 269
Daily Show, The, 47, 51
Davis, R., 105
Dean, D. L., 248
Dean, Howard, xvii, 4, 16, 59–79, 150, 168
Dearstyne, B., 106
Deci, E. L., 86
Defamation, 206–208, 213–215, 219, 224, 241
Deliberation, 53, 60–62, 65–71, 77, 265
Delli Carpini, M. X., 110
Delwiche, A., 3, 5, 16
Democracy, 39, 41, 52, 62, 83, 190, 215, 225, 235
Deuze, M., 241–242, 263, 269
Dewey, J., 61, 226
Diary format, 28, 31, 35, 36
Dimmick, J., 130–131, 141
Distributed labor, 50, 53
Dominick, J., 21, 22
Domke, D., 51,
Dong, O., 178
Donohew, L., 127, 131–132, 140
Downing, J., 226
Drezner, D., xiv, 4–5, 40, 64, 66, 263
Drudge Report, 40, 53–54, 188, 190, 241
Drum, Kevin, 40, 52
Dryzek, J., 60, 67
Dube, J., 240
Dunn, D. G., 127, 131, 140
Dunwoody, S., 106
Dyer, C., 206
Dyk, T. B., 194

E

Ebert, Roger, 50
Edwards, H. H., 264
Edwards, John, 45, 47, 60, 77
Edwards, L., 213, 218
Eighmey, J., 127, 130–131, 140, 142–143
Eko, L., 212, 216–218

Elaboration likelihood, 61
Elshtain, J. B., 17
Embrey, T. R., 40
Emotions, 33, 98, 154, 160
Empowerment, 60, 74
Engle, E. A., 218
Entertainment, 23, 32, 130, 143, 151, 199, 251, 263, 266
Erbring, L., 21
Ethnography, 3
Eveland, W. P., Jr., 106, 122, 167, 169, 179, 264, 266–267
Expressiveness, 33–34

F

Fact-checking, 39–42, 46, 53–54, 270
Fagin, M., 213, 216, 219
Fallows, D., 5, 128, 165, 167, 169
Family communication, 24, 28, 31–32, 34
Fan, D. P., 51
Farrell, H., xiv, 4, 5, 40, 64, 66, 263
Feedback, 22, 27–36, 89, 91, 97, 99, 129, 137, 198, 227–231, 270
Felder, J. L., 90
Female, 12, 34, 158, 160, 173
Ferguson, D. A. 127, 129–130, 143
Ferguson, T., 89
Filter blogs, x, 3, 6–8, 13–17, 91, 219
Firestone, C., 149
First Amendment, 187, 190–194, 199, 209, 213, 215, 218, 220
Fishkin, J. S., 60, 61, 67
Fitzsimons, G. M., 85
Flanagin, A. J., 150–151
Fleishman, G., 150
Flickr, 97, 245, 252
Forrest, E. J., 127
Fotheringham, M. J., 89
Fourth Estate, 50–51
Fox, S., 51, 128, 169
Fraser, N., 226
Frauenfelder, M., 127, 130, 140, 142
Freimuth, V. S., 91
Friendster, 76, 97

Fuentes, A., 129, 130, 143
Funk, C. L., 63

G

Gannon, Jeff, 52, 54
Gans, H., 41, 51
Garnett, N. W., 213–215, 220, 224
Garramone, G., 130–131, 133, 143
Garrison, B., 270
Gastil, J., 60–61
Gatekeeping, 84, 134, 137, 141, 150, 242, 270
Gegax, T. T., xv
Gender,
    blog authors 7–8, 12, 25
    blog readers, 110–119, 154–158, 161, 170–171, 176–177
    health communication, xv, 87, 91–94, 97–98
    public/private dichtomy, 17
Gibson, R., 60
Gieryn, T. F., 142
Gill, K. E., 39
Gillmor, D., 3, 5, 15, 241, 254, 262–263
Giuliani, Rudloph, 45
Glance, N., 64–65, 263
Glaser, M., 39, 40, 128, 241–242
Google, 47, 84, 132, 210–211, 217, 268, 270
Grabowicz, P., 227
Granovetter, M., 78
Grant, D., 207, 214–215
Gratifications, 21–25, 29, 31, 35, 127, 129, 131–132, 137, 140–147, 167
Greenberg, B. S., 127–132, 140, 143
Greenspan, R., 128, 143, 148, 170, 172, 177
Grossman, L., 40, 165
Gruhl, D., 106
Grusin, R., 50, 54
Guha, R., 106
Gumbrecht, M., 3, 85
Gutmann, A., 60–61, 67

H

Ha, L., 8, 26
Habermas, J., 60, 67, 226
Halavais, A., x, xvi, 40, 261, 264
Hamdy, N., 166
Hamilton, A., 130, 165–166, 177
Hardy, B. W., 179, 266
Harp, D., 267
Harris, A., 130
Harvill, J. G., 127
Hastert, Dennis, 60, 77
Hastings, M., 130, 166, 177
Helm, D. M., 127
Henning, J., 5, 18
Henson, S., 189
Herring, S. C., x, xvii, 3–5, 7–9, 15, 17, 21, 23, 25, 35, 37, 263
Hersh, A., 98
Hesser, K. M., 160
Hewitt, H., 44, 200
Hill, K. A., 62, 65
Hofmokl, J., 7, 20
Hofstetter, C. R., 105
Homer. P. M., 153
Homophily, 62
Horrigan, J. B., 5
House, J. S., 40, 48, 52, 60, 88, 195
Hovland, C. I., 152–153
Howard, P., 143
Hu, Y., 178, 264
Huckfeldt, R., 63, 65, 78
Huffaker, D. A., 90
Hughes, J. E., 62, 65
Humor, use of, 28–29, 31, 34–36, 43, 48, 133, 137
Hyun, K., 87, 106, 261

I

Identities, 90, 96–97, 99
Identity, 90, 95
Informality, 15, 24, 28, 31, 34, 36, 63, 105, 189, 227, 265
Innovation, 23, 26–27, 30, 32, 46, 239

Instapundit, xiv, 39, 42–43, 46–48, 50–51, 64, 111, 168, 189, 228, 267, 269
Interactivity, 26, 27, 32, 35, 59, 85, 150, 160, 225–230, 242, 267
International, 205–211, 219, 223, 226, 258
Interpersonal communication, 66, 73, 76, 152, 160, 275
Intimacy, 33, 34
Investigative reporting, 50, 51, 193, 196
Iraq, 4, 6, 16–17, 62, 105, 165–181, 265
Irony, use of by bloggers, 29, 31, 34–35
Iyengar, S., 160

J

Jackson, M., 215, 218
James, E. L., 8, 26
James, M. J., 127–131, 133, 140, 143,
Jamieson, K. H., 66, 160
Janis, I. L., 152–153
Jarvis, Jeff, 40, 262
Jarvis, S., 40
Jeong, J., 87, 106, 261, 265
Jesdanun, A., 128, 166
Johnson, A., 211
Johnson, S., 228–229
Johnson, T. J., xiii, xvii, 84, 87, 105–108, 120–121, 127–132, 140–143, 150–152, 160, 166–169, 177–180, 263–266
Jokes, use of, 31
Jones, D. A., 108
Jones, K., 210
Journalists, bloggers as, xiv, 3, 5–6, 39–41, 51, 53, 150, 166–167, 177, 187–201, 205–220, 225–236, 263, 267

K

Kahle, L. R., 153
Kaid, L. L., 264, 267
Kakutani, Michiko, 50
Kalis, A., x, 261
Kalyanaraman, S., 160

Kang, M., 127, 129–131, 140, 142–143,
Katz, E., 63, 129
Katz, J. E., 21, 166
Kaus, Mickey, 21, 52
Kawachi, I., 87
Kaye, B. K., xiii, xvii, 85, 87, 105, 107–108, 120–121, 127–132, 136–143, 150–153, 160, 167–169, 177–178, 180, 263–266
Kean, T. J., 91
Keeter, S., 110, 121
Kelley, H. H., 152,165
Kelly, K., 127, 130, 140, 142, 228
Kelman, H. C., 152
Kelshaw, T., 60
Kendall, K., 66
Kenny, C., 63
Kerbel, M. R., 4, 6, 19
Kerry, John, 4, 16, 60
Kestnbaum, M., 107
Kim, J., 63–64, 66
Kinsley, M., 269–270
Kiousis, S., 83, 152
Kippax, S., 127, 131, 140
Kirk, R., 6, 19
Kirschner, P., 153
Kline, S., 130–131
Klinenberg, E., 59
Knobloch–Westerwick, S., 84
Korgaonkar, P. K., 130–131, 143,
Kouper, I., 5, 7, 17, 21, 23, 25
Kramer, S., 128
Kraut, R., 21
Krishnamurthy, S., 5, 19
Kuehn, S. A., 29
Kurtz, Howard, x, v, 51, 127, 140, 168, 179, 268
Kwak, N., 122

L

Laird, J. D., 153
Landreville, K., 266
Larson, E., 250
Lasica, J. D., xii, 3, 5–6, 39, 40, 150, 168, 178, 227, 262
Lasker, J. N., 89

Lasswell, H. D, 41
Lawson–Borders, G., 6, 19
Lazarsfeld, P. F., 41, 62
Lee, J. K., 265
Leigh, L., 25
Lemert, J. B., 152
Lenhart, A., 5
Leo, J., 127, 140, 168, 178
Levy, M. R., 130, 142–143, 148, 166–168,
    177–178
Libel, 205–209, 212–215, 219–220, 223,
    241, 255
Liben–Nowell, D., 106
Library science, 40
Lin, C. A., 127, 129, 131, 140, 142, 168
Link analysis, 64
Lippman, Walter, 36
Liptak, A., 192
Lott, Trent, 5, 39, 52, 128
Lu, S., 8, 11, 18
Lukose, R. M., 54
Lum, P., 129
Lurkers, 85–86

M

Madrid, 4, 16
Magazines, 136, 170–171, 174–176, 192
Mainstream media, 3, 5–6, 21, 31, 34,
    39–42, 46–48, 50, 53, 64, 83,
    99, 107–108, 114, 121, 165–169,
    170, 178, 187–188, 191, 195,
    200, 241, 249, 261–271
Manheim, J. B., 51, 54
Manovich, L., 50
Marcus, B. H., 89
Mardsen, P. V., 63
Marlow, C., 64, 66
Martin, J. D., 64–65, 266
Massey, K. B., 131, 227
Matthews, D., 61
McBride, K., 271
McCain, John, 45
McChesney, R. W., 51
McGuire, W. J., 153
McKenna, K. Y. A., 85, 89–90
McLeod, J. M., 63–64, 66, 129, 131, 180

McMillan, S. J., 8, 91
McPherson, M., 62
Mediated reporting, 50
Memogate, 39, 41, 44, 49–52, 54
Merton, R. K., 41, 62
Mertz, R. J., 152
Metzger, M. J., 150–151
Meyer, P., 225
Milbank, D., 149
Mill, J. S., 61
Miller, C. R., 3, 62
Milton, J., 213
Mindich, D., 225
Mobarak, R., 166
Mobilizing, 59, 77
Mooney, P., 217, 223
Morris, H. J., 127, 129, 136, 140, 258
Motivations, xvii, 3, 29, 86–88, 97,
    127–147, 154, 263, 266
Murray, J. P., 127, 131, 140
Mutz, D., 63–65, 77
MySpace, ix, 76, 97

N

Naik, G., 207, 223
Nardi, B., 3, 85, 88–89
Networks, 21, 50, 53, 61–66, 77, 85–89,
    97, 134, 138, 189, 192, 225–235,
    262
Neustadtl, A., 108
New York Times, 39, 45, 46, 179, 199, 217,
    234, 268
Newhagen, J. E., 29, 129, 136
Newspapers,
    bias, 111, 138, 139
    blog links to, 73–75
    blog references in, 105
    credibility, 152, 160
    expense of, 136
    online, 167–168, 268
    press protection, 188–189, 192, 196
    profitability, 256
    use, measure of, 112
    war coverage and use, 170–179
Newsweek, 74, 148
Nie, N., 21

Nir, L., 62–63
Nisbet, E., 63, 110
Nisbet, M. C., 63, 64, 110
Noelle–Neumann, E., 61
Noonan, P., 41
Norris, P., 60, 108
Northwest Voice, 240–241, 243, 253, 256–257

O

Obama, Barak, 60, 77
Objectivity, 40, 135, 141, 150, 225, 227, 230, 242
Oh, Y. H., 239–240
OhMyNews, 239–241, 243, 257–258
Olsen, D. R., 248
Outing, S., 40
Owen, N., 89

P

Page, Clarence, 50
Palmgreen, P., 127, 129, 131–132, 140
Palser, B., 130, 165–166
Papacharissi, Z., xvii, 3, 7, 15, 21–23, 26–27, 61–62, 90, 127, 129–131, 142–143, 166, 263
Park, D., 3, 6
Patterson, T., 66
Paul, N., 165, 258
Pax, Salam, 39, 165–166
Pein, C., 128
Perloff, R. M., 152
Perreault, W., 25
Perrin, A., 59
Perse, E. M., 127, 129–131, 140, 143
Personal information, 10, 22, 24, 29, 31, 33–34, 36, 134, 165
Personal journals, 5, 13–14
Personalization, 23, 36
Peterson, T., 212,
Petty, R. E., 61, 153–154, 159
Pew Research, 40, 59, 86, 106–114, 123, 126, 141, 148–152, 165, 266
Phillips, A. F., 129, 206, 209
Political ideology, 108, 113, 116, 117

Political knowledge, 61, 109–110, 113–114, 121, 169–170, 266
Political participation, 61, 63, 109–125, 169, 266–267
Popkin, S. L., 159
Postelnicu, M., 264, 266–267
Price, V., 62–63
Professional advancement, 23, 32
Pseudonyms, use of, 10, 65
Public journalism, 225, 226, 269
Punditry, 50–52, 54

R

Radio, 12, 40, 54, 67–68, 74–75, 105–123, 142, 167–179, 233, 261, 264, 266
Rafaeli, S., 26, 29, 62, 129, 136
Raines, Howell, 39, 139
Rainie, L., 128, 143, 148, 165, 167, 169–172, 177–181, 249, 266
Rakowski, W., 91
Random sampling of blogs, 4, 7, 8, 17, 21, 23–24, 43, 67, 91, 99, 132, 143, 170, 180, 228–229, 264
Rayburn, J. D., 127
Reese, S. D., 87, 106, 188, 261, 268
Regan, T., 39
Revkin, A., x
Reynolds, Glenn, 39, 42–43, 47–48, 52, 64, 165–166, 168, 179, 269
Rhetorical analysis, 3
Richards, Ann, 40
Ridgway, P., 89
Riou, P., 208–209, 223
Roberts–Miller, T., 62
Robinson, J. P., 107
Rogers, E. M., 26, 106
Rosen, J., 190, 225, 227
Rosenberg, S., 127, 130, 140, 142, 165, 179
Rosengren, K. E., 129
RSS, 83
Rubin, A. M., 29, 127, 129, 130–132, 140, 142–143, 153
Ruggiero, T. E., 127, 132

Rutigliano, L., xviii, 87, 106, 261, 263, 265, 267
Ryan, M., 128, 130, 165, 166, 168, 177
Ryan, R. M., 86
Ryfe, D. M., 60

S

Safire, William, 50
Salon.com, 47–48, 68, 148, 184
Sandburg, P., 206
Sanders, L. M., 61
Sapp, A., 7, 20
Sarcasm, 29, 31, 34–35, 53, 199
Schauer, F., 190, 191
Scheidt, L. A., x, 3, 5, 7, 8, 15, 21, 23, 35, 263
Scheufele, D. A., 63–64, 66, 110, 179, 266
Schiano, D., 3, 85
Schiavo, Terri, 54
Schramm, W., 212
Schrobsdorff, S., xiv
Scodari, C., 90
Scott, L. C., 84, 227
Seipp, C., 130, 142–143, 148, 165, 168, 178, 181
Self-efficacy, 61, 71, 74, 170–172
Self-fulfillment, 32, 35
Self-representation, 22
Severin, W., 188
Shachtman, N., 19
Shah, D. V., 51, 122
Sham–Shackleton, Y., 217
Sharim, R. R., 89
Shepherd, D., 3, 19
shield law, 193, 195, 199, 203
Shiffrin, S. H., 191
Shirky, C., 227–228
Shoemaker, P. J., 188
Siebert, F. S., 212
Sifry, D., 16, 20
Simon, A., 64, 66
Simon, E., x, 261
Simon, S., 166
Singer, J. B., 268
Smith, M. J., 22
Smith–Lovin, L., 62

Smolkin, R., 150, 165
Smolla, R. A., 198
Soames, M., 206
Sogolow, E. D., 89
Spector, J., 216
Speed, x, xi, 86, 265, 270
Spiral of silence, 61
Spratt, A., 255
Stafford, L., 130–131, 143
Standeford, D., 219
Stein, J. A., 91
Steinberg, J., 41
Step, M. M., 127, 131, 140
Steuer, J., 26
Stewart, Jon, 51
Stewart, P., 47, 52, 190
Stoll, C., 106
Stone, B., 5, 19
Strohecker, C., 242
Stromer–Galley, J., 63, 65, 108, 160
Su, N. M., 87–88
Subjectivity, 29, 43, 90, 143
Sullivan, Andrew, 21, 42–46, 48, 53, 168, 209, 224
Sundar, S. S., xvii, 83–85, 160, 264
Sunstein, C., 62, 76, 78, 106
Surveillance function of media, 41–44, 49–50, 130–131, 136, 139–140
Sutton, M. F., 213, 219
Swartz, L., 85
Swope, C., 203
Sydell, L., 167

T

Tait, N., 207
TalkingPointsMemo, 42–43, 46, 48, 111, 179, 267
Tankard, J. W., 188
Tannenbaum, W., 223
Tarkowski, A., 7, 20
Technorati, x, xi, 5, 106
Tedjamulia, S., 248
Television, 21, 54, 64, 67–68, 73–75, 107, 110–112, 131, 142, 150, 152, 160, 167–168, 170–172, 176–179, 189, 192, 199, 241, 263, 268; see also TV news

Terdiman, D., 240
Terrorist attacks, 105, 128
Thompson, D., 60–61, 67
Thompson, G., 6, 166, 168, 178–179
Thomsen, E. B., 40
Tomkins, A., 106
Trammel, K. D., 83, 90
Trammell, K. D., 3, 6, 7, 17, 83, 90–91,
    149–154, 266
Tremayne, M., 261, 265, 267–268
Trippi, J., 150
Turkle, S., 89–90, 96, 129–130, 143
Turnbull, G., 4, 20
TV news, 123, 174–175, 255
Tyler, T., 208

U

Ugland, E. F., 190–191, 194
Ulbig, S. G., 63
Ustinova, A., 151

V

Van Houweling, M. S., 219
Venkatesh, A., 142
Viégas, F. B., 87
Vincent, R. C., 127, 131, 140
Vitalari, N. P., 142
Vividness, 26, 27, 30, 32

W

Walker, J. R., 21–22, 26, 127, 131–132,
    140, 149, 223
Wall, M., 6, 41, 47, 106, 167–168, 177,
    206–207, 217, 223
Wallsten, P., 40
Walther, J. B., 89
Wanta, W., 178
Warblogs, 6, 165, 168, 177–178
Ward, S., 60
Warren, M. E., 61
Washington Monthly, 40

Washington Post, 45–46, 52–53, 107, 208,
    217, 268
Wasserstein, B., 40
Watchdogs, 40, 53, 128, 187, 200, 270
Watts, M. D., 51
Weaver, D., 77, 180
Weintraub, D., 40
Weiss, J., 40
Weiss, W., 152
Welch, M., 5, 40, 223–224
Welsch, P., 64–65
Wenner, L. A., 129
Whelan, D., 40, 168, 172, 178, 181
Whitehead, J. L., 152
Wikipedia, 53, 84, 270
Wilkerson, K., 59
Williams, F., 40, 129, 226, 245, 266
Winer, David, 5, 149, 188
Witt, L., 225, 227, 263, 269–270
Witte, J., 143
Wolcott, J., 130, 142
Wolin, L. D., 130–131, 143
Women, 6, 17, 87, 97–98, 128, 160, 266;
    see also Gender
Wotring, C. E., 127
Wright, C. R., 41
Wright, E., x, 3, 5, 21, 23, 263
Wyatt, R. O., 63

X

Xalabarder, R., 211
Xenos, M., 64, 66

Y

Yelvington, S., 258
Yousefzadeh, P., 128, 165
Yu, P. K., 211

Z

Zhang, L., 54
Zheng, N., 265